JAPANESE STUDIES IN BRITAIN:
A SURVEY AND HISTORY

SOAS – Entrance to the Russell Square campus

Japanese Studies in Britain

A Survey and History

———○———

Edited by

Hugh Cortazzi *and* Peter Kornicki

RENAISSANCE BOOKS

JAPAN SOCIETY PAPERBACK EDITION Not for resale

JAPANESE STUDIES IN BRITAIN
A SURVEY AND HISTORY

First published 2016 by
RENNAISANCE BOOKS
PO Box 219
Folkestone
Kent CT20 2WP

Renaissance Books is an imprint of Global Books Ltd

ISBN 978-1-898823-58-2 [Hardback]
     978-1-898823-59-9 [E-book]

SPECIAL THANKS

The Chairman and Council of the Japan Society together with the
Publishers wish to express their thanks to The Great Britain Sasakawa
Foundation for their support in the making of this book.

British Library Cataloguing in Publication Data
A CIP catalogue entry for this book is available
from the British Library

Set in Adobe Garamond Pro 11 on 12.5 pt by Dataworks
Printed in England by CPIAntony Rowe, Chippenham, Wilts

To the memeory of Sir Peter Parker's contribution
to furthering Japanese Studies through his 1986 report
Speaking for the Future

Contents

○

Preface   xi
Acknowledgements   xvii
List of Contributors   xix
List of Relevant Biographical Portraits   xxvii

Part I: History   1

1   A Brief History of Japanese Studies in Britain –
    from the 1860s to the Twenty-first Century   3
    Peter Kornicki
2   British Missionaries and Japanese Studies in Pre-war Japan 41
    Hamish Ion
3   British Consular and Military Officers in Japan Before 1941 52
    J. E. Hoare

Part II: Japanese Studies at Universities   71

4   Cambridge University   73
    Richard Bowring
5   Japanese Library Collections: Cambridge and Elsewhere   87
    Koyama Noboru
6   Cardiff University   89
    Christopher Hood

7   Durham University   94
    Don Starr

8   University of East Anglia   108
    Simon Kaner

9   University of Edinburgh   112
    Ian Astley, Helen Parker and **Urs Matthias Zachmann**

10 University of Leeds   117
    Mark Williams

11 London School of Economics   128
    Ian Nish and **Janet Hunter**

12 Manchester University   139
    Jonathan Bunt

13 University of Newcastle   144
    James Babb and **Joanne Smith Finley**

14 Oxford University   148
    Roger Goodman and **Arthur Stockwin**

15 Oxford Brookes   166
    Joy Hendry

16 Sheffield University   172
    Gordon Daniels

17 SOAS, University of London   187
    Andrew Gerstle and **Alan Cummings**

18 The White Rose East Asia Centre:
    Collaboration in Japanese Studies Between the
    Universities of Leeds and Sheffield   212
    Glenn Hook

19 Japanese Studies at Other Universities in Britain   227
    Hugh Cortazzi

Part III: Foundations and Other Organizations   233

20 The British Association for Japanese Studies (BAJS)   235
    Caroline Rose

21 The Daiwa Anglo-Japanese Foundation and
    Japanese Studies in UK Universities   243
    Jason James

22 The Great Britain Sasakawa Foundation: Japanese Studies
Funding and Policy, 1985–2016   253
Stephen McEnally

23 The Japan Foundation's Support for
Japanese Studies in Britain   267
Ishikawa Yui

24 The Japan Society and Japanese Studies in the UK   278
David Warren

25 Japanese Studies in the UK: The Role of the
Japan Society for the Promotion of Science   285
Polly Watson

26 The Sainsbury Institute for the Study of Japanese
Arts and Cultures   294
Nicole Coolidge Rousmaniere

27 The Tanaka Fund and its Impact on Japanese Studies
Library Collections in the UK through the
JFEC and the JLG Cooperative Acquisitions Scheme   302
Gill Goddard

Bibliography   *307*
Index   *309*

Preface

○

JAPAN HAS BEEN a relevant and significant partner for Britain for much of the last 150 years. Some British politicians and businessmen have, however, recently been giving so much attention to China that Japan's importance for Britain has sometimes seemed to be overlooked or at least given less priority. This is unwise.

Japan has the third largest economy in the world in GDP terms and in GDP per person Japan far exceeds China. Japan has a population over double that of the United Kingdom. It has a well-educated workforce, including a high proportion of technically qualified engineers. Its culture, both historical and contemporary, attracts worldwide interest and admiration. Trade between Britain and Japan is significant to both countries. Japanese direct investment in Britain has not only ensured the survival of the British motor manufacturing industry but has contributed significantly to the improvement of quality standards. Japanese firms have provided numerous jobs in areas of high unemployment and have helped to revive areas in Scotland and Wales as well as in the northeast, the northwest and the midlands in England. Japanese banks and security houses have a significant presence in the City of London and Japanese funds and financial strength have been vital factors in the growth of the British economy.

The Japanese market is not as large as that of China, but it is mature and Japan has a sophisticated economy. It is true that today Japan faces testing times. Prime Minister Abe's 'three arrows' (fiscal stimulus, monetary easing and structural reforms) have not yet overcome deflation. Japan feels threatened by the growth of China's defence capability and troublesome issues with China have yet to be resolved. But, through its location and its economic and political power, Japan is of strategic importance to peace in Asia. Japan is moreover a parliamentary democracy and the rule of law prevails. The same cannot be said of China.

As a country with world political and economic interests, it is important that British people should have a good understanding of modern Japan. Britain needs a corps of Japanese experts to work in business, diplomacy, finance and education.

It is sometimes argued that business in Japan can be done in English both in government and in commerce and that knowledge of the Japanese language is a luxury. Anyone who has lived or worked in Japan knows that this is nonsense. Japanese are meticulous in negotiations and interpreters and translators may not be able to convey the nuances correctly. Moreover, those who deal with Japanese officials and businessmen know the importance of understanding Japanese ways of thinking. What is more, few Japanese politicians are fluent in English. These are some of the reasons why the Foreign and Commonwealth Office every year arranges for members of the diplomatic service to study Japanese and ensures that a high proportion of officers serving in Japan are qualified in the language.

Provision for Japanese studies has been the subject since the war of a number of official reviews, which are summarized in the introduction by my co-editor Peter Kornicki. The last such review was by Sir Peter Parker in 1986. His report entitled 'Speaking for the future' drew attention to the poor supply of experts in Japanese and recommended that a monitoring group should be set up to keep an eye on developments in Japanese studies. This, unfortunately, did not happen.

This book takes an in-depth look at the study of Japan in contemporary Britain concentrating on the universities where Japanese studies are an honours degree subject. It also summarizes the history of Japanese scholarship in Britain and draws attention to the key players and benchmarks that facilitated and underpinned the quality of scholarship achieved.

It grew out of an essay on Japanese studies at Cambridge University prepared by Richard Bowring for another purpose. This suggested the need for a survey of current provision across the country and the contributions made by foundations and other organizations. A further spur to investigating the present state of Japanese studies was a report last year that the Japanese government was considering putting funds into the promotion of Japanese studies in other countries. There was no early prospect of Japanese government funds becoming available for Japanese studies in the UK, but no British or Japanese organization seemed at the time to have a clear picture either of the present state of Japanese studies in the UK or of how they had developed in the past. Hence the need for a book such as this.

Peter Kornicki and I are indebted to the many scholars and other writers who contributed to this volume, all of whom were asked to write to the same brief. Their contributions provide insights into both the strengths and weaknesses of the study of Japan in Britain. Several of the writers have drawn attention to the structural problems in British universities. In his historical survey and introduction Peter Kornicki, my co-editor, summarizes not only the history of Japanese studies by British scholars but also their present state.

What do we mean by Japanese studies? In the first instance it means learning the language in its spoken and written forms, but while language ability is an essential tool, it is for most people the beginning not the end of Japanese studies. Anyone who wants to understand Japan needs also to study Japanese culture and history. By culture we mean to encompass society and behaviour as well as literature and art. Since society is governed by the political and economic systems of the day, Japanese studies are accordingly inextricably bound up with multiple academic disciplines.

Unfortunately, studying a foreign language is no longer a requirement in schools and universities in Britain and we are in danger of becoming a nation of monoglots. This is in spite of the fact that expertise in foreign languages is in the national interest and at the same time the only way to come to grips with the mentalities of people whose mother tongue is not English. And of course, studying a foreign language is an essential tool to understanding English and recognizing the nuances in meanings and constructions.

Are Japanese studies in Britain in a healthy state? This survey may seem to show that there are a sufficient number of universities where Japanese studies can be taken to degree level to meet student demand. But while the main centres teaching Japanese language to degree level have staff with knowledge of the main aspects of Japanese culture, some of the newer centres with limited staff may find it difficult to ensure that their students gain as broad an understanding of Japanese history and culture as in my view they should. The situation would be much worse if it had not been for the generous help given by Japanese organizations such as the Japan Foundation, the Great Britain Sasakawa Foundation and the Daiwa Anglo-Japanese Foundation.

A comparison with the state of Japanese studies in other Western countries shows that there is no basis for British complacency. In France and Germany an increasing number of young people are studying Japanese and levels of scholarship are high. Japanese studies in the USA are main stream in most universities and scholarly publications about Japan have proliferated.

What are the principal problems and weaknesses? The main centres are constrained by the government insistence that the only criterion for funding is meeting the demands of the market. It is right that students who are likely to be saddled with significant debts on graduation should dictate aspects of their university education. But they will understandably be inclined to choose courses which are likely to help them find gainful employment. Finding a job has in the past been a particular problem for graduates in Japanese studies as British firms involved in the Japanese market have looked more for business training and commercial skills than language ability. One positive result of this has been the development of joint honours degrees in Japanese with business studies and other subjects. Japanese investment in Britain and the growth in the tourist trade have helped to provide more opportunities for graduates in Japanese studies, making the job problem now less acute. But, if the job opportunities decline, Japanese studies centres will be forced under the present market-driven system to cut staff and coverage of Japanese studies. This could be damaging to the long-term national interest and reinforces the case for official protection to maintain Japanese and other 'minority' subjects of national interest for which demand declines or for which jobs are difficult to find.

One result of leaving everything to the market is that universities will decide on courses they will offer and on staff they will employ solely on the basis of cost and income earned. Decisions will be accordingly be made without considering the long-term strategic interests of the UK and of the importance of Japanese studies to this country. The most egregious example of this sort of short-term thinking was the decision to close the East Asia Centre at Durham University in 2003.

In our view there should be a body tasked with maintaining oversight over the provision of Japanese studies and other subjects of strategic and national importance in Britain and ensuring that decisions taken by universities take due account of the national interest

The costs of taking a degree in Japanese studies, which include the costs of a year in Japan, and the consequent student debt burden have further consequences. They are likely to deter all but those aiming to make a career in academia from staying on at university to take masters degrees or doctorates. This means that the pool of potential applicants for the most senior academic posts is restricted and universities may have to depend on applicants from the United States where greater resources are available for Japanese studies. However, universities have recently had significant difficulty in getting visas and work permits for teachers and researchers from outside the EU. This affects their ability to provide both the teaching and research needed for the healthy development of Japanese studies in this country.

The problems facing Japanese studies are not solely caused by reliance on student demand and restrictive visa policies. Some issues are the result of the way in which Japanese studies in Britain have developed over recent years. If Britain were starting Japanese studies courses from scratch would we have chosen the present division and allocation of teaching and research posts or would we have decided on a more logical and perhaps more streamlined system with most work in a specific field concentrated in one university? Specialisms have from time to time developed because an academic at an institution has an interest or bent for some particular aspect of Japanese studies. This is understandable and inevitable but it may mean that some aspects of Japanese studies particularly relevant to the national interest may be overlooked or not given the attention they deserve and need.

The British Association for Japanese Studies (BAJS) provides a forum for coordination and collaboration. The Japan Library Group ensures that limited library sources can be shared. Increased availability of digitalized texts and books has significantly helped. There are close links between the Universities of Sheffield and Leeds, which were cemented by the establishment of the White Rose Centre.

SISJAC in Norwich works closely with SOAS. Is there scope for closer cooperation elsewhere?

In guiding researchers in their choice of topics is enough thought given by supervisors and students to national interests? It may be argued that any study, which contributes to a better understanding of some aspect of Japanese culture and society, is in the national interest. But the Treasury is unlikely to see this as justifying funding out of national taxation. The Economic and Social Research Council, on whose board I once served, tends to take a more focussed approach, but its funding is inevitably more responsive than purposive. Those directing and encouraging research, while taking a broad and liberal approach, which will encourage research, need to ask themselves – and prospective researchers will need to think carefully about – how the area of their proposed research contributes to the national interest. It would be wrong to focus too narrowly on utility but anyone undertaking research who is dependent on public funds needs to bear in mind that he/she has a duty to justify what he/she is doing and to be able to show that it is of benefit to others as well as to himself/herself.

One area of national interest, which has so far been overlooked in our universities, or at least has been given inadequate attention, is the history of Britain's relations with Japan in the second half of the twentieth century. Trade friction was a major factor particularly in the 1960s and 1970s. Japanese finance has been significant in the city. Japanese investments in British manufacturing industry have not only increased employment opportunities but improved quality and engineering skills. British investment in Japan has been an important factor in our trade with Japan. And yet there is no centre in the UK focusing on research in these important areas of Anglo-Japanese interest.

Peter Kornicki and I hope that this book will provide a useful snapshot of the state of Japanese studies in Britain today. We also hope that it will prompt discussion by those responsible directly and indirectly for Japanese studies in the UK and will lead to deepening and strengthening those studies in ways that will contribute to better understanding and closer cooperation between the UK and Japan today and in the future.

HUGH CORTAZZI

Acknowledgements

○

THE EDITORS WISH to thank all the contributors for the time and effort they have devoted to preparing accounts of Japanese studies at their institutions. They also wish to thank the representatives of organizations which have done so much to help and promote Japanese studies in the United Kingdom for providing descriptions of the contributions which their organizations have made.

Special thanks are due to the Japan Society and to the Great Britain Sasakawa Foundation for sponsoring the publication of this book and to Stephen McEnally for his help and advice during the development of this project.

List of Contributors

O

Ian Astley completed his PhD degree at Leeds and then worked at the Institute for the History of Religions at Aarhus University in Denmark. From 1991 he taught at the University of Marburg, Germany, and then in 1997 became senior lecturer at the University of Edinburgh. He has published on Japanese religions, especially Japanese Buddhism, in English, German and Danish.

James Babb is senior lecturer in Politics at the University of Newcastle upon Tyne. He is the author of *Tanaka: The Making of Postwar Japan* (2000) and *Business and Politics in Japan* (2001) and has recently edited *The SAGE Handbook of Modern Japanese Studies* (2014). For several years he has been working on a long-term project on the evolution of Japanese conservatism producing a number of referred journal articles on the subject.

Richard Bowring is Emeritus Professor of Japanese at the University of Cambridge. He taught in Australia (Monash) and the United States (Columbia and Princeton) before moving to Cambridge in 1984. He was the foundation professor of Japanese from 1985 to 2012 and was also Master of Selwyn College (2000–2013). Amongst his many publications are *Murasaki Shikibu: Her Diary and Poetic Memoirs* (1982), *Murasaki Shikibu, The Tale of Genji* (1988) and *The Religious Traditions of Japan 500–1600* (2005) and he co-edited *The Myotei Dialogues: A Japanese Christian Critique of Native Traditions* (2015) and other works.

Jonathan Bunt studied English at Bristol and after a PGCE there decided to spend a year teaching English abroad and ended up in Japan on the JET programme. His one year became two and he stayed for 8 years teaching in schools, colleges and universities, returning to the UK for one year to do an MA at UEA. He returned to the UK in 1996 and the following year came to the Greater Manchester Centre for Japanese Studies (GMCJS), a partnership of the then five universities in the city (UMIST, Salford,

Manchester, MBS, MMU), and worked to develop teaching in the partnership. When the GMCJS was taken over by the University of Manchester in 2008 he helped to set up the new department of East Asian Studies and its new Japanese undergraduate programme. He has written a grammar and a learner dictionary (both published by OUP) and also teaches on film.

Sir Hugh Cortazzi studied Japanese at SOAS during the Second World War and later joined the Diplomatic Service. He served as British Ambassador to Japan from 1980 to 1984 and was subsequently a long-serving Chairman of the Japan Society amongst many other roles. He has published many works on Japan, including *Isles of Gold: Antique Maps of Japan* (1983), *Victorians in Japan: in and Around the Treaty Ports* (1987), *Japan in Late Victorian London: The Japanese Native Village in Knightsbridge and 'The Mikado', 1885* (2009). He edited *Britain & Japan: Biographical Portraits, vols IV–X.*

Alan Cummings is a Senior Teaching Fellow in Japanese at SOAS, where he completed his PhD. He has published *Haiku: Love* (2013) with the British Museum Press and various articles on kabuki in the Edo period.

Gordon Daniels was Lecturer and then Reader in Japanese History at Sheffield University. He was the British Convenor of the Social and Cultural Section of the Anglo-Japanese History Project 1996–2002. His major publications are *Sir Harry Parkes: British representative in Japan, 1865–1883* (1996) and several co-edited volumes, *Britain and Japan, 1859–1991: Themes and Personalities* (1991) and *The History of Anglo-Japanese Relations, 1600–2000*, vol. 5 'Social and cultural perspectives' (2002). *The Collected Writings of Gordon Daniels* were published in 2004. He edited *Japanese Women: Emerging from Subservience, 1868–1945* (2005) with Hiroko Tomida.

Andrew Gerstle is Professor of Japanese Studies at SOAS. He previously taught at the Australian National University, where he was also Professor of Japanese. He has published extensively on Japanese theatre and more recently also on Japanese erotic art. His publications include *Chikamatsu: Five Late Plays* (2001) and *Edo onna no shungabon: tsuya to warai no fūfu shinan (Shunga books for Edo-period women; charm and humour for couples)*; he co-authored *Kabuki Heroes on the Osaka Stage 1780–1830 (2005)* and was the co-compiler of *Shunga: Sex and Pleasure in Japanese Art (2013)*, which accompanied the British Museum exhibition on *shunga*.

Gill Goddard is the former East Asian Studies Librarian at the University of Sheffield. She is a long-standing member of the Japan Library Group, and continues to offer cataloguing and bibliographic data services to Japanese Studies collections in the UK.

Roger Goodman is a social anthropologist by training who specialises in the study of Japanese education and social policy. He held a Readership in the Department of Sociology at the University of Essex and a Lectureship in the Department of Anthropology at the University of Oxford before taking up the Nissan Professorship of Modern Japanese Studies at Oxford University in 2003. His main publications include the monographs *Japan's International Youth: The Emergence of a New Class of Schoolchildren* (1990; also published in Japanese), and *Children of the Japanese State: The Changing Role of Child Protection Institutions in Contemporary Japan* (2000; also published in Japanese). He has edited many books including most recently *A Sociology of Japanese Youth* (2011) and *Higher Education and the State* (2012).

Joy Hendry is Professor Emerita of Oxford Brookes University, founder of the Japan Anthropology Workshop, and a Senior Member of St. Antony's College, Oxford. She has held visiting associations with Tokyo, Doshisha and Keio universities and carried out long-term fieldwork in Kyushu and a seaside town south of Tokyo. Her many books and articles on Japan include *Wrapping Culture: Politeness, Presentation and Power in Japan and Other Societies* (1993) and *The Orient Strikes Back: A Global View of Cultural Display* (2000) and four editions of *Understanding Japanese Society* (1987–2012).

James Hoare joined the Foreign and Commonwealth Office Research Cadre in 1969, and has a PhD from SOAS (1971). He retired as a Research Counsellor in 2003. He served in Seoul and Beijing, and was Chargé d'Affaires in Pyongyang after Britain established diplomatic relations with North Korea. He has been President of the Korea Branch of the Royal Asiatic Society and of the British Association for Korean Studies. He has published a number of books on East Asia, most recently *Historical Dictionary of the Republic of Korea* (2015). He edited *Britain and Japan: Biographical Portraits,* vol. III (1999).

Christopher Hood is Reader in Japanese Studies at Cardiff University. He is the author of *Shinkansen: From Bullet Train to Symbol of Modern Japan* (2006), *Dealing with Disaster in Japan: Responses to the Flight JL123 Crash* (2011), *Education Reform in Japan: Nakasone's Legacy* (2001), *Japan: The Basics* (2014) and *Osutaka: A Chronicle of Loss in the World's Largest Single Plane Crash* (2014).

Glenn D. Hook is Toshiba International Foundation Anniversary Research Professor in the School of East Asian Studies at the University of Sheffield, and Director of the National Institute of Japanese Studies, part of the White Rose East Asia Centre, a collaboration between the universities of Sheffield and Leeds. His most recent publication is *Regional Risks and Security in Japan: Whither the Everyday* (co-author; Routledge, 2015).

Janet Hunter is Saji Professor of Economic History at the LSE. She has published widely on the economic and social development of modern Japan, particularly on the female labour market and the history of Anglo-Japanese economic relations. Amongst her many publications are *The History of Anglo-Japanese Relations, 1600–2000 - Economic and Business Relations (2002)* and *Women and the Labour Market in Japan's Industrialising Economy: The Textile Industry Before the Pacific War* (2003). She has also co-edited *The Historical Consumer: Consumption and Everyday Life in Japan, 1850–2000* (2011) and other works. She is currently researching on the economic impact of the Great Kanto Earthquake of 1923.

Hamish Ion is Professor Emeritus, History Department, Royal Military College of Canada. He completed a PhD in Japanese Studies at the University of Sheffield. Among his books are *The Cross and the Rising Sun. Volume 2: The British Missionary Movement in Japan, Korea and Taiwan, 1869–1945* (1993) and *American Missionaries, Christian Oyatoi and Japan 1859–1873* (2009).

Ishikawa Yui was Deputy Director of the Japan Foundation in London with responsibility for Japanese Studies until 2015.

Jason James has been Director General of the Daiwa Anglo-Japanese Foundation since 2011. A graduate of the Japanese Department at Cambridge, he was previously Head of Research at HSBC's Tokyo office, and Director of the British Council in Japan.

Simon Kaner is Director of the Centre for Japanese Studies at the University of East Anglia and Head of the Centre for Archaeology and Heritage at the Sainsbury Institute for the Study of Japanese Arts and Cultures. He has been a Fellow of the Society of Antiquaries of London since 2005 and has undertaken archaeological research in Japan, the UK and elsewhere. His recent publications include *The Power of Dogu: Ceramic Figures from Ancient Japan* (2009); he is currently completing an edited volume, *An Illustrated Companion to Japanese Archaeology*, to be published in 2016.

Peter Kornicki is Emeritus Professor of Japanese at the University of Cambridge. He taught at the University of Tasmania and Kyoto University from 1978 to 1984. He is a fellow of the British Academy, where he is chair of the East and Southeast Asia Panel. His publications include *The Book in Japan: A Cultural History from the Beginnings to the Nineteenth Century* (1998) and *The Female as Subject: Women and the Book in Japan* (co-edited, 2010) as well as catalogues of collections of Japanese books in libraries in Britain and elsewhere in Europe.

Noboru Koyama was Head of the Japanese Collections at Cambridge University Library from 1985 to 2015. He is the author of many books on relations between Britain and Japan including *Kokusai kekkon daiichigō* (1995), *Nihon no shisei to eikoku ōshitsu* (2010), *Rondon nihonjin mura o tsukutta otoko* (2015).

Stephen McEnally was the British Council's Regional Director in Kyoto between 1979 and 1982. After serving in a variety of Council posts at home and overseas he moved to the Japan Foundation, London, with a particular remit for its Japanese studies' work. He was Chief Executive of the Great Britain Sasakawa Foundation from 2006 until 2016.

Ian Nish is Professor Emeritus of International History at LSE. He learned Japanese during the Second World War at Simla and Karachi and in 1946 was posted to the Combined Services Detailed Interrogation Centre in Kure. He completed his PhD at SOAS and taught at the University of Sydney until 1962. He is the author of several books on the Anglo-Japanese Alliance and the Russo-Japanese War and more recently has written Japanese foreign policy in the interwar period (2002). He has also edited or co-edited numerous books including *Japanese Envoys in Britain, 1862–1964* (2007) and *War, Conflict and Security in Japan and the Asia-Pacific, 1941–52: The Writings of Louis Allen* (2011). His most recent work is *The History of Manchuria* (2016).

Helen Parker was an undergraduate student of Japanese at Oxford, where she completed her doctorate in 1993. Since 1990 she has been lecturer in Japanese at the University of Edinburgh where she teaches classical literature among other subjects. She is a specialist on Japanese drama and has published *Progressive Traditions: An Illustrated Study of Plot Repetition in Traditional Japanese Theatre* (2006).

Caroline Rose is Professor of Sino-Japanese Relations at the University of Leeds and Deputy Head of the School of Languages, Cultures and Societies. She is also Executive Director of the White Rose East Asia Centre and President of the British Association for Japanese Studies. She is the author of *Interpreting History in Sino-Japanese Relations* (1998) and *Sino-Japanese Relations: Facing the Past, Looking to the Future?* (2004).

Nicole Coolidge Rousmaniere is IFAC Handa Curator of Japanese Art at the Department of Asia, British Museum. She is also the founding Director of the Sainsbury Institute for the Study of Japanese Arts and Cultures and Professor of Japanese Art and Culture at the University of East Anglia. In 2012, she wrote *Vessels of Influence: China and the Birth of Porcelain in Medieval and Early Modern Japan*. In addition to her work at the British Museum from Summer 2011, she is the Research Director of the Sainsbury Institute.

Joanne Smith Finley is senior lecturer in Chinese studies at Newcastle University. After completing an undergraduate degree in modern Chinese studies at Leeds, she spent three years studying Japanese and teaching English in Japan. She then completed a PhD at Leeds on changing identities among the Muslim Uyghur people of Xinjiang, Northwest China, before joining Newcastle in 2000. She has published *The Art of Symbolic Resistance: Uyghur Identities and Uyghur-Han Relations in Contemporary Xinjiang* (2013) and is co-editor of *Situating the Uyghurs between China and Central Asia* (2004) and *Language, Education and Uyghur Identity in Urban Xinjiang* (2015).

Don Starr is lecturer in Chinese studies and Director of Studies for Japanese in the School of Modern Languages and Cultures at Durham University. He has mostly published on Chinese language and literature, including the co-authored book *Du's Handbook of Classical Chinese Grammar* (2009). He was head of the Department of East Asian Studies at Durham from 2000 until its closure in 2007.

Arthur Stockwin was Nissan Professor of Modern Japanese Studies and Director, Nissan Institute of Japanese Studies, University of Oxford between 1982 and 2003. He is now Emeritus Professor at St Antony's College. Between 1964 and 1981 he taught in the Department of Political Science, Australian National University, Canberra. His publications include *The Japanese Socialist Party and Neutralism* (1968), and *Governing Japan* (fourth edition, 2008).

Sir David Warren has been Chairman of the Japan Society since December 2012, and was British Ambassador to Japan from 2008 to 2012. He studied Japanese for the Foreign and Commonwealth Office at SOAS and Kamakura from 1976 to 1978, and served in the British Embassy in Tokyo for over twelve years during his Foreign Office career. He is also an Associate Fellow of the Royal Institute of International Affairs.

Polly Watson is International Programme Coordinator at the Japan Society for the Promotion of Science, London. She has a background in civil engineering, joined JSPS London in April 2008 and is responsible for the international programmes and the activities of the UK and Republic of Ireland Alumni Association.

Mark Williams has been Professor of Japanese Studies at the University of Leeds since 2004. He studied Japanese at Oxford and then did his PhD at the University of California at Berkeley. From 2008 to 2011, he was President of the British Association for Japanese Studies and from 2011 to 2014 he was Vice President for Academic Affairs at Akita International University in Japan. He has published *Endo Shusaku: a literature of reconciliation* (1999), plus several translations of novels by the same author. He has also co-edited *Japan and Christianity: Impacts and Responses* (1996), *Representing the Other in Modern Japanese Literature: A Critical Approach* (2006) and *Imag(in)ing the War in Japan: Representing and Responding to Trauma in Post-war Japanese Literature and Film* (2010).

Urs Matthias Zachmann is the Handa Chair in Japanese-Chinese relations at the University of Edinburgh. He completed his undergraduate and postgraduate studies at the University of Heidelberg. He taught at the Japan Center of Munich University before taking up his present position in 2011. Amongst other works he has published *China and Japan in the Late Meiji Period: China Policy and the Japanese Discourse on National Identity, 1895–1904* (2009) and edited *Asia after Versailles: Asian Perspectives on the Paris Peace Conference and the Post-war World, 1919–1933* (2015).

List of Relevant Biographical Portraits

O

ROMAN NUMERALS REFER to the volumes in the series *Britain and Japan: Biographical Portraits*; B.ENV refers to Hugh Cortazzi, ed., *British Envoys in Japan, 1859–1972* (Folkestone: Global Oriental, 2004); T & P refers to Hugh Cortazzi and Gordon Daniels, eds, *Britain and Japan 1859–1991: Themes and Personalities* (London: Routledge, 1991); EXP refers to Hugh Cortazzi, ed., *Japan Experiences: Fifty Years, One Hundred Views: Post-war Japan Through British Eyes 1945–2000* (Richmond, Surrey: Japan Library 2001).

Alcock, Sir Rutherford	II and B.ENV
Allen, G. C.	T&P
Allen, Louis	V
Anderson, William	V
Aston, W. G.	T&P and B.ENV
Batchelor, John	II
Beasley, W. G.	VII and EXP
Blacker, Carmen	VII and EXP
Bownas, Geoffrey	EXP
Boxer, Charles	IV
Brinkley, Francis	III
Britton, Dorothy	X and EXP
Calthrop, Lt.Col. R.F.	VIII
Ceadel, Eric	V and EXP
Chamberlain, Basil Hall	X and T&P
Craigie, Sir Robert	I and B.ENV
Daniels, Frank and Otome	I
Davidson, Sir Colin	X
Dening, Sir Esler	T&P and B.ENV
Dening, Walter	VII

Dickins, F. V.   III
Dunn, Charles J.   VIII

Eliot, Sir Charles   T&P and B.ENV

Faulds, Henry   IV

Gardner, Kenneth   VII and EXP
Gubbins, J. H.   II and B.ENV

Hall, John Carey   X
Hawley, Frank   V

Kennedy, Malcolm   T&P

Lloyd, Arthur   VII
Longford, Joseph   VI

McEwan, John R.   X
Mills, Douglas   X
Mitford, A.B.   VIII
Munro, Gordon   I

O'Neill, P. G.   VIII

Parker, Sir Peter   VI and EXP
Parkes, Sir Harry   I and B.ENV
Piggott, Maj. Gen F. S. G.   T&P and VIII
Pilcher, Sir John   III and B.ENV

Redman, Sir Vere   II and EXP
Riddell, Hannah   II

Sansom, Sir George   T&P and B.ENV
Satow, Sir Ernest   T &P and B.ENV
Shand, W.J.   X
Shaw, Alexander Croft   III
Stopes, Marie   T&P
Storry, Richard   V and EXP

Waley, Arthur   T&P
Warre, C.F.   X
Weston, Walter   T&P

Part I

History

1

A Brief History of Japanese Studies in Britain – from the 1860s to the Twenty-first Century

O

Peter Kornicki

THE CORE OF this book shows how the study of Japan has developed in a number of British universities, but almost all of that development took place after the Second World War. Before the War, the study of Japan, such as it was, was spread very thinly and achieved most of its successes in terms of research and publication outside the universities. Although it is, of course, true that the School of Oriental and African Studies (SOAS) began teaching Japanese in 1917, in the entire pre-War period only two students graduated with degrees in Japanese, one in 1938 and the other in 1939; on the other hand, many others took short courses, including Army and Navy officers, and the foundations of the university teaching of Japanese in Britain were laid down at SOAS.

The fact is, however, that few undergraduates were drawn to the study of the Japanese language before the War, even though the history of the flourishing Japan Society founded in London in 1891 shows that there was already a lot of interest in Japan. A small number of British men and women acquired a good knowledge of Japanese in Japan over the subsequent decades, but, after 1941, wartime requirements dramatically transformed the need for and the value of people with a reliable knowledge of the language, and this led to the introduction of accelerated courses to increase the supply. Many of those whose introduction to Japanese and the study of Japan came about in this way went on to play a fundamental role in the development of Japanese studies in the universities after the War. This chapter will present an overview from the beginnings in the nineteenth century up to the present day, taking into account changes in government policy and examining the prospects for the future.[1]

BEFORE 1941

William Adams (1564–1620), thought to have been the first English person to visit Japan, seems to have learnt to speak Japanese during his long residence in Japan from 1600 to his death 1620, but it is highly unlikely that he learnt to read Japanese and no clear sign of his Japanese literacy survives. Much the same is true of Richard Cocks (1566–1624) and his colleagues at Hirado, where the East India Company operated a trading post from 1613 up to its closure in 1623. None of them studied the language like the Portuguese Jesuit, João Rodrigues, who published his grammar of Japanese in Nagasaki in the first decade of the seventeenth century.

The first British citizens to acquire a thorough command of written and spoken Japanese were, therefore, members of that intrepid band who went out to Japan in the closing days of the Tokugawa Bakufu and the early years of Meiji Japan. The best known of those early scholars of Japan are Sir Ernest Mason Satow (1843–1929) and William George Aston (1841–1911), who first went to Japan in 1861 and 1864 respectively.[2] As student interpreters in the Japan Consular Service, their first job was to learn the language and they

---

[1]   For other valuable accounts of the history of Japanese studies in Britain see Frank J. Daniels, *Japanese Studies in the University of London and Elsewhere: An Inaugural Lecture Delivered on 7 November 1962* (London: School of Oriental and African Studies, University of London, 1963); Ian Nish, 'The growth of Japanese studies in Britain', *Hosei Occasional Papers* 6 (1989), pp. 1–12, 'Introducing Japanese studies in Britain', in J. W. M. Chapman, ed., *European Association for Japanese Studies 1973–88* (Ripe, E. Sussex : Saltire House Publications Society, 1988), pp. 52–57, and 'Japanese Studies in Britain', in Yu-ying Brown (ed.), *Japanese Studies* (London: British Library, 1990).

[2]   Peter Kornicki, 'William George Aston (1841–1911)' and 'Ernest Mason Satow (1843–1929)', in Hugh Cortazzi and Gordon Daniels, eds, *Britain and Japan 1859–1991: Themes and Personalities* (London: Routledge, 1991), pp, 64–75, 76–85.

both subsequently became pioneers in Japanese bibliography and other fields; Aston wrote grammars of the spoken and written languages, which went through several editions each as he gradually gained a better understanding of the language.

Aston and Satow were not alone, however. Even before them Sir Rutherford Alcock (1809–1897), who was Britain's first resident diplomatic officer in Japan as consul-general in Edo from 1858 to 1864, used the opportunity to study the language and explore Japanese art, publishing *Elements of Japanese grammar, for the use of beginners* (1861) and *Art and art industries in Japan* (1878).[3] By 1867 Trübner and Co., the booksellers of Paternoster Row in London, had not only published two new works by Alcock, his *Practical grammar of the Japanese language* and *Familiar dialogues in Japanese*, but also had on sale in London several Japanese-English dictionaries published in Japan and, remarkably, even some thirty-eight books and maps written in Japanese and imported from Japan in woodblock-printed editions. These included the *Tale of the Heike*, an illustrated version of the story of the forty-seven rōnin (*Ehon chūshingura*) and an illustrated account of the sights of Edo (*Edo meishozue*).[4] The romanized transcriptions of the titles in Trübner's lists are much mangled so it is difficult to imagine that Trübner might have been selling to the small number of Japanese resident in London in 1867, but if not them then whom?

Aston and Satow were followed by many other members of the Japan Consular Service. One of them was John Harrington Gubbins (1852–1929), who served in various British consulates in Japan from 1871 to 1908 and was in 1909 appointed lecturer in Japanese at the University of Oxford; he translated the Civil Code of Japan into English and wrote several books on the recent history of Japan.[5] Another was Sir George Sansom (1883–1965), who

3   Hugh Cortazzi, 'Sir Rutherford Alcock, the first British minister to Japan 1859–1864: A reassessment', *Transactions of the Asiatic Society of Japan* (4th series) 9 (1994): 1–42.

4   *Trübner's American and Oriental Literary Record*, 31 January 1867, p. 391, and 15 May 1967, p. 21. I am grateful to my wife, Francesca Orsini, for having drawn Trübner's monthly record to my attention.

5   Ian Nish, 'John Harrington Gubbins an "old Japan hand", 1871–1908', and J. E. Hoare, 'Britain's Japan Consular Service, 1859–1941', in Hugh Cortazzi, ed., *British Envoys in Japan, 1859–1972* (Folkestone: Global Oriental, 2004), pp. 241–249, 260–268. Gubbins wrote *The Progress of Japan, 1853–1871* (Oxford: Clarendon Press, 1911) and

spent most of his career in the Japan Consular Service from 1904 to 1935, apart from the years of the First World War: by 1935 he had published *An historical grammar of Japanese* and *Japan: a short cultural history*, and he was the first scholar-diplomat to teach on Japan at university level, albeit not in Britain. He taught at Columbia University in New York before and after the Second World War; during the War itself he was attached to the British Embassy in Washington as an expert on Japan.[6]

Few of the diplomats (as opposed to members of the Japan Consular Service) who served in the British Embassy in Tokyo before the outbreak of the Second World War became serious scholars of Japan. One exception was Sir Ernest Satow, who had transferred from the Japan Consular Service to the Diplomatic Service, but there was also Sir Charles Eliot (1862–1931), whose major study of Japanese Buddhism was published posthumously in 1935.[7]

In 1872 the Asiatic Society of Japan was founded in Tokyo and the regular meetings of the Society provided a forum for British and other residents of Japan to engage seriously with the culture and history of Japan. The early volumes of the *Transactions* of the Society contain many British contributions and testify to the considerable number of British residents of Japan who had acquired a good knowledge of Japan and Japanese.[8] Some of them were missionaries, like the Reverend Professor Arthur Lloyd (1852–1911), who reached Japan in 1884 and remained there until his death: in addition to studies of Japanese Buddhism he also published in 1917 a translation of Ozaki Kōyō's sensational novel *Konjiki yasha* under the title *The gold demon*. Other missionaries who engaged in the study of Japan include Walter Dening (1846–1913), who wrote *The life of Toyotomi Hideyoshi* (1888) and other works and who was

---

The Making of Modern Japan: An Account of the Progress of Japan from Pre-feudal Days to Constitutional Government & the Position of a Great Power, with Chapters on Religion, the Complex Family System, Education, &c. (London: Seeley, Service, 1922).

[6] Gordon Daniels, 'Sir George Sansom: pre-eminent diplomat and historian', in Cortazzi, ed., *British Envoys in Japan, 1859–1972*, pp. 250–259.

[7] Dennis Smith, 'Sir Charles Eliot: ambassador to Japan 1919–1925', in Cortazzi, ed., *British Envoys in Japan, 1859–1972*, pp. 114–122.

[8] Douglas Moore Kenrick, 'A century of Western studies of Japan: the first hundred years of the Asiatic Society of Japan 1872–1972', *Transactions of the Asiatic Society of Japan (TASJ)*, Third Series, vol. 14 (1978).

the father of Sir Esler Dening (1897–1977), the first British ambassador to Japan after the Second World War, and John Batchelor (1855–1944), who lived in Hokkaido from 1877 to 1941 and was a pioneer scholar of Ainu language and culture.[9] Many other missionaries became scholars of Japan, as Hamish Ion's contribution to this volume shows.

Other important contributions came from Frederick Victor Dickins (1838–1915), who spent two periods in Japan firstly as a doctor and secondly as a lawyer and was the first to write on Hokusai in any language, and Basil Hall Chamberlain (1850–1935), who was Professor of Japanese at Tokyo Imperial University from 1886 and produced many pioneering studies of the languages and literature of Japan.[10] Chamberlain was an *oyatoi*, a foreign employee of the Meiji government, and he was by no means the only one to use the opportunity to learn Japanese and take up the study of Japan.[11]

In the first half of the twentieth century the army and navy Language Officer scheme, which came into operation in 1903 following the initiation of the Anglo-Japanese Alliance, created a steady stream of capable officers with a good knowledge of Japanese, some of them staying for as long as four years in Japan. By 1922, forty-eight British Army officers, two Royal Air Force officers and (from 1906 onwards) twenty-nine Indian Army officers had spent at least one year in Japan studying the language; an unknown number of Royal Naval officers had also studied in Japan.[12]

---

[9]   Hamish Ion, 'Walter Dening (1846–1913) and Japan', in *Britain and Japan: Biographical Portraits* [hereafter referred to as *BJBP*], vol. VII (Folkestone: Global Oriental, 2010), pp. 384–401; Roger Buckley, 'Sir Esler Dening: ambassador to Japan, 1951–57', in Cortazzi, ed., *British Envoys in Japan, 1859–1972*, pp. 173–8; Cortazzi, 'John Batchelor: missionary and friend of the Ainu, 1855–1945', in Ian Nish, ed., *BJBP*, vol. II (Richmond: Japan Library, 1997), pp. 216–232.

[10] Hamish Ion, 'Arthur Lloyd (1852–1911) and Japan: dancing with Amida', in Hugh Cortazzi, ed., *BJBP* vol. VII, pp. 402–419; Kornicki, 'Frederick Victor Dickins (1838–1915), in J. E. Hoare, ed., *BJBP* vol. III (London: Japan Library, 1999), pp. 66–77; Richard Bowring, 'An amused guest in all: Basil Hall Chamberlain (1850–1935)', in Cortazzi and Daniels, eds, *Britain and Japan, 1859–1991*, pp. 128–136

[11] On the *oyatoi*, see E. R. Beauchamp and A. Iriye, eds, *Foreign Employees in Nineteenth-Century Japan* (Boulder, Colorado: Westview Press, 1990) and O. Checkland, *Britain's Encounter with Meiji Japan, 1868–1912* (London: Macmillan, 1989).

[12] For the Army, Indian Army and Royal Air Force officers up to 1922 see the list in Captain M. D. Kennedy, *The Military Side of Japanese Life* (London: Constable and Co.,

The number of RAF officers is low because before 1918, when the
RAF was formed, officers in the Royal Flying Corps counted as
Army officers; one of them, however, spent the years 1905–1907
in Japan and was later to become Air Chief Marshal Sir Geoffrey
Salmond KCMG DSO. One of the first group who arrived in
1903 was Major Charles Yate (1872–1914), who spent three
years in Japan. He died on 20 September 1914 while in captivity and won the Victoria Cross: he was one of eight former
Language Officers to die in the First World War.[13] Captain
Kennedy, who was himself a Language Officer and wrote a number of books on Japan, records that in 1917 six officers were
selected to undergo a preliminary course at the School of Oriental Studies (as SOAS was then called) and that as a result of an
examination he and one other officer were sent out to Japan; he
spent the years 1917–1920 in Japan and later had an important
part to play in the training of young men and women for work at
Bletchley Park during the Second World War.[14]

After the First World War the Language Officer programme
continued. Between 1922 and 1939, when the programme was terminated owing to the outbreak of war in Europe, at least twenty-
two British Army officers, ten Indian Army officers, ten Royal
Navy officers, eight Royal Air Force officers and two Royal Australian Navy officers had taken part.[15] The Language Officers spent
the first year on intensive language work with a private teacher but
in subsequent years, while continuing their studies, they also spent
time attached to units of the Japanese Army if they were officers of

Ltd, 1924), pp. 357–359. Arrangements were put in place in 1904 for naval officers
to pursue language training in Japan and in 1905 Captain Jones of the Royal Marines
Light Infantry and Oswald Tuck were already studying in Japan. See National Archives:
ADM 1/7728 Gubbins to Sir Claude Macdonald, 16 December 1904 and 10 January
1904 [sic:1905].

13   On the reverse of the title page of the work cited in the previous note Kennedy reproduces
the text of a tablet to the memory of the eight and of one who died in 1919 that was
unveiled in St Andrew's Church in Tokyo in 1922 by the Prince of Wales; the church was
destroyed by bombing in 1945. On Yate see Yahya Shaigiya-Abdelsamad, 'Major C. A.
L. Yate VC (1872–1914): a gallant British officer and admirer of Japan', in Cortazzi, ed.,
BJBP vol. IX (Folkestone: Renaissance Books, 2015), pp. 524–530.

14   Kennedy, The Military Side of Japanese Life, p. 3.

15   See the tables in Antony Best, British Intelligence and the Japanese Challenge in Asia,
1914–1941 (Basingstoke, Hants.: Palgrave Macmillan, 2002), pp. 94–95, 108; not all
completed their studies, and not only those who arrived in 1939.

the British or Indian armies.[16] A few of them later in their career became Military or Naval attachés. Two of the most significant attachés in terms of the development of Japanese studies were Captain Oswald Tuck RN (1876–1950) and Major-General Francis Piggott (1883–1966).[17] Tuck was summoned out of retirement in 1942 to teach Japanese at the Inter-Service Special Intelligence School in Bedford, while Piggott taught on the SOAS courses during the War.

The Language Officer who made the most important contributions to scholarship was undoubtedly Major Charles Boxer (1904–2000). He was sent to Japan in 1930 and in 1933 qualified as an Army Japanese Interpreter. Between 1937 and 1941 he was a member of the Far East Combined Bureau, a British intelligence organization in Hong Kong that monitored Japanese wireless traffic. After the capture of Hong Kong he became a prisoner of war and remained in captivity until 1945. His academic career began in 1951 when SOAS appointed him as its first Professor of the History of the Far East, and in the same year his famous study of *The Christian century in Japan, 1549–1650* was published.

There were many others who lived in Japan in the first half of the twentieth century and learnt Japanese to a high level. Sir Robert Craigie (1883–1959), who was British ambassador in Japan from 1937 to 1941, wrote several reports in early 1941 on the availability of Britons with a good knowledge of Japanese to meet the needs of the authorities in Singapore, India, Ceylon and Burma, who were pressing him for people to act as interpreters or censors of posts and telegraphs. He could only come up with forty names, half of whom were missionaries; four were employees of the Rising Sun Petroleum Company (now Showa Shell Sekiyu), which required employees to learn Japanese, and four were teachers, including Frank Daniels

---

[16] Kennedy, *The Military Side of Japanese Life*, pp. 25–28; James Weymouth (pseud.), 'The language officer in Japan', *United Services Magazine*1030 (1914), pp. 646–650.

[17] See Sue Jarvis, 'Captain Oswald Tuck RN (1876–1950) and the Bedford Japanese School', in Hugh Cortazzi, ed., *BJBP*vol. V (Folkestone: Global Oriental, 2005), pp. 196–208, and Carmen Blacker, 'Two Piggotts: Sir Francis Taylor Piggott (1952–1925) and Major General F. S. G. Piggott (1883–1966)', in Cortazzi and Daniels, eds, *Britain and Japan, 1859–1991*, pp. 118–127. Piggott *père* was an employee of the Japanese government for many years as legal expert to Itō Hirobumi and wrote on Japanese art and gardens.

(1899–1983) and Frank Hawley (1906–1961).[18] Craigie deplored the shortage:

> It will be observed that the number of British subjects with the requisite knowledge of Japanese is comparatively small. ... I regard this development as very serious both from the general point of view in times of emergency and also in connexion with the future cultural and social relations between the two countries. There can be no doubt that a good knowledge of the Japanese language makes an incalculable difference to the understanding of this country.[19]

Few though they may have been, some of them put their skills and knowledge to use as part of the war effort.

One who did so was Frank Daniels, who was later to become the first professor of Japanese at SOAS. Daniels had taught English at Otaru Commercial High School from 1933, and was succeeded there by Richard Storry (1913–1982), who later as an army major commanded one of the Combined Services Detailed Interrogation Centre (India) mobile sections in Burma during the War and later taught at Oxford University and wrote on Japanese history.[20] Another person whose knowledge of Japanese contributed to the war effort was Captain Martin, who had spent three years in Japan as superintendant of the Blue Funnel Line and later taught on the Japanese courses run in the Naval Section at Bletchley Park.[21]

British interest in Japan was, of course, by no means confined to the British community in Japan. The formation of the Anglo-Japanese Alliance in 1902 seems to have stimulated growing interest in Japan, for in 1903 William Shand (1850–1909), who had worked in banking and insurance in Yokohama for twenty-seven years, opened a School of Japanese Language and Literature in London. By 1908 more than seventy students had passed through

---

[18] Ronald Dore, 'Frank and Otome Daniels', in Ian Nish, ed., *BJBP* (Folkestone: Japan Library, 1994), pp. 268–278; Manabu Yokoyama, 'Frank Hawley, 1906–61: scholar, bibliophile and journalist', in Cortazzi, ed., *BJBP* vol. V, pp. 409–417.

[19] National Archives: FO 371/27953, 24 March 1941, 26 April 1941, April 1941; the quotation comes from his report to the Foreign Office of 26 April 1941.

[20] Ian Nish, 'Richard Storry, 1913–82: a life-long affair with Japan', in Cortazzi, ed., *BJBP* vol. V, pp. 326–336.

[21] National Archives: HW 8/51, H. R. Foss, 'The origin and development of N.S. I J', (nd) p. 19.

his hands: nearly half of them were military officers who then proceeded to Japan under the Language Officer scheme but there were also women intending to go to Japan as missionaries and assorted commercial and private students. Shand also published *Japanese self-taught and grammar* (1907), one of a number of books for learners published in London after 1902.[22]

The most well known self-taught scholar of Japan between the wars in Britain was undoubtedly Arthur Waley (1889–1966), whose translation of the *Tale of Genji* (1921–1933) brought Japanese classical literature to the attention of literary circles in Britain for the first time. During the war he worked in the Ministry of Information in London, which was based in the Senate House of the University of London.[23]

Throughout the early twentieth century an important venue for the study of Japan was the Japan Society, which was founded in 1891 during the International Congress of Orientalists, held in London that year.[24] Many of the scholar consular officials such as Aston and Gubbins became members, and the first chairman of the Society was William Anderson (1842–1900): Anderson had taught at the Imperial Naval Medical College in Tokyo from 1873 to 1880 and had continued to practise medicine in London while simultaneously filling the post of Professor of Anatomy at the Royal Academy of Art and publishing pioneering studies of Japanese art.[25] The *Transactions and Proceedings of the Japan Society* preserve a valuable record of the papers read at the Society's meetings. Some of these were travellers' tales but others were more serious, such as a lecture on translating Noh plays by Arthur Waley in 1920: this lecture was chaired by Marie Stopes (1880–1958), who is famous as a birth control pioneer but had also visited Japan and written on Noh. The Society was inevitably suspended in 1942 but resumed activities in 1949.[26]

[22] Noboru Koyama, 'William J. S. Shand (1850–1909) and Henry John Weintz (1864–1931): "Japanese self-taught"', in Cortazzi, ed., *BJBP* vol. X, pp. 362–370.

[23] Philip Harries, 'Arthur Waley (1899–1966): poet and translator', in Cortazzi and Daniels, eds, *Britain and Japan, 1859–1991*, pp.214–222.

[24] Hugh Cortazzi, 'The Japan Society: a hundred-year history', in Cortazzi and Daniels, eds, *Britain and Japan, 1859–1991*, pp. 1–53.

[25] John Rawlins, 'William Anderson, 1842–1900: surgeon, teacher and art collector', in Cortazzi, ed., *BJBP* vol. V, pp. 3–12.

[26] Carmen Blacker, 'Marie Stopes (1907–1958) and Japan', in Cortazzi and Daniels, *Britain and Japan, 1859–1991*, pp. 157–165. The year 1907 was the year in which Stopes went to Japan, not the year of her birth.

Although it is certainly true that most expertise on Japan was, before 1941, to be found outside the universities, a few universities had begun to show an interest in Japan. In Oxford, Gubbins had held a lectureship in Japanese from 1909 to 1912 and Frederick Victor Dickins was made reader in Japanese at the University of Bristol, but in neither case were undergraduate courses in Japanese given. When Ernest Satow wrote to the Vice Chancellor of Cambridge University in 1912 to express his delight that his books had found a home in Cambridge, he wrote that he hoped the University would in due course start teaching Japanese history and literature but he added that 'the language is of no examination value'.[27] More active as a teacher than either of these was Joseph Henry Longford (1849–1925), who, like Gubbins, was a former member of the Japan Consular Service: he served as Professor of Japanese at King's College, London, from 1902 to 1916.[28]

From the late nineteenth century onwards there had been a succession of committees, reports and public statements calling for a 'school of oriental languages' in Britain. The most significant of these had been the report of a committee appointed by the Treasury and chaired by Lord Reay 'to consider the organization of Oriental Studies in London', which was published in 1909.[29] Satow had in fact given evidence to that committee and expressed himself in favour of the teaching of Japanese history, civilization and religion.[30] However, it was not until 1916 that the recommendations of the Reay Committee were finally acted upon and the School of Oriental Studies, as it was initially called, was inaugurated.

---

[27]   Cambridge University Library Archives: Library Syndicate Appendix to Minutes 1909–1919, Satow to Vice-Chancellor, 30 October 1912.

[28]   Ian Ruxton, 'Joseph Henry Longford (1849–1925: consul and scholar', in Hugh Cortazzi, ed., *BJBP* vol. VI (Folkestone: Global Oriental, 2007), pp. 307–314.

[29]   *Report of the Committee Appointed by the Lords Commissioners of His Majesty's Treasury to Consider the Organisation of Oriental Studies in London* (London: HMSO, 1909). On previous efforts, see P. J. Hartog, 'The origins of the School of Oriental Studies', *Bulletin of the School of Oriental and African Studies* 1:1 (1917), pp. 5–22.

[30]   *Report of the Committee Appointed by the Lords Commissioners of His Majesty's Treasury*, pp. 69, 73.

In response to the opening of the School, an article in *The Spectator* lamented the fact that it came many years after similar institutions had been established in various European countries.

> It is, indeed, little short of a public scandal that whilst for a long time past Germany, Austria, France, Russia and Italy have possessed establishments where Oriental languages are taught, Great Britain, with her three hundred and fifty millions of Asiatic and African subjects, and her huge trade with the East, involving a turnover of more than two hundred millions a year, should have lagged behind, and should not long ago have established any adequate system for instructing British administrative and commercial agents in either the languages, customs, religions or history of the populations with whom they were destined to be brought in contact.[31]

This was not the first time that provision in Britain was to be compared unfavourably with that in other countries. It is worth remembering at this juncture that Johann Joseph Hoffmann (1805–1878) had been appointed to a chair of Chinese and Japanese at Leiden University in 1855, that Antelmo Severini (1827–1909) had been appointed Professor of Far Eastern Languages at the Scuola Regia in Florence in 1863, and that Léon de Rosny (1837–1914) had been appointed Professor of Japanese at the École des langues orientales in Paris in 1868.[32] In 1916 Britain certainly was behind.

Japanese was offered consistently at the School of Oriental Studies from 1917 onwards, as Andrew Gerstle's essay in this volume shows. As in the case of many of the other courses offered by the School before the Second World War, however, few students were following degree courses, although many took short courses. It was, then, the outbreak of the Pacific War in 1941 that transformed the study of Japan in Britain, and that in turn had a profound impact upon the development of university courses in Japanese in post-war Britain.

---

[31] 'The School of Oriental Studies', *The Spectator*, 16 June 1916, p. 8.
[32] Ivo Smits, 'Japanese studies in the Netherlands', in Leonard Blussé, Willem Remmelink and Smits, eds, *Bridging the Divide: 400 Years of the Netherlands-Japan* (Leiden: Hotei, 2000), p. 241; Adolfo Tamburello, 'Japanese studies in Italy', *The Japan Foundation Newsletter*, 4. iv (1976), p. 3; Bénédicte Fabre-Muller, Pierre Leboulleux and Philippe Rothstein, *Léon de Rosny: 1837–1914; de l'Orient à l'Amérique* (Villeneuve-d'Ascq: Presses Universitaires du Septentrion, 2014).

WARTIME STUDIES

In 1941, not only had the war in Europe left Britain isolated but also there was a growing sense of the inevitability of war with Japan. In the United States the shortage of Japanese speakers had already begun to cause alarm: in 1940, the US Navy had only twelve officers with a good knowledge of Japanese so efforts were made to identify civilians with suitable knowledge that could be drawn upon and then to introduce language courses for naval officers.[33] SOAS had already been making efforts in 1939 and again in 1941 to draw the attention of the War Office to the need to anticipate any language needs in the case of war with Japan, but to no avail.[34]

The attack on Pearl Harbor on 7 December 1941 brought the United States into the Second World War and symbolically marks the beginning of the Pacific War. However, shortly before the attack on Pearl Harbor, although seemingly on the following day owing to the effect of the International Date Line, Japanese troops launched their invasion of Malaya and some hours later they attacked Hong Kong. The invasion of these two British colonies was followed by the sinking of the battleship *Prince of Wales* and the battlecruiser *Repulse* on 10 December 1941, the surrender of the colonial authorities in Hong Kong on 25 December 1941 and the surrender of the colonial authorities in Singapore on 16 February 1942. It was at this point that Britain woke up to its woeful deficiencies in Japanese expertise.

The first to act was the Government Code and Cypher School (GC&CS; renamed Government Communications Headquarters in 1946), which had been established in Bletchley Park in 1938. In December 1941 Colonel John Tiltman (1894–1982), one of Britain's leading cryptanalysts, proposed the creation of a special Japanese school at the Inter-Service Special Intelligence School at Bedford. Tiltman was at this time head of the Military Section at GC&CS and from 1933 he had in fact been working on Japanese diplomatic codes with some success: in June 1939

---

[33] As reported in the *New York Times*, 12 December 1943.
[34] National Archives: ED 54/123 Ralph Turner (Director of SOAS) to Board of Education, 11 February 1942.

Tiltman's team cracked one of the new Japanese naval codes.[35] In June 1942 Tiltman explained the genesis of the Bedford Japanese School:

> Qualified Japanese interpreters whom I consulted criticized the idea on the grounds that, owing to the extreme complexity of the language and the very large number of Chinese characters to be memorized, responsible translation could not be expected of students who had not studied the language for at least three years. It seemed to me, however, that an effective result might be achieved if students at the most receptive age were carefully chosen, and if the scope of the course were severely limited to our immediate requirements. After consultation with senior members of Oxford and Cambridge Universities I became convinced that the most suitable material for the experiment would be carefully selected Classical Scholars between the ages of eighteen and twenty. I formed the opinion that, other things being equal, the discipline of training in the Classics would be of more value for the desired purpose than modern language training, with the added advantage that the classical qualifications had no other immediate value for the war effort.[36]

The 'qualified interpreters' Tiltman consulted were most likely qualified Army or Navy interpreters, who had usually themselves undergone a three-year period in Japan as Language Officers. The view that three years were needed was shared by the embassy in Tokyo: as Craigie wrote in 1938, 'The experience of this Embassy has led to the conclusion that three years is the minimum period during which even reasonable proficiency in the Japanese language can be attained, and then only as a result of very serious application.'[37]Although it has been commonly assumed and often stated that it was SOAS he consulted, Tiltman's own account gives the lie to this.

The person he chose to run the courses was Captain Oswald Tuck RN, who has already been mentioned above.[38] By this time he was

---

[35] Ralph Erskine and Peter Freeman, 'Brigadier John Tiltman: one of Britain's finest cryptologists', *Cryptologia* 27 (2003), pp. 295–296.

[36] National Archives: HW 67/3, typescript 'The Japanese language course at Bedford' by John Tiltman, dated 26 June 1942.

[37] National Archives: FO 371/22192, item 4200 on ff. 197–200, Craigie to Lord Halifax, 19 March 1938.

[38] See Sue Jarvis, 'Captain Oswald Tuck R.N. (1876–1950) and the Bedford Japanese School', in Cortazzi, ed., *BJBP* vol. V, pp. 196–208. Jarvis assumes that it was SOAS that Tiltman consulted.

already sixty-five years old and had last been in Japan in 1909 as Assistant to the Naval Attaché in Tokyo. One of the most capable students on the first course, Eric Ceadel (1921–1979), was retained to help Tuck teach the subsequent courses; in 1947 he was to become the first lecturer in Japanese at Cambridge. In all, eleven six-month courses were run at the Bedford School and 225 men and women were trained there. At first young students of Classics from Oxford and Cambridge were chosen but some came from other backgrounds and for the later courses some were recruited straight from school.

The students at the Bedford School were not told that they were learning Japanese for cryptographic work, but it gradually dawned on them when they were given decrypts or intercepted messages sent in Japanese morse code to translate. Here is an example of the kind of text they had to get to grips with:

> Message sent from Sofia to Budapest on 7 December 1942 by a Japanese diplomat.
>   shoo konpan kichoosu kokoni atuku zaioochuu no gokonjoo shasi setuni gokenshoo inoru sakakibara

This does not make a lot of sense even to seasoned students of Japanese! The word breaks were inserted by those transcribing the message, who did not know Japanese. This is how Patrick Field, a student on the eighth course, translated it, after less than six months studying Japanese:

> I am just returning home. I hereby warmly thank you for your kindness to me while I have been in Europe. I earnestly hope you are well. Sakakibara

He had been taught to deal with the bizarre word breaks and the truncated style of military messages and had managed to produce an accurate translation.[39]

After completing their course the students were sent to Bletchley Park, where they were initiated into the mysteries of decryption. Some stayed at Bletchley Park for the remainder of the war while

---

[39] Personal papers of Patrick Field, Bishop's Stortford. I am indebted to Mr Field for his hospitality and willingness to share his papers with me.

others were posted to the so-called Wireless Experimental Centre at Delhi, which was really a Bletchley Park outpost, or the listening and decrypting stations in Kilindini (Mombasa), HMS Anderson outside Colombo, or Australia. Most of them were engaged not only in translating decrypted messages but also in decrypting the original messages.

In later life some of the students made contributions to Japanese studies, such as David Bentliff (1926-), who later worked as a civil servant and on retirement became a senior lecturer in Japanese at the Polytechnic of Central London (now the University of Westminster), Geoffrey Bownas (1923–2011), who in 1954 became the first lecturer in Japanese at Oxford and then was the foundation Professor of Japanese Studies at Sheffield University (1965–1980), and Eric Ceadel, who has already been mentioned. There were many others, however, who achieved distinction in other fields but for most or all of their lives were obliged by the Official Secrets Act to make no mention of their Japanese studies or their work at Bletchley Park. Amongst them are the following: Michael Dummett FBA (1925–2011), who became Wykeham Professor of Logic at Oxford; David Hawkes (1923–2009), who became Professor of Chinese at Oxford; Sir Hugh Lloyd-Jones FBA (1922–2009), who became Regius Professor of Greek at Oxford; Michael Loewe (1922-), who taught Chinese at Cambridge for many years; Denise Newman (1924-), who became a champion diver and swimmer and took part in the 1948 London Olympics; Wilfrid Noyce (1917–1962), who was a member of the successful 1953 Everest expedition and died climbing in the Pamirs; Donald Russell FBA (1920-), who became Professor of Classical Literature at Oxford; Michael Screech FBA (1926-), who became Professor of French at University College London; William Skillend (1926–2010), who became Professor of Korean at SOAS; Peter Stein FBA (1926–), who was Regius Professor of Civil Law at Cambridge; and Maurice Wiles FBA (1923–2005), who was Regius Professor of Divinity at Oxford.

Although the Bedford Japanese School worked hard to provide Japanese linguists for Bletchley Park, there was always a need for more. As a consequence, the Naval Section in Bletchley Park in 1943 began running its own short courses for its cryptographers including many from the Women's Royal Naval Service (Wrens).

Among those on the first course was a Wren officer, E. J. W. Kirby, who already had a command of colloquial Japanese, presumably from residence in Japan, while most of those on the second course were Wrens.[40] The course was taught by John Lloyd (1914–1982), who had joined the Japan Consular Service in 1937, and made use of a specially printed booklet entitled *The Elements of Written Japanese,* by Arthur Cooper: Cooper had lived in Japan for some time, had worked in intelligence in Singapore and somehow managed to escape to Australia after the fall of Singapore and make his way back to England.[41] Although the courses were designed to produce linguists with no more than a command of naval Japanese as quickly as possible, it was recognized that some knowledge of Japan was necessary to be an efficient cryptographer. To this end the Naval Section organized a series of lectures in August 1943: these covered not only the history of the Japanese army and navy but also four lectures on the history of Japan given by Captain Kennedy and lectures on Japanese culture and Japanese law by a future ambassador to Japan, Sir John Pilcher (1912–1990) and Sir Vere Redman (1901–1975), who resided in Japan from 1927 and after the war became Information Counsellor in the United Kingdom Liaison Mission during the Occupation.[42] Amongst those who took these courses at Bletchley Park itself was John Chadwick FBA (1920–1998), who was later to team up with Michael Ventris to solve the puzzle of the Linear B script used to write Mycenaean Greek.

Only a couple of weeks after Tiltman launched his programme to prepare Japanese linguists for intelligence work at Bletchley Park, the War Office took steps to meet likely wartime needs. In January 1942 the War Office consulted the Board of Education with a view to a scheme of scholarships to provide a supply of young men with expertise in Chinese, Japanese, Turkish and Persian.

---

[40]   National Archives: HW 50/78, 'Jap translators Naval Section course'.

[41]   Michael Smith, *The Emperor's Codes: Bletchley Park's Role in Breaking Japan's Secret Cyphers* (London: Dialogue, 2000), pp. 102–103; Kevin Jackson, *Humphrey Jennings* (London: Picador, 2004), p. 75. Cooper later published translations of Chinese poetry.

[42]   National Archives: HW 8/125 typescript copies of lectures given in August 1943 for Naval Section Japanese course. Cortazzi, 'Sir John Pilcher GCMG (1912–90)', in Hoare, ed., *BJBP* vol. III, pp. 296–310; Cortazzi, 'Sir Vere Redman, 1901–1975', in Nish, ed., *BJBP* vol. II, pp. 283–300.

The right policy seems to be to catch them young and teach them before the age for military service. Our idea is to pick, say, fifty boys at Public or other secondary schools, aged 17–18 and with a marked aptitude for languages, and give them special facilities to study one of these languages at the School of Oriental Studies ... while continuing their general education. [43]

With astonishing rapidity a printed memorandum was sent in February to all headteachers seeking applications for these scholarships: applicants had to have obtained a credit in one or more foreign languages (ancient or modern) in the School Certificate examination and they had to give an undertaking that they would be at the disposal of the Government for a period of not more than five years after the termination of their scholarship.[44] There were 660 applicants, far more than had been expected, and after interviews it was decided to award more scholarships than originally planned. Of these, twenty-seven scholarships in Japanese were awarded although only a few had chosen Japanese: amongst them were Sir Peter Parker (1924–2002), who later became Chairman of British Rail, Patrick O'Neill (1924–2012), who was later to become Professor of Japanese at SOAS, and Ronald Dore FBA, the distinguished sociologist of Japan.[45] The students were accommodated in Dulwich College and took their courses at SOAS, and have been known as the 'Dulwich Boys' ever since.[46]

On 1 May 1942 the Dulwich Boys began their courses at SOAS, with nineteen months allowed for those doing Japanese or Chinese. SOAS at the time had three teachers of Japanese: Yoshitake Saburō, a linguist who worked on both Mongolian and Japanese, Commander N. E. Isemonger, a retired naval officer who had

---

[43] National Archives ED 54/123, W. H. Ottley (War Office) to Board of Education, 17 January 1942.

[44] National Archives ED 54/123, printed memorandum.

[45] National Archives ED 54/123, 'Scholarships in Oriental languages 1942', Board of Education report prepared 31 March 1942; 'State Scholarship Courses/Japanese/ Report March 31st, 1943.' (typescript); 'Dulwich Students: finally agreed division of Chinese and Japanese students between the three services 4.3.43' (typescript)

[46] For a more detailed account see Sadao Ōba, *The 'Japanese' War: London University's WWII Secret Teaching Programme and the Experts Sent to Help Beat Japan*, trans. Anne Kaneko (Folkestone: Japan Library, 1995); the sources used in the book and in the original Japanese version are not fully made clear.

published *The Elements of Japanese Writing* in 1929, and Frank Daniels, who had taught English in Otaru, Hokkaido.[47] Daniels's wife, Otome, was also appointed a temporary lecturer in March 1942, and a number of other temporary appointments were made to deal with the influx of scholarship students, including Major-General Piggott, Mr John Pilcher, and three men with Japanese names, who seem to have been Nisei (people of Japanese descent) seconded from the Canadian Army.[48] There were also two Japanese London-based journalists, Matsukawa Baikin and Yanada Senji, who were released from internment to act as teachers.[49] The students finished their course in late 1943 and by 1944 most of them were in India employed either in SEATIC (South East Asia Translation and Interrogation Centre), where Japanese translators and interpreters from the three services were employed, or in the Combined Services Detailed Interrogation Centre (India).

In addition to the Dulwich Boys there were many other courses run at SOAS for serving members of the armed forces, although precise numbers are not available.[50]

In 1941–1942 there were 295 part-time and eighty-eight occasional service students taking courses in Chinese, Japanese and phonetics, and in 1942–1943 162 full-time, 114 part-time and thirty-four occasional students following the same courses; in 1943–1944 there were 212 following a Japanese course in the SOAS phonetics

[47] F. J. Daniels, *Japanese Studies in the University of London and Elsewhere*, Inaugural lecture delivered on 7 November 1962 (London: School of Oriental and African Studies University of London, 1963), pp. 18–19. On the wartime staff and students see also Daniels, 'Japanese studies in England and Japan', *Bulletin of the Japan Society of London* 3 (1951), pp. 15–21.

[48] On Frank and Otome Daniels, see Ōba, *The 'Japanese' war*, pp. 17–9, 24–25, and Ronald Dore, 'Frank and Otome Daniels', in Nish, ed., *BJBP* [vol.I], pp. 268–278. For the additions to the staff, see *Report of the Governing Body, Statement of Accounts and Departmental Reports for the year ending 31st July 1942* (SOAS, 1942), p. 41. Later, in 1942, they were joined by Frank Hawley and others: *Report of the Governing Body, Statement of Accounts and Departmental Reports for the year ending 31st July 1943* (SOAS, 1943), pp. 7, 41, 43. For the three Japanese-Canadians, see *Report of the Governing Body, Statement of Accounts and Departmental Reports for the year ending 31st July 1946* (SOAS, 1946), p. 55. On Piggott see Antony Best, 'Major-General F.S.G. Piggott (1883–1966)', in Hugh Cortazzi, ed., *BJBP* vol. VIII (Leiden: Global Oriental, 2013), pp. 102–116.

[49] *Collected writings of P.G. O'Neill* (Richmond: Japan Library, 2001), p. 2.

[50] According to the Scarbrough Report, 850 service students were sent to SOAS from 1942 onwards, but this figure appears to include those studying Chinese: *Report of the the Interdepartmental Commission of Enquiry on Oriental, Slavonic, East European and African Studies* (London: His Majesty's Stationery Office, 1947), p. 103.

department.[51] The phonetics course used records which had been specially prepared with sentences of increasing difficulty but exclusively of military content, such as *bakugeki kaishi yotei jikoku shirase* ('information on the expected time when bombing is to commence'). They were intended to train students to be able to listen to live clear broadcasts from aeroplanes.[52] In addition to the phonetics courses there were separate courses for interrogators and for translators, both of which lasted 12–18 months.[53] There were more than a dozen teachers including John Firth (1890–1960), who was later to become the first professor of general linguistics in the UK at SOAS, Kenneth Strong, who was later to teach Japanese literature at SOAS, and Eileen Evans, who taught in the Phonetics Department and compiled a detailed guide to the contents of the records, which was labelled 'secret'.[54]

Amongst the hundreds of students of these SOAS courses were many who achieved eminence in later life. The two Dulwich Boys, Sir Peter Parker and Ronald Dore, have already been mentioned, but there were many others. Louis Allen (1922–1991) served in Burma during the War after studying Japanese at SOAS and later taught French at Durham while playing a leading role in efforts to reconcile former combatants.[55] Carmen Blacker FBA (1924–2009), who had already been studying Japanese before the War with Major-General Piggott, did one of the SOAS courses before going on the Bletchley Park; later she was to teach at Cambridge University and achieved fame with her study of religious practices in rural Japan, *The Catalpa Bow* (1975).[56] Sir Hugh Cortazzi, who completed a sixteen-month course at SOAS in December 1944, was posted to India and then served at the South East Asia Translating and Interrogation Centre in Singapore before going to Japan in 1946, became British ambassador in Tokyo in 1980 and then

---

[51] SOAS archives: SOAS/REG/01/01/01.
[52] Bletchley Park archives, uncatalogued item: 'Handbook to the records', typescript prepared in 1944.
[53] Cortazzi, *Japan and Back and Places Elsewhere: A Memoir* (Folkestone: Global Oriental, 1998), pp. 18–19.
[54] SOAS archives: SOAS/REG/01/01/01.
[55] Phillida Purvis, 'Louis Allen (1922–91) and Japan', in Cortazzi, ed., *BJBP* vol. V, pp. 344–357.
[56] See her entry in the *Oxford Dictionary of National Biography*.

had a second career as the author of many books on Japan. Peter Laslett FBA (1915–2001) was recruited to Bletchley Park and later served in Washington before becoming a historian at Cambridge; he became famous for his book *The World We Have Lost: England Before the Industrial Age* (1985). Guy de Moubray (1925–2015) was a Dulwich Boy and was one of the first allied soldiers to reach Singapore after the Japanese surrender where he found both his parents alive: later he became Chief Economist at the Bank of England and after his retirement and the death of his wife he published a number of recipe books.[57]

Some learnt their Japanese in India, for a course was established in Simla, which was later transferred to Karachi. Ian Nish, later to be professor at the London School of Economics and famous for his studies of the Anglo-Japanese Alliance and the Russo-Japanese War, was despatched to India to learn Japanese and later took part in the Occupation, as did many other graduates of the various Japanese courses in Britain.[58]

Those who learnt their Japanese as part of the war effort found themselves using their knowledge of the language in a variety of ways. Some found themselves translating captured documents or decrypts while others listened to clear wireless transmissions or interrogated prisoners of war or, after the war, suspected war criminals. In the cryptographic war it is, inevitably, the cryptographers who have attracted the most attention, but without translators the decrypts would have had no meaning. The role of the translators has long been a forgotten part of the story: they are not even mentioned in Boyd's study of the decrypted messages sent by Ōshima Hiroshi (1886–1975), who was entrusted by Hitler and Ribbentrop with critical intelligence that he passed on to Tokyo not realizing that all his despatches were being decrypted.[59] The quantity and volume of these messages, which relayed critical information about German plans and preparations for dealing with the expected Allied invasion, placed heavy demands on the Japanese translators.

---

[57]   Guy de Moubray, *City of Human Memories* (Stanhope: Memoir Club, 2005), pp. 75–76.

[58]   Vivienne Kendrick, 'Ian Nish', *The Japan Times*, 18 September 2004.

[59]   Carl Boyd, *Hitler's Japanese Confidant: General Hiroshi Ōshima and Magic Intelligence, 1941–1945* (Lawrence, Kansas: University Press of Kansas, 1993).

During the five years from 1942 to 1945 it is likely that there were more people studying Japanese in Britain than in any five-year period up to the 1990s. The lives of some changed completely, as their wartime experiences awakened their interests in East Asia, while others returned to the paths they had been following before 1942. And those at Bletchley Park never mentioned their studies until the 1980s.[60] For a short while, then, the intellectual and linguistic horizons of hundreds of young men and women were broadened unimaginably, but for most they contracted again after the War was over. Nevertheless, that wartime generation produced sufficient men and women whose interest in Japan was lasting to provide the first generation of postwar teachers in British universities. It was thanks to the efforts of William Beasley, Carmen Blacker, Geoffrey Bownas, Eric Ceadel, Frank Daniels, Charles Dunn, John McEwan, Ian Nish, Patrick O'Neill, Richard Storry and others that the growth of Japanese studies in British universities was possible at all.

POST-WAR DEVELOPMENTS UP TO 1985

As early as December 1944, well before the end of the war could be safely predicted, the Foreign Office established an Interdepartmental Commission of Enquiry on Oriental, Slavonic, East European and African Studies under the chairmanship of the Earl of Scarbrough. The introduction to the report ('Scarbrough report'), which was published in 1947, made it clear what the context was in late 1944:

> The under-developed state of our store of knowledge and the small numbers of our countrymen with any detailed acquaintance with the culture and economy of the people of Africa and the East stood in marked contrast to the intimacy of our contact with them in the joint struggle to save the world from a return to the dark ages. The demands to be made against us by the final struggle against Japan were still unknown, but it was already apparent that an excessive preoccupation with western affairs and civilisations would prove

---

[60] Timon Screech, Professor of Art History at SOAS, studied Japanese at Oxford and his moral tutor at St John's College was Professor Donald Russell, who has been mentioned earlier: Russell never dropped a hint that he had studied Japanese during the war. Timon Screech, personal communication.

to be an obstacle to the effective mobilisation and deployment of military power in the Far East. Such were the circumstances which gave rise to this enquiry. ... A significant part of our contribution to world peace is to understand and know our neighbours both near and distant. Western and Eastern civilisations have been brought together by a revolution in communications and must not remain separated by superstition and ignorance. The East makes great efforts to know and understand the West and our interests and traditions require that among the Western powers we of all peoples should reciprocate.[61]

The introduction went on to refer to British 'responsibilities' towards British colonies and the dominions of Australia and New Zealand, and it is clear, therefore, that it was partly military considerations in connection with British interests in East Asia that prompted the enquiry. Nevertheless, the dangers of ignorance had clearly been driven home by the war.

The remit of the enquiry was, 'to examine the facilities offered by universities and other educational institutions in Great Britain for the study of Oriental, Slavonic East European and African languages and culture' and the object was to make recommendations for their improvement.[62] To this end sub-committees were formed to look at the separate areas of study. The sub-committee focusing on 'Far Eastern studies' consisted of scholars and diplomats with expertise on China, but evidence was submitted by four individuals who knew Japan well: Frank Daniels, Frank Hawley, Major-General Piggott and Sir George Sansom.[63] After surveying current provision, the Scarbrough Commission drew attention to the failure to attract students in substantial numbers and the poor Government provision for the study of 'living Oriental languages' in Britain compared with that of many other countries, both points which have not lost their edge today, more than sixty years later.[64] These studies were, however, the Report insisted, of 'national importance', for, 'If we are to preserve close and intimate relations

---

[61]   *Report of the the Interdepartmental Commission of Enquiry on Oriental, Slavonic, East European and African Studies* (London: His Majesty's Stationery Office, 1947), p. 5.

[62]   *Ibid.*, p. 5.

[63]   *Ibid.*, pp. 78, 172–5.

[64]   *Ibid.*, p. 22.

with the nations of Asia we must develop in our own country an interest in the cultures of the East.'[65] Japan was not explicitly mentioned, but given the close ties between Britain and Japan during the years of the Anglo-Japanese Alliance, Japan must have been in the Commission's collective mind.

The Report emphasized the need for language study as the basis of scholarship but argued that philological studies should not predominate and that there should be a balance between classical and modern studies. To achieve its aims the Commission recommended earmarked grants to universities and a programme of 195 postgraduate studentships over five years to encourage further study. It hoped that an academic tradition in 'Oriental studies' would be built up and that in schools the imagination of boys and girls would be led beyond the countries of Western Europe, but no specific recommendations for the creation of posts were made. Early in 1945 a questionnaire had been sent to universities and, in connection with the study of Japan, SOAS had made an ambitious proposal for the expansion of the study of China, Japan and Korea while Cambridge had asked for a lecturer in Japanese, but that was all. Perhaps because Britain was still at war with Japan, no other bids specifically for the study of Japan were made, though St Andrews, Manchester and Liverpool all expressed an interest in 'Far Eastern studies'.[66]

As a result of the Scarbrough Report, the teaching of Japanese at SOAS gradually expanded after the end of the war and in 1947 a lectureship in Japanese was created at Cambridge, which was followed by two further lectureships by 1950. Elsewhere there were few developments until somewhat later. Those who were appointed to teaching positions in Japanese studies as a result of the Scarbrough Report were men and women who for the most part had learnt their Japanese during the war. The one exception was SOAS, where many of the staff had been busily occupied during the war teaching Japanese for the war effort. At Cambridge the three posts were first held by Eric Ceadel, John McEwan, who was one of the Dulwich Boys, and Donald Keene, who had learnt his Japanese in the US Navy Japanese Language School at Boulder, Colorado.

[65]   *Ibid.*, pp. 24–26.
[66]   *Ibid.*, pp. 62, 69–70, 103.

Geoffrey Bownas was a typical case: he had gone up to Oxford with a scholarship in Classics at The Queen's College, but was recruited to learn Japanese, along with many other young classicists, at the Bedford School of Japanese. From there he was sent to Bletchley Park, where he was assigned to the section dealing with the Japanese military codes, but after a while, along with several of his classmates, he was sent out to the Wireless Experimental Centre in Delhi: this innocuous name concealed the real purpose of this Bletchley Park outpost, which was monitoring Japanese wireless traffic, decrypting it and translating the messages. After the war was over Bownas returned to Oxford in 1946 to complete his degree in Classics but then he did a degree in Chinese followed by two years in Kyoto. In 1954 he was appointed to a lectureship in Chinese and Japanese at Oxford, and this marks the beginning of the undergraduate course in Japanese there.[67]

By 1960 the University Grants Committee considered that it was time for an assessment of the progress made in studies of Asia and Africa and appointed a sub-committee under Sir William Hayter, a former British ambassador to the Soviet Union. The Hayter Report, which was published in 1961, expressed disappointment in developments since 1947: although numbers of staff had increased, student numbers were still low and the system of earmarked grants had come to an end in 1952. What is more, the Report considered the British educational system 'anachronistic' in its focus on western Europe, North America and the Commonwealth.[68] The Report, which contains a useful survey of developments since 1947, was based not only on an assessment of Britain's needs but also on the findings of a visit to universities in the United States and Canada: already the Report expressed its fear of a 'drain' of teachers to American universities.[69] The Report argued that 'the universities should now be encouraged to pay more attention to studies related to Asia, Africa and eastern Europe', and not so much in language departments as in the history, geography, law, economics and other social science departments; to this end it

---

[67] Obituary in *The Guardian*, 13 March 2011.
[68] *Report of the the Sub-Committee on Oriental, Slavonic, East European and African Studies* (London: Her Majesty's Stationery Office, 1961), p.3.
[69] *Ibid.*, p. 61.

recommended the creation of a fund that universities could draw upon to make new appointments of these kinds and argued for more teaching of spoken languages and for the cooperative buying and cataloguing of books.[70]

Many of the recommendations made by the Hayter Report made a lot of sense but it was to be many years before they were implemented. For example, in the case of library resources, the Japan Library Group was founded in 1966 but it was only from 1975 that it was able to operate a cooperative acquisitions scheme, and that depended on financial help from the Japan Foundation Endowment Committee. In the case of Japanese studies, which in the Hayter Report was subsumed under 'Far Eastern studies', the Sub-Committee did not see much room for expanding language provision beyond SOAS, Oxford and Cambridge with the exception of Durham, but it did wish to see the development of centres of area studies including the 'Far East'.[71] The only such proposal in the case of Japanese studies came, rather fortuitously, from Sheffield University, and this development dramatically changed the landscape of Japanese studies in Britain. A Centre for Japanese Studies was created in 1963 with funds made available by the University Grants Committee and in 1966 Geoffrey Bownas was appointed Professor of Japanese, but the real innovation was to introduce courses linking language study to the study of history, economics and the social sciences.

The establishment of the Centre for Japanese Studies at Sheffield, and the title of Geoffrey Bownas' inaugural lecture in 1966, 'From Japanology to Japanese studies', were emblematic of a shift that was then still taking place. Bownas outlined the difference between the two terms, describing Japanology as 'almost pretentious in its breadth', 'inward-looking', and 'sometimes a little amateurish'.[72] On the other hand, Japanese studies, he insisted, 'must be professional, specialist, permitting concentration on a concise sphere of interest', and 'directed to a comparative, multi-disciplinary

[70]   *Ibid.*, pp. 68–70, 87, 106–107.
[71]   *Ibid.*, pp. 83, 87.
[72]   Bownas, 'From Japanology to Japanese studies', inaugural lecture, University of Sheffield, 14 December 1966, p. 6. The lecture is reprinted in Bownas, *Japanese Journeys: Writings and Recollections* (Folkestone: Global Oriental, 2005), pp. 228–246.

treatment of Japan'.[73] He was really advocating a change in out-
look more than anything else, but by the 1970s the term 'Japanese
studies' had become standard, with the foundation of the European
Association for Japanese Studies in 1973, of the British Association for Japanese Studies in 1974 and, in the United States, of the
Journal of Japanese studies also in 1974. The term was not altogether
new, however: it had been used in 1937 by the Kokusai Bunka
Shinkōkai, in 1947 the University of Michigan had established a
Center for Japanese Studies and in 1963 Daniels had used the term
in his inaugural lecture.[74] The increasingly common use of 'Japanese
studies' from the 1970s onwards, however, did signify the coming
of age of an area studies focus on Japan with due weight given to
disciplinary approaches. Just how important the change of terminology was is perhaps debatable: the equivalents of Japanese studies
in German and French, *Japanstudien* and *études japonaises*, are relatively recent coinages and have not replaced the older terms, *Japanologie* or *Japanistik* in Germany and *Japanologie* in France. This has
not, however, deterred French and German scholars from pursuing
disciplinary studies of Japan.

The hallmark of 'Japanese studies' has been an expansion
beyond the earlier focus on language, literature and history to
include anthropology and the social and political sciences. The
lead set by Sheffield was later followed by other universities such
as Stirling and Essex, and the Nissan benefaction at Oxford
enabled the creation of new posts in the social and political sciences there in the 1970s; in Cambridge, where the study of Japan
almost came to an end in the 1980s, it was in the late 1980s and
1990s that new posts were created in Japanese society, politics and
international relations. SOAS is a slightly different case, as there
already were Japan specialists in some of the social and political
science departments, and much the same was true of the London
School of Economics.

Although the study of Japan remained concentrated in departments of Japanese studies, by the early 1980s there were not only

---

[73] *Ibid.*, p. 12.
[74] *A guide to Japanese studies. Orientation in the study of Japanese history, Buddhism, Shintoism,
art, classic literature, modern literature* (Tokyo: Kokusai Bunka Shinkōkai, 1937). Frank J.
Daniels, *Japanese studies in the University of London and elsewhere.*

new developments based in non-language departments but also growing outreach, with courses on the history, economy, sociology and politics of Japan being offered to those with no knowledge of the language. This was, at the undergraduate level, the beginning of a process of reducing the eurocentric bias of disciplinary courses which tended to focus on Europe and North America.

It was during this same decade that courses in Japanese and Japanese studies began to mushroom. In 1980 the Scottish Centre for Japanese Studies was founded as part of the Scottish Business School and in 1984 a Japanese Business Policy Unit was founded at the University of Warwick, with plans to incorporate it in a new East Asia Centre. Durham added Japanese studies to Chinese studies in the 1980s, and the Contemporary Japan Centre at the University of Essex was founded in 1989 with the aim that 'Japan should not be studied simply *sui generis* but that students need to combine a solid training in social scientfic approaches, theories and methodologies with a good control of language sources (written and spoken) in their approach to the country'.[75]

POST-WAR DEVELOPMENTS AFTER 1985

Although the Hayter Report tried to hammer home some much needed lessons and it did at least make possible the creation of the new Centre at Sheffield, its recommendations for a special fund for posts, for 100 earmarked postgraduate awards and for six or eight new centres of 'areas studies' were not implemented.[76] What is more, its continued use of terms such as 'Far Eastern studies' rather undermined the attempt to present the study of East Asia as urgent and pressing for Britain. It was only the third and last of the three major postwar enquiries into Asian and African studies in Britain that adopted different, less-eurocentric language. This was another report prepared for the University Grants Committee, this time under the chairmanship of Sir Peter Parker (1924–2002), who had been a Dulwich Boy studying Japanese in 1942 and had

---

75   Roger Goodman and Ian Neary, eds, *Case Studies on Human Rights in Japan*, 2nd printing (London: Curzon Press, 2003), p. x.
76   *Report of the the Sub-Committee on Oriental, Slavonic, East European and African Studies*, p. 4.

gone on to become Chairman of the Board of British Rail. The so-called Parker Report was properly entitled 'Speaking for the future: a review of the requirements of diplomacy and commerce for Asian and African languages and area studies' and it was published in 1986. In the twenty-five years since the publication of the Hayter Report, decolonization had mostly run its course and Britain's influence in the world was undeniably declining, but it was precisely for this reason, Parker argued, that Britain's commercial and diplomatic efforts needed ever more mastery of the languages and cultures of the world: 'A Government which is concerned for the development of Britain's overseas trade must therefore be prepared to take a view of the long-term languages and areas studies provision needs on behalf of business.'[77] However, in a section entitled 'The system at risk', Parker argued that the 'system [of education in Asian and African studies] whose benefits the country is still enjoying is already gradually breaking down'.[78]

In response to the Parker Report, the University Grants Committee agreed to fund posts in a variety of subject areas covered in the Report. The 'special factor' funding, as it was called, ran for five academic years from 1987 to 1992 and was mainly used for the creation of new posts, around half of which were in Arabic, Chinese or Japanese which Parker considered were 'likely to remain of both major political and commercial significance'.[79] Simultaneously, additional funding was made available to SOAS outside the Parker initiatives: 'because of its specialist nature, [it] was funded substantially by special factor allocation'.[80] Some of the new posts were created in existing centres and some in new centres. The new centres included the Cardiff Japanese Studies Centre, which was established in 1989 as part of the Cardiff Business School, and Leeds, where Japanese studies was grafted on to the existing provision in Chinese and Mongolian studies to create a new Department of East Asian Studies. The new posts in Japanese

---

[77] *Speaking for the future: a review of the requirements of diplomacy and commerce for Asian and African languages and area studies* (1986), p. 8.

[78] *Ibid.*, p. 11.

[79] *Evaluation of HEFCE funding for minority subjects: a report to HEFCE by Universitas* (2005), p. 6: http://heer.qaa.ac.uk/SearchForSummaries/Summaries/Pages/CDS63.aspx

[80] *Ibid.*, p. 6. See also National Archives: UGC 30/1, 'The Parker Report and SOAS' (12 March 1990). This file is marked 'Closed until 2022'!

studies created when the Parker Report was implemented were distributed as follows: Cambridge (1), Newcastle (2, one being a chair), Oxford (1), Sheffield (2), SOAS (3), Stirling (2). The UGC subsequently made allocations to Cardiff for 3.5 posts and to Essex for 2 posts in the expectation that 'both institutions will raise a considerable proportion of their funding from non-UGC sources'.[81]

The 1990s were undoubtedly a time of growth, at least in the number and range of institutions teaching on Japan in one way or another. A survey of Japanese studies in British universities carried out in 1996–1997 revealed the development of courses in Japanese studies as an option or a minor subject at Aston, Birmingham, Bradford, Nottingham, Ulster and other universities as well as King's College London, the University of Central Lancashire and King Alfred's College of Higher Education.[82] Meanwhile Japanese studies was being firmly established in Essex University, where Japanese had been available as an option since 1983 and then became a postgraduate degree subject; the chair in Japanese was funded by Sanwa Bank. Japanese studies was also flourishing at Durham, with Gina Barnes as NSK Professor of Japanese: between 1993 and 1999 six posts in Japanese were created there, one as a result of funds received from the Japan Foundation. Furthermore, the Department of Trade and Industry launched a 'Japanese Training Initiative' in 1989 in the hope of doubling the numbers of graduates in Japanese and thereby increasing the numbers of people in UK industry able to do business effectively with Japan; a key part of this was to make sure that all students spent a substantial period in Japan. The DTI supported four new postgraduate courses, at SOAS, Stirling, Bath and the North-West Centre for Japanese Studies at Manchester and enhanced existing courses at Sheffield, Essex and Liverpool.[83] Unfortunately, however, the funding came to an end in 1994, as has happened so often.

---

[81] National Archives: UGC 30/1, University Grants Committee, Summary of provision for Japanese (undated typescript, *c.* 1990).

[82] *Japanese degree courses in universities and other tertiary education institutions in the United Kingdom 1996/7* (London: Japan Foundation and Daiwa Anglo-Japanese Foundation, 1997)

[83] *The DTI Japanese Language Training Initiative (JLT): evaluation* (typescript, nd [*c.* 1993]).

In Scotland, courses on Japan were taught at Stirling in the early 1970s by James Valentine in Sociology and Social Anthropology and Jean-Pierre Lehmann in History. A centre for providing language courses and business services to the public was set up but there was no further development until a Japan Foundation staff expansion post was created in Japanese religions in the early 1980s and this was held for six years by Dr Brian Bocking. In 1987, Stirling was awarded two posts for the establishment of Japanese degrees from the Funding Council and it was also decided to appoint in addition a Director and professorial Post. Ian Gow was appointed to the Directorship and the other two posts were filled by Ian Reader and Tessa Carroll. Joint degrees were established quickly in a number of subjects including business studies and languages. NatWest Bank provided funding for the Chair in Japanese Studies which was held by Ian Gow, and Stirling also won major funding for the masters in Japanese Business programme funded by the Department of Trade and Industry. Approval was obtained from the Secretary of State for Scotland to name the Stirling centre the Scottish Centre for Japanese Studies. Ian Gow was succeeded by Joseph Moran and John Crump but student numbers dropped, posts were not renewed and then joint degrees and the masters degree were also dropped.

Anybody wondering what happened to all these courses need only turn to the subsequent survey, carried out in 2001–2002, which revealed that most of these courses had shrunk or been discontinued. In 1997, Essex 'discontinued the teaching of Japanese at undergraduate level in any form because it was no longer economically viable', the Scottish Centre for Japanese Studies ceased to exist in 1999 and from 2002 there was a phased withdrawal of all Japanese courses there and at Ulster.[84] At Durham the Department of East Asian Studies was axed in 2003, in spite of widespread and high-level protests.[85]

In 1991 the University Funding Council (UFC), the successor to the University Grants Committee, had introduced a programme of Minority Subject funding to protect imperilled

---

[84] *Japanese degree courses 2001–2002: a directory of Japanese degree courses in universities and other tertiary education institutions in the United Kingdom* (London: Japan Foundation and Daiwa Anglo-Japanese Foundation, 2002), pp. 106, 211, 224.

[85] *Times Higher Education Supplement*, 3 October 2003.

subjects and languages. As a result, courses in Japanese and other languages enjoyed some budgetary protection. In 1992 the UFC was succeeded by four new funding councils. The Higher Education Funding Council for England (HEFCE), the Higher Education Funding Council for Wales and the Scottish Funding Council at first maintained the Minority Subject funding: only HEFCE persevered with the scheme, however, while the Welsh and Scottish Funding Councils phased out Minority Subject funding. Although the Minority Subject funding arrangements were reviewed and renewed in 1994 and 1999, Japanese and Chinese were no longer consider 'minority subjects' and were therefore not eligible for further tranches of funding.[86]

In the first decade of the twenty-first century, however, a new initiative for Language Based Area Studies was launched by the Economic and Social Research Council, the Arts and Humanities Research Council, the Scottish Funding Council and HEFCE. The objective was to enhance national understanding of the Arabic-speaking world, China, Japan and eastern Europe (including the former Soviet Union) by creating new centres of excellence staffed by researchers who combined the necessary language skills and disciplinary expertise. In 2006 five new centres were created, selected from a larger number of bids, and they were funded at a combined cost of £15M, but the only one with a component related to Japanese studies was the White Rose East Asia Centre, which was hosted by the University of Leeds with the University of Sheffield as a partner institution.

The White Rose East Asia Centre epitomized a new regional focus on East Asia rather than just on Japan. This new focus is also to be found in the universities of Leeds, Sheffield and Cambridge, where new departmental nomenclature has sought to represent this shift in approach.

THE PRESENT AND THE FUTURE

As the essays contained in this volume show, there is much to celebrate in the growth of Japanese studies in Britain since 1945 and

---

[86] *Evaluation of HEFCE funding for minority subjects* (downloadable from http://dera.ioe. ac.uk/5876/), p. 30 and *passim*.

particularly over the last thirty years. This is true both in terms of scholarship and in terms of the development and growth of Japanese studies courses. The scholarship is evident from the publications mentioned in the essays, but it is worth remembering that not a few British scholars working on Japan have done so outside Britain: Ivan Morris (1925–1976) taught at Columbia for many years, Hamish Ion, a contributor to this volume, teaches at the Royal Military College of Canada, and Martin Collcutt at Princeton University. Conversely, many who were born and educated outside Britain have contributed to Japanese studies in Britain. Particularly important have been the talented language teachers who have brought their expertise in the teaching of Japanese as a second language to British universities and the librarians who have curated some of the best collections of Japanese books in Europe. There have also been teachers such as the Americans Donald Keene, who taught at Cambridge from 1948 to 1954, and Andrew Gerstle, who has contributed to this volume and is Professor of Japanese at SOAS, and many others from Austria, Germany, Italy, Japan, the United States and elsewhere, some of whom have done their graduate work in Britain. Collectively they have enriched Japanese studies in Britain by bringing different approaches and teaching methodologies with them, but it is a concern that few British undergraduates go on to undertake graduate work and seek academic employment in Britain.

As for Japanese studies courses, graduates now typically leave university not only with language skills honed during a year's residence in Japan but also with disciplinary expertise in one or more of a number of disciplines ranging from literature to business studies, anthropology and the social sciences to classical Japanese. In spite of these successes, we need to remember that Japanese is taught in an ever-changing environment for higher education in Britain and therein lie some problems.

Since 1945, Japanese studies, like other Asian, African and East European studies, have benefitted from the encouragement given by the Scarbrough, Hayter and Parker reports, but the funding that resulted from these reports was short-lived. As Parker put it in a letter to Sir Peter Swinnerton-Dyer, chairman of the UGC, on 18 February 1986:

It cannot be right that every other decade the country goes into a spasm of concern. I must hope that this Enquiry, the latest of them, will offer an opportunity to develop a more coherent policy – with stamina.[87]

Alas, that opportunity was not taken.

It is true that the study of Japan has weathered the storms rather better than other subjects thanks to the extraordinary generosity of Japanese corporations, foundations and individuals over the last couple of decades. The Japan Foundation, the Japan Foundation Endowment Committee, Daiwa Anglo-Japanese Foundation, the Great Britain Sasakawa Foundation, the Nippon Foundation, the Keidanren and the Nissan Motor Company (Oxford), Sanwa Bank (Essex), NSK (Durham), along with other individuals and charitable bodies, have underwritten posts and in other ways provided financial support that has not been forthcoming from universities or funding bodies. In addition, the Japan Society, the British Association for Japanese Studies and the Japan Library Group have lobbied on behalf of Japanese studies, facilitated the growth of library collections and done much else to support the study of Japan in Britain. Finally, the superb resources of the British Library and the British Museum, as well as those of many libraries, museums and art galleries around Britain, constitute a national collection of material relating to Japan that is of staggering scope and depth. We have much to be grateful for.

Nevertheless, the loss of earmarked funding and the end of special treatment has made departments of Japanese studies vulnerable to the calculus of student numbers, to the rhetoric of value for money and to the demands of the market. In the United States, on the other hand, the National Defense Education Act of 1958 has served to protect vulnerable subjects seen as of strategic value to the US irrespective of student demand and market sustainability, but there is no such protection in Britain.[88] Parker pointed out by way of contrast that by 1986 SOAS had had its income cut by 37% and had lost 25% of its academic staff over the previous five years and lamented the lack of 'systematic planning of provision' or of

---

[87] Appendix to Parker Report.
[88] *Speaking for the Future*, pp., 12, 78–80

'monitoring of the national stock of expertise in studies of Africa and Asia'.[89] There is still no planning or monitoring on a national level, and areas of expertise have already been lost, though Chinese and Japanese studies seem safe for the time being, thanks to reasonably buoyant student numbers. Unfortunately, the protection that substantially higher student numbers would bring is unlikely to materialize in the near future.

It must also be admitted that the growth of Japanese studies in the UK has not been impressive in terms of numbers of undergraduates, especially when compared with the United States, France or Germany. The Japan Foundation has carried out regular surveys of Japanese studies in the United Kingdom and these 'snapshots', taken at intervals of five or more years, make it possible to identify the shifts that have taken place over the last thirty years. The 1988 survey revealed that the number of undergraduates taking single honours degrees in Japanese in that year was 16 and that had risen to 56 by 1995; the projection in 1993 was that the number would rise to over 100 by 2000, though the actual number in 2001 was 58. Similarly, in the case of joint or combined honours degrees there were 7 graduates in 1988 rising to 145 in 1995; the projection in 1993 was that this number would rise to 250 by 2000, but the actual number in 2001 was 122.[90] Since then, however, the numbers have indeed risen and in 2015 there were 222 taking single honours degrees and 305 taking joint or combined honours degrees, bringing the total over 500 for the first time.[91] It is clear, then, that there has been slow but steady growth in student numbers. To some extent this can be attributed to the rising numbers of pupils being exposed to the Japanese language at schools, some of whom go on to take GCSE or further qualifications in Japanese but other factors include the popularity of Japanese popular culture with teenagers, which has the effect of reducing the unfamiliarity of Japan.

---

[89]   *Speaking for the Future*, p. 11.
[90]   *Japanese degree courses in universities and other tertiary education institutions in the United Kingdom 1996/7*, p. 13; *Japanese degree courses 2001–2002*, p. 15.
[91]   *Japan Foundation Japanese Studies Survey 2015: A Survey of Japanese Studies at University Level in the UK* (London: Japan Foundation, 2016; downloadable from http://www.jpf. org.uk/japanesestudies/survey.php), p. 13.

In the twenty-first century much of the growth has been in new centres and departments, such as those at Oxford Brookes and Leeds and more recently the University of East Anglia and the University of Central Lancashire, amongst others. Altogether 35 universities are listed in the latest Japan Foundation survey, four more than in the previous survey. Of these 15 offer courses leading either to single honours or joint/combined honours degrees in Japanese studies, while the rest either offer stand-alone modules relating to Japan or have staff and/or postgraduate students working on Japan-related topics. From this it is clear that more students than ever before are having the opportunity to include at least some study of Japan in their degree courses.

The 2015 Japan Foundation survey also includes the result of a survey of undergraduates studying Japanese, based on the replies of 293 respondents. These reveal that 30% were not UK nationals and that as many as 49% had undertaken some study of Japanese before going to university. Of those who had studied Japanese before only 20% had studied at school while 50% had studied independently. For 92% of all undergraduates the most important factor prompting them to opt for a degree in Japanese was unsurprisingly the desire to learn the Japanese language; for this reason a high degree of importance was attached to the year spent in Japan during the course. The areas of Japanese studies that attracted most interest were the language, 'traditional culture' and history, and the area of least interest was the Japanese economy.[92]

A particular problem for courses in Japanese studies as for all language-based subjects in the UK has been the steady decline in the numbers of boys and girls taking A levels in languages. To some extent this can be attributed to the removal by the Labour government in 2004 of the requirement to study a modern foreign language at Key Stage 4. This led to a major decline in the numbers taking languages at GCSE level: in 2001 78% of Year 11 pupils took a modern foreign language but by 2011 that had dropped to 40%. Inevitably, fewer pupils then went on to take A level languages: more than 22,000 took A level French in 1996, but in

---

[92]   *Ibid.*, pp. 189, 192, 199, 201–202, 204.

2013 fewer than 10,000.[93] At the same time the introduction of an annual fee of £9000 in most universities has led to an understandable reduction in the number of EU students coming to Britain. For these various reasons most university language-based courses have experienced falling numbers of enrolments.

On the other hand, the teaching of Japanese in secondary schools has become less uncommon and major new commitments to Japanese studies were made by the University of Manchester in 2007 and the University of East Anglia in 2011, the latter building on the foundations provided by the Sainsbury Institute for the Study of Japanese Arts and Cultures. What is more, the study of Japan, along with the study of other Asian societies, has undoubtedly contributed to the process of reducing the eurocentric bias of disciplines such as history, the history of art, sociology, and so on. This process, of course, is still far from complete: it is far from uncommon in the UK for historians of Japan, for example, to be placed in departments of Japanese studies rather than in history departments, though this has long ceased to be the case in North America. Similarly, most departments of the history of art pay little attention to Asian art, and the same can be said of music, philosophy, and so on. This is not so in SOAS, and elsewhere there have been signs of the opening up of traditionally eurocentric departments. The appointment of Craig Clunas, a sinologist, to the professorship of the history of art at Oxford represented a significant step in the right direction. At Nottingham the two representatives of Japanese studies, Andrew Cobbing and Sue Townsend, are both based in the Department of History, while at Oxford Brookes courses on Japanese society are embedded in the teaching of anthropology.

In spite of the problems mentioned above, which relate mostly to undergraduate provision and the new university funding structures, in one respect Japanese studies certainly has flourished in Britain, and that is in research and publications. Whereas before 1945 almost all writing on Japan was produced outside the universities, the balance has shifted dramatically since 1945. The publications of

---

[93]   Debra Malpass, 'The decline in uptake of A-level modern foreign languages: literature review', in *A Review of Modern Foreign Languages at A level* (Joint Council for Qualifications, 2014; downloadable from http://www.jcq.org.uk/).

university-based scholars are mentioned in the various chapters that follow, but other contributions there certainly have been. Amongst them are the writings of two librarians, Kenneth Gardner of the British Library and Koyama Noboru of Cambridge University Library: Gardner produced a magnificent catalogue of the pre-1700 Japanese books in the British Library, while Koyama has produced well-researched books on such subjects as international marriages in Meiji Japan, Japanese tattooists and the British royal family and the Japanese village in late-nineteenth-century London.[94] Among the diplomats, James Hoare, who served for many years in the British Embassy in Seoul and was Britain's first diplomatic representative in Pyongyang, and Sir Hugh Cortazzi, who was British ambassador to Japan from 1980 to 1984, have both written on relations between Britain and Japan. Cortazzi has also written many historical studies, including *Isles of Gold: Antique Maps of Japan* (1983), *Victorians in Japan: In and Around the Treaty Ports* (1987), *Japan in Late Victorian London: The Japanese Native Village in Knightsbridge and 'The Mikado', 1885* (2009), and has been one of the most effective defenders of Japanese studies in Britain over the last 30 years.[95]

In a recent lecture, Arthur Stockwin, emeritus professor of Japanese at Oxford, said that, 'Studying Japan, even in what we might consider an ideal world, is at best a minority pursuit, widely regarded as non-mainstream, and therefore potentially expendable.' In that context, he argued, 'those of us who study and teach about Japan ought not to be complacent' and need to be ready to make the case for the need to study Japan.[96] Japan of course remains today a compelling subject of study and there is no reason to suppose that its significance on the world stage will diminish in the short or medium term. The changing dynamics of the Pacific Rim

---

[94] Gardner, *Descriptive catalogue of Japanese books in the British Library printed before 1700* (1993); Koyama, *Kokusai kekkon daiichigō* (1995), *Nihon no shisei to eikoku ōshitsu* (2010), *Rondon nihonjinmura o tsukutta otoko* (2015). Yu-ying Brown, 'Kenneth Gardner (1924–95): librarian and bibliographer', in Cortazzi, ed., *BJBP* vol. VII, pp. 230–239.

[95] Hoare, ed., *Britain and Japan* (1999); much of Hoare's work has focussed on British relations with Korea. So far, ten volumes of the series *BJBP* have appeared, of which the first two were edited by Ian Nish, the third by Hoare and the remainder by Cortazzi alone.

[96] J. A. A. Stockwin, 'The future of Japanese studies: a personal perspective', paper delivered at the Canon Foundation in Europe Regional Fellow Meeting, EHESS Paris, 21 November 2014.

economy, the changes in the balance of power in East Asia and the globalization of Japanese culture by means of translations, touring theatre companies and the like have all worked together to make Japan better known, worth studying and impossible to ignore. Many will study Japan without learning the language, but how far can you go without knowledge of the language? The needs of diplomacy, business, informed journalism and scholarship are such that the ability to converse and debate in Japanese, to make use of Japanese written documents and to function in Japanese society are likely to remain indispensable. However those skills are taught in the future it will be alongside the necessary disciplinary skills, and those with the disciplinary skills will need to continue helping to remove the eurocentric bias of so many subjects of study in the United Kingdom.

2

British Missionaries and Japanese Studies in Pre-war Japan

O

Hamish Ion

INTRODUCTION

ALONG WITH COMMERCE and diplomatic recognition, the British set out to bring the benefits of Christianity to the Japanese in the mid-nineteenth century.[1] For the ordinary Japanese, who had little chance to travel, the British missionary was a microcosm of British society. The missionary, on the other hand, was engaged in personalized diplomacy, conducting Anglo-Japanese relations at a different level from the government-to-government variety practiced by Foreign Office diplomats. The Christian presses and missionary society journals and magazines in Britain ensured that

---

[1] The vast bulk of British missionaries in Japan belonged to the major Anglican and Scottish Presbyterian missionary societies: the Church Missionary Society (CMS, Low Church Anglican) which established a permanent British missionary society presence in metropolitan Japan in 1869; the Society for the Propagation of the Gospel in Foreign Parts (SPG, High Church Anglican) which opened its Japan work in 1873, and the Japan mission of the United Presbyterian Church of Scotland which began in 1874. For a history of the British missionary effort in Japan and its colonial empire, see A. Hamish Ion, *The Cross and the Rising Sun*, Volume 2, *The British Protestant Missionary Movement in Japan, Korea, and Taiwan, 1865–1945* (Waterloo, Ontario: Wilfrid Laurier University Press, 1993). The standard history of the Nippon Seikōkai remains Nippon Seikōkai rekishi hensan iinkai, ed., *Nippon Seikōkai hyakunenshi* (Tokyo: Nippon Seikōkai Kyōmuin Bunsho Kyoku, 1959).

missionary views reached a large audience. One of the results of this activity is the accumulated records of the work of British missionary societies in Japan and the papers of individual missionaries held in British archives, university libraries and church organizations as well as the enormous canon of published literature about Japan by missionaries. This represents a major source of information held in Britain about Japan perhaps only third to formal government Foreign Office and Admiralty-War Office materials.[2]

While American Protestant missionaries challenged Japanese culture, British Anglicans were different and sought to affirm Japanese society. Cyril Powles (1918–2013), a former Canadian Anglican missionary turned academic, has argued that Anglicans 'preferred to serve Japan as the Established Church of England served its own society, by engaging in a wide variety of social and cultural pursuits'.[3] Powles also has stressed that missionaries led by the Americans James Curtis Hepburn (1815–1911), the American Presbyterian lay doctor, and William Elliot Griffis (1843–1928), the Congregationalist pastor, but including the Britons John Batchelor (1854–1944), Walter Dening (1846–1913), and Arthur Lloyd (1852–1911), should be ranked as a second group alongside diplomats like Ernest Mason Satow (1843–1929), William George Aston (1841–1911) and Algernon Mitford (1837–1916) or scholars and journalists like Basil Hall Chamberlain (1850–1935) and Frank Brinkley (1841–1912), who were trailblazers responsible for the first competent works on the language, history and literature of Japan.[4]

This paper focuses on Batchelor, Dening and Lloyd not only because of their pioneering importance to the development of Japanese Studies but also because their writings embody characteristics and interests also found in the works of other British missionaries or their contemporary secular Japanologists in the culture, history

---

[2]   The library catalogues of the School of Oriental and African Studies, University of London, of University of Birmingham, and the Bodleian Library, Oxford University are helpful in identifying the relevant libraries and holdings. See also Robert A. Bickers and Rosemary Seton, eds., *Missionary Encounters: Sources and Issues* (Richmond: Curzon Press, 1995).

[3]   Cyril Hamilton Powles, *Victorian Missionaries in Meiji Japan: The Shiba Sect, 1873–1900* (Toronto: University of Toronto-York University Joint Centre on Modern East Asia, 1987), p. 9.

[4]   Powles, p. 47.

and religions of Japan. Batchelor was concerned with recording and capturing the language, grammar, customs and manners of a dying indigenous society in remote Hokkaidō; Dening was interested in the mental characteristics of Japanese in the sixteenth century that still might be seen in Japanese of the Meiji period; and Lloyd was fascinated by Japanese Buddhism and comparative religion. Underpinning the work of Batchelor and Lloyd was their Christian intent that their pursuits would facilitate respectively the conversion of the Ainu and Christian dialogue with Buddhists. In the case of Dening, it was his time as a CMS missionary in isolated Hakodate that provided him with the opportunity to acquire the facility in Japanese that was a hallmark of his literary work after he had ceased to be a missionary. It was traditional Japan and its attributes rather than modern Japan that attracted them most, which would also appear to be true of their scholar diplomat contemporaries, Satow, Aston and Mitford. Batchelor, Dening and Lloyd were at their most productive at the apogee of the British missionary endeavour in Japan, which was the last years of the Meiji period.

MISSIONARY PIONEERS IN TRANSLATION

The foundation of British missionary interest in Japanese Studies lay in Bible translation and the creation of English-Japanese dictionaries and other aids to Japanese language study.[5] The first British missionary attempts to study the Japanese language began with Walter Henry Medhurst (1796–1857), the English Congregationalist missionary, who began studying Japanese in Batavia, and as early as 1830 had

---

[5]   It was the Leiden University secular academic, Johann Joseph Hoffmann (1805–1878) who made the most significant lexicographical contributions together with the lay American Presbyterian lay medical missionary, Hepburn, in the nineteenth century and Andrew Nathaniel Nelson (1893–1975), the American Seventh Day Adventist missionary in the twentieth century, See Andrew Nathaniel Nelson, *The Modern Reader's Japanese-English Character Dictionary* (Rutland, Vermont: Charles E. Tuttle, 1962). See also James Curtis Hepburn, *A Japanese and English Dictionary, with an English and Japanese Index* (Shanghai: American Presbyterian Mission Press, 1867). Hoffmann published a grammar in Dutch and English in 1867 and a dictionary in 1875, see Cynthia Vialle, 'Japanese Studies in the Netherlands', in Nanyan Guo, ed., *Japanese Studies Around the World 2013: New Trends in Japanese Studies* (Kyoto: International Center for Japanese Studies, 2013), pp. 117–126.

printed an English-Japanese Japanese-English vocabulary.[6] Karl Friederick August Gützlaff (1803–1851) published in Singapore in 1837 the first Japanese version of the Gospel of John by a Protestant missionary.[7] Bernard Jean Bettelheim (1811–1870), the pioneer missionary of the Loochoo Naval Mission resident in Naha between 1846 and 1854, translated parts of the New Testament into the Ryūkyūan language.[8] Aids to Japanese language use were also helpful: John Liggins (1829–1912), the Wiltshire-born Protestant Episcopal missionary who arrived in Nagasaki in 1859, published in Shanghai in 1860 *Familiar Phrases in English and Romanized Japanese.*[9] Yet more important because it allowed educated Japanese familiar with Chinese language the possibility to read the Bible was the publication in Shanghai of a combined edition of the New and Old Testament in Chinese in 1864.[10]

The translation of the Bible into Japanese by missionaries resident in Japan reached a crucial stage in 1872 when an interdenominational Translation Committee for the publication of the New Testament was formed in Yokohama. Although this was led by the American missionaries Hepburn, Samuel Robbins Brown (1810–1880) and Daniel Crosby Greene (1843–1911), it also came to include William Ball Wright (1843–1912) of the SPG and John Piper (1840–1932) of the CMS.[11] This committee was able to publish the major works of translation between 1876 and 1880 as the various parts of the New Testament were finished.

In 1878 a permanent translation committee with representatives of all missionary denominations was formed for the translation of the Old Testament. Like the New Testament, the bulk of

6   See Sugimoto Tsutomu, *Seiyōjin no Nihongo hakken: gaikokujin no Nihongo kenkyūshi* (Tokyo: Kodansha, 2008), pp. 302–303.
7   See Ebisawa Arimichi, *Nihon no seisho: seisho wayaku no rekishi* (Tokyo: Nihon Kirisutokyōdan Shuppankyoku, 2005 edition), pp. 107–108.
8   See, Ebisawa, p. 126, 128. See also *Nihon Seisho Kyōkai hyakunenshi*, p. 28. See also Hamish Ion, 'James Curtis Hepburn and the translation of the New Testament into Japanese: a case Study of the impact of China on missions beyond Its borders', *Social sciences and missions*, 27 (2014), pp. 25–54.
9   See Sugimoto, pp. 321–324.
10   *Ibid.*, p. 103.
11   See Hamish Ion, 'British Bible Societies and the translation of the Bible into Japanese in the nineteenth century', in Hugh Cortazzi, ed., *Britiain and Japan: Biographical Portraits* [hereafter cited as *BP*], vol. IX (Folkstone, Kent: Renaissance Books, 2015), pp. 185–196, especially pp. 186–188.

translation work was carried out by relatively few people: among them was Philip Kimball Fyson (1846–1928) of the CMS, who later became Bishop of Hokkaidō, and the Americans Hepburn, Guido Verbeck (1830–1898) and David Thompson (1835–1915). Other British missionaries involved to a greater or lesser extent in the translation process were Piper, Wright, Dening and Robert Young Davidson (1846–1909) of the Scottish UPS mission. Like the New Testament, the Old Testament was published in stages beginning in 1882 and continuing until 1888 when the complete Old Testament was finished. As well as the interdenominational Bible translation effort, individual denominations were also concerned with their own denominational needs for Japanese language prayer books and hymnals. Archdeacon Charles Frederick Warren (1841–1899), the CMS missionary in Osaka, was much involved in the translation of the Anglican Book of Common Prayer.

Bible translation was not restricted to Japanese, for John Batchelor, a CMS missionary in Hokkaidō, began publishing his Ainu Bible translation in 1889, and by 1897 the complete Ainu New Testament was published.[12] Batchelor's pioneering work on Ainu language, custom and manners clearly made a major contribution to the development of Ainu studies, and helped pave the way for others like Neil Gordon Munro (1863–1942), the Scottish doctor and amateur archaeologist, whose Ainu studies were not underpinned by a desire to convert the Ainu to Christianity.[13] More than any other foreigner, however, it was Batchelor who drew British attention to the Ainu.

Batchelor was not the only British missionary in Japan to look at disappearing societies. Lionel Cholmondeley (1858–1945), the SPG missionary and honorary chaplain to the British Embassy in Tokyo, wrote a history of the English community in the Bonin Islands and Walter Weston (1861–1940), the CMS missionary and mountaineer, was clearly attracted to the simplicity and purity found in the ways of the hunters and rural folk he met in the mountains

---

[12]   Sir Hugh Cortazzi, 'John Batchelor, missionary and friend of the Ainu', in Ian Nish, ed., *BP*, vol. II (Folkestone, Kent: Japan Library, 1997), pp. 216–232.
[13]   For Munro, see Jane Wilkinson, 'Gordon Munro: ventures in Japanese archaeology and anthropology', in Ian Nish, ed., *BP*, vol. I (Folkestone, Kent: Japan Library, 1994), pp. 218–233.

of the Japan Alps.[14] Nostalgia for a simpler past was strong among
many British missionaries, and after the First World War there was
a tendency to look back on the Meiji period as a golden age before
the emergence of a modern industrialized and urbanized Japan in
the Taishō and early Shōwa eras, and to look for escape into rural
Japan where a more traditional Japan still existed. Batchelor chose
to live for over half a century in Hokkaidō away from the clamour
of modernizing Honshū, Hannah Riddell (1855–1932), the CMS
missionary who cared for lepers, worked in Kumamoto, and Barclay Fowell Buxton (1860–1946), the founder of the Japan Evange-
listic Band, formed his first Band of Christian converts in Matsue.[15]
In their writings to their supporters back in Britain, missionaries
provided a window into the world of provincial Japan.

Walter Dening, the CMS missionary in Hakodate in 1877 when
Batchelor first arrived in Hokkaidō, had already begun to study
Ainu language and made contact with the Ainu villagers at Piratori,
outside Hakodate, who would prove key to Batchelor's early Ainu
language study.[16] Theological differences between Dening and the
authorities of the CMS led him to leave the CMS's service in 1883
and embark on a new career as a teacher, journalist, and scholar.
Like other missionaries or former missionaries, he came to serve as
an interpreter of things Japanese to a Western audience.

MISSIONARIES AS INTERPRETERS AND CULTURAL
BRIDGES BETWEEN JAPAN AND BRITAIN

Dening possessed indefatigable energy and productivity for he wrote
an enormous amount in newspaper columns, articles and books
about Japan in which he helped to set the tone for the sympathetic
study of Japanese culture that has characterized much of the best of

---

[14] For Weston, see A. H. Ion, 'Mountain high and valley low: Walter Weston (1861–1940)
      and Japan', in Sir Hugh Cortazzi and Gordon Daniels, eds, *Britain and Japan 1859–1991:
      Themes and Personalities* (London: Routledge, 1991), pp. 94–106. For Cholmondeley, see
      Hamish Ion, 'Lionel Berners Cholmondeley: a chaplain in Tokyo, 1887–1921', in Ian
      Nish, ed., *BP*, vol. II, pp. 180–189.

[15] For Riddell, see Julia Boyd, 'Hannah Riddell, 1855–1932', in Nish, ed., *BP*, vol. II,
      pp.120–136.

[16] For Walter Dening, see Hamish Ion, 'Walter Dening (1946–1913) and Japan', in Hugh
      Cortazzi, ed., *BP*, vol. VII (Folkestone, Kent: Global Oriental, 2010), pp. 384–401.

British writings on Japan over the century since his death. Of his writings, Dening's study of Hideyoshi Toyotomi stands out as a pioneering attempt based upon an impressive collection of Japanese texts, which aimed through studying Toyotomi's life to reveal the mental characteristics of the Japanese that continued to persist from the late sixteenth century into the Meiji era.[17] Clearly, there was a Western audience eager to find out what traditional mental characteristics of the Japanese helped to bring success to Meiji Japan. Unfortunately for Dening, it was Nitobe Inazō (1862–1933), the American-educated Quaker and educator, who was able to provide the popular answer with his best-seller *Bushido: The Soul of Japan*.[18] Dening, however, was at the forefront of the British exploration of the late sixteenth century. Dening's language ability, already demonstrated in his translation work on the Old Testament, allowed him to research deeper into Japanese history than many of his former missionary colleagues. His work in the field was in keeping with that of James Murdoch (1856–1921), the historian, and he was also on friendly terms with Lafcadio Hearn (1850–1904) with whom he shared an interest in traditional tales, and with Basil Hall Chamberlain.

Arthur Lloyd, the SPG missionary, teacher and pioneer in the study of Japanese Buddhism, rivalled Dening in literary output and energy.[19] Unlike most of his European contemporaries who approached Buddhism from Indian studies, Lloyd investigated Buddhism from Japan, primarily the indigenous Shin and Nichiren traditions. Like some of Batchelor's more technical Ainu studies and Dening's literary surveys, much of Lloyd's early work was published in the 1890s in the *Transactions of the Asiatic Society of Japan*, for the Asiatic Society of Japan wanted to ensure that valuable information that could not find a publisher elsewhere was put on record. Later Lloyd's articles on Buddhism were coming off the

---

[17]   Walter Dening, *The Life of Toyotomi Hideyoshi*, third Edition with preface, notes and an appendix by M. E. Dening (London: Kegan Paul, Trench, Trubner, 1930). The first edition of this book was published by Hakubunsha in Tokyo in 1888.

[18]   Nitobe Inazō, *Bushido: The Soul of Japan: An Exposition of Japanese Thought* (Philadephia: The Leeds & Biddle Co., 1900).

[19]   For Arthur Lloyd, see Hamish Ion, 'Arthur Lloyd (1852–1911) and Japan: dancing with Amida', in Hugh Cortazzi, ed., *BP*, vol. VII (Folkestone, Kent: Global Oriental, 2010), pp. 402 419.

presses of at least five countries in English, German and Japanese.[20] By the time of his death, Lloyd was at the forefront in the effort to open a dialogue between Christians and Buddhism. In hindsight, his work on Buddhism can be seen to be flawed and should be seen more as an early sympathetic attempt at comparative religion rather than a straightforward analysis of Japanese Buddhism. Powles has pointed out that, 'Arthur Lloyd represented at his best the British ability to see intrinsic value in an alien culture. His unscientific approach to Buddhism need not leave the reader dissatisfied. Scientific method is of limited value to the study of religion.'[21]

While Lloyd had a Christian motivation behind his Buddhist studies, he was sympathetic and interested in Japanese religion and philosophy and willing to search out advice and help from Inoue Tetsujirō (1856–1944) and Anesaki Masaharu (1873–1949), which other Western Christians were not doing at that time. Powles noted Lloyd's failings were 'his inability to settle down to concentrated study and his confidence in his own linguistic ability led him to rely on facility with words when he might have spend more time trying to understand the concepts involved. In common with many liberals of his day, he never grasped completely the problems involved with the relativity of history and cultures.'[22] Anesaki noted about Lloyd's *The Creed of Half Japan*, in which Lloyd attempted to show that Shingon Buddhism was greatly influenced by Manichaeism (which Anesaki found inconclusive), that his 'work is often marked by hasty conclusions; yet his suggestions are valuable and await further investigation'.[23] While Lloyd's ideas about Buddhism might be flawed, they were thought provoking and worthy of further investigation. It was left, however, to August Karl Reischauer (1879–1971), the American Presbyterian missionary, and Sir Charles Norton Edgecumbe Eliot (1862–1931), the diplomat, to write studies of Japanese Buddhism that garnered more popularity than Lloyd's thought-provoking work.[24]

---

[20]   Powles, *Victorian Missionaries*, p.81.

[21]   *Ibid.*, pp. 82–83.

[22]   *Ibid.*, p. 81.

[23]   Masaharu Anesaki, *The History of Japanese Religions* (London: Kegan Paul, Trench, Trubner & Co., 1930), p. 130, footnote 1. Arthur Lloyd, *The Creed of Half Japan: Historical Studies of Japanese Buddhism* (London: Smith Elder, 1911).

[24]   A. K. Reischauer, *Studies in Japanese Buddhism* (New York: Macmillan; revised edition, 1925); Sir Charles Eliot, *Japanese Buddhism* (London: E. Arnold, 1935).

Lloyd was an acute observer of Japanese life surrounding him as seen in his *Every-day Japan*, which remains an interesting depiction of Japan society at the end of the Meiji period.[25] This book can be classified as part of a missionary genre of Japanese customs and manners of which *Nine Years in Nippon* by Henry Faulds (1843–1930), the Scottish United Presbyterian missionary doctor, is another example. Faulds' book was written for the general public and projects a positive impression of the Japanese people as well as a confident hope that the continued progress and development of Japan along modern lines would lead to a bright future.[26] The books, photographs, and journal articles that Walter Weston (1860–1940), the mountaineering CMS missionary, began to write within ten years of Faulds' *Nine Years* were not concerned with the future progress of Japan but with capturing what remained of the past. In 1921 Canon Walter Frederick France (1887–1963), an SPG missionary and later Overseas Secretary of the SPG, lamented the disintegration of past standards and ideals which had helped to make life in Japan so pleasant in the pre-war period.[27] Yet, he was not above writing about changing Japan as seen in his book about industrialism in Japan.[28] John Cooper Robinson (1859–1926), a Canadian Anglican missionary resident in Nagoya and amateur photographer, made a large collection of photographs covering the transitional years from Meiji to Taishō which was described by the late Marius Jansen (1922–2000) of Princeton University as having laid 'to rest many of the questions East Asian scholars have debated for years'.[29]

Missionaries were also a British presence in metropolitan and provincial Japan. In 1878 Isabella Bird Bishop (1831–1904), the

[25] Arthur Lloyd, *Every-day Japan: Written After Twenty-five Years' Residence and Work in the Country* (London: Cassell, 1909).

[26] Henry Faulds, *Nine Years in Nipon: Sketches of Japanese Life and Manners* (Boston: Cupples & Hurd, 1888).

[27] Ion, *The Cross and the Rising Sun*, p. 197. Canon France and Audrey M. Henty (1878–1970), a CMS missionary and niece of the famous author, taught Japanese to servicemen students at the School of Oriental and African Studies in London, and so could take some credit for teaching some of those who would later in civilian life go on to become leading figures in post-war British Japanese Studies. See Ōba Sadao, *Senchū Rondon Nihongō gakkō* (Tokyo: Chuōkoronsha, 1988), p. 51.

[28] Walter F. France, *Industrialism in Japan* (Westminster: Society for the Propagation of the Gospel in Foreign Parts, 1928).

[29] 'From Wycliffe to Japan: John Cooper Robinson', Wycliffe College (University of Toronto) *Insight* (Winter 2012), p. 1. The over 2,500 photographs are destined to be housed at the Museum of Anthropology at the University of British Columbia, Vancouver, B.C., Canada.

British explorer and author, visited Walter Dening's house in Hako-date at the start of her travels in Hokkaidō which also included a stay with the Ainu at Piratori.[30] For later newcomers to Japan such as George Cyril Allen (1900–1982), the academic economist, who stayed with Robinson when he first arrived in Nagoya in 1922, a sea-soned missionary like Robinson could provide valuable initial assis-tance and advice by functioning as a cultural bridge between Japan and the British world that they had just come from.[31] Churches like St. Andrew's, Tokyo, All Saint's, Kobe, and Christ Church, Yokohama, with English congregations served as focal points for the British community in those cities.

CONCLUSIONS

The negative impact of the First World War on British missionary families as well as its economic, social and religious consequences on the British missionary movement in Japan meant it was in decline by the early 1920s. Nevertheless, scholar missionaries like Ronald Duncan Shaw (1883–1972) continued to work on Buddhist texts and Japan still continued to attract talented clergymen like Wil-liam Howard Murray Walton (1890–1980), George Noel Strong, Charles and James Stranks (1901–1981) into the 1930s. How-ever, one consequence of the weakening of the British missionary endeavour in Japan during the interwar years was the limited influ-ence of British missionaries on the development of Japanese studies in post-War Britain. This stands in stark contrast to the experience in the United States where mish-kids (children of missionaries born in Japan) played very significant roles in the expansion of Japanese studies in the United States from the late 1940s onwards into the 2000s, and were responsible for the training of many of the next generation of Japanese studies specialists.[32]

---

[30]   Isabella L. Bird [Bishop], *Unbeaten Tracks in Japan: An Account of Travels in the Interior Including Visits to the Aborigines of Yezō and the Shrines of Nikkō and Ise*, first edition (London: John Murray, 1880, vol.II), p. 155. Bishop stayed at Biratori (Piratori) and described the Ainu there, p. 149.

[31]   G. C. Allen, *Appointment in Japan: Memories of Sixty Years* (London: Athlone Press, 1983), p. 10.

[32]   Among them were, Edwin O. Reischauer (1910–1990, Harvard), John Whitney Hall (1916–1997, Michigan and Yale), Donald Shively (1921–2005, Berkeley), Otis Cary

This does not detract, however, from the considerable role that British missionaries in Japan made to the development of Japanese studies before the War. The British Anglican affirmation of Japanese society led to a missionary approach to Japanese culture and religion based on sympathy, tolerance and appreciation for many Japanese traditional values. British missionaries helped to lay the foundations of British Japanese studies through Bible translation and through the pioneering work of individual missionaries like Batchelor, Dening and Lloyd. The British missionary endeavour in Japan has left behind an enormous resource for the study of pre-war Japan in its accumulated records, and the contribution of British missionaries to the development of British Japanese studies will continue to grow as researchers make use of this resource.

(1922–2006, Amherst and Dōshisha), and among the younger generation are Fred G. Notehelfer (b. 1939, UCLA) and Mark R. Mullins (Sophia and Auckland).

3

British Consular and Military Officers in Japan Before 1941

○

J. E. Hoare

THE CONSULAR SERVICE

AT THE TIME of the 'opening' of Japan in the 1850s, Britain had three consular services. The general service operated in most of the world. Older and better regarded was the Levant Service, covering parts of the near and middle east. Its staff were systematically recruited, properly paid, exercised jurisdiction over their countrymen, and some at least were expected to know the local languages. The China Consular Service that emerged in the 1840s resembled the Levant Service rather than the general service. The 1842 Treaty of Nanking (Nanjing) opened five ports for trade and residence, with a consulate at each. The need for efficient communication led to a professional Chinese-speaking consular service. By 1858, the China Service had developed a structure that would survive until the 1940s. Senior positions in the Service were no longer filled by missionaries and other outsiders with a knowledge of the language but by officers who qualified as interpreters; there were proper salaries and allowances during an officer's employment and a pension at the end;

and the rules against trading were strictly enforced. This was the model for the Japan Service.[1]

In the early years in China, the availability of missionaries and others filled the gap until a professional cadre could be trained. Japan had remained more isolated, however, and there were few Westerners who had any knowledge of the language. The person with probably the best Japanese was based in the Ryūkyū Islands, but seemed to be unhinged by the mid–1850s. Members of the China Consular Service studied Japanese but the only one who had made real progress died in 1851. Harry Parkes, later minister in Tokyo, had tried but had not advanced far.[2]

From the start, therefore, it was assumed that there would be a need to train language staff . In preparation for the opening of Japan to foreign residence, several university colleges were approached in 1854 for nominations. Those selected went to Hong Kong as 'supernumerary interpreters'. It is not clear if any went to Japan. Instead A. J. Gower, private secretary to Sir John Bowring, the Superintendent of the China Trade, was assigned to Japan as it was understand that he had ' ... directed his attention to Japanese'. Whatever Gower's language abilities, they proved no match for reality: he proved incapable of running the legation or learning Japanese and retired in 1874 with general good wishes.

At first, reliance was placed on Dutch–speaking staff. Dutch was the only Western language widely known in Japan and it was widely believed to be some form of lingua franca. Four Dutch speakers were selected: A. Annesley, C. F. Myburgh, F. M. Cowan and Richard Eusden. Martin Dohmen, a supercargo on a Dutch ship, later joined them. Another Dutch–speaking Briton, J. J. Enslie, was appointed in 1861. Cowan died in the autumn of 1860, Myburgh in 1869. The others stayed, even though it was obvious that officers who understood Japanese would be essential. As early

---

[1]   D. C. M. Platt, *The Cinderella Service: British consuls since 1825* (London: Longmans, 1971); P. D. Coates, *The China Consuls: British consular officers 1843–1943* (Hong Kong: Oxford University Press 1988). For Japan see J. E. Hoare, 'Britain's Japan Consular Service 1859–1941', in Ian Nish, ed., *Britain and Japan: Biographical Portraits* vol. II, (Richmond, Surrey: Japan Library, 1997), pp. 94–106, 350–353, where full references will be found.

[2]   W. G. Beasley, 'The language problem in the Anglo–Japanese negotiations of 1854', *Bulletin of the School of Oriental and African Studies*, 13 (1950), pp. 746–758.

as 1861, Alexander von Siebold (1846–1911), who had reached Japan in 1859 with his father, was employed as a supernumerary interpreter because he had learnt Japanese. Ernest Satow, joining the legation in 1862, found that Eusden, although designated 'The Japanese Secretary', knew not a word of Japanese, yet was supposed to provide language supervision for the students. In 1867, a consular post was found for him, and Satow took over as Japanese Secretary. The other Dutch interpreters served on although their lack of Japanese was a barrier to promotion. Annesley eventually left to become consul at Réunion and then at Portland, Maine. Only Enslie, who passed an oral examination in 1878, made any attempt to learn Japanese. He never qualified in the written language and that, plus other issues, blocked his promotion prospects.[3]

The need for Japanese was clear. Few Japanese had any knowledge of English, and the consular officers had to conduct business in the local language. Soon the rule against no promotion without a language qualification was strictly enforced. Those recruited in 1861 were sent to China initially, since Rutherford Alcock, the first British minister in Japan, believed this would help them with Japanese. Urgent need cut short the experiment, which was not repeated, and Ernest Satow, R. A. Jamieson and Russell Robertson set out for Japan in August 1862. Jamieson left at Shanghai to become a newspaperman. The other two arrived in Japan to find that there were no arrangements for teaching them. Western books on Japanese were few, out of date and not easily obtained in Yokohama. There were no teachers, and no funds to pay for them. The students had to devise their own methods. At first they worked on their own, but were eventually allowed to employ the American missionary the Reverend S. R. Brown for two hours a week at public expense. A Japanese teacher was also provided at public expense; they paid for a second themselves.[4]

---

[3]   See J. E. Hoare, 'Mr Enslie's grievances: the Consul, the Ainu and the bones', Japan Society of London *Bulletin*, no. 78, (March 1976), pp. 14–19.

[4]   E. M. Satow, *A Diplomat in Japan: An Inner History of the Japanese Reformation* (London, 1922; reprinted Rutland, Vermont: Tuttle, 1983), pp. 55–56; Brown's daughter married J. F. Lowder, another member of the Consular Service: J. E. Hoare, 'John Frederic Lowder (1843–1902): Consul, Counsel and *o-yatoi*', in Hugh Cortazzi, ed. *Britain and Japan: Biographical Portraits* vol. X (Folkestone, Kent: Renaissance Books).

Time for study proved difficult. Satow may have had it in writing that his task was to learn Japanese, but the prevalent view before the days of typewriters was that the best way to learn about current issues was by copying out despatches and notes. It took much effort to persuade his seniors otherwise. As late as 1885, the British Foreign Office expressed concern that constables rather than junior consular staff were doing the copying; the minister successfully argued that it gave the former something to do, while allowing the latter to keep up their Japanese.[5]

For some years, consular staff continued to acquire Japanese by puzzling out the language with books and a Japanese teacher, a method Satow remained wedded to for the rest of his life. By June 1863, he could provide an adequate translation of a Japanese document. In 1865, on the recommendation of the new minister, Sir Harry Parkes, he was appointed as 'Interpreter for the Japanese Language', with a salary of £400 per annum, double that of a student, but less than that of the senior Dutch interpreter, the Japanese Secretary. When Eusden finally moved in 1868, Satow took over, with a salary of £700. In status, he ranked with but after the diplomatic second secretaries.

Passing the interpreters' examination and moving on to an assistant's post, however, was no easy task, and it was never achieved in the two years allowed. Even though copying gave way to more modern methods, there were always other requirements which took the student interpreters away from their main task. Yet, having passed the examination, officers were not required to re–qualify, and there was concern that they would sit on their laurels or 'devote their leisure to dissipation and extravagance'.[6]

In the early 1860s, more systematic arrangements were in operation for recruitment. A. B. Mitford (later Lord Redesdale), a diplomatic service officer, told a Commission of Enquiry in 1870 that student interpreters in China and Japan were of a higher class than 'dragomen' (interpreters) in the Levant: '... young gentlemen who come out principally from the Irish universities'. Asked if they were of the same class as diplomatic attachés, Mitford said they were not. The First Civil Service Commissioner put it more gently in 1914: recruits for the Far Eastern Consular Services were like diplomats 'but not so highly qualified'.[7] In fact, the social origins of entrants to the Japan Service were firmly middle to upper class and educational levels were high. 'Irish universities' and schools were indeed well represented but so were other areas, including occasionally Oxford and Cambridge.

After two years, students became assistants. There were three assistant grades, at £300, £350 and £400 respectively. In addition, an allowance of £100 was paid to up to six officers who had passed the interpreter's examination. Parkes drew up a training scheme in 1870 under which third-class assistants spent one year at the court at Kanagawa (Yokohama) for legal training, and one year at a consulate for practical experience. At junior levels office hours could be long, a minimum of five or six hours a day, and an assistant's lot was not exciting. (At the senior levels, staff had a much less exacting schedule, sometimes as little as two hours a day.) Apart from the ubiquitous copying, there was much translation. Parkes discouraged the Japanese from writing in English, and it was not until his departure that such communications were generally accepted. Plunkett, Parkes' successor, noted in 1885 that a first assistant kept accounts, prepared despatches and letters to the Japanese authorities, kept the land and other registers, undertook notary acts, and might act as judge. Junior assistants looked after the Japanese-language archives, prepared translations, registered claims, and copied the outward letters and despatches. Each level took two to three years. An officer then become a vice-consul, or, if good at the language, assistant Japanese Secretary. It normally took at least ten years to became consul. Some took longer. Periods as acting consul softened the blow of delayed promotion.[8]

---

[7]   *Report from the Select Committee on Diplomatic and Consular Services*, Parliamentary Papers House of Commons (PPHC), 1870 (382), vii, pp. 300–301; Minutes of Evidence, *Fifth Report of the Royal Commission on the Civil Service*, PPHC 1914–1916, (Cd 7749), Q.38,820.

[8]   Hoare, 'Britain's Japan Consular Service, 1859–1941'.

Language training continued to dominate. Although the Japanese Secretary argued for better teachers as early as 1910, new recruits were left without guidance and expected to teach the teachers how to teach, just as in the 1860s. Before a commission of enquiry in 1913, Satow in retirement argued that there was no other way. In 1933, George Sansom, the commercial counsellor, and W. B. Cunningham, the Japanese Secretary, both good linguists, argued the same. The Foreign Office thought this was complacent. It was true that the language skills of many officers attracted praise and officers such as Sansom and Colin Davidson were admired for their excellent Japanese. Yet others found difficulty in meeting the standards. Esler Dening, son of a missionary with good spoken Japanese and a post–war ambassador to Tokyo, had not passed the examination after ten years. One particular hurdle was the requirement of a serious study of some aspect of Japan, not unlike a modern master's thesis. Working in Tokyo or Yokohama might make this a relatively easy task. Further away, with the demands of the job pressing, many complained that they had not been able to qualify only because they had failed to complete this task. No new system had been devised by 1941. Nobody drew any lesson from the fact that British language students, after four years, were failing to reach a standard others did in two.[9]

Japan was a difficult place to live, especially in the early years. It was remote and there was the fear of assassination. Local communities were small and faction-ridden. Consular officers found themselves the targets of local jealousies and tensions, to which they sometimes contributed. There was much sickness, some mental breakdowns and early deaths. Hyōgo (Kobe), Nagasaki, Niigata and Yokohama were unhealthy posts, and attracted added years for superannuation purposes. Most officers left well before the official

---

[9]   Minutes of Evidence, *Report of the Committee on Oriental Studies in London*, PPHC 1909, (Cd 4561), XXXV, Q.470; FO 369/308, Sir C MacDonald to Lord Grey, no. 4 consular, 5 January 1910; FO 369/595/42565, Sir C. Greene to Consular Dept, semi-off., 19 August 1913; FO 369/2151/K2207, minutes 3 February 1930; FO 369/2323/K4122, correspondence and minutes, 1933. For an approach more akin to modern teaching, see Richard Bradford, 'Learning the enemy's language: U.S. Navy Officer language students in Japan, 1920 – 1941' *International Journal of Naval History*, vol 1, no. 1 (April 2002), at www.ijnhonline.org/wp-content/uploads/2012/01/pdf_bradford. pdf (accessed 2 February 2016).

retiring age of 70, later 65. Few questions were asked about the medical reasons offered.

After 1900, new posts were added. In 1895 Japan acquired Taiwan, where Britain had a consulate. Dairen (Dalian) in the Liaotung peninsula was added in 1905, and Seoul and Chemulpo in Korea in 1910. Manila (1903) and Honolulu (1904) were also added to the Japan Service, to improve career prospects. But they were a mixed blessing. It was not easy to keep up Japanese and different terms of service applied.

Promotion remained slow. Economic constraints in the 1920s and 1930s hit hard, both in reductions in salaries and in the poor physical environment in which staff worked. The consular premises at Yokohama, destroyed in the 1923 earthquake, were not rebuilt until the late 1920s, and the consular residence not until 1937. There were long delays in providing new accommodation in Tokyo after 1923. At Kobe, the poor state of the consulate was a standing joke. There were battles over minor improvements. Like other specialised services, the Japan service was creaking to a halt. Reports and committees concluded that the solution was amalgamation, which came in 1932; China remained outside the amalgamated service. After 1934, other consular staff would be recruited to one service. The new arrangements had barely begun when a new war threw everything into chaos. After the war, the Japan Consular Service was no more, but several former members continued involvement with Japan as members of a united diplomatic service.[10]

Where did scholarship fit into all this? The general ethos of treaty port society laid a heavy emphasis on sport, horse–riding and other robust pursuits. Students were advised to bring sporting equipment with them. 'Studying', even for those officially employed to do so, was not highly regarded. Yet it was not surprising that some among a group of well–educated young men with little else to do would turn to intellectual occupations. Under Alcock and his temporary replacements there was little encouragement, although Alcock himself would eventually be a prolific writer on things Japanese, even producing a guide to Japanese grammar. The new service was too young and its members too taken up with the need to acquire

---

[10]   Platt, *Cinderella Service*, pp. 221 *et seq.*

language skills to have time to produce learned papers. After 1868, the situation changed. There was a new minister, Harry Parkes, who had tried his hand at learning Japanese in Shanghai in the 1840s. Parkes, who had been neither to a public school nor to university, was no scholar but he was interested in scholarly work and encouraged his staff to take it up.[11] So too did the Japanese Secretary, Ernest Satow. Satow was an assiduous scholar, who had published translations from Japanese and encouraged his charges to follow his example both as students and when they moved on to more regular work. He was regularly disappointed at their unwillingness to do so.[12]

There was another stimulus that would play a major role in encouraging scholarship. By the 1860s, the London–based Royal Asiatic Society had branches in places further east. Parkes had been active in the North China Branch in Shanghai, for example. The idea of a Japanese branch came up in 1866 soon after Parkes moved to Japan but came to nothing. Revived in 1872, mainly under the auspices of American missionaries but with active British participation, the idea, took off – although early on it was noted that it was not a good idea to organize meetings around the time of the races. In deference to American susceptibilities, the 'Yokohama Branch of the Royal Asiatic Society', quickly became 'Asiatic Society of Japan', which it still remains today.[13]

Members of the British diplomatic and consular services played a prominent role in the new Society. Its historian places Parkes at the head of this group, noting that if he had not been in London awaiting the Iwakura mission, he would have chaired the early meetings. Instead, the chargé d'affaires, R. G. Watson, became the first presi-

---

[11] Douglas Moore Kenrick, 'A century of Western studies of Japan: the first hundred years of the Asiatic Society of Japan 1872–1972', *Transactions of the Asiatic Society of Japan*, Third Series, 14 (1978), pp. 70–73. Parkes made two unpublished presentations.

[12] John Carey Hall, among Satow's earliest students, was a disappointment for his failure to produce work on the pre–modern Japanese legal system until long after Satow had retired: J. E. Hoare, 'John Carey Hall (1844–1921), a career In Japan (1868–1913) and the Japan Consular Service', in Cortazzi, ed., *Britain and Japan: Biographical Portraits* vol. X.

[13] *Far East*, vol. 6 (1874–75), p. 286; Kenrick, 'A century of Western studies of Japan', pp. 38–50; Hoare, *Japan's Treaty* Ports, pp. 44–46. A similar society organized in Korea in 1900 with many American members remains the 'Korea Branch of the Royal Asiatic Society'.

dent for a relatively brief period. When Parkes returned to Japan in 1873, he and W. G. Aston, who had also accompanied the Iwakura mission in Britain, joined the Society. Aston would become a leading figure. By 1873, some of his translations from the Japanese had already appeared in British government publications. His *Short grammar of the Japanese spoken language*, published in 1869, had gone into several editions, including a French translation.[14]

There were other outlets for scholarly or quasi–scholarly papers on Japan but the Asiatic Society and its *Transactions* were the first wholly dedicated to Japan. British officials were major contributors: both Satow and Aston had papers in the first set of *Transactions*, and both were to be prolific contributors in later years. Satow's total was 21 as sole author and one jointly with F. V. Dickins. Aston contributed 19 as sole author and one joint paper. Two other members of the Consular Service, J. H. Gubbins and J. C. Hall contributed six each. Parkes' nephew, T. R. McClatchie wrote five and J. J. Troup four. Others contributed between one and three papers. Some of these were probably based on the interpreter's exam essays. They covered a wide range of subjects, with much on literature, archaeology, history and legal studies both past and present. Not all were scholarly and neither were they all published. Nor were they confined to Japan. The Society was willing to hear travel accounts and Korea and China occasionally featured. British officials served as officers of the Society, with the British minister or one of his colleagues as president. The number of papers by British officials dropped away from about 1914 onwards, as work demands intensified with the war and the increased use of the telegraph. Only G. B. Sansom kept up the tradition producing 12 papers between 1910 and 1941, with one after retirement in 1950. Involvement in running the Society did not diminish however. British ambassadors (after 1902) still took the presidency and even produced papers.[15]

In addition, several officers published papers elsewhere, in the proceedings of societies such as the London Royal Asiatic Society, the Japan Society of London (now the Japan Society), the Royal

---

[14]   P. F. Kornicki, 'William George Aston', in H. Cortazzi and G. Daniels, eds., *Britain and Japan 1859–1991: Themes and Personalities* (London: Routledge, 1991), pp. 64–75.

[15]   D. M. Kenrick, *A Century of Western Studies of Japan* (Tokyo: Asiatic Society of Japan, 1978) pp. 346–446, gives the details.

Geographical Society and many others. These included papers on linguistics and history, and the geography of Japan and the Japanese empire. After the establishment of the Korea Branch of the Royal Asiatic Society in 1900, several members of the Japan Consular Service who served there contributed papers to its meetings and *Transactions*, and also served as council members and officers.[16]

As mentioned, Alcock wrote a number of works about Japan, including his two–volume account of his time in the country, *The Capital of the Tycoon*, which appeared in 1863. In 1878, he published *Art and Industries of Japan*. Aston had published his first grammar in 1869; he went on to produce another in 1872, which also went into several editions. The 1870s and 1880s saw Korea take a major role in his life, as the first resident British official in 1884. This interest led to several papers on the Korean language. After a brief period as Japanese Secretary, he retired on health grounds in 1889. But his main work was still to come, in the form of a translation of the *Nihon shoki* (*Chronicles of Japan*) in 1896, published by the Japan Society of London, and a *History of Japanese literature*, which appeared in 1899. His last work was *Shinto* (*The Way of the Gods*), which appeared in 1905.[17]

J. H. Gubbins, another founding member of the Asiatic Society and Japanese Secretary from 1889, was the chief negotiator of the 1894 revised treaty between Britain and Japan. His *Dictionary of Chinese–Japanese Words in the Japanese Language* appeared in 1889. In retirement, he became a lecturer at the University of Oxford for a short period. He produced two major works on Japan, *The progress of Japan 1853–1871* in 1911, and *The Making of Modern Japan* in 1922. He also produced a handbook on Japan for use at the 1919 Peace Conference.[18] Gubbins' books received much praise when they appeared and can still be read with profit. The same cannot be said of those by his contemporary J. H. Longford, who took up a university appointment at King's College London on retirement.

[16] J. E. Hoare, 'The centenary of Korean–British diplomatic relations: aspects of British interest and involvement in Korea, 1600–1983, *Transactions of the Korea Branch Royal Asiatic Society*, vol. 58 (1983), pp. 1–34.

[17] Kornicki, 'William George Aston', esp. pp. 71–73.

[18] Nish, 'John Harrington Gubbins', in I. Nish, ed., *Britain and Japan: Biographical Portraits* vol. II (Richmond, Surrey: Japan Library 1997), pp. 107–119.

He wrote three major books, *The Story of Old Japan* (1910), *The Evolution of New Japan* (1913) and *The Story of Korea* (1915). Well–received at the time, they now seem very old–fashioned and have little more than antiquarian value. In 1916, Japanese studies moved from King's College to the new School of Oriental Studies (now School of Oriental and African Studies). Longford did not transfer to the new institution and his post came to an end. When James Murdoch died in 1922 with his *History of Japan* unfinished, Longford was asked to take over the production of the third volume and apparently planned a fourth but he too died before this could be achieved.[19]

Satow, whose reputation as a Japanese scholar remains high, by contrast published very little apart from his papers for the Asiatic Society. His nearest approach to a Japanese grammar was *Kaiwa hen: Twenty–five Exercises in the Yedo Colloquial*, which appeared in 1873. (One cannot help wondering if the *Exercises in the Yokohama Dialect*, produced in 1879 by the 'Bishop of Homoco' – a red light district – was not a spoof on Satow's volume, produced by one of his fellow Japanologists.) With a Japanese diplomat, he co–edited a major English–Japanese dictionary published in 1876. This continued in use, in modified form, until the early 1940s. Together with Lt A. G. S. Hawes, he published *A Handbook for Japan* in 1881, which benefitted greatly from his wide–ranging travel throughout the country. From 1884, when he moved to a diplomatic appointment in Siam (Thailand), he was busier but still managed to produce two papers for the Asiatic Society, although new interests were beginning to take over. Some of his old enthusiasm revived when he returned to Tokyo as minister in 1896 and he was president of the Asiatic Society, for which he produced his last two papers before he left for China in 1900.

In retirement, he did little on Japan and disposed of most of his collection of Japanese books. However, he did contribute the chapter on Japan to the *Cambridge modern history* series. In 1921, he published *A Diplomat in Japan: an inner history of the Japanese*

---

[19]   Kenrick, *A Century of Western Studies of Japan*. p. 120. See also the contribution by Andrew Gerstle and Alan Cummings in this volume, and the introduction to James Murdoch, *A History of Japan* (London; Kegan Paul, Trench and Trubner, 1926), vol. III, pp. xvii–xviii.

Reformation, based on the diaries and notes that he had kept between 1862 and 1869. It was not scholarly, in the sense that it had neither notes nor bibliography, yet it remains a readable and useful guide to those turbulent years. His last great work was *A guide to diplomatic practice* in 1917. Much modified over the years, it remains in print.[20]

Two consular officers carried forward the tradition of scholarship in the 1930s. One was M. Paske–Smith. The other was George Sansom. Paske–Smith (1886–1946) joined the Consular Service in 1907 and served in a number of the more remote posts including Manila, Taipei and Dalian. Like Satow, Gubbins and Sansom, he was not university educated but he was clearly of a scholarly mind. He presented two papers to the Asiatic Society, one unpublished, a translation of *Hōgen monogatari*, the other, in 1913, which dealt with Japanese in the Philippines in the Spanish period. His major work, *Western Barbarians in Japan and Formosa in Tokugawa Days, 1603–1858* (1930), is still widely cited. He also edited much material relating to the East India Company's interests in Japan, including a two–volume edition of Peter Pratt's *History of Japan Compiled from the Record of the English East India Company* (1931) and Sir Stamford Raffles *Report on Japan to the East India Company* (1930), as well as a collection of material on the persecution of Japanese Christians at the end of the Tokugawa period, and other works.

Paske–Smith would be seen now as an antiquarian perhaps, rather than an historian. No such charge can be brought against Sansom (1883–1965), who arrived in Japan in 1904. Not only was he a highly successful officer, winning high praise for everything that he undertook, but he also produced a series of books that have stood the test of time. Like the pioneers such as Aston and Satow, both of whom he admired, Sansom embraced Japanese culture and history as his own, which greatly helped him in what started as a hobby but would become his second career. Sansom got on well with Sir Charles Eliot, ambassador from 1919 to 1925, whose

20   Satow features prominently in Kenrick, See also P. F. Kornicki, 'Ernest Mason Satow (1843–1929)' in Cortazzi and Daniels, eds., *Britain and Japan, 1859–1991*, pp. 76–85; Bernard M. Allen, *The Rt. Hon. Sir Ernest Mason Satow, G.C.M.G: A Memoir* (London: Kegan Paul, Trench and Trubner, 1933). Ian Ruxton has edited many of his letters and diaries, while former ambassador to Tokyo, Sir David Warren, plans a full–scale biography.

secretary he was. He completed Eliot's unfinished *Japanese Buddhism*, which appeared in 1935. By then, Sansom had already published two major works, *An Historical Grammar of Japanese* (1928) and *Japan: A Short Cultural History* (1931), probably his most famous work. While still in government service, he was invited to lecture at Columbia University in New York, where he spent six months while on leave in 1935. His plan to retire in 1940 was thwarted by the war, which he spent in South-East Asia before the Japanese invasion in 1941–1942 and then in Washington. After his retirement in 1947, he returned to Columbia as professor of Japanese studies. Later, he moved to Stanford University, where he worked on his three-volume *History of Japan*.[21]

The Japan Consular Service's high reputation for linguistic skills and Japanese scholarship perhaps owed more to a few bright stars than to the mass of its members. It must have been hard as a junior officer to come back from the office and begin reading Japanese for pleasure. The siren calls of sports and other outdoor activities remained strong – though some were active in both areas. Middle-ranking managers such as Satow or Gubbins might encourage the acquisition of knowledge about Japan but senior officers were more concerned that the copying was done or the official translation completed than that a junior should shine at the meetings of the Asiatic Society. That 'scholar diplomats' were encouraged to be knowledgeable about Japan is a myth. As one official noted in the 1930s: 'We did not send Mr Paske–Smith to Formosa [Taiwan] to write books.'

Some former members of the Japan Consular Service continued to use their language skills after retirement. A number (and several serving officers) joined the intelligence services in both wars and in the intervening peace. Only two, Longford and Gubbins, became university lecturers. Longford's post at King's College London ended in 1916; Gubbins' post at Oxford, created for him in 1909, lasted only until 1912, since few students took the courses he

---

[21]   Ian Nish, 'Sir George Bailey Sansom (1863–1965)', *Oxford Dictionary of National Biography* (Oxford University Press, 2004) at http://www.oxforddnb.com/view/article/35944, accessed 31 January 2016; Gordon Daniels, 'Sir George Sansom: pre-eminent diplomat and historian', in Hugh Cortazzi, ed. and comp., *British Envoys in Japan, 1859–1972*, (Folkestone, Kent: Global Oriental: 2004), pp. 250–59.

offered. Oxford did not re–establish a post in Japanese until 1954 and it was only in 1963 that teaching for a degree in Japanese began. One of the last entrants to the Japan Consular Service, Henry Sawbridge (1907–1990), spent a short time as deputy director of the newly established centre of Japanese studies at the University of Sheffield, where he did some language tutoring.[22]

MILITARY OFFICERS

It was naval officers who began to add to the meagre details of Japan known in Britain up to the mid–eighteenth century.[23] Before then, some information came from European publications derived from missionary accounts. Japan was known to the East India Company but its information was not widely shared. Naval explorations added more, even if the main purpose was to aid navigation. With the opening of Japan to foreign residence after the second round of treaty–making in the late 1850s, British naval and military officers became a more permanent feature in the country. Some such as Thomas Blakiston had resigned their commissions before coming to Japan. Others came either as part of the British garrison at Yokohama from 1863 until 1875 or were seconded to the Japanese government. A number of these stayed on in Japan. They included F. V. Dickins, Frank Brinkley and Lt A. S. G. Hawes. Many became serious students of things Japanese, active in the Asiatic Society and publishing books and papers on Japan. Another group were the naval officers who regularly called at Yokohama. At the first meeting of the Asiatic Society, it was Admiral Sir Charles Shadwell, Commander-in-Chief of the China Station, who drew attention to the folly of holding meetings that coincided with race days. Shadwell seems to have attended on other occasions, as did his colleagues, and he was one of the earliest elected honorary members of the society. Naval officers gave papers from time to time, mostly about voyages around the Pacific. These 'entertained and informed' the society but were perhaps not great scholarship. They tended to appear less and less frequently as the years went by.[24]

---

22   'Sawbridge, Henry Raywood', in *Who was Who 1907–1990*, p. 669.
23   The *Encyclopedia Britannica* published in 1771 has two lines on Japan, and two pages on 'japanning' (lacquer)! See vol. II, pp. 826–828.
24   Kenrick, *A Century of Western Studies of Japan* gives details. Dickins and Blakiston have *Oxford Dictionary of National Biography* entries.

There was no connection between these military or ex–military scholars and the British government, which did not see the need for Japanese language training until after the signing of the Anglo–Japanese Alliance in 1902. Once Japan assumed more importance as Britain's ally, however, it was decided that there was a need for officers who could understand Japanese and who could work along-side the Japanese military. The concept of 'military attachés' or military officers who would supply expert knowledge to diplomatic posts was relatively new but was seen as of growing importance. Such officers would need to know the languages of the countries in which they served, and this led the Army Council to seek officers for training in Japan. The first four left in late 1903, and the second group the following year. Between then and the outbreak of the Pacific War, around 100 officers of the British and Indian armies would learn Japanese.[25] There were also naval officers, whose course of training followed similar lines.[26]

Initially, officers were only to spend a year in Japan. This quickly increased to two and by 1910 had become three. Some did longer but that was exceptional. The first year was spent in formal language training, at the end of which they took the same examination as consular staff. Failure meant returning to Britain. There followed an attachment to a Japanese regiment or military institution. In the early years, with the Anglo–Japanese Alliance still fresh, officers found themselves well received by their Japanese counterparts. Later, they were regarded with much more suspi-cion, especially on the part of the police, and their movements were closely monitored.

As with the Consular Service, no particular arrangements seem to have been made for teaching. Lt Calthrop, in the first group to go, had some lessons in advance from J. H. Longford. On arrival in Tokyo, Gubbins, by now Secretary of Legation, provided a list of teachers, and explained what the examination required and that was that. Lt F. S. G. Piggott, one of the second batch in 1904, who had

---

[25]   See Anthony Best, *British Intelligence and the Japanese Challenge in Asia, 1914–1941* (Basingstoke: Palgrave, 2002). The Indian Army stopped sending officers for training in 1930: F. S. G. Piggott, *Broken Thread*, (Aldershot: Gale & Polden, 1952), p. 250.

[26]   Sue Jarvis. 'Captain Oswald Tuck RN (1876–1950) in Hugh Cortazzi, ed. *Britain and Japan: Biographical Portraits* vol. V (Folkestone, Kent: Global Oriental 2005), pp. 196–208.

been partly brought up in Japan, found a teacher in the same way. Thus the system that had operated since the 1860s carried on. Most of the military students continued to live in Western style as far as possible, though there were exceptions, including Calthrop, whose language skills and knowledge of Japan benefited accordingly. He was the only officer to attend the Japanese Staff College, although even he found himself dragooned into helping with embassy amateur dramatics.[27]

Many of those who trained in Japan had successful military or naval careers. Both Calthrop and Piggott became military attachés in Tokyo, the latter twice. Calthrop might well have gone back to Japan but he was killed in 1915. It is hard to know how many maintained their language skills after leaving. Most would have gone back to their regiments where it would have been difficult to do so. At the outbreak of the Pacific War, few former language officers were willing to come forward as teachers despite the urgent needs of the time.[28]

Like their consular colleagues, some became interested in Japan beyond their official duties, and they produced books and papers reflecting this. Understandably, there were many military–related publications. Even before the language scheme began, A. G. Churchill, military attaché at the time of the Boxer uprising, produced a *Dictionary of Military Terms*, as did Calthrop, both with assistance from Japanese scholars. Calthrop, more controversially, published a translation of the *The Art of War*, the Chinese classic study of strategy and tactics. Here he was helped by Sansom as well as by Japanese. First published as *Sonshi. The Chinese Military Classic* in Tokyo in 1905, it reappeared as *Sonshi. The Book of War, the Military Classic of the Far East* 'translated from the Chinese',

---

[27]   For Calthrop, see Hamish Ion, 'Something new under the sun: E. F. Calthrop and the Art of War', *Japan Forum* vol. 2, no. 1 (April 1990), pp. 29–41; Sebastian Dobson, 'Lieutenant–Colonel Everard Ferguson Calthrop (1876–1915), in Hugh Cortazzi, comp. and ed.., *Britain and Japan Biographical Portraits* vol. VIII, (Leiden: Global Oriental, 2013), pp. 85–101. For Piggott, *Broken Thread*, pp. 24 et. seq. Piggott's father had been a legal adviser to the Japanese government: Carmen Blacker, 'Two Piggotts: Sir Francis Taylor Piggott (1852–1925) and Major General F. S. G. Piggott (1883–1966)', in Cortazzai and Daniels, *Britain and Japan*', pp. 118–127. See also Anthony Best, 'Major–General F. S. G. Piggott (1883–1886), in Cortazzi, com. and edit., *Britain and Japan: Biographical Portraits* vol. 8, pp. 102–116.

[28]   Sadao Oba, trans. Anne Kaneko, *The 'Japanese' War* (Folkestone, Kent: Japan Library 1995, pp. 4–8. Some of those who might have been eligible were either killed or prisoners in East Asia.

in London in 1908. This brought down the wrath of Lionel Giles, assistant curator at the British Museum and a noted scholar of Chinese, who had also translated the work. Calthrop published a number of other minor translations.[29]

Piggott published *The Elements of Sosho*, the Japanese cursive script, in 1913, which received praise from Basil Hall Chamberlain, professor of Japanese at Tokyo Imperial University and from George Sansom. Unlike his father, he never presented a paper to the Asiatic Society – few military people did after 1900 – but he was later active in the Japan Society of London, where he gave papers mostly of an ephemeral nature. During the Pacific War, Piggott was a senior lecturer at the School of Oriental and African Studies (SOAS), teaching Japanese to military and naval staff.[30]

Malcolm Kennedy, also a language officer, was invalided out of the army after the First World War; he became a businessman, then a journalist and later a code-breaker at Bletchley Park, and published several books about contemporary Japan. The naval officer Captain Oswald Tuck taught Japanese to recruits for code-breaking and later contributed papers on cultural subjects to the Japan Society. But the star was Charles Boxer (1904–2000), an officer in the Lincolnshire Regiment. Boxer was in Japan from 1930 to 1933. Thereafter, he specialized in intelligence work and towards the end of the 1930s he was in Hong Kong. Boxer had begun the study of early European contacts with Japan in his spare time in the 1920s, which led to the publication of *Jan Compagnie in Japan* in 1936, as well as many other works. In Hong Kong, he was at every party, but would appear next day as neat as ever, having gone home to work on another academic paper. He was wounded and taken prisoner in December 1941. He left the army after the war to become Professor of Portuguese at King's College London, where he produced major works on Europe in the age of exploration and on Japan. In addition to his chair at King's, he spent two years at SOAS as Professor of the History of the Far East (1951–1953), 12 years at Indiana University and from 1969 to 1972 was a professor at Yale.[31]

---

[29] Ion, 'Something new under the sun: E. F. Calthrop and the Art of War'.

[30] Oba, *'Japanese' War*, p.8; Blacker, 'Two Piggotts', pp. 102–106.

[31] James Cummins, 'Charles Boxer (1904–2000) in Hugh Cortazzi, ed., *Britain and Japan: Biographical Portraits* (London: Japan Library, 2002), pp. 265–276.

CONCLUSION

The work of these pioneers was important not just in Britain. Dictionaries, grammars and other aides to language learning were the bedrock on which Japanese studies could develop. Historical, linguistic and legal studies, if sometimes they made little immediate impact, would be fruitful sources for more advanced studies later. Men of the Japan Consular Service, and their military and naval counterparts, with their wide contacts in Japan and in the rest of the world, helped provide the basis for the courses that can now be found in many major universities. Today's students may not read Aston, Satow or Calthrop but they might read Gubbins, Sansom and Boxer, and even the forgotten efforts of the pioneers can be discerned beneath contemporary works. All helped make known to the world the richness and complexity of Japan.

PART II

JAPANESE STUDIES AT UNIVERSITIES

4

Cambridge University

○

Richard Bowring

THE FIRST FORTY YEARS

WHEN THE STUDY of Japan and Japanese finally came to be introduced at Cambridge in 1948 it was established in what was then called the Faculty of Oriental Languages.[1] The Faculty was subsequently renamed Oriental Studies in 1955, but remained in essence devoted to the study of a wide range of languages, including Hebrew, with a prime interest in those of the Middle East and India. The common thread was an interest in philology and religion that ultimately went back to colonial and imperialist times. The regius professorship in Hebrew was founded in the time of King Henry VIII and the first chair in Arabic had been established in the 1660s. There were also chairs for Sanskrit and Egyptology while the chair in Chinese dates from 1888. Japanese was a newcomer and had been added not because of student demand but as a matter of strategic priority. Nevertheless Faculty politics ensured that it remained a minority subject for many years. As late as the 1970s it was considered more important to fight for the retention of a post in Ancient Iranian than to create a new one in modern Japanese history.

---

[1] For a more substantial account of the period 1947–97, see Richard Bowring, ed., *Fifty Years of Japanese at Cambridge*, Faculty of Oriental Studies, University of Cambridge, 1998. http://www.ames.cam.ac.uk/postgraduate/japanese/fifty-years.pdf/view

The first lecturer in Japanese was Eric Ceadel, who was appointed in October 1947.[2] By 1948 he had persuaded the university authorities to agree to the establishment of Japanese as a subject, which could lead to a BA degree. He had graduated in 1941 with First Class Honours in Classics and had published three articles on metrical problems in Greek tragedy in the *Classical Quarterly* while still an undergraduate. In January 1942 he was posted to the inter-service course in Japanese held at Bedford and was made an instructor there in November 1942, a position that he held until October 1945. Twenty years later in 1967 he resigned his post as lecturer in Japanese in order to take up the post of University Librarian where he ensured that the university library had an extensive and valuable collection of Japanese books. He also devised the library's system of arranging and cataloguing its Japanese books. He died in 1979, an early example of what is now known in Japan as *karōshi* or 'death through overwork'. His academic work in Japanese centered on the *Kokinshū* and its prefaces.

Two more appointments in Japanese studies were made soon after Ceadel; thenceforth a complement of three lecturers was considered adequate. Given that there were few students this is perhaps not surprising, but 'three' became fixed in stone and was not altered until after 1984. One of the two was J. R. McEwan, known for his work on Ogyū Sorai, who taught from 1948 to 1959.[3] The other was Donald Keene, who was a lecturer from 1949 to 1954: Columbia University in New York was prepared to offer him a longer spell of sabbatical leave in Japan than Cambridge could agree to, so he moved back to the United States and was replaced in 1955 by Carmen Blacker, who was to become famous for *The Catalpa Bow* (1975), a study of shamanistic practices in Japan.[4] In 1960 Charles Sheldon, a historian, replaced McEwan, and in 1967 Douglas Mills, a specialist in Japanese literature, replaced Ceadel.[5]

[2]   For details of Ceadel's life and achievements see the Foreword to Nozomu Hayashi and Peter Kornicki, *Early Japanese Books in Cambridge University Library* (Cambridge University Press, 1991) and the biographical portrait in Hugh Cortazzi, ed., *Britain and Japan: Biographical Portraits,* volume V (Global Oriental, 2004).

[3]   See portrait by Peter Kornicki in Hugh Cortazzi, ed., *Britain and Japan: Biographical Portraits,* volume X (Renaissance Books, 2016).

[4]   See biographical portrait by Peter Kornicki in Hugh Cortazzi, ed., *Britain and Japan: Biographical Portraits,* volume VII (Global Oriental, 2010).

[5]   See biographical portrait by Richard Bowring in Hugh Cortazzi, ed., *Britain and Japan: Biographical Portraits,* volume X (Renaissance Books, 2016).

Sheldon had written *The Rise of the Merchant Class in Tokugawa Japan* (1958) and Mills was later to write *A Collection of Tales from Uji* (1970).

It was only after 1957 that moves were made to employ a Japanese national to teach the modern language, but the list of scholars who then arrived to carry out this task contains some illustrious figures: Itasaka Gen (1957–1960), Torigoe Bunzō (1962–1964) and Yamanouchi Hisaaki (1968–1973), the first Japanese to be awarded a Cambridge doctorate in English Literature.

The initial course of study reflected the fact that Ceadel was a classicist and that 'Oriental Languages' was still closely tied to the discipline of philology. One began at, or near, the beginning: first-year students in 1949 started with Heian-period classics such as *Taketori monogatari* and *Tosa nikki*, proceeded in the second year to the *Man'yōshū*, *Makura no sōshi*, and finally had to tackle passages from the *Kojiki*. This in itself would be tough enough, but one of the compulsory papers in the early years was composition *into* Classical Japanese. From the viewpoint of a classicist this would have been seen as quite a normal requirement; in the context of Japanese, it was bizarre.

The speaking and reading of modern Japanese was introduced only later and even then in somewhat haphazard fashion; it was not until 1965–1966 that an oral examination was introduced. The emphasis at Cambridge had initially been on classical Japanese. One reason for this had been the difficulty of finding native speakers who could teach spoken Japanese. Another was the dearth of modern Japanese books in the immediate post-war years. In a letter dated 10 June 1947 to Captain J. Clifford, who was stationed at the time in Kuala Lumpur and was to become one of the first students at Cambridge, Eric Ceadel had occasion to write as follows:

> I wonder if you have any contacts, official or unofficial, with anyone in Japan now who could help me get some Japanese books – mainly works of reference, dictionaries, and editions of the Classics? I have tried four or five times to get some of these books by writing to people in Japan (mainly officers in the Occupation Forces) but with no success. If you know of any means to help me, I would be very glad.

Copying machines were not available in those days; as one copy of each book was needed for each student, the choice of reading matter was limited. This state of affairs did not last very long but even in 1965 when I arrived as a student, we were still using copies of hand-written material in purple ink produced on a Gestetner machine and there was no hope of ever seeing a Japanese newspaper, let alone tasting a Japanese meal.

In these early years the three lecturers had only a handful of students in each year. In 1971 ten students arrived in the Faculty, but the number quickly leveled out and double figures were not reached again until the mid-1980s.

By the late 1960s Japan was well on its way to becoming a major economic power and this did not go unnoticed in Britain at large. In accordance with the 1947 Scarbrough report, funds had become available for the development of modern Japanese studies. The School of Oriental and African Studies (SOAS) in London expanded its provisions. Oxford University began to focus on the importance of Japan and a new centre was opened at Sheffield, concentrating on modern Japanese studies.[6] The University of Cambridge with its high reputation in economics, engineering and the sciences as well as in core humanities subjects such as English, history, philosophy and classics, was unfortunately slow to recognize the importance of an understanding of modern Japan and to adapt to what was happening in the wider world. The comparison to the United States and, in particular, Australia, where students were being introduced to Japanese at Junior School level, is striking.

Inevitably when funds for higher education began to dry up, Japanese at Cambridge began to look vulnerable. The early 1980s were a time of crisis. Stringent cuts in the education budget meant that the University had to look for savings and Oriental Studies, with its unrealistic staff-student ratio, came in for close scrutiny. In 1980 the University established a sub-committee to look into the matter. The report was produced on the assumption that overall funding for Japanese studies would not be increased.

---

[6]   See separate account of Japanese studies at Sheffield by Gordon Daniels, at Oxford by Roger Goodman and Arthur Stockwin, and at SOAS by Andrew Gerstle and Alan Cummings in this volume.

By the time that the report was submitted in 1981, it had become clear that the whole financial position of the University was set to deteriorate further and in short order. Decisions on funding for the Faculty were therefore postponed, but the Faculty Board was asked to investigate ways of increasing student intake and to take a careful look at teaching provision. The gravity of the situation was underlined by the fact that the first recommendation was that discussions take place with the equivalent Board at Oxford on how certain subjects with very low student numbers might be shared out between the two universities to avoid unnecessary duplication. In particular they asked that 'the future pattern of Japanese in the two Universities' be investigated.[7]

The situation became critical when it was announced that Oxford had received a large benefaction for Japanese studies from the Nissan car company. Unfortunately no one in authority at Cambridge had thought about seeking funds from Japan or had tried to push the case for strengthening Japanese studies at the University. Then, as part of an attempt to reduce staff, the University encouraged teachers near the end of their tenure to take early retirement on very advantageous terms. In September 1982 both Charles Sheldon and Douglas Mills decided to accept this offer. In both cases the decision was made for entirely understandable reasons, but the effect was to put a large question mark over the whole future of Japanese studies at Cambridge, given that the University authorities, looking for further cuts, might refuse permission to fill the posts and simply allow the subject to wither away.

The result of discussions by what became known as the Joint Working Party (Oxford and Cambridge) was revealed in a further report to the University dated 16 March 1983. On the subject of Japanese, it said:

> The position of Japanese at Oxford and Cambridge presented the Joint Working Party with a particularly difficult problem. The small number of undergraduates in recent years hardly justifies, on financial grounds, the provision of courses at both Universities. Cambridge has the larger establishment of offices supported by U.G.C. funds, with three University Lectureships, two of which are now

---

[7]   *Cambridge University Reporter*, 16 March 1983, p. 392.

vacant, and a Lectorship. Oxford has only two such posts, with considerably younger incumbents, but the recent establishment of the Nissan Institute of Modern Japanese Studies on a benefaction supporting a Professorship, two University Lectureships, and an Instructorship, has strengthened the subject immeasurably so that it is clearly guaranteed at Oxford for the foreseeable future, even though the resources of the Institute are outside the Faculty and almost entirely non-linguistic. Furthermore, it is possible that the establishment of the Institute may further deplete student numbers at Cambridge. On the other hand, although the pattern of retirements at Cambridge, recent developments at Oxford, and the possibility of even fewer undergraduates must put into question the continuation of Japanese Studies at Cambridge, its strength in classical Japanese is unique in the United Kingdom, and it has, in the University Library, probably the largest single Japanese library collection in Western Europe. Moreover, Chinese would be weakened, and its credibility diminished outside the University, without the support of Japanese, which is an essential research tool for Chinese scholars. The termination of Cambridge Japanese would undoubtedly dismay senior academics in Japan, and would also be at odds with other international influences and trends. In the present financial circumstances, however, the Board feel obliged to accept the view of the Joint Working Party that the Cambridge Japanese course could be maintained adequately with an establishment of two University Lectureships and a Lectorship. The Board accordingly propose the suppression of one of the vacant University Lectureships, and they intend, subject to the approval of that proposal, to give permission to fill the remaining vacancy. They look to the Faculty Board, however, to review the working of the proposed new arrangements and to inform the Board accordingly.[8]

These recommendations were accepted. Charles Sheldon's post was suppressed and the other, held by Douglas Mills, was advertised. At this point, October 1983, the balance had shifted markedly in Oxford's favour. Cambridge had only two active posts: one University Lectureship (Carmen Blacker) and one Lectorship (Haruko Laurie). Despite the stated view of the Joint Working Party that 'the Cambridge Japanese course could be maintained adequately with an establishment of two University Lectureships and a Lectorship', this was clearly not a realistic proposition in

---

8   *Cambridge University Reporter*, 16 March 1983, p. 396.

the longer term, and there was a distinct possibility that Japanese studies would collapse when Carmen Blacker herself reached the retirement age.

Carmen Blacker, who was much concerned about the threat to Japanese at Cambridge, drew the attention of Sir Hugh Cortazzi, then British Ambassador in Tokyo, to the seriousness of the matter and asked for any help he could give. He decided that efforts must be made to try and raise money in Japan for the endowment of a Chair and save Cambridge Japanese. He accordingly raised this with the *Asahi shinbun* on 29 April 1983. This brought a response on 14 May and the next day the famous column '*Tensei jingo*' took up the subject. By the end of that year and as the result of much work by many people, a benefaction for a Chair of Modern Japanese Studies was received from the Keidanren. The then Chairman of the Keidanren, Hiraiwa Gaishi, was a prime mover and it is known that TEPCO was by far the largest donor. The Chair was established at the end of July 1984 and advertised in October.

In the meantime, the vacant Lectureship was eventually advertised in December 1983. Richard Bowring, who had already published books on Mori Ōgai and the diary of Murasaki Shikibu, was appointed and returned from Princeton to take up the appointment on 1 June 1984.[9] By that time it was clear that the Keidanren benefaction had been promised and that the prospects for Japanese studies at Cambridge looked rosier than they had done a year earlier.

In a separate but related development, work had been proceeding on another front. The Japan Foundation had been concerned that Japanese Studies might disappear at Cambridge and, in collaboration with St John's College, they eventually agreed to part-fund a senior studentship for three years with teaching duties in the Faculty. David McMullen, a lecturer in Chinese and fellow of St John's, was particularly active in ensuring the success of this particular subvention. This post was advertised and filled in October 1984 by Peter Kornicki, who was at that time a researcher at the *Jinbun kagaku kenkyūjo* in Kyōto, the first foreigner to hold an established position at this kind of Japanese state institution.

---

[9] *Mori Ōgai and the Modernization of Japanese Culture* (1979) and *Murasaki Shikibu: Her Diary and Poetic Memoirs, a Translation and Study* (1982).

Carmen Blacker decided not to apply for the newly established chair in Japanese at Cambridge although she was well qualified for the post. It was instead offered to Richard Bowring. On 19 February 1985 he was duly appointed to the chair, and the lectureship, which he had held, immediately became vacant; it was offered to Peter Kornicki in April 1985. This, in turn, left the Senior Studentship open and both the Japan Foundation and St John's College generously agreed to fund this post as of new, for a full three years.

It was filled soon afterwards by Mito Takamichi, a PhD student from Toronto working on Japanese oil policy and international relations. It was his job to begin to fill the gap in modern studies and he did this by starting a course in Japanese politics. By spring 1985, therefore, the situation had been transformed: the establishment had suddenly grown from two to five, and Eric Ceadel's dream of creating a substantial centre for Japanese studies was beginning to look achievable.

The lure of benefaction led in 1985 to the university being almost taken in by a Japanese Walter Mitty type fraudster who went under the name of Ijuin Kimitaka. As this episode is marginal to the theme of this article but is indicative of the problems of fund raising, the story has been consigned to a footnote.[10]

---

[10] In the spring of 1985 someone calling himself Dr Ijuin Kimitake, introduced by a scholar of English theatre from Waseda University, visited us. Dr Ijuin announced that he was on a hush-hush, private mission from Prime Minister Nakasone. The Japanese Embassy would not know of his visit because it had been arranged by the PM's private office; he would be obliged if we did not contact the Embassy to avoid embarrassment. Things were a little delicate, he explained. As everyone knew, Japan was worried at the size of its trade imbalance with Europe and the United States. Plans were afoot to set up a major Japan Studies Institute in Kyoto (this eventually came to fruition as the *Nichibunken*) and he had been sent to inquire what could be done about setting up a similar institute in Cambridge. He handed us a four-page proposal for a 'Euro-Japan Institute of Cambridge', which would involve purchasing land in the city. The proposal was in English. He had already had a meeting with the University Treasurer, who had, perhaps unwisely, revealed the existence of a suitable site in the city. It turned out he was referring to the empty shell of the old city hospital, known as the Old Addenbrooke's Site, which eventually became the Judge Institute of Business Studies. A meeting with the Vice Chancellor had also been set up. We were duly impressed. Dr Ijuin produced a description of his own Japanese Cultural Arts Institute (Getsuritsu-yo) in Yamanashi prefecture, in which he described himself as 'pottery master, author, international lecturer and mathematician'. In conversation it turned out that he had studied at Princeton, knew Marius Jansen there, and had a PhD from Dallas. Having passed him my card at the very beginning of the proceedings, I now asked him for his. After some hesitation ('*ma, ii daro*' [well, I suppose it's safe], he said quietly) he gave me his card.

At the time I was a little taken aback but assumed that the secrecy of his mission meant that he had to be careful about handing his card to all and sundry at this stage.

Soon after he left, we began to have second thoughts. A number of things did not quite add up. His name card was a very individualistic one; it had panache but carried no information apart from the name and an address in Yamanashi, not quite the kind of thing one expected from someone connected to the PM's office. And then there was the matter of the name. It was a curious mixture: Ijuin was an aristocratic name from Kyushu, but Kimitake, his personal name, was the same as the real personal name of the Japanese author and suicide Mishima Yukio. He had been at Princeton but had relied on an interpreter. Most curious of all, he had combined a sober suit and tie with brown leather cowboy boots. Well, I thought, this may be what special envoys from Nakasone were wearing these days, but I doubted it. I rang the Embassy. No, they said, they did not know of an Ijuin, but they would check and get back. Meanwhile the meeting with the Vice Chancellor went ahead. All the top university officers were present. The plan to buy land and put up a large institute was presented. The meeting lasted forty minutes. I told the Vice Chancellor of my concerns at the end of the meeting and we agreed to wait and see what happened.

The Embassy rang later that week to say that they had no knowledge of Ijuin but were still checking. I had the opportunity to discuss things with Prof. Marius Jansen from Princeton, who was on a short visit to Cambridge University Press, and he confirmed that he knew Ijuin, but not as a student. Ijuin had approached him in similar circumstances and mention had also been made of a similar Institute in the States. He had even visited Ijuin's mansion in Yamanashi. I heard nothing for a week, and then came a call from Interpol: could they come and discuss a recent Japanese visitor, please? Apparently he was wanted in Tokyo on fraud charges.

The tale that eventually emerged told of the power of personal introductions, the ways in which Japanese institutions can be manipulated, and of the kind of atmosphere that sudden richness in Japan had generated. It also said something about the reputation of Nakasone, in that the whole yarn of being a personal emissary had seemed so plausible. In the end it was a sad story, but one had to admire the genius of a man who could pass himself off in front of the Vice Chancellor without batting an eyelid. It turned out that Ijuin (aka Kido Kazuo, Sakata Kazuo, Sakata Kimitake) was the eldest son of a Kyushu miner. Born in 1937, he had dropped out of high school, gone to work at the US base at Ashiya and picked up English. He returned home in 1962 just when the mines at Kaijima were closed. Borrowing his father's golden handshake, he married and went to America for his honeymoon. He was divorced in 1967. Off to America again, where he eventually ended up in jail for three years for fraud and embezzlement. Released in 1971, he returned to Japan. Going to see a famous Hagi potter called Sakata, he asked to be taken on as an apprentice. When this failed, he approached and eventually married the daughter. They had three children but he was again divorced in 1981. How he had cooked up the idea of becoming a Nakasone envoy I do not know, but it was a touch of genius. What did he hope to get out of it from Cambridge? A letter signed by the Vice Chancellor perhaps? Or was it just the thrill of fooling the whole world and his brother?

While he was acting his new role in Cambridge (and he tried Oxford the next month), things were quickly unraveling in Tokyo. On 26 May, 1985 the *Sankei Shinbun* revealed that the upmarket Tokyo Department Store Wakō had begun to recall all pottery sold at a one-man exhibition held three years previously. The potter's name was one Ijuin Kimitake. About eighty pieces had been sold at an average of ¥200,000 a piece. It had recently come to light that some of the pieces were by a rank amateur and had been exhibited without his knowledge. It turned out that 'Ijuin' had managed to pass himself

THE RECENT PAST

The years from 1985 to 1995 brought steady expansion based on a successful search for funding outside the University. Starting in the summer of 1985 fund-raising approaches were made via former students working in the City of London, primarily in merchant banks. Miss Haruko Fukuda, then working at James Capel & Co, and Patrick Gifford of Robert Fleming were central figures in raising this fund. They wanted to raise the money from British rather than Japanese institutions. James Capel and Robert Fleming gave substantial amounts and other British instructions helped, but the British response was disappointing and Haruko Fukuda and Patrick Gifford had to seek help from Japanese financial institutions to ensure that a sufficient fund was provided. In all £350,000, was subscribed including contributions from major Japanese financial houses.

This allowed the creation of another language teaching post known as an Instructorship, to which Haruko Laurie was appointed in 1987. At the same time, the results of the Parker Report entitled 'Speaking for the Future: a Review of the Requirements of Diplomacy and Commerce for Asian and African Languages and Area Studies', commissioned by the then University Grants Committee, gave Cambridge a further lectureship in Japanese. The modern historian Stephen Large, who moved from a Readership in History at Adelaide to start teaching in October 1987, filled this post. He had already published *The Rise of Labor in Japan: The Yūaikai, 1912–19* (1972) and *Organized Workers and Socialist Politics in Interwar Japan* (1981) and was later to make a major contribution with *Emperor Hirohito and Shōwa Japan: A Political Biography* (1992).

---

off as a master potter, had persuaded Wakō to hold an exhibition of his work, and had made a tidy profit from the proceeds. Takashimaya and Daimaru, two of Tokyo's largest department stores, had also been taken in and run similar exhibitions. The fraud only came to light when an amateur potter in Okayama called Itō, who had never sold a piece in his life, just happened to see some of his own pieces in the catalogue of the Wakō exhibition. He then recalled that Ijuin had visited him some years back saying that he was in politics but was getting fed up with the rat race and wanted to study as a potter. Could he please have some advice as to how to begin as an amateur and could he please borrow some pieces as examples? It was these examples that eventually ended up in the Wako exhibition. A year later I heard that our friend Ijuin had been arrested at Narita and was now serving yet another sentence for fraud. Red faces all round.

In 1988 Mr. Mito left Cambridge to take up a position in banking in London. By October 1988 the teaching strength was up to six, with one additional unexpected bonus: Gina Barnes, who had previously been an Assistant Lecturer in the Department of Archaeology, won a Senior Studentship at St John's College to continue her research and teaching. Dr Barnes was uniquely a specialist in Japanese and Korean archaeology, and Cambridge had the benefit of her presence, her research and her teaching until she left in 1996 to become Professor of Japanese at Durham. 1988 also brought a personal benefaction from the Japanese educationalist Kawashima Hiroshi, which allowed the university to create one more lectureship, to which Mark Morris was appointed in April 1989: he was well known for a series of seminal articles in the *Harvard Journal of Asiatic Studies*.

Carmen Blacker was due to retire in 1991, but permission was obtained to fill the prospective vacancy well in advance and Hugh Whittaker, now a professor at Oxford and the author of many books on the sociology of Japan, was appointed in August 1989. The following year saw the establishment of the Fuji Bank Lectureship in Modern Japanese Studies, which was first filled by Barry Keehn and is now held by John Nilsson-Wright, who has written *Unequal Allies?: United States Security and Alliance Policy Towards Japan, 1945–1960* (1998).

At the same time the balance in the first fund raised increased to the point where it was possible to think about improving the position of Haruko Laurie as the person in charge of language teaching. The treatment of language teachers in universities has always been problematic. Dedicated, born language teachers are not always born researchers and so tend to become trapped in positions that do not reflect their worth to the University. Eventually, after much consultation and many committees, Bowring finally succeeded in persuading the University that it made sense to establish a post, entitled Senior Language Teaching Officer, that would attract a stipend that would more truly reflect the contribution made, while treating any research done by the officer to be an added bonus rather than a requirement. Haruko Laurie was appointed to this new post in October 1991.

Further benefactions were received from, among others: Yasuda Trust and Banking for a five-year Research Fellowship in the

Faculty; the Daiwa Anglo-Japanese Foundation for a five-year Research Fellowship at Downing College; Mitsui Kaijō Kasai for a microfilm collection of all printed books from the Meiji period held in the National Diet Library; and Mr Aoi Tadao of Marui Co. Ltd. This last gift of £3 million allowed us to build a new wing on the University Library to house Japanese, Chinese and Korean resources together with an East Asian reading and reference room.

Student numbers at Cambridge have always been sensitive to developments in the countries in question: they rose dramatically at first in line with the Japanese economy and then fell again when the Japanese bubble burst. The average has been fairly constant at 10–15 per year. Given the rise of China, interest in Japan might have declined further had it not been for Japanese pop culture, *manga* and *anime*, which have kept things Japanese in the forefront of the minds of school children. Whether a fascination with *anime* can carry one through the rigours of actually learning how to read Japanese is another matter.

THE SITUATION TODAY

Richard Bowring retired in 2012 not long after publishing *The Religious Traditions of Japan 500–1600* (2008) and was replaced by Peter Kornicki, who had published *The Book in Japan* in 1998. He, in turn, retired in 2014, and the third professor of Japanese at Cambridge, Mikael Adolphson, took up the post in January 2016. He is the author of *The Gates of Power: Monks, Courtiers, and Warriors in Premodern Japan* (2000) and *The Teeth and Claws of the Buddha: Monastic Warriors and Sōhei in Japanese History* (2007) amongst other works and brings expertise on Japanese medieval history to Cambridge for the first time.

Following the retirement of Haruko Laurie, who had produced a valuable new textbook, *An Introduction to Modern Japanese*, in two volumes in 1993, and of Mark Morris, who had published both on Japanese literature and Korean cinema, in 2015, several new appointments were made. In addition to Professor Adolphson and John Nilsson-Wright, the current members of staff are Toshimi Boulding, who teaches language, Miki Kawabata, who is Haruko

Laurie's replacement as senior language teaching officer, Barak Kushner, who is the author of *The Thought War: Japanese Imperial Propaganda* (2006) and *Men to Devils, Devils to Men: Japanese War Crimes and Chinese Justice* (2015), Laura Moretti, who is the author of a large number of articles in English and Japanese on Edo-period literature, Matthew Shores, who works on premodern Japanese literature and is also a *rakugo* performer, and Brigitte Steger, who has written *Sekai ga mitometa Nippon no inemuri. Tsūkin densha no utouto ni mo imi ga atta!* [The world has recognised Japanese inemuri. There was a meaning in napping on commuter trains!] (2013) and *Japan Copes with Calamity. Ethnographies of the Earthquake, Tsunami and Nuclear Disasters of March 2011* (2015, edited with Tom Gill and David Slater).

With student interest at its present level, any further expansion of Japanese studies at Cambridge will have to be via endowment, but the twenty-year deflation and stagnation in Japan are not propitious. The result is a steady state but at a less-than-desirable level. Perhaps the greatest problem that faces the subject in Cambridge is its continued isolation within the broader University. Thanks to the Nissan benefaction, Oxford has managed to create Japan-related posts in politics, social sciences, history and economics. Cambridge has a strong central core but lacks this further presence in other larger faculties, which restricts the subject from growing. It is here where comparisons with the United States are so stark. It would be rare to find a major US university where there were only six academics working on Japanese subjects. The other area in need of improvement is postgraduate studies. The superb resources of the University Library at Cambridge remain underused. Not enough funding is available to support graduates, who increasingly gravitate towards the United States where the subject is far better resourced at this level. This has two knock-on effects. A vibrant community of graduate students can make a big difference to a subject; and there are signs that the next generation of lecturers will be coming from outside the UK. It is a good sign that we can still attract such people but the matter is surely serious when there are no UK applicants for jobs when they do become available.

The University Library has a good collection of books relating to Japan. If the funding problems can be solved, we are confident that good graduates will be attracted by its treasures and its resources, which are all available on open-stack. The first Japanese book arrived in the Library in 1715. It took 233 years for the subject itself to be taught.

5

Japanese Library Collections: Cambridge and Elsewhere

O

Koyama Noboru

JAPANESE LIBRARY COLLECTIONS in Britain are associated with two major historical events in modern Japan - the Meiji Restoration and World War Two. Their collections originated after these turning-points when Japanese books were at particularly low-prices. Ernest Mason Satow (1843–1929), one of three great pioneers of Japanese studies together with William George Aston (1841–1911) and Basil Hall Chamberlain (1850–1935), was a prominent collector of Japanese books and most of the important early Japanese books in research libraries in Britain derived from Satow's collection including those of Cambridge University Library, the British Library (formerly the British Museum Library), the Bodleian Library, etc.

Satow collected Japanese books enthusiastically in Japan in the early part of the Meiji period and probably the size of his collection reached around several thousand titles, but in the mid-1880s (1883–1886), he started to disperse his books to the British Museum and his friends. He took a post at Bangkok, Siam, in 1884 to move from the consular to the diplomatic services and, in order to finish his 'Japanese days' (his youth), he disposed his collection of Japanese books mainly from Bangkok, confirming his determination to make a new career.

Satow's best samples of early printings including early movable type editions found a home in the British Museum in 1884–1885 through sale and donation. Satow also sent his Japanese books to Chamberlain in Tokyo and his Japanese books on Buddhism to James Troup (1840–1925) in Kobe and Thomas Watters (1840–1901), but the majority of his collection was dispatched to Frederick Victor Dickins (1838–1915) in London and those books were subsequently lent or given to Aston for his Japanese studies in 1892. When Aston died in 1911, his library of 1,978 Japanese books, 82% of which had been Satow's books, ended up in Cambridge University Library. In the same year, Cambridge University Library received a donation of 721 Japanese books which belonged to the former library of Heinrich Philipp von Siebold (1852–1908). Also Satow directly donated 433 Japanese books to Cambridge University Library in the following years (1912 and 1913). In 1991, *Early Japanese Books in Cambridge University Library: A Catalogue of the Aston, Satow and von Siebold Collections,* edited by Nozomu Hayashi and Peter Kornicki, was published by Cambridge University Press. The catalogue lists 2,474 items of Japanese, Chinese and Korean books at Cambridge University Library.

After receiving the collections of early Japanese books in 1911–1913, Cambridge did not acquire a substantial amount of Japanese books until the Scarbrough Report of 1947 which promoted Asian and East European studies including Japanese studies following World War Two. Cambridge received a grant of £6,000 for acquiring Chinese and Japanese books based on the Scarbrough Report. Cambridge spent £3,500 on purchasing Japanese books in 1949 and 1950 and acquired 2,542 items (13,653 volumes) of Japanese books from Japan in order to establish the modern Japanese library collection. *Classified Catalogue of Modern Japanese Books in Cambridge University Library* by Eric B. Ceadel was published by W. Heffers & Sons (Cambridge) in 1961 and, finally, the collection was ready to fully support Japanese studies at Cambridge University.

6

Cardiff University

O

Christopher Hood

THE PARKER REPORT of February 1986 entitled 'Speaking for the Future' highlighted the need in the long-term national interest to expand the study of Japanese language, history, economy and culture. In the light of this report the University Grants Committee agreed to fund the establishment of new posts. One objective was to ensure that Japanese could be studied at degree level at a number of universities where Japanese had not hitherto been taught at this level.

The time was right, if not overdue. The Japanese economy was expanding fast and there was increasing interest in Japanese management techniques. Japanese investment in Britain was bringing significant benefits to the UK economy. There had been a Japanese presence in Wales since the early 1970s but its importance grew in the 1980s.

Cardiff University, or the University of Wales, Cardiff College, as it was then called, recognized the importance of Japan to the development and prosperity of Wales. In 1987 the new Cardiff Business School was established. At the first meeting of the School Board it was agreed that the School should bid for funding to appoint new lecturers in Japanese studies as well as staff to teach the Japanese language as there were already a number of staff in the Business

School who were researching aspects of Japanese management and Japanese investment in the UK. The bid was successful.

In 1989 the Cardiff Japanese Studies Centre was established as part of the Cardiff Business School. Its director was Douglas Anthony who came to Cardiff from the Japanese Studies Centre at Sheffield University. Based on his experience at Sheffield, he concentrated on establishing a number of joint honours programmes and other combined degrees. In 1990 the Cardiff Japanese Studies Centre accepted its first students who were able to choose from one of six degree programmes combined with Japanese: business, French, German, Italian, Spanish and Law. Despite the subsequent deflation in the Japanese economy and a reduction in the level of Japanese investment in Wales, Cardiff University continued to attract a good number of students throughout the 1990s, many of whom were attracted to the Centre by the presence in the school of prominent academics such as Gaye Rowley and Mark Teeuwen as well as Douglas Anthony. However, by the end of the 1990s, all these specialists had left and a decision was taken to cease accepting students to do Law with Japanese. Doubts were even cast on whether Japanese should continue to be taught at Cardiff.

In 2000 Cardiff Business School, however, appointed Christopher Hood to become the new director of the Cardiff Japanese Studies Centre. Hood, an associate fellow of Chatham House and a graduate of the business studies and Japanese studies programme at Sheffield, changed a number of features of the Centre with the aim of reinvigorating the Centre's activities. The first goal was to upgrade the Business with Japanese programme into the Centre's flagship joint honours programme. Within a few years Cardiff saw the number of students on the programme rise to a level where there were more students in one year on this programme than were studying the same programme across all four years at Sheffield. The intake across the five programmes regularly was over 20 students and in some years was over 35.

In 2000 the Centre had a number of exchange agreements with universities in Japan, but in principle students on, for example, the Business and Japanese programme would all go to the same university. It was decided, however, that it would be better for students to be split up and to attend different universities. This policy would encourage them to interact more in Japanese, and with other students from around the world. It would also increase the likelihood of their becoming involved in extra-curricula activities at the host university, and would help them to diversify their experiences whilst in Japan. This should in turn enhance the level of class discussions upon their return to Cardiff. Increasing the number of agreements with Japanese universities would also help to ensure that the number of Japanese exchange students coming to Cardiff could be maintained at an appropriate level. By the end of the decade the number of agreements had risen to twelve.

The Cardiff Japanese Studies Centre also appointed new lecturers. In 2001 David Williams, author of *Japan: Beyond the End of History* (1994) and Takeda Hiroko, author of *The Political Economy of Reproduction in Japan* (2005), were appointed as the Centre looked to develop new activities. However, by this time it was becoming clear that students preferred to study in a single honours Japanese studies programme rather than in the joint honours programmes where Cardiff had become one of the leading universities in Japanese studies in the UK. It was, however, difficult to develop a single honours programme within the Cardiff Business School, especially when there was a cap on the number of students that the School could recruit. Meanwhile the Centre continued to strengthen the work done with the rest of the Cardiff Business School programmes and research. This was greatly helped by the appointment of Umemura Maki, author of *The Japanese Pharmaceutical Industry: Its Evolution and Current Challenges* (2011). Christopher Hood's own research, particularly his books *Shinkansen: From Bullet Train to Symbol of Modern Japan* (2006) and *Dealing with Disaster in Japan: Responses to the Flight JL123 Crash* (2012), helped to act as a bridge between the interests of the Business School and broader interests in Japanese Studies.

Umemura Maki's appointment had been made possible by funds provided by the GB Sasakawa Foundation and the Nippon Foundation as part of a significant programme to provide new posts in Japanese studies at UK universities. Her appointment under this programme confirmed the importance attached to Japanese studies at Cardiff University.

After his appointment as director of the Centre, Hood worked on reinvigorating and professionalising the teaching of Japanese language at Cardiff University. The underlying ethos was that in order for Cardiff to be a leading provider of Japanese language in higher education it was necessary to recruit and keep highly qualified and experienced staff who specialised in teaching the Japanese language. Over a number of years there was a shift from 'teaching assistants' to 'teaching instructors' and then to 'Japanese language lecturers'. This saw Cardiff University employ leading specialists, some with doctorates, in the field of teaching Japanese language and Japanese linguistics. Meanwhile other lecturers and staff, including Rosemary Smith who had joined the Centre when it was established, supported Japanese language teaching as needed.

In 2014 the biggest change in Japanese studies at Cardiff University since its establishment took place. The University's School of Modern Languages was established and this became home to all of the Japanese degree programmes. As a result the Cardiff Japanese Studies Centre, which had been supported throughout by Janet Richards, effectively ceased. The prior restrictions relating to degree programmes were removed and the school could look to establish new programmes and increase the number of options on other programmes to study Japan and Japanese.

In its first year the School provided a Japanese option through the innovative 'Languages for All' programme that allows any undergraduate student to study a language during their time at Cardiff University. There are also Japanese options within the translation studies programme of undergraduate and postgraduate degrees. All of these changes and developments are also being reflected in changes in staffing with Japanese studies specialists in the School of Modern Languages as well as in other schools around the University. Christopher Hood joined the new School while Umemura Maki remained in the Business School. In 2013 the School of History, Archaeology and Religion appointed a new lecturer in Japanese history, Ian Rapley. The School of Modern Languages also appointed a new lecturer, Dr Ruselle Meade, in Japanese studies in 2015. With others around the University also continuing to research aspects of Japan, Cardiff University is well placed to attract PhD students.

Graduates from Japanese programmes at Cardiff University have gone on to many different careers. One graduate returned to Kitakyūshū, where he had been an exchange student during his studies and while working there was appointed as honorary British Consul. Another graduate in Law and Japanese was awarded an MBE in 2012 for her services to enterprise. In recent years there has been an increase in the number of graduates who have continued their studies by doing an MA, for example in translation studies, or doing an MPhil/PhD. Another trend in recent years has been the significant increase in numbers of those going to Japan upon graduation to seek full-time jobs. Until recently many students had regarded the demand for employment in Japan as limited and often restricted to teaching English, for example on the JET Programme. However, with Japan facing a skilled labour shortage and with companies beginning to prefer hiring those with a knowledge of Japanese language and culture, the opportunities for employment in Japan upon graduation have risen.

7

Durham University

O

Don Starr

IN DURHAM'S RECENT history Louis Allen was the first person to offer instruction in the Japanese language and to publish on Japan. Louis was a reader in French but in the war had been sent to SOAS on a crash course in Japanese and was then despatched to Burma as an intelligence officer. Those courses consisted of studying either speaking and listening or reading, since only limited skills could be taught in the time. Louis revelled in telling how lucky it was he had done the reading course since a Gurkha soldier had come back from fighting with a bedraggled document that Louis was able to identify as a Japanese battle plan, and alert his superiors to its contents. After the fighting ended he remained in Burma to interrogate Japanese prisoners and as a result of that began a long term collaboration with a former Japanese soldier. Louis went on to publish a number of books on the war with Japan and became deeply involved in the reconciliation movement. Just before his death we were approached by the Japanese Embassy over their plan to recommend him for an award, but sadly he died before this could happen. In the 1960s and 1970s Louis offered Japanese classes to all-comers on Wednesday afternoons as informal non-credit courses.

The School of Oriental Studies (SOS) at Durham was established in 1951 by Professor T.W. Thacker, a semitic philologist fluent in

German who had worked with the code-breakers at Bletchley Park during the war. The funding for SOS came partly as a result of the Scarbrough Report of 1947, an attempt to ensure that Britain did not in the future find itself once again desperately short of qualified linguists, as it had been during the war. The first lecturer in Chinese, Raymond Dawson, was appointed in 1952; when he returned to Oxford he was replaced by Archie Barnes. A second lecturer in Chinese, Keith Pratt, was appointed in 1964, and a third, Don Starr, was appointed in 1971. The latter two brought interests and expertise in Korean and Japanese to the School.

Formal teaching of Japanese for credit began in 1981 when a student of Chinese at the School of Oriental Studies (SOS), Michael Jenkins, expressed a keen interest in taking Japanese as a subsidiary subject. Don Starr, who himself had 'majored' in Chinese but taken Japanese as a subsidiary at SOAS under Patrick O'Neill and subsequently under Carmen Blacker and Douglas Mills at Cambridge, agreed to teach Michael. This soon developed into a regular 'main plus subsidiary' pattern with a small group of students, around half a dozen, taking the 'Chinese Studies with Japanese' course each year. This course offered modules in Japanese to third and fourth year students. Thanks to funding from Japanese sources we were able to send some of the students to Nanzan University for a summer course in the language. This was enormously helpful in raising standards and making students feel at home in Japan, so that many returned to Japan to work or study after they graduated. At this time the course relied on Don Starr as the only regular member of staff, teaching Japanese grammar alongside a succession of part-time teachers, many recruited from among the Japanese wives of staff at the new Nissan factory.

As a result of one of the 'reorganisations' that convulse our subject area with monotonous regularity in the name of efficiency, the School of Oriental Studies was dismantled in 1989 and the staff teaching on the Ancient Near East (Egyptology, Coptic, Hebrew, Akkadian, etc.), Persian, Classical Arabic, Indian Studies and Turkish were retired or transferred elsewhere. Two subject areas from SOS were reprieved: Chinese studies and modern Arabic studies. This was in no small measure the result of the 1986 Parker Report which pushed the University Grants Committee, the university funding body at that time, into offering extra support for so-called 'minority' languages, but specifically targeted at their usefulness in the areas of 'diplomacy and commerce'. The parts of SOS that were retained were those that met these criteria and were relatively successful in attracting students; those that were axed had been very successful in research terms, but this was only just becoming recognised in funding terms (the first Research Assessment Exercise was 1986). The result was that Arabic was transferred to a new unit, the Institute for Middle Eastern and Islamic Studies (which combined language and literature specialists from SOS with social scientists working on the Middle East), and Chinese remained in the original Elvet Hill House location, which was renamed the Department of East Asian Studies (DEAS) with a remit to develop a specialist undergraduate course in Japanese studies, something we had been urging on the University for many years. We had taken regular advantage of the generous Japan Foundation book grant scheme in the 1980s to supplement the limited existing collection of works on Japan in the University Library. By the time the BA in Japanese Studies degree started in 1992 there was a useful basic collection that expanded quickly through the funds generated by a full course. It was also supplemented by additional grants, such as the one from the Daiwa Foundation that allowed the University to acquire the library of Louis Allen after his death.

This period coincided with the establishment of the Teikyo University of Japan in Durham in 1990. A delegation from Teikyo University had visited the UK several years before with a view to establishing a branch campus in the UK to enable Teikyo students to spend part of their study period abroad. Teikyo's aim was to make its university more competitive in an era of declining student numbers in Japan. Teikyo chose Durham for its UK campus and built blocks of living accommodation for 120 male and female students and a teaching block containing a library. One of Teikyo's reasons for choosing Durham was the latter's plans to develop Japanese studies and Teikyo offered to provide a much more extensive library, containing 30,000 volumes, mostly in Japanese, than their own students required, for the benefit of Japanese studies in Durham. Teikyo also gave financial support for the first lectureship in Japanese studies in 1994 and later supported the St Mary's College

Japanese teaching fellow programme. Durham students formed an Anglo-Japanese Society to bring together Durham students of Japanese and Teikyo students for language exchange and social activities. One of the first social activities was a visit to Gateshead's dog track for an evening of greyhound racing.

The BA in Japanese Studies accepted its first cohort of students in October 1992 for a specialist four-year degree in Japanese with the second year spent studying at a Japanese university. These students were taught initially by the existing staff teaching on the Chinese with Japanese programme, but two full-time Japanese specialists were recruited for the second year, starting from January 1994. These were William McClure, who had completed a PhD in Japanese linguistics at Cornell, as lecturer in Japanese, and Naomi Cross, from Newcastle, as Language Instructor. These were followed a year later in January 1995 by John Weste, who had completed a PhD in modern Japanese history at Cambridge. This appointment enabled DEAS to rethink its history courses, changing them from Chinese history to East Asian history with all students expected to study the history of both China and Japan (with some limited Korean input, too). This applied to first year undergraduate survey courses, both history and culture, and to third and fourth year modules, where we had, for example, a course entitled 'Modern East Asian Political Thought'. As a result all DEAS students studied the history and culture of both China and Japan, giving them a comparative perspective. The appointment of John Weste also enabled DEAS to offer a Japanese component on the MA in Modern East Asian Research. This degree had originally been set up as a joint degree with Newcastle's Department of Politics as part of a successful post-Parker funding bid with a collaborative element. Newcastle provided the Japanese expertise and Durham the Chinese, and the students commuted between the two universities. It was very good to work with colleagues in Newcastle, but there were considerable practical problems in offering a split-campus degree, and it was not popular with students. John Weste's appointment enabled Durham to create a stand-alone degree which very successfully recruited up to 10 taught MA students per year.

DEAS was then able in 1996 to appoint Gina Barnes as professor of Japanese Studies. She was an expert in Japanese, and more broadly East Asian, archaeology. She had been a senior research fellow at St. John's College, Cambridge, for a number of years. This appointment was made possible by the generosity of a local Japanese company, NSK. It had set up one of the earliest Japanese factories in the north-east 25 years earlier and wanted to mark its anniversary with a contribution to the locality. Lord Dennis Stevenson, who had been Chairman of the Newton Aycliffe and Peterlee New Town Development Corporation from 1971 to 1980, helped to arrange a £250,000 gift from NSK to establish the chair of Japanese studies.

Recruitment to the Japanese undergraduate degree went well with around 20 new students starting each year. This enabled Durham to expand the staff numbers. A priority was a specialist in Japanese literature. With the support of a staff expansion grant from the Japan Foundation, Durham was able to advertise a lectureship in Japanese literature in 1998. Dr Carol Hayes, who completed a PhD on Hagiwara Sakutarō at Sydney University, was recruited from a lectureship at ANU in 1998. This was followed in 1999 by the appointment of Mika Kizu, who had just completed a PhD in Japanese linguistics at McGill University. Mika was a replacement for Bill McClure who returned to the US in 1997. Two additional full-time language instructors were taken on, Kazuki Morimoto in 2000 and Hideki Saigō in 2001. These posts allowed DEAS to expand its MA course portfolio to include an MA in Teaching Japanese as a Foreign Language and an MA in Translation (Japanese). The MA in Teaching Japanese as a Foreign Language recruited 6–8 students a year. Professor Toshiko Ishida, a specialist in teaching Japanese as a second/foreign language from Tsukuba University, acted as consultant on this course, and she spent part of a year at Durham supported by a Japan Foundation Visiting Professorship grant. Professor Ishida was instrumental in arranging for a series of teaching fellows to come to Durham for a year from Tsukuba, ICU and Nihon Joshi Daigaku. The MA in TJFL course was primarily taught by Naomi Cross, Mika Kizu and Kazuki Morimoto. We wished to offer some of the graduates of this course a year of practice teaching after the course. The Principal of St Mary's College, Joan Kenworthy, took a special interest in this and successfully applied to the Great Britain Sasakawa Foundation UK for three years of funding to support a St Mary's Japanese teaching fellow. The College was thus able to offer free accommodation and food and a small allowance to one graduate from the MA in TJFL each year. After the three years, Teikyo University, which has close links with St Mary's College, offered continued support for this venture. In terms of professional development, this MA course was very successful with many of its graduates entering Japanese language teaching posts at universities in the UK, the US and Japan.

By the early 2000s Japanese Studies at Durham was thriving with seven full-time members of staff: a professor, three lecturers and three language instructors, plus a number of part-time staff. There were over 70 undergraduate students, 15 taught MA students taking Japanese courses and a small number of research students. DEAS was receiving up to 150 applications a year for the undergraduate courses in Japanese studies. This suite of courses included Japanese studies (with Classical Japanese), Modern Japanese Studies (no Classical Japanese) and Japanese with a subsidiary subject (including: Chinese, Korean, a European language, Linguistics, History, Philosophy, Geography, Management – the latter technically a joint honours course). All students spent their second year at a Japanese university on an exchange basis. These partner universities, which because of Mombushō regulations could only take a couple of students each, numbered around a dozen including ICU, Sophia and Nihon in Tokyo, Yokohama, Tsukuba, Nanzan, and Kumamoto.

However, university finances in the UK were worsening in spite of the introduction of a £1000 p.a. fee from 1998–1999. When Carol Hayes decided to return to Australia in 2001, it was only with a struggle that we persuaded the University to allow us to advertise for a Japanese literature replacement in 2002. The decisive factor was that the post had been funded by the Japan Foundation and the University had given an undertaking to maintain it. Robert Khan was appointed from September 2002; he had previously been assistant professor at the University of Texas at Austin. Universities responded to the worsening finances by taking a number of measures to introduce structural changes intended to make the institutions more efficient. One popular measure was 'schoolification': getting rid of departments and faculties and grouping subjects into large schools. Another was devolving finances to lower level units, nominally offering greater autonomy, but actually intended to make departments more financially accountable by including all costs and income in departmental budgets. This would show which departments were profitable and which were loss-making. It would also give ammunition to 'profitable' departments to demand that their profits were retained to fund additional staff in their subjects, rather than subsidising other 'loss-making' departments. The message that went around Durham at the time was that Durham had too many departments and needed to concentrate its resources on a smaller number of subjects in order to be successful. Success was largely measured in Research Assessment Exercise (RAE) terms. DEAS was one of twelve Durham units of assessment awarded a grade 4 rating in the 2001 RAE.

Between 2001 and 2003, University officials held several meetings with DEAS members as part of a 'change agenda' to address the future, and invited DEAS to reinvent itself. No guidance was given over the form such 'change' might take, and no specific performance targets were set. Having one of the most popular and successful programmes in the country, DEAS saw little reason to embark on change just for the sake of change. The problem was compounded by the lack of robustness of central data as the University moved to new systems. The financial data painted a worse financial situation for DEAS than the reality, and the University's student demand figures suggested a national pool of just over 100 qualified applicants, whereas DEAS knew it was receiving over 300 applications per year, mostly from qualified applicants.

The results of the 'Strategic Improvement Programme' review were announced by the Dean to shocked DEAS staff at a hastily convened meeting immediately after the final Board of Examiners meeting in June 2003. East Asian Studies had been recommended for 'disinvestment' along with Linguistics (with an RAE 5 rating). The document argued that East Asian studies was not a key part of the 'Durham brand' and although it had reached an RAE rating of 4, it was a 'falling 4', down from a previous 5 rating. A number of other departments were to be restructured in more limited ways. The outcome was that Linguistics was transferred to Newcastle, and the only staff ultimately made redundant from the University were DEAS staff. The University had initially suggested that DEAS staff would be allocated to other departments, but did little to facilitate this, with the result that other departments saw no reason to take DEAS staff, and they were not redeployed.

The savings from the DEAS closure were to be invested in departments that offered better prospects for research success in the next RAE. In the Arts Faculty the big winners were English and History, two 5* units in the 2001 RAE. English would be given 4 new posts over the next two years, including a chair, and History 3 new posts. The only department to oppose DEAS closure and express a willingness to forgo additional posts to save DEAS was the Department of Philosophy. DEAS fought against the decision over the summer and received very strong support from alumni, colleagues in other universities and representatives of the countries concerned. Over 300 protest letters were received by the University. Japanese sources were particularly supportive. In one instance, a diplomat from the Japanese Embassy in London arranged to come to Durham to meet the Vice-Chancellor, where he told a shocked VC that the Japanese people would never forgive him for this decision. The University leadership was taken aback by the level of opposition, which it had not expected, but it did not back down on its decision.

The University initially considered relocating DEAS students to other universities, but no other university expressed a willingness or an ability to accept them, hence the University decided it would have to teach out existing students, including the cohort due to arrive in October 2003, but to disallow the recruitment of any further students, including one-year MA students which DEAS staff had already offered to take. The financial savings plan envisaged axing one-third of the DEAS staff each year over the following three years, achieving full savings of the total DEAS budget by 2006/7. We pointed out that it was a four-year course, so the full savings would not be possible until 2007/8 after the last cohort had graduated in 2007. We also pointed out that to ensure that the students received a similar quality of provision to previous cohorts DEAS needed the full range of teaching expertise until the department was closed. The University agreed to abandon its plans for staged redundancies, and to allow all staff to remain in post until

September 2007. It also agreed to take on temporary full-time staff if vital existing staff left before 2007. Over the following years John Weste, Mika Kizu, Robert Khan and Kazuki Morimoto left for posts elsewhere, Hideki Saigō returned to Japan at the end of his contract, and Gina Barnes took early retirement. They were replaced by Hiromi Sasamoto-Collins, teaching Japanese history, Kazuki Takada, teaching literature, and Robert Kasza, teaching language and linguistics.

DEAS staff were all offered 'voluntary' severance when DEAS closed in 2007 on terms that were typically five times the legal minimum they would have received under compulsory redundancy. Two members of staff refused to accept these terms, obliging the University to initiate compulsory redundancy proceedings. One of these, Don Starr, was subsequently offered the two years of research leave he argued was his due having been head of department for 7 years without any leave. The other, Hiromi Sasamoto-Collins, later agreed to accept the University's terms having made the point that for all DEAS staff 'voluntary severance' did not mean they were leaving voluntarily.

When Senate passed the 'Strategic Improvement Programme' in 2003, the University management had undertaken to 'retain elsewhere in the University ... provision for the teaching of Chinese and Japanese language'. Arabic had been moved to the School of Modern European Languages (subsequently renamed the School of Modern Languages and Cultures - MLaC), but that School had refused to accept Chinese and Japanese on the grounds that there were no synergies or cultural connections with Europe, as there were with Arabic. The University investigated offering these languages through the Language Centre but discovered that the number of potential students at that time was not large enough to finance the two language instructor posts in each language considered necessary for TQA (Teaching Quality Assurance) reasons: back-up was required in case of illness or other problems, and a second examiner was required. This meant any teaching would be limited to non-credit bearing LfA (Languages for All) evening classes. The problem could be parked while DEAS existed, since it had offered for-credit single module option courses in Chinese, Japanese and Korean to students of other departments ever since modularisation, but when it ceased to exist a solution would need to be found. A new executive dean, renamed Pro Vice Chancellor for Arts and Humanities, was appointed in 2005 from the University of Aberdeen. This was Professor Seth Kunin, an American with a family background in *ukiyoe* woodblock print art. From the outset he expressed doubts about the wisdom of closing DEAS in the way it had been handled, and he argued the case that a university with Durham's international profile and global aspirations should offer serious engagement with the languages and cultures of China and Japan. By then Japan and China were ranked second and third in the world economic league tables, and the closure decision was looking increasingly bizarre. The decision had generated a lot of very negative publicity for Durham without producing the projected savings, the whole rationale for the exercise. In fact, by keeping DEAS open for four years and giving staff generous severance payments, the exercise had cost, not saved, the University money.

The PVC resolved to split the Language Centre, relocating the teaching of foreign languages in a new unit (the Centre for Foreign Language Study – CFLS) within MLaC, while the English language section remained as a separate entity. He also decided to create a post in Chinese to enable CFLS to offer Chinese as part of its institution-wide language provision (IWLP), i.e. for-credit courses for non-specialists. In the meantime MLaC had set up an MA in Translation Studies offering Chinese as one of the languages taught. This MA course began in 2008 with 3 Chinese students, with Don Starr teaching the first term and the new lecturer, Binghan Zheng, the second term, following his arrival in January 2009. We took the opportunity to introduce a Japanese strand to the MA in Translation Studies degree in 2012. This has been taught by Angus Turvill and Etsuko Okahisa, who had previously taught on an MA in Translation course at Newcastle University. It has run each year since 2012, successfully but with limited numbers.

The financial success of the MA in Translation Studies generated a favourable atmosphere for the re-introduction of undergraduate courses in Chinese, and ultimately Japanese. CFLS was also thriving under the new fee regime: the University was encouraging more students to take a language module as part of their undergraduate courses, as a result IWLP Chinese rapidly went from a single beginners' courses to three beginners' level courses in Durham (plus another in Stockton) and four higher level courses. We proposed the introduction of a for-credit Japanese beginners' module from 2011, to be taught by Ritsuko Koso, a graduate of the DEAS MA in Teaching Japanese as a Foreign Language, with Don Starr as back-up and second examiner. Ritsuko had settled in Durham and had taught on LfA 'evening class' Japanese courses since 2004. This new beginner's Japanese module immediately recruited above its 15 student quota. The following year a second level was added plus a second beginners' class, and in subsequent years stage 3 and stage 4 Japanese were added. The total number of students taking CFLS courses was more than 800 in 2015/2016, including 70 for Japanese.

Seth Kunin, the PVC, kept on Don Starr year by year after his 2009 leaving date to set up the new undergraduate courses. These had to be distinct from the DEAS courses, hence it was decided that MLaC would provide the core language and culture modules and the History Department would provide the core history modules, and the third year would be spent in East Asia. Other departments would take on specialists on China and Japan, or at least be able to offer some relevant modules so that students could become specialists in the economy, anthropology, art, history, politics, etc. of their chosen country. The PVC offered the History Department two posts in East Asian history; after initial reluctance they took on two specialists in Chinese history, and found the modules were oversubscribed. The Chinese undergraduate degree began in 2011 with two students, rising to the quota of 20 over the next three years. The Japanese studies course began from October 2014 following the same pattern, with a year studying at a Japanese university in the third year to fit the MLaC structure. With a favourable environment in Japan for international collaboration, Durham's International Office has been able to negotiate exchange agreements with a number of Japanese universities. An existing agreement with Tokyo University has been extended, and the first cohort of students will go there in 2016–2017. Agreements are under discussion or signed with Kumamoto, Nagoya, Osaka and Waseda universities for subsequent years once student numbers have increased.

Ritsuko Koso was made a full-time teaching fellow in 2014, and a Japanese lecturer, a specialist in manga from Japan, was appointed. Unfortunately she was taken ill in the summer of 2014 and decided she could not take up the post. Don Starr, as back-up, was then called upon to teach the Japanese culture module, with Gina Barnes and David Hughes helping out too. The Japanese history course was taught by Paul Bailey, professor of Chinese history, who had previously taught Japanese history at Edinburgh. The first year there were just three students initially, later dropping to two; the second year, 2015, started with eight students. Applications for 2016 are double the number for 2015 so we are hopeful of reaching the quota of 20 students. Seth Kunin unfortunately returned to Aberdeen at the beginning of 2014 but his successor as PVC of Arts and Humanities, Professor David Cowling, a French specialist from MLaC, has continued to support Japanese strongly. A lectureship in Japanese studies was advertised in 2015. At the interviews Professor Cowling announced that he had secured additional funding so it would be possible to appoint two candidates. These were Rebekah Clements and Fusako Innami. Dr Clements completed her PhD on the impact of translation on pre-modern Japan at Cambridge University and was a Junior Research Fellow at Queens' College; she published a monograph based on her research, *A Cultural History of Translation in Early Modern Japan*, in 2015. Fusako Innami completed her D.Phil. at Oxford University in 2014 on touch in modern/contemporary Japanese literature and subsequently taught for a year at the University of East Anglia before coming to Durham in September 2015. In addition to these two posts at MLaC, Durham's Department of History has advertised a post in Japanese history to start from September 2016. This, together with a second teaching fellow in Japanese language at MLaC from September, means Durham will have five full-time specialists in Japanese plus a number of part-time staff to run the Japanese studies degree programme, the CFLS Japanese language courses, and the Japanese strand of the MA in Translation Studies, to contribute to other Translation Studies modules and a new culture MA and to offer research supervision.

Another positive development has been in the Japanese art field. The Durham University Oriental Museum collection goes back to the late 1940s when Professor T.W. Thacker, founding head of the School of Oriental Studies, negotiated the acquisition of the Northumberland Collection of ancient Egyptian antiquities. Subsequently the first lecturer in Chinese, Raymond Dawson, arranged the exhibition of a loan collection of Chinese bronzes for the 1953 Coronation. This resulted in further loans and gifts of Oriental art. The need for a permanent exhibition and storage space was met by the provision in 1960 of a purpose-built museum building funded by a grant from the Gulbenkian Foundation. The first curator of the museum, from 1960 to 1975, was Philip Rawson, an inspired choice who brought to the task great enthusiasm and a highly honed aesthetic sense. Japanese art was one of the areas in which Rawson had a particular interest: he published *Japanese Buddhist Painting* in 1963. He and his wife, Barbara, scoured antique shops and auctions looking for objects, and cajoled collectors into offering loans and gifts. The Japanese collection was built up in this way rather than through the acquisition of major collections. There was always on permanent display a small collection – swords and armour, *netsuke* and *inro*, pottery and furniture - but no appropriate space for displaying the good collection of *ukiyoe*.

This remained the case until interest was rekindled, partly through the suggestion of the then Vice-Chancellor, Professor Chris Higgins, that the Museum produce a glossy book to showcase the Museum's collection, something that could be given to official visitors to the University. The task of commissioning the articles and editing the volume was undertaken by the Curator, Craig Barclay, the Deputy Curator, Rachel Grocke, and the Acquisitions Manager, Helen Armstrong. Five representative Japanese objects were chosen to be included and two were written up by Craig Barclay, and three by external contributors. The book was published as *Treasures of the Oriental Museum, Durham University* in 2010. Subsequently the Oriental Museum successfully applied for funding to set up a permanent Japanese gallery, which opened in October 2013. This houses a growing collection of contemporary Japanese art and cultural objects, and special funding has allowed the acquisition of twentieth-century material culture. This project brought Oriental Museum staff into contact with staff from the Japanese National Museum of Japanese History resulting in a proposal for the NMJH, supported by their parent body, the National Institute for the Humanities, to carry out a six-year project based at the

Oriental Museum to create a Japanese and English on-line catalogue of the Japanese historic collections held across the north of England, including the Oriental Museum's 3,350 items. It is planned that there will be a major exhibition in 2020 to coincide with the Tokyo Olympics.

There have been government enquiries into UK university provision of 'Oriental' languages for over a hundred years. These have resulted in short-term initiatives but no long term solutions. Japanese is more expensive to teach than History or English but this is not reflected in the fees received by the universities, a situation made worse under the £9,000 fee regime. It could easily be resolved by a more dirigiste, or more calibrated, approach by HEFCE. In the development of Japanese studies at Durham over the last 35 years we have been indebted to the Japanese community for their constant support, practical, financial and psychological, especially the Japanese Embassy in London and the Consulate General in Edinburgh, the Japan Foundation, the Daiwa Anglo-Japanese Foundation, the Great Britain Sasakawa Foundation, Teikyo University and NSK. When the Japanese studies programme was relaunched in October 2014, Ambassador Keiichi Hayashi made a special effort to attend a dinner in Durham in a show of support and this was greatly appreciated.

8

University of East Anglia

○

Simon Kaner

THE UNIVERSITY OF East Anglia was established in Norwich in 1963, and the first Japanese students arrived in the 1970s. Since then, Japan has been regarded as a trusted and reliable friend of the University, but it has really been over the past few years that UEA's relationship with Japan has truly blossomed.

In 2012 Norwich was designated a UNESCO City of Literature, the first English city to receive this honour. One of the University's great strengths lies in literature and creative writing: the famous MA in Creative Writing was set up by Angus Wilson and Malcolm Bradbury in 1970, and the second student was one Kazuo Ishiguro, who went on to pen such masterpieces as *The Artist of the Floating World*. The first graduate from this course was Ian McEwan, now regarded as one of the best current writers. UEA's connection with Japanese literature continues, and in recent years, with the generous support of the Nippon Foundation, many distinguished Japanese authors and their translators have featured at the annual Summer School run by the British Centre for Literary Translation, established by W. G. Sebald in 1989. A recent Director of this centre, Dr Valerie Henitiuk, who is now a professor at McEwan University in Edmonton, Canada, was herself a specialist in the translation of classical Japanese literature and published *Worlding Sei Shōnagon: The Pillow Book in Translation* (2012).

Building on the reputation for Japanese studies established by the Sainsbury Institute for the Study of Japanese Arts and Cultures (SISJAC) discussed elsewhere in this volume, UEA embarked on a new phase of engagement with Japan in 2011, with the creation of a Centre for Japanese Studies and new degree-level programmes in Japanese. With the generous support of Yakult UK, a University Lecturer in Japanese Language was appointed, Dr Nana Sato-Rossberg, a specialist in the burgeoning field of translation studies. At the time of writing, the fourth cohort of undergraduates studying for a degree in Japanese language has just started, and the first cohort has just returned from their year abroad, at one of 14 Japanese universities. The University now has four lecturers in Japanese language in the School of Politics, Philosophy and Language and Communication Studies, led by the Yakult Lecturer and Head of Japanese, Mika Brown. Japanese is currently the most popular foreign language taught on campus, with the subsidiary Japanese language programmes repeatedly oversubscribed.

These developments followed on from the inspired investment by the Great Britain Sasakawa Foundation, in 2008, in a Sasakawa Lectureship in Contemporary Japanese Visual Media, a post shared between the Sainsbury Institute and the Faculty of Arts and Humanities at UEA, one of 13 such posts created across the country in response to the closure of a number of departments of Japanese studies. The first post-holder was Dr Ulrich Heinze, a sociologist working on manga, anime and broadcasting. These posts were complemented in 2011 with the appointment of Dr Akira Matsuda as Lecturer in Japanese Artistic Heritage in the School of Art History and World Art Studies, a post generously supported by the Japan Foundation through their Staff Expansion Scheme. Dr Matsuda has gone on to take up a new appointment in the Department of Cultural Resource Studies at the University of Tokyo, and Dr Heinze has now returned to Germany to pursue his research interests. The search is currently on to secure replacements.

The Centre for Japanese Studies was inaugurated in September 2011 with a lecture by Professor Yakushiji Katsuyuki of Toyo University, former political editor of the *Asahi Shinbun,* who addressed a capacity audience in the largest lecture theatre on the campus, on the theme of politics and society six months on from the Great East Japan Disaster. The director of the Centre for Japanese Studies was in Japan on that fateful day, joined just a day later by the dean of students, Annie Grant, on a mission to explore relations with Japanese partner universities. Our plans had to be shelved as the full impact of the disaster became apparent.

The Centre for Japanese Studies provides a degree of coordination in Japan-related teaching and research across the campus, and a bridge between the University and the Sainsbury Institute, and works to link up the community across Norfolk and East Anglia with activities at the University. As well as arranging various Japan-related events across the campus, the Centre, in conjunction with the University's international programmes office, also organises a Japanese studies summer school, with the generous support of the Toshiba International Foundation, which provides bursaries for students from eastern and central Europe. To date two such Summer Schools have been held, with a third planned for 2016.

Another of UEA's strengths is climate research. The Tyndall Centre for Climate Research is the centre of a global network of research and policy making in this area. One current initiative is Future Earth, a major international research platform encouraging the transformation to a truly sustainable world, for which UEA is the European Hub, and the Research Institute for Humanity and Nature in Kyoto is the Asian hub.

UEA is also renowned for its programmes in International Development, and each year on average 30–35 Japanese students are registered on degree programmes in this area, some taking advantage of the joint Masters' programme offered by Kobe University and UEA, brokered by Reader Emeritus Dr John Thoburn. A new initiative, including a joint venture capital fund between the ADAPT agri-technology group at UEA led by Professor John French, and the Tsukuba Seed Company and Tsukuba University, will see a new generation of start-up companies in the field of sustainable development housed in UEA's new Innovation Centre.

The international office at UEA strives to encourage Japanese students to come and study in our beautiful city, and in conjunction with the University's study abroad office and partnerships office seeks out the best opportunities for UEA students to spend time in Japan. Currently some 100 students from Japan are enrolled at UEA. The University's joint venture with INTO UEA provides grounding in British higher education and English-language assistance for international students, including many from Japan, who want to study here. In addition, many Japanese universities, including Meiji and Ritsumeikan, send students to UEA for bespoke short-term programmes. Many UEA students join a range of Japan-related societies at the University, including the Japan Society, which arranges informal Japanese language classes, and the Anime Society. There are regular film screenings of Japanese movies, and talks by movie directors. Film and TV Studies is a strong area at UEA, and Dr Rayna Denison has attracted many students since her appointment as Lecturer in Japanese cinema in the School of Film, TV and Media Studies.

Although a relative newcomer in offering Japanese Studies at degree level, UEA is building on its tradition of welcoming Japanese students over the decades, and the established reputation of Japan-related partners such as the Sainsbury Institute for the Study of Japanese Arts and Cultures (SISJAC) to create distinctive high-quality programmes on Japan that make the most of UEA's founding precept of interdisciplinarity and of our reputation for high levels of student satisfaction. Our current vice chancellor, Professor David Richardson, a distinguished biochemist, has identified Japan as one of a small number of countries around the world with which the University plans to develop strategic international research partnerships. We work hard to engage with the Japanese Studies community elsewhere in the UK, for example hosting the British Association for Japanese Studies Conference twice in the last 10 years (2008 and 2012). And we maintain close links with our Japanese alumni network, supported by our indefatigable ambassadors in Japan, Professor Hayasaka Makoto of Gakushuin University and Professor Ando Mikio, Executive Assistant to the President of Kobe University: Japanese alumni are active especially in the areas of language teaching, development and museology.

9

University of Edinburgh

O

Ian Astley, Helen Parker and *Urs* **Matthias Zachmann**

JAPANESE WAS FIRST taught at Edinburgh in 1976, when it was offered to students on the MA Honours in Chinese programme as part of their degree. In Scotland undergraduate degrees usually take four years and lead directly to an MA degree. In the late 1980s, with the appointment of Dr Nobuko Ishii, a specialist in mediaeval Japanese narratives, to a lectureship in Japanese, pre-Honours courses in Japanese language (Japanese 1 and Japanese 2) were set up. Japanese 1 had a limited number of places, but was open to students on any undergraduate programme, while Japanese 2 was open to students who had performed well in Japanese 1. Students on the MA Honours in Chinese programme were allowed to take these courses as Honours options in their third and fourth years, and this arrangement continued until the year abroad for MA Honours in Chinese was moved from second year to third year.

In autumn 1990, full undergraduate degree programmes (MA Honours) were established in Japanese and Japanese & Linguistics in a Centre for Japanese Studies within East Asian Studies. Dr Helen Parker, who works on traditional Japanese theatre, was appointed as a second Lecturer in Japanese: the post was supported by the Japan Foundation for the first three years. The first intending

Honours students were admitted to the first year at this stage and, in addition, one or two students who had successfully completed Japanese 1 and Japanese 2 were allowed to progress straight to the third year of the newly established degree programme (i.e., the year abroad in Japan), so the first graduates were awarded their degrees in 1992. Professor Ron Asher (Linguistics and Dean of the Faculty of Arts) presented theatre director Ninagawa Yukio for an honorary degree at the degree ceremony in the same year.

In October 1993, Ms Hiromi Kawahara was appointed as the first Foreign Language Assistant, succeeded during the following year by Ms Kazuyo Igarashi. From January 1994, Dr Margaret Mehl, whose specialism was historiography and Meiji history, was appointed as a Lecturer in Japanese Civilization, and her mission was to set up a pre-Honours course in Japanese Civilization and a fourth year Honours course in Japanese History. Dr Mehl's post was funded by the Japan Foundation.

Following Dr Ishii's retirement in 1995, Dr Yoko Matsumoto-Sturt (Applied Linguistics and Japanese language pedagogy) was appointed as a temporary Lecturer in Japanese and Ms Tomoko Yoshikawa joined the programme as the next Foreign Language Assistant (succeeded by Ms Reiko Hoshino from September 1996). Both posts were funded by the University. Dr Mehl resigned to take up a position at the University of Stirling in autumn 1995, but in 1995/6 and 1996/7, Dr Kweku Ampiah, also of the University of Stirling, contributed a fourth year Honours course in Japanese History as a visiting lecturer. The pre-Honours Japanese Civilization course was integrated with Chinese Civilization to create an East Asian Civilization course from 1996/7. Undergraduate students from Edinburgh participated for the first time in the Japan Foundation spoken Japanese competition for university students in 1996, and won prizes in both 1996 and 1997.

In 1995 and 1996 there was acute concern about the future of Japanese studies at Edinburgh, both internally (students and staff directly involved with the programme) and externally (external examiners, professional bodies, the Japan Foundation and the Japanese Consulate in Edinburgh). The support of these parties enabled two new appointments in autumn 1997: Dr Ian Astley, who works on Japanese religions and the history of ideas, was appointed as a

Senior Lecturer (a post partially funded by the Japan Foundation for the first five years) and Dr Yoko Matsumoto-Sturt as a Lecturer (funded by the University). This modest expansion of research staff provided the opportunity to start developing postgraduate studies, admitting small numbers of students to study for an MSc in Japanese: most students took the degree on a research programme, although a taught programme was also established. We were also able for the first time to offer PhD supervision: the first PhD students were admitted in 1999 and were awarded their degrees in 2004. Other activities to foster research in Japanese studies included a seminar series in collaboration with the Scottish Centre for Japanese Studies at the University of Stirling and smaller subject-specific workshops and conferences in Japanese religions, theatre, women's history and language teaching pedagogy. Asian Studies also hosted the triennial Joint East Asian Studies Conference (for members of the three British Associations of Japanese, Chinese and Korean studies) in 2001. At undergraduate level, too, material was introduced that reflected the expertise of new colleagues in pre-modern history and culture and that included academic writing in Japanese.

Also from autumn 1997, the Japan Foundation appointed and directly employed Ms Ryoko Onishi as a junior lecturer with the remit to contribute to Japanese language teaching at the University of Edinburgh. This was initially a two-year appointment, but the Japanese language courses at all levels actually benefited from the input of a Japan Foundation junior lecturer for a total of six years: Ms Onishi's contract was renewed for a third year, then Ms Mikiko Kurokawa was employed in the same post for another three years. These members of staff, working with Dr Matsumoto-Sturt, made important developments in course design and teaching materials for the Japanese language side of the programme.

From autumn 2004, Ms Fumiko Narumi-Munro (teaching Japanese as a foreign language and e-learning/game-based learning) was appointed to a 0.5 position as Language Instructor to continue and build on the work of the Japan Foundation junior lecturers. She was upgraded to a full-time Language Instructor position in September 2005, both positions being funded by the University. In order to meet student demand from outside the School of Literatures, Languages and Cultures for tuition in Japanese without undertaking the heavy workload required for intending Honours students, Ms Narumi-Munro set up one-semester courses for non-language students, starting in 2009.

In 2009/2010, Japanese Studies collaborated with the School of Education and Information Services to develop the HaNABI (Handheld-device enhanced learning with Nintendo's Applications Beyond Institution and country) project. This teaching and learning initiative was funded primarily by JISC, a not-for-profit organisation providing digital services for higher education institutions in the UK, and used Nintendo DSi games consoles as a learning tool to link third-year students on exchange in Japan to co-students elsewhere in Japan and their tutors in Edinburgh.

In January 2011, Dr Chris Perkins, who works on Japanese society, especially Japanese media, was appointed to a lectureship in Japanese, funded by the Japan Foundation and the University. This allowed the undergraduate and taught postgraduate programmes to begin to diversify, with fourth-year Honours and Masters options now offered in the social sciences. Dr Perkins has also been active in redesigning the elements of Japanese Studies taught in the second year as a foundation for study in Japan.

In October 2011, Professor Urs Matthias Zachmann, who works on the intellectual and cultural history of modern Japan within the context of East Asian international relations, was appointed to the new Handa Chair in Japanese–Chinese relations. This appointment was particularly welcome in that it redressed a balance between Chinese and Japanese by introducing a specialist dealing with Japan at professorial level, as well as enabling further development in the areas of modern history, politics and international relations.

Ms Sakie Chiba-Mooney and Ms Sakino Kelbie were also added to the teaching staff for Japanese language in 2013, giving us a sound basis for accommodating the growing numbers of students on undergraduate courses in the language. These are both intending Honours students and the considerable numbers from other departments who are interested in pursuing their study of the Japanese language as an adjunct to their main subjects.

Another complement to the study of the Japanese language was the setting up of a JLPT (Japanese Language Proficiency Test) Test Centre, directed by Dr Matsumoto-Sturt. This is the only such centre in the UK outside London and serves not only Scotland but also the north of England, offering people from all walks of life a more convenient opportunity to sit for these important qualifications. Our own students are also encouraged to take these tests.

To meet the desire to draw Korean Studies into the ambit of the department's work and to respond to the popularity of courses in International Relations in East Asia, Lauren Richardson joined us in 2015 as a Teaching Fellow in Japanese-Korean relations and politics. This has also opened up the prospect of developing Korean Studies at the department.

The disciplinary side of our research and teaching now has a commendable balance of social sciences and arts and humanities, as well as of pre-modern and modern specialists. We work closely with our counterparts in Asian Studies – Chinese and Sanskrit – at Edinburgh. Besides various collaborations in research and teaching, this has led to the establishment of an MSc in East Asian Relations in co-operation with Chinese Studies and the Politics department. This course augments the MSc in Japanese Society and Culture, which has been running in its current guise for four years now.

Our recruitment of PhD students has been helped by the Sasakawa Japanese Studies Postgraduate Studentship Programme. We currently have three doctoral candidates under this scheme.

Whilst there have been long periods when the subject was constrained to offer a full programme with a very limited staffing base, the developments over the last five years, kick-started by the kind provision of the Japan Foundation Staff Expansion Scheme, have brought us to a situation where we have a closely knit team of researchers and teaching staff who are well equipped to accommodate the growing interest in studying Japanese at Edinburgh, a situation that holds great promise for the coming years.

10

University of Leeds

O

Mark Williams

WHEN SIR WILLIAM Hayter was commissioned by the UK government in 1960 to produce a report on the state of 'Oriental, Slavonic, East European and African Studies' education in the UK higher education system, few can have anticipated the consequences of his report. At the time, courses designed to nurture the next generation of East Asian specialists were extremely limited in scope, with those interested largely restricted to programmes in which the inevitable focus, given the exigencies of the time, lay in providing a sound linguistic and philological perspective.

Hayter's main recommendations included securing a better balance in the programmes available 'between linguistic and non-linguistic studies and between classical and modern studies', to be secured through implementation of a 10-year programme of development, centred on the establishment of new centres for the study of East and Southeast Asian languages and societies beyond the golden triangle centres.[1] Within months of publication of this report, plans were in place to ensure that the series of new centres for area studies Hayter envisaged for the north of England were

---

[1] 'The Future of Asian Studies after the Hayter Report', *Asian Studies* 12:3 (1981), pp. 245ff.

duly inaugurated – and, when the special funding for this purpose was released in 1962, the Universities of Leeds, Sheffield and Hull all moved quickly to bring these ideas to fruition; the centres for Chinese studies at Leeds, for Japanese studies at Sheffield and for South-East Asian studies at Hull were duly established.

Effective leadership for these new centres was crucial – and, to this end, Leeds moved quickly to secure the appointment of Owen Lattimore as its inaugural professor of Chinese Studies. Lattimore was a British-educated American, who had served during WW2 as President Franklin D. Roosevelt's appointed personal political adviser to Chiang Kai-Shek and later as Director of Pacific Operations in the Office of War Information in San Francisco. Fluent in Chinese, Russian, Mongolian and French, Lattimore was lured from his post as Professor of International Relations at Johns Hopkins University in the US and by 1963 he had succeeded in establishing the Department of Chinese Studies at the University of Leeds. He brought with him not only years of experience working in China-related posts but also some trenchant opinions as to how best to implement a teaching and research programme in area studies. More specifically, he arrived with a commitment to ensuring that any new programme in Modern Chinese Studies would be predicated on a thorough understanding of both the linguistic and cultural underpinnings of the society, a training that in his eyes required a period of study in mainland China, as soon as this became feasible.

The degree programme in modern Chinese studies quickly flourished and it was not long before Leeds was sending a group of students to a series of language programmes in the PRC on an annual basis. One particular aspect of this arrangement was the decision, taken very soon after such arrangements became practicable, to send students to China for their second year of study. This was a carefully considered decision, one that put the department out of synch, not only with the majority of Chinese studies courses in the UK at the time, but also with the other (European) language programmes at the University of Leeds, all of which operated a third year programme of study abroad. Lattimore's rationale behind this decision was, however, clear: fully conversant with the latest second language learning pedagogy, he was persuaded that the most effective means of ensuring that his students would leave Leeds with the optimum understanding of the contemporary situation in China was to send them to the country as soon as they had mastered the fundamentals of the language and to provide them with the opportunity to familiarise themselves with real, live Chinese sources at the earliest possible opportunity. This in turn was designed to allow the students to return from China with a heightened linguistic confidence, affording greater scope for the examination of more complex documents in their third and fourth year courses.

The philosophy was deemed a success – and, to this day, Leeds continues to send all students from its now multifarious East Asian programmes to East Asia for the entirety of their second year. The decision has not been without its issues, and there remain some who believe that students with only a single year's exposure to what remains, for the majority of the cohort, a new and considerable challenge require more than a year's training in the fundamentals of the language before being left to their own devices *in situ*. On balance, however, Leeds is persuaded of the benefits of undertaking the early stages of language acquisition in the appropriate linguistic context, and 'Year 2 in East Asia' remains a considerable attraction to the majority of our applicants.

The future of the department came in for widespread debate at Leeds – and the issue resurfaced in the 1980s when, in the wake of the Parker Report (which reiterated most of the decisions of the Hayter Report and called for renewed governmental support for modern area studies in particular), the decision was taken to diversify beyond Chinese (and the small, bespoke offering in Mongolian Studies that represented another of Lattimore's significant legacies) and to consider the broader East Asian context. The main tangible upshot of this was the decision to introduce a full degree level programme in modern Japanese studies. It was my privilege to be hired to work on this project in conjunction with Penny Francks and, having successfully persuaded the powers that be that the launching of this new enterprise required a re-branding of the department – as the Department of East Asian Studies, work progressed rapidly on the development of a programme in modern Japanese studies that was modelled on the existing Chinese curriculum.

In all this, the timing could not have been more propitious: no sooner had the University Senate approved these moves in early 1989, than events in China, culminating in the horrors perpetrated in Tiananmen Square on 4 June, took over. It was immediately apparent that business as usual for our students was not an option – and for several years following this popular uprising, Leeds was obliged to send all its modern Chinese studies students for language training in Taiwan. Another consequence of this situation at Leeds, however, was the facility to offer all new students enrolling onto the Chinese programme the option of transferring onto the recently approved joint honours offering in Chinese and Japanese studies. The response was immediate: despite the lack of any serious marketing and the fact that in those days the notion of 'web presence' was still no more than a dream for some in Silicon Valley, this option was immediately taken up by a handful of intrepid students – and when this programme was opened up for general admissions from the following Autumn, it was not long before the quota had been filled and we were obliged to go to the University authorities with a request for increased student numbers. The trend was clear, our logical response equally evident: within a year of commencing Japanese studies at Leeds, we had initiated firstly a joint honours package whereby Japanese could be combined with a range of other social science and humanities disciplines and, shortly thereafter, a single honours programme in modern Japanese studies. And still the numbers snowballed!

I can still vividly remember a series of crisis meetings (admittedly a nice 'crisis' with which to be confronted!) called to determine how to cope with this unexpected surge in demand for Japanese. In light of this upsurge in interest, clearly there were issues that did need to be carefully managed – most notably with regard to ensuring the smooth operation of the compulsory year abroad element within the programme. And it is certainly true that, having made a strategic commitment to Japan, Leeds proceeded to invest heavily in seeking to raise its profile in the country by entering into a series of exchange agreements designed, not simply to ensure that there was a sufficient number of placements to enable all of our second year students to study in Japan, but also, with the research assessments exercise process changing the way in which academic research was managed and evaluated in the UK, to seek to focus on those partnerships that would allow faculty members at both ends to reap the benefits of research collaboration.

So where did all these students come from? And what became of the mantra, repeated endlessly by worried bureaucrats at the embassy and at the multifarious symposia that were convened to consider how the community should respond to the fact that students had bought into the vision of the impending twenty-first century as the 'era of China', that Japanese studies in the UK should prepare for a significant drop in numbers? That was certainly not the experience of us in Leeds, nor that of colleagues at several of the other centres with whom I was in contact at the time. Maybe one factor influencing this impression was the fact that, whereas a quick search of the relevant course offering lists revealed a plethora of UK universities with some kind of Chinese studies offering, Japanese studies was limited, by and large, to the small number of established centres. Yes, the 1990s did see the closure of several East Asian programmes. But, with vice chancellors of the day increasingly at the mercy of internal markets, this was a trend reflected in provision of all the so-called 'hard', and thus high-cost, language areas.

Related to this is the issue of the motivations leading this new generation to embark on a programme of study of Japan. Again the conventional wisdom held that it was the *manga* and *anime* boom of the day that was enticing a small, but significant cohort of teenagers to pursue this interest to degree level. And it is true that analysis of the reasons cited on personal statements does reveal frequent mention of this aspect of Japanese popular culture as one of the impetuses behind the decision. If asked, however, whether there was evidence of a significant shift in motivation away from the reasons traditionally cited by earlier generations (more specifically 'excellent job opportunities' and 'prior connections with Japan') towards a more generic 'fascination with Japanese popular culture', I am not persuaded that the supporting evidence is available. Yes, courses focusing on Japanese popular culture did become – and remain – almost *de rigueur* as an integral part of most of the undergraduate programmes in Japanese from the 1990s onwards. But, given the diversity of career opportunities that remain available to modern linguists – and to those with knowledge of the strategically important, non-European languages in particular – we underestimate the importance of the variety of other motivational factors in this process at our peril.

The 1990s have been dubbed as Japan's 'lost decade' by a series of commentators.[2] And there can be little doubt that, with the bursting of the economic bubble, commemoration of the 50th anniversary of VJ Day, the collapse of the LDP's stranglehold on the levers of power starting in 1993, etc., popular perceptions of Japan were radically transformed around this time – and this reality could not be ignored by the various Japanese studies programmes around the country. The demand for rigorous intellectual engagement with the factors behind these realities continued, however, unabated, and this was reflected, in Leeds and elsewhere, in a strengthening of the position of the intensive core language programme, including a mandatory period of study abroad in Japan, as the central pillars of the various degree programmes on offer. At Leeds, for example, a good passing grade on the final year Japanese language modules became, not simply a desired outcome, but was elevated into a formal graduation requirement. To this end, these modules were carefully revamped – to reflect new language acquisition pedagogies in which all four linguistic skills (reading, writing, listening and speaking) were prioritised equally. At the same time, moreover, considerable attention was paid to bridging the divide that had emerged between language and 'studies' modules – with the resulting new modules, specifically marketed as 'Advanced Japanese in Context' (including variants for literature, history, politics, economics, etc.), specifically designed to move students away from reliance on textbook analysis and to familiarise them with texts and other documents drawn from a variety of everyday contexts.

The next major development in the development of Japanese Studies as a significant presence at the University of Leeds came with the decision to incorporate all the area studies/language programmes into a single School of Modern Languages and Cultures (SMLC) towards the end of the 1990s. The move was initiated by the decision to create nine, large faculties at Leeds – and the concomitant creation of a Faculty of Arts comprising four Schools,

[2]   Cf. eg. Tim Callen & Jonathan Ostry (eds) *Japan's Lost Decade: Policies for Economic Revival*. IMF, 2003.

English, History, Humanities and Modern Languages. The SMLC soon emerged as second only to Medicine in terms of overall student numbers at the University. Inevitably the move towards integrating a series of hitherto small, yet discrete, language departments into a unitary school was no minor challenge – with the anticipated opposition to all change exacerbated by the speed with which the operation was conducted (with departmental secretaries replaced by school officers seemingly overnight) and by the economic and fiscal constraints that underpinned this move. Tony Blair's mantra of 'Education, Education, Education' may have offered the prospect of welcome support for a fundamental shift in the Higher Education landscape; but the fact remained that such major reforms were designed primarily to ensure the financial viability of the institution as a whole – and we, along with the vast majority of UK schools of languages, were not immune from the requirement to persuade others of our contribution to the University's overall strategic plan: the era of 'impact' had dawned.

One factor that languages at Leeds could use to their advantage was the sheer size of the consequent school. With the decision made early to include the language centre, into which considerable investment had been poured during the previous decade, as a core constituent member, the school represented by far the largest such unit in the UK – and there were certain economies of scale that could usefully be applied. Indeed, with the exception of certain Indian languages, the school could justifiably claim to offer degree level programmes in the thirteen most widely spoken languages in the world,[3] and it was not long before module offerings, drawing on expertise from across the school, became an accepted part of the undergraduate curriculum. Colleagues with an interest in religion in Russia now found themselves sharing a classroom with those with a background in other world religions, those working on the twentieth-century German novel could now co-teach with colleagues working on contemporary Chinese literature. And so on, and so on – in ways that would have seemed unimaginable within the old departmental structures with their artificial area studies boundaries.

---

[3]   See the Wikipedia 'List of languages by total number of speakers'.

The possibilities were exciting – and two areas in particular were selected by the faculty for development through specific strategic investment. The first of these, the centre for translation studies, quickly developed a series of cohesive school-wide MA programmes, in both translation and interpreting studies. And in both these endeavours, Japanese played a prominent role – with the strand in translating to and from Japanese (which included both practical training alongside a carefully devised core module in which students from all language pairings came together to explore the latest translating software and machine translation technology) soon securing an annual stream of highly motivated, would-be professional translators, mostly from Japan. The other, the Centre for World Cinemas, was the first of its kind in the UK when inaugurated in 2000, and sold – and continues to sell – itself on providing a 'positive, inclusive and democratic approach to film studies' (CWC website). Again, colleagues from the Japanese section have provided regular input into both its teaching and research programmes at both the undergraduate and postgraduate levels.

Numbers on all Japanese programmes, but particularly on the core undergraduate degree level offerings remained buoyant as we moved into the new millennium – and the unit received a further boost in 2003 when the decision was taken, with backing from HEFCE, to transfer the Centre for South-East Asian Studies from Hull to Leeds. The transfer – of some six posts, considerable library offerings, etc. – envisaged a significant expansion of the East Asian Studies programme at Leeds (which already offered a variety of courses on South-East Asia and the Asia Pacific, including the successful and, at the time, pioneering online MA in Asia Pacific studies). And for the next few years, there was a small but steady cohort of students opting to study Japan in its regional context by availing themselves of some of the new courses that resulted from this transfer. The real benefit of this amalgamation, however, was in cementing Leeds' reputation as an important regional centre for the study of East and South-East Asia writ large, ensuring that it was well prepared for the call, issued in 2005 following the extensive review of UK expertise in the various 'strategically important, yet vulnerable' language areas initiated by the Blair government, for the establishment of a series of 'Language-based Area Studies' (LBAS) national centres of excellence.

With the call specifically naming Japanese and Chinese (in addition to Arabic and Slavonic) as language areas in which there was a compelling need for national investment – and stipulating that bids should incorporate a minimum of two established centres in that particular area, Leeds, given the recent expansion of its East Asian Studies programme and its historical ties and geographical proximity to the School of East Asian Studies at the University of Sheffield, was ideally placed to respond. The call was issued from HEFCE, but received considerable financial support from both the ESRC and the AHRC, and, in drafting this bid, the two units were greatly assisted by the breadth of their pre-existing expertise across the humanities and social sciences spectrum. At the same time, the proposed centre was able to draw heavily on the burgeoning reputation of the Centre for International Business at the University of Leeds (CIBUL), established in 1995 but already attracting a serious international reputation.

There were, however, two related issues to be addressed in drafting the application for a mooted White Rose East Asia Centre (WREAC). These related to the requirement, clearly stipulated in the call for expressions of interest, that consortia bid for a centre in one of the four designated linguistic areas. Not only did this seem to militate against the very notion of a composite East Asia Centre; it also seemed to encourage study of China and Japan in isolation, ignoring their geopolitical contexts in East Asia and implications for the wider South-East Asian area. This represented a serious challenge to two departments that had spent the past few decades making a transition in the opposite direction – and our drafting team spent several lengthy evenings, holed up in a conveniently situated hostelry off the M1, seeking to persuade the selection committee to exercise flexibility in its own stipulations by making the case for an integrated centre.

The rationale was carefully drafted, with the envisioned centre comprising two parallel National Institutes (for Japanese and Chinese Studies respectively) deliberately subsumed under an overarching East Asian umbrella. Our argument was carefully scrutinised at the interview stage – and it would be another six months before announcement of the success of our application suggested that our vision had been shared by the evaluators.

Establishment of WREAC changed the landscape at Leeds and, with the majority of the funding being channelled into a series of PhD studentships – with all recipients co-supervised at both Leeds and Sheffield, this enabled us to complement our vibrant undergraduate programme in Japanese Studies with a welcome influx of graduate students. Not only did this new cohort represent an invaluable resource from which the undergraduate community benefitted considerably, it also resulted in a breadth of interests, especially when combined with colleagues from Sheffield, to organise Japan-related workshops and seminars on a previously unimaginable range of topics.

After the initial five-year period of funding from HEFCE, the ESRC and AHRC, WREAC has received continued support from the AHRC with the aim of developing and strengthening our humanities-based research. This has enabled us to continue our advanced language-based training in Chinese and Japanese, and to invest in new and exciting research projects on Chinese theatre, new Chinese writing, East Asian soft power, and memory and representation in East Asia. In addition, in conjunction with the Nippon Foundation, the GB Sasakawa Foundation has provided invaluable ongoing support to Leeds and the other major centres, firstly in the guise of its Sasakawa lectureship programme and, more recently, the series of Sasakawa studentships. The former scheme enabled Leeds to appoint Irena Hayter in 2008 (a post that was duly funded as a permanent position following expiration of the bespoke funding); under the latter, Leeds has been able to offer funding to support three postgraduate research projects on Japan-related topics for the past two years.

So where does that leave us in 2015? On balance, it would seem that Japanese studies continues to hold its own in an increasingly competitive market. Indeed, with applications for traditional European language degrees struggling to recruit to quota in the brave new world of high tuition fees, not only do applications for Japanese continue to hold firm;[4] but also,

---

[4]   Latest (2015) admissions figures for Leeds show 20 students enrolled onto the Single Honours programme in Japanese Studies, twice as many as the next most popular

as attested by the recent inclusion of Japanese Studies in the recent *Daily Telegraph* list of 'top 10 degree subjects in terms of expected life-time salary',[5] the 'excellent employment prospects' argument persists as a powerful lure to potential candidates. It is thus noticeable that, when our recently revamped School of Languages, Cultures and Societies (renamed in 2014 to reflect the incorporation of Classics into the School) is looking at ways to increase undergraduate student enrolment, the Japanese unit is one area to which it tends to turn. Coping with this perennial demand with an ever-rising staff student ratio was never going to be easy. But we remain grateful for a continuing flow of highly motivated students – and seek to ensure that, for them too, career prospects remain bright.

---

modern languages, French and Spanish. Numbers for the new intake are then more than doubled by the cohort of students who have enrolled onto one of the many Joint Honours programmes involving Japanese.

[5]   http://www.telegraph.co.uk/education/university education/9552659/Graduate-jobs-Top-10-degree-subjects-by-lifetime-salary.html?frame=2344221,.

11

London School of Economics

O

Ian Nish and Janet Hunter

THE LONDON SCHOOL of Economics and Political Science was founded in 1894. By the time of the First World War it had an established reputation as an international centre for research and teaching in the social sciences with special emphasis on the contemporary world. Japan had come onto the international scene during these two decades as a successful economic and political power. Economically it had completed a programme of modernization and established itself as a major industrialized and trading power; politically it had set up a quasi-democracy with political parties and parliamentary institutions.

It was not surprising that Japan should attract interest overseas. The Japanese government was anxious to project the country's image as a modernized progressive country and it encouraged Japanese scholars to travel around the globe in order to project a favourable image of their country. LSE had the funds from the Martin White Foundation Lectureship which enabled them to invite prominent academics from abroad in the field of Sociology. Thus it invited Lafcadio Hearn, an Irishman educated partly in Britain and a long-term teacher in Japan, to deliver a course of 8 public lectures on Japanese civilization in 1904 just before the outbreak of the Russo-Japanese War. Hearn, a prolific publicist, was gratified by the invitation but confessed that he did not fancy writing 'a serious thesis on the Sociology' of Japan. He declined the invitation and died in September 1904.

Okakura Yoshisaburō, younger brother of the famous publicist, Okakura Kakuzō, himself no stranger to international lecturing circles, took his place. His three lectures on the 'Spirit of Japanese Civilization' were delivered to a large audience the following year. Two years later one of the most eminent Japanese academics of the day, Baron Dr Kikuchi Dairoku, president of the Imperial University of Tokyo, gave a course of 15 lectures on 'Education in Japan' in which he drew the attention of a surprised world to the high educational standards of the Japanese people and to how their system balanced and combined the modern with the traditional. In these two instances LSE introduced Japan to a wider world. It showed itself to be an institution not limited to parochial subjects. But LSE did not include in the curriculum any teaching specifically about Japan, far less any suggestion of teaching the Japanese language. It did have a select number of Japanese graduate students, the most notable of whom was Uehara Etsujirō, who studied at LSE from 1907 under the leading sociologist and social psychologist Graham Wallas, and completed a thesis on the contemporary Japanese political system. This thesis was later published by the School under the title *The Political Development of Japan, 1867–1910*. This was a signal honour for Uehara, but also a politically risqué subject bearing in mind the fate of radical thinkers in Japan.

Two of the influential founders of the school, Sidney and Beatrice Webb, chose at this time to proceed on an Asian tour.[1] They fitted in visits to East Asian countries, including Japan, Korea, Manchuria and China. They were hosted in Japan by both Kikuchi and Uehara and they made contact with the graduates and associates of the School in these countries. A number of members of the faculty were in the 1920s following in the footsteps of the Webbs and visiting the countries of what was then called the Far East. We can follow the teaching exploits of the ethnologist Charles Seligman, the economic historians R. H. Tawney and Eileen Power, and

---

[1]   A portrait of Sydney and Beatrice Webb and Japan by Colin Holmes is contained in Hugh Cortazzi and Gordon Daniels, eds, *Britain and Japan 1859–1991: Themes and Personalities* (London: Routledge, 1991).

(if the LSE may claim him as one of our own) Bertrand Russell, one of the spiritual and financial founders of the School. Their priority was to study and teach in China but they all also included trips to Japan.[2]

After 1919 it would have been most remiss of LSE if it had not included some study of Japan, but the methods of teaching often made it hard to fit in any country-by-country analysis. One staff member in the 1930s reported that he had to integrate Japan within his lecture courses on world history of the 1930s. However, a Department of International Studies was set up at LSE in 1927 and in 1932 (Sir) Charles Webster became the first holder of the Stevenson Chair in International History of the interwar period. That was a significant year because East Asia was enflamed by the Manchurian and Shanghai crises. The League of Nations decided to send a commission of enquiry, which naturally looked to the universities of its European members for help from people with suitable expertise. Only the Netherlands and the non-League Americans were able to supply their need for expertise on the Sino-Japanese problem. It was a salutary moment and the coverage of Japanese subjects in lectures and book collections in Europe improved thereafter.

Not much information exists about Japanese students who attended LSE in the 1930s. It had always been the practice of the Japanese Embassy in London to allow its staff to attend LSE courses on a part-time basis, and it was particularly the Ministry of Finance officials who took advantage of this opportunity to become occasional students at LSE. Such were Watanabe Takeshi, who subsequently became the first LSE honorary fellow in Japan, and Fukuda Takeo, later to become prime minister in 1976–1978. There were also university visitors, especially those associated with liberal or left-wing causes. Among the first were Professor Yanaihara Tadao, then a researcher into Japanese colonialism, and later to become president of Tokyo University (1951–1957), and also Professor Oka Yoshitake, whose recent diaries *Rondon Nikki 1936–8* (University of Tokyo Press, 1997) show that, while most of his time was

---

[2]   A biographical portrait of Bertrand Russell by Toshihiko Miura is contained in Hugh Cortazzi, ed., *Britain and Japan: Biographical Portraits*, volume VII (Global Oriental, 2010).

spent at the Public Record Office, he identified in the evenings with causes associated with the LSE.

With the end of the Second World War and the return of LSE from Cambridge to its buildings in central London, the total number of students rose gradually from 4000 in 1950 to 5000 in 1990. Over the same period teaching on aspects of Japan gradually expanded. From the 1960s such teaching has included courses on Japanese sociology and industrial relations by Ronald Dore and Keith Thurley; courses on Japanese history by Ian Nish and Antony Best; and courses on Japanese economic history by Malcolm Falkus and Janet Hunter. The International Relations department has always had a Japanese component in its teaching and research, and has benefited from teaching by Japanese visitors. Professor Hosoya Chihiro of Hitotsubashi University taught a year's course on Japanese foreign policy, while Chiba Kazuo, former Japanese ambassador in London, was appointed as one of LSE's first centennial professors, and gave a course of lectures on Japanese foreign policy.[3] Japan as a country has of course also featured largely in courses on the international economy and trade on account of her spectacular economic growth. Hamada Kōichi, formerly one of the Japanese government's senior advisers on the Japanese economy, and now emeritus professor at Yale, taught economics at LSE in the late 1970s. Specific aspects of the Japanese experience have also figured in courses in other disciplinary areas, such as anthropology, social policy and media studies.

Over recent years the provision of Japanese language tuition by LSE's Language Centre has also expanded significantly as part of its broader programme to make language learning more available to a wide range of students and researchers. Japanese language study is not available for credit as part of a degree programme, but the language is taught at four levels from beginner to advanced as part of our foreign language certificate programme. Some of the courses are fast track, whereas others progress more slowly, allowing for a range of abilities and needs. Demand for these courses from LSE students prepared to study language in addition to their degree programmes has been buoyant, stimulating expansion in provision, and the courses are also open to students from other

---

3   A biographical portrait of Kazuo Chiba is contained in Hugh Cortazzi, ed., *Britain and Japan: Biographical Portraits,* volume X (Renaissance Books, 2016).

parts of the University of London and other individuals. Japanese language provision does not, however, currently extend to teaching for students who wish to engage in full-time, or nearly full-time, language study.

For a while from the 1960s there was a regular Japanese seminar at LSE. Organized by Ronald Dore, who was appointed Reader in Japanese Sociology in 1961, it took advantage of the large number of senior Japanese professors on research leave at the School. This was an opportunity to hear the concerns of the Japanese academics and exchange views with them in small groups.

SUNTORY AND TOYOTA CENTRES (STICERD)

On 2 June 1978 LSE was given substantial donations from the Suntory Company and the Toyota Motor Company (through the Japan Foundation), which enabled the setting up of LSE's International Centre for Economics and Related Disciplines. Its title was later expanded to include the names of the donors, hence the name STICERD by which it is now generally known. It was fitting that Professor Morishima Michio, who held the Sir John Hicks Chair in Economics, should become the founding chairman, since it was he who had negotiated with the two companies, the Japanese government and the Japan Foundation.[4] Professor Morishima defined the functions of the new Centre as follows:

> The Centre shall undertake (i) research into applied economics and related fields, including especially studies of the Japanese economy, comparative studies involving Japan and other economies... (ii) research into studies of economies in which Japan has a major trading or political interest...(iv) historical, sociological, legal, political and other work leading to the above ends

STICERD was to be a research rather than a teaching institute, and this is one thing that differentiates it from approaches on other campuses. A second distinctive feature was the desire to embed any study of Japan within a broader disciplinary framework and

---

4   A biographical portrait of Professor Morishima by Janet Hunter is contained in Hugh Cortazzi, ed., *Britain and Japan: Biographical Portraits*, volume IX (Renaissance Books, 2015).

disciplinary excellence. Studying Japan has become only a small part of the overall discipline-based work in STICERD, albeit an important one. Apart from the work of individual academic members of the School on Japan, notably Ian Nish, Keith Thurley, Janet Hunter and Antony Best, STICERD's Japanese Studies Programme's contribution has come in several key areas: the organization of workshops and symposia on Japan-related topics; the issuing of working papers and discussion papers embodying research on Japan, much of it previously presented at STICERD symposia; the hosting of visiting Japanese academics and researchers, and of academics from other countries specializing in the study of Japan; financial support for particular research projects with a Japanese element; and support for graduate students working on a doctoral thesis related to Japan.

From the outset, regular symposia on international studies and Japanese studies were held at STICERD every year, providing a forum for discussion on Japan for both academics and non-academics with an interest in Japan. It is not possible here to give a comprehensive list of these events, but a good idea of their range can be obtained from the lists of working papers available on the internet.[5] The diversity of these events, however, can be suggested by giving two examples. A conference on interwar Japan, held in 1988 to commemorate the 10th anniversary of STICERD's founding, included among its eminent speakers Professor James Morley of Columbia University and Professor Nakamura Takafusa of the University of Tokyo. A major symposium was held in 1995 on 'Indigenous innovation and comparative industrialization', in which discussion focused mainly on the development of textile, textile machinery, automobile and semi-conductor industries in the USA, Europe and Japan. Leading speakers included Ronald Dore of the University of Sussex, David Hounshell of Carnegie Mellon, Richard Samuels of MIT and Wada Kazuo of the University of Tokyo. While some symposia were attended by 10–20 people, many other events attracted significant audiences of over 50. By the early 1990s the number of individuals included in the mailing list for Japan-related events stood at around 250, ensuring a significant core of attenders for the events that were put on. Apart

---

5   http://sticerd.lse.ac.uk/_new/publications/series.asp?prog=JS and http://sticerd.lse.ac.uk/_new/publications/series.asp?prog=IS.

from these more Japan-dedicated events, STICERD has also offered support for general LSE events that concern Japan, for example a lecture in 2010 by Adam Posen, a member of the Monetary Policy Committee of the Bank of England, on 'Realities and relevance of Japan's Great Recession' and a lecture by Itō Motoshige of Tokyo University in 2014 on 'Why Abenomics matters'. Both lectures filled large lecture halls, testifying to the ongoing interest at LSE in the workings of the Japanese economy.

It should also be noted that over the years 1987–1996 STICERD supported a joint seminar on Japanese economic history in comparative perspective. While the seminar had to be discontinued in 1996 when the SOAS co-organiser, Sugihara Kaoru, returned to Japan to take up a post at Osaka University, the seminar hosted some of Japan's leading economic historians during its existence. Speakers such as Odaka Kōnosuke and Saitō Osamu of Hitotsubashi University and Suzuki Yoshitaka of Tōhoku University attracted an enthusiastic group of researchers and students from across the London area.

The considerable volume of discussion papers and working papers issued by STICERD on Japan-related topics is testimony to the success of the symposia and the research that was articulated at them. The International Studies and Japanese Studies series have been mainly, though not exclusively, focused on history and economic history. They have now been digitized and a complete record is available to consult on the websites indicated above. The work of many leading scholars of Japan is represented in these working papers. Well- known names include Akira Iriye and Albert Craig (Harvard), Richard Smethurst (Pittsburgh) and William Beasley (SOAS). Other publications on Japan were also supported. In 1980 there was a publication from Keith Thurley's work on 'Development of personnel management in Japanese enterprises in Great Britain', and in 1991 a working paper by Michael Hebbert and Norihiro Nakai on 'How Tokyo grows: land development and planning on the metropolitan fringe', which offered an analysis of the mechanisms of urban land development in Japan and a review of current policy measures.

Academic visitors have also been a key part of STICERD's work in relation to Japan, as they have been to the strategy of LSE as a whole. Some of those visitors have been Japanese academics working in specific disciplinary areas, while others have focused their research on Japan. Particularly distinguished visitors have included the social anthropologist Nakane Chie, development economist Gustav Ranis, the labour economist Tachibanaki Toshiaki, the historian and President of Nanzan University Johannes Hirschmeier, and the economist Moriguchi Chikashi, Director of the Institute of Social and Economic Research at Osaka University. Kōji Taira of the University of Illinois at Champaign-Urbana spent time at STICERD, as did Masahiko Aoki of Stanford. Visits by early-career scholars from Japan, in some cases for extended periods, helped to establish publication records and cement international contacts for a number who subsequently built up formidable academic reputations. Yasutomi Ayumu's monograph on the finances of Manchukuo in the 1930s was awarded the 1997 Nikkei Prize for Economics while he was a visiting research associate at STICERD.

STICERD has in a number of ways supported Japan-related research across LSE. In its very early days, in the late 1970s, it offered financial support to assist in the final stages of the compilation of an index to the records of the Tokyo War Crimes Trials, and to work in the Geography Department on the sub-national impact of the Japanese multinational industrial firm. Through an ongoing programme of research grants for researchers across LSE a number of projects with some kind of Japan element have been facilitated. It has in addition throughout its existence offered support to Japanese studies as one of its core programmes, and this has included the employment of early career researchers, support for translation of a small number of Japanese-language works, and help for more specific research projects. Early career scholars employed as researchers have included the economic historian Sugiyama Shin'ya (now emeritus professor at Keiō). More recently financial support helped with the translation into Japanese of *The Historical Consumer*, a book co-edited by Janet Hunter and Penelope Francks.

Last, but not least, STICERD has made a significant contribution to supporting doctoral level research by Japanese students and by students from different departments working on Japan. In some cases this has been done through research assistant posts, but in many through the provision of graduate student scholarships. STICERD's first annual report to its donors reports on an allocation to a PhD student working on Japanese history, and doctoral students working on Japan have on a number of occasions benefited from STICERD studentships. Most recently doctoral students working on Japan from across LSE have been invited to become affiliated to the Japanese Studies Programme. This not only provides them with access to a small amount of research funding, but also brings them together on the basis of their shared interest in Japan, complementing the disciplinary community that is offered by their different departments. The total numbers remain small, but this strategy helps to support Japan-related research at LSE.

Turning from STICERD back to its host institution, two final points should be made about research and teaching on Japan at LSE. The first is that LSE has never claimed to offer itself as an area studies institution. 'Area studies' at LSE is, to use the words of the 1961 Hayter Committee's report on its visit to North America, 'a group of scholars....who are all using their own disciplines to pursue studies related to that area'.[6] While LSE contains within it a number of centres and programmes that help to bring together research interests on particular geographical regions, the disciplinary focus remains paramount. Both faculty and students working on Japan at LSE identify themselves as historians, economists, political scientists, etc., whose research or study focuses on Japan, rather than as any kind of 'Japanologist'. In this context a significant number of LSE academics with leading profiles in their disciplines, but with no claim to Japanese studies expertise, have also made visits to Japan and have had recurrent links with the country. Particularly in the financial and economic fields, LSE faculty members have acted as advisers and consultants for the Japanese government and other institutions. Other LSE researchers interact with Japanese academics on the basis of shared disciplinary interests. Expertise on, and interaction with Japan is not, therefore, limited to the small number of Japan specialists.

---

[6]   *Report of the Sub-Committee on Oriental, Slavonic, East European and African Studies* (London: HMSO, 1961), p. 122.

Secondly, and following on from this, much of the teaching and research on Japan at LSE has involved some kind of broader international and comparative context, whether it is Japan in the context of East Asia or international relations, or Japan as a model of economic development or social welfare to be compared with the experience of other economies and systems. In this context the narrowing of the institutional divide that has historically existed between area studies and disciplines in the UK is greatly to be welcomed, although the complementarity of different approaches to the study of Japan is likely to remain central to its vitality.

During the period from the 1980s to the early 1990s LSE concluded framework agreements for collaboration with a number of Japanese universities, including the University of Tokyo, Keiō University, Hitotsubashi University and Kyōto University. These agreements were a recognition by LSE of Japan's increasing importance in the global world. More recently LSE has focused on the conclusion of more concrete ways of cooperating with Japanese institutions of higher education. The Language Centre now has formal language student exchange agreements with both Waseda and Keiō universities. The Economic History Department has a research student exchange programme with the Faculty of Economics at the University of Tokyo, while the Master in Public Affairs programme at LSE is part of a global consortium of top MPA universities of which the University of Tokyo is also a part. Annual lectures in both London and Tokyo take place under the auspices of the Hitotsubashi-LSE lecture programme, and further collaborative efforts with Hitotsubashi have been under discussion. Individual academics, of course, have their own personal networks with universities and academics in Japan.

It has to be acknowledged that the extent of teaching and research on Japan at LSE is at the present not as extensive as many at LSE would like it to be. It will also be apparent that much of what has been achieved in this area over the past few decades has been due to the contribution of individual academics and the teaching and structures that they have created. The death of Professor Morishima Michio in 2004 left LSE without its leading Japanese academic, while the stagnation of the Japanese economy helped to reduce

Japan's international image as a topic worthy of study by social scientists and undermined student interest. Recent efforts by individuals, by STICERD and by the School as a whole are seeking to redress what is a disproportionately low coverage of one of the world's major economies. LSE fully recognizes that Japan still matters, and is working to maintain its past tradition of close involvement.

12

Manchester University

O

Jonathan Bunt

JAPANESE STUDIES AT Manchester University grew out of a
long-term collaborative language-teaching and business development centre run by what were then the four universities in Greater
Manchester (the University of Manchester Institute of Science and
Technology [UMIST], Salford University, Manchester Metropolitan University and the Victoria University of Manchester). After
early attempts to establish an MA foundered, the so-called Greater
Manchester Centre for Japanese Studies was largely a business and
teaching service operation until in 2006 it was finally absorbed into
the new Manchester University, which was created following the
2004 merger of the Victoria University of Manchester and UMIST.
The formation of the new University of Manchester was significant
in providing opportunities to reach out into new areas of scholarship and teaching. Japanese Studies was developed along with Chinese Studies (established a year earlier, in 2006) through internal
university development funds.

Ian Reader was appointed as the foundation professor in 2007
and he worked with Professor Steven Parker (then head of the
School of Languages, Linguistics and Cultures) and Jonathan
Bunt, who formerly worked at the Japan Centre developing language-teaching programmes and has published a dictionary and

grammar of Japanese for learners, in order to develop a full department and programmes of study. The new department has had a focus on modern and early modern Japan from the outset. Professor Reader, who is an expert on modern Japanese religion and the author of *Sendatsu and the Development of Contemporary Pilgrimage* (1983) and *Religious Violence in Contemporary Japan: The Case of Aum Shinrikyō* (2000), was joined by two lecturers who were specialists on modern Japanese society, Dr Peter Cave, an anthropologist who works on education and has written *Primary School in Japan: Self, Individuality and Learning in Elementary Education* (2007), and Dr Mara Patessio, a historian of Meiji Japan who wrote *Women and Public Life in Early Meiji Japan: The Development of the Feminist Movement* (2011). With language tutors from the former Japan Centre, a degree programme was launched in 2007 and although the programme had not been fully advertised nearly twenty students were enrolled.

Initially the programmes in Japanese and Chinese were combined in a single department of East Asian Studies but they have now been formally separated. However, despite this formal separation, Japanese and Chinese continue to work closely together, developing East Asian Studies as a degree programme and allowing students to benefit from several courses taught by lecturers with a wider East Asian perspective in their research and teaching.

The development of Japanese Studies was greatly aided by generous grants from the Japan Foundation for materials and from the Sasakawa Foundation for an additional lectureship in Japanese visual cultures, to which Dr Sharon Kinsella was appointed in 2008; she is the author of *Schoolgirls, Money and Rebellion in Japan* (2013). The Japan Foundation contributed again to appointing a further language tutor and a full department was finally in existence. Funding from the Wellcome Trust added a further post-doctoral position. To this Dr Aya Hōmei was appointed in 2009: she specializes in the history of medicine and science and with Michael Worboys has written *Fungal Disease in Britain and the United States 1850–2000* (2013): this post was converted into a full lectureship in 2015.

The academic staff in the new Japanese Studies programme were impressed to find that Manchester University Library already possessed a comprehensive collection of literature on Japan in English

– a tribute to the wide horizons of those developing the library over the decades. However, when the programme was inaugurated, there were few if any Japanese-language books, and developing this collection has been one of the priorities of the department in its first years. This was aided by the early acquisition of three important collections: the personal library of Professor Ronald Dore, one of the leading scholars of postwar Japanese society, the library of Gyōsei College at the University of Reading, and a generous and supportive donation of duplicate volumes from the University of Cambridge thanks to Professor Peter Kornicki and Professor Richard Bowring. The University now has very substantial holdings on Japan in Japanese, English and other languages and has a specialist library team who catalogue and develop the collections.

In addition, Manchester is fortunate that the John Rylands Library, which is also part of the university, has a fine collection of Japanese woodblock books, prints and maps, which have excited students when they have been used in undergraduate teaching. A digitalisation of some of these resources (in particular the maps) is currently underway in a project led by Dr Erica Baffelli in collaboration with the curatorial team at the John Rylands Library.

A decision was taken early on not to develop a Japan Studies MA programme for the foreseeable future, concentrating instead on undergraduate teaching and research students and, in spite of some fluctuations, undergraduate numbers have been reasonably consistent (around 45–50 admissions each year). Alongside single-honours students, there are joint-honours students reading other languages, business, or mathematics along with Japanese. It should also be noted that Manchester has run a programme for Life Sciences and Japanese since 2001; students on this programme spend a year in Japan in science labs at either Nagoya or Tsukuba universities.

The establishment of exchange partnerships for the main Japanese Studies programme was an early priority, and to date about 25 partnerships have been set up with Japanese universities from Kyushu to Hokkaido, with the majority in the Tokyo and Kansai areas. We have been very happy to see that numbers of Japanese exchange students coming to Manchester have been similar to the numbers the programme sends to Japan, and there have been excellent relationships between the Japanese exchange students and the Japanese Studies programme students in Manchester, aided by plenty of student-run social events.

The department has gradually been building up its numbers of PhD students (7 current students as of September 2015), and it has been good to see that doctoral students have had an excellent record of successful completion within a four year period, with a number being appointed to postdoctoral and permanent academic positions in the UK and overseas thereafter.

Academic staff changes in recent years have seen the retirement of Ian Reader, who is now an Emeritus Professor. Dr Erica Baffelli, an expert on new religions in Japan, has taken up teaching and research in the field of religion, where there are excellent synergies with Manchester's celebrated and long-established department of Religions and Theology.

In 2013 a major structural change saw the merger of two schools to create a new School of Arts, Languages, and Cultures, which is larger than some of our partner universities in Japan. The merger has created opportunities for further development of joint-honours programmes and other major programmes.

Manchester has scholars working on Japan in departments outside Japanese Studies, notably in fields such as history, business and social anthropology, and there have been fruitful collaborations with colleagues across departments, both in research projects and in the supervision of doctoral students. One such collaboration, on the history of childhood, education and youth in Japan between 1925 and 1945, involves the creation of a digital archive of original sources – both documents and oral history interviews – a new initiative with potential for future development. This project has attracted interest in Japan as well, with academic staff featuring on national television and newspapers. Other notable recent initiatives have included a conference looking back on the Aum Shinrikyō sarin gas attack after 20 years, which was covered prominently on the NHK News 9 programme.

Although the Japanese Studies department at Manchester is relatively new, it has benefited greatly from being situated in one of Britain's largest, best-resourced, and most internationally known universities and one of the country's most globally prominent cities.

Links between Japan and the Manchester area are both deep and long; it is well known that Lancashire technology helped to power the Japanese textile industry, and in the early twentieth century it was patent sales to Platt Brothers of Oldham that provided Toyota with the funds to enter vehicle manufacturing. The Manchester department looks forward to being part of this dynamic continuing relationship.

13

University of Newcastle

O

James Babb and Joanne Smith Finley

PRIOR TO 1963, King's College, which became the University of Newcastle-upon-Tyne in 1963, was originally part of the University of Durham. The University of Durham had a long established programme in East Asian Studies, but for the first two decades of its existence the University of Newcastle did not have any formal East Asian Studies programme. It was not until 1984 that a degree in Politics and East Asian Studies (PEAS) was created in the Department of Politics at the University of Newcastle and run by the East Asian Centre, which was then part of the Department of Politics.

James Cotton and David Goodman were the main academics behind the degree and the Centre, and recruited a new lecturer in Japanese Politics, Ian Neary. The move was given added impetus by the decision of Nissan to locate a large automobile factory in the north-east of England and this brought with it a large number of Japanese firms as suppliers. The role of Japan in the world seemed to be on the rise, and Sir Peter Parker was commissioned in 1985 to report on the state of Japanese studies in the UK with the aim of enhancing the development of Japanese studies. Interest in and funding for Japanese studies increased.

Goodman, Cotton and Neary all left Newcastle in the late 1980s to pursue successful careers elsewhere, culminating in prominent professorial positions. There was also turnover in the lecturership in Japanese politics, with two coming and leaving in quick succession, including Dr Jin Park, who left to assume a job as press spokesperson for the President of Korea. On the other hand, a chair of Japanese Studies was established in 1989 at the University of Newcastle and Reinhard Drifte was selected to fill it: he served as Director of the Newcastle East Asian Centre from 1989 to 1996. Originally, all the language teaching (Chinese, Korean and Japanese) was undertaken by staff in the East Asian Centre, but in the early 1990s the language teaching was moved to the Language Centre, a service department providing tuition in non-European languages and English for Speakers of Other Languages in the University.

In 1993, the East Asian Centre comprised three lecturers in Politics, covering China (Shaun Breslin), Korea (Roland Wein) and Japan (James Babb), and under the leadership of Professor Drifte the Centre was poised for growth. A former lecturer on Korea, Barry Gills, remained in the Department of Politics as a lecturer in International Political Economy, and maintained a strong focus on East Asia. The number of students on the PEAS degree slowly expanded. The joint MA in East Asian Studies with Durham University was closed and replaced by a new MA in East Asian Politics located in the Department of Politics at the University of Newcastle. The number of research students obtaining PhD degrees also increased at this time.

The expansion was, however, short-lived. The departure of two members of staff undermined the PEAS degree. One was Roland Wein, Lecturer in Korean Politics (1993–1995) who left the University to work in an NGO; the other was Shaun Breslin, Lecturer in Chinese Politics (1987–1997), who moved to the University of Warwick. The loss of Breslin, and the inability of the Politics Department to replace him at a time when the market for Chinese specialists was so strong, meant that the PEAS programme was no longer viable and was phased out. Breslin had been core to the programme as an early PEAS degree undergraduate who completed his PhD at Newcastle in 1993 and then became a member of the teaching staff. Without the larger number of students studying Chinese politics, the number of students on the Japan strand of the PEAS degree was not high enough to justify its continuation. The MA in East Asian Politics was withdrawn in 1998, and the final cohort of students on the PEAS degree graduated in 2000. From this time on, the main channel of undergraduate recruitment for Chinese and Japanese language studies was the University's Combined Studies programme.

Professor Drifte took early retirement in 2003 when the University of Newcastle was restructured and the Department of Politics was merged with Geography and Sociology into a 'School', though he continued his association in an Emeritus capacity. The East Asian Centre was then also phased out, first by a review of East Asian Studies conducted by the University in 2000 which resulted in the loss of its funding, and then by a policy to convert Centres into Faculty Research Groups, for which the East Asian Centre did not qualify.

One very positive development in 2002 was that the teaching of East Asian languages was moved from the Language Centre to the School of Modern Languages, where it was again housed in a research-active environment. The number of programmes within which Japanese could be taken as a subject then increased significantly. In 2003, Joanne Smith in the School of Modern Languages (now Smith Finley, Lecturer in Chinese Studies since 2000) and Naomi Standen in the School of Historical Studies (also appointed in 2000) took the initiative to bring together staff teaching East Asian subjects across the Faculty of Humanities and Social Sciences, and launched a new Single Honours programme in Chinese/Japanese and Cultural Studies (later re-titled Chinese Studies/Japanese Studies). From this time on, they worked with James Babb in Politics to coordinate and enhance East Asian teaching provision at Newcastle, and made the case for internal and external funding to increase the number of research-active colleagues in East Asian studies. In 2006, the University was successful in hiring a new Lecturer in Chinese Politics, Michael Barr. In 2007, the School of Modern Languages invested in a new Lecturer in Japanese studies, Dr Andrea Germer. In the same year, Standen was successful in applying for Sasakawa Foundation funding for a new post in modern Japanese history, taken up by Martin Dusinberre in 2008.

Also in 2008, the School of Modern Languages hired an additional lecturer in Chinese Studies, Sabrina Yu, and in 2011, it was successful in attracting Japan Foundation funding for an additional lecturer in Japanese Studies, Shiro Yoshioka. There has been considerable staff turnover at Newcastle owing to the departure of staff as they successfully obtained positions at a higher level elsewhere. In the School of Modern Languages, Germer was succeeded by Laura Moretti in 2010, who was in turn succeeded by Gitte Marianne Hansen in 2013. In the School of History, Classics and Archaeology, Dusinberre was succeeded by Philip Garrett in 2014. On the Chinese studies side, Standen was succeeded by Joseph Lawson in 2013. Japanese can currently be studied within the following undergraduate programmes: Japanese Studies; Modern Languages; Modern Languages, Translating and Interpreting; Modern Languages and Linguistics; Modern Languages and Business Studies; Combined Honours; Linguistics with Japanese; and International Business Management. Japanese Studies can also be pursued at postgraduate level via a one-year Master of Letters (MLitt) research degree. In 2015, the Faculty of Humanities, Arts and Social Sciences approved and funded an Asian Studies Research Group at Newcastle University, as well as applying for a language-based area studies funding pathway in East Asian Studies within the ESRC North East Doctoral Training Centre jointly based at Newcastle and Durham Universities.

Japan-related research by current staff covers a wide range of fields from medieval history (Philip Garrett, published in the *Journal of Japanese Studies* in 2015) to contemporary politics, represented by James Babb who has published *Tanaka: The Making of Postwar Japan* (2000) and *Business and Politics in Japan* (2001). Gitte Hansen has published *Femininity, Self-harm and Eating Disorders in Japan: Navigating Contradiction in Narrative and Visual Culture* (2016) and Shiro Yoshioka works on contemporary cultural history (particularly animation film).

14

Oxford University

O

Roger Goodman and Arthur Stockwin

EARLY BEGINNINGS

ANY HISTORY OF the development of Japanese studies at Oxford
needs to start, as with many other subjects, with the history of the
Japanese collection at the Bodleian library. The first known accession of Japanese printed material was three volumes of the so-called
Saga-bon, books printed with moveable-type in the Saga district of
Kyoto in the early seventeenth century, which were presented to the
Library in 1629 by Robert Viney, rector of Barnack, who studied at
Oxford in 1621–1625.[1] The Bodleian also possesses some very rare
examples of missionary literature of the Jesuit Mission Press in Japan,
collectively known as Kirishitan-ban, that were produced from 1590
until the expulsion of the missionaries from Japan in 1614.

The Japanese manuscript collection, numbering about 100
titles, contains over 20 Nara-ehon (Nara picture books), decora-
tively illustrated literature hand-produced in either book or scroll
format from the seventeenth to the eighteenth centuries, including
a unique picture scroll of Urashima. The library also has a copy of
the *shuinjō* (vermilion seal document) of 1613 that was issued by
Shōgun Tokugawa Ieyasu to grant the English East India Company

---

[1]   *Nipponica*, 131–133.

trade privileges in Japan, as well as the log-book of William Adams (1564–1620), the first Englishman known to have visited Japan.

The Bodleian has a rich collection of pre-1850 books in European languages dealing with Japan. This includes examples of the published correspondence of the Jesuit fathers, accounts of the early travels to Japan in various published records of European voyages overseas, material relating to the East India Companies of England and Holland, and works of European explorers of the eighteenth and nineteenth centuries. This material vividly illustrates Europe's contacts with Japan from the sixteenth century to the mid-nineteenth century.

All of this material, of course, pre-dates not only the formal study of Japan at Oxford but also indeed the arrival of Japanese students in Oxford, the first of whom appeared in 1873: he was Iwakura Tomotsune, the third son of Iwakura Tomomi, then Minister of the Right in Japan and the man who led the famous Iwakura Mission. The first female student was Tsuda Ume who studied at St Hilda's College in the 1890s and went on to found Japan's first private women's school of higher education.

As Brian Powell said in his survey of 'Oxford and Japan', 'While there was no-one in Oxford giving regular courses of lectures on Japan in the nineteenth century, the facilities for certain types of research were increasing impressively. The Bodleian had books, the Ashmolean various types of Japanese art, and from the mid-1880s these were joined by the ethnographic collections of the Pitt Rivers Museum'.[2] Basil Hall Chamberlain (1850–1935), who was Professor of Japanese at Tokyo Imperial University, was a particularly important collector of everyday Japanese artefacts for the Pitt Rivers Museum.

The first person who formally taught about Japan at Oxford (as opposed to Japanese visitors who gave the occasional talk) was John Harrington Gubbins (1852–1929). Ian Nish has praised Gubbins for his work, in particular for his role in revising the unequal treaties between Britain and the UK in the mid-1890s.[3] In 1909, Lord Curzon, then Chancellor of the University, leant

---

[2]   Brian Powell, 'Oxford and Japan', unpublished seminar paper presented at the Nissan Institute of Japanese Studies, 13 November 2009, p. 5.

[3]   Ian Nish, ed., *Britain and Japan: Biographical Portraits*, volume II (Japan Library, 1997).

on Oxford to appoint Gubbins as a Lecturer in Japanese. He was attached to Balliol College, but his lectures did not attract enough students and his three-year appointment was not renewed. The teaching of Japan at Oxford did not pick up again until more than forty years later.

The two figures who should be most credited for the building of a programme for teaching Japanese in Oxford in the post-war period are Richard (Dick) Storry (1913–1981) and Geoffrey Bownas (1923–2011).[4] Bownas was appointed lecturer in Chinese and Japanese Studies in 1954 (the date which has ever since been taken as the foundation of Japanese Studies in Oxford) and Storry was elected to a special fellowship at St Antony's College the following year.

THE DEVELOPMENT OF THE BA IN JAPANESE

While Bownas and Storry between them can be seen as responsible for the subsequent development of Japanese Studies, their separate involvement explains why the pre-modern and modern trajectories of the discipline often appeared to move in an apparently uncoordinated fashion. Bownas' efforts were focussed in the Faculty of Oriental Studies and the creation of a BA degree in Japanese. This was not easy, not least because his post involved a lot of teaching in Chinese and overall resources were thin on the ground. The fact that he had a dual responsibility, however, proved to be the way forward. Japanese was first made an optional part of the Chinese BA degree in 1957 and grew from there until it was given its own stand-alone degree status in 1964 (first examined in 1965). In relation to the issue of lack of resources, Bownas was one of the early fundraisers in Oxford's history, writing literally hundreds of letters to organisations and companies which he thought might be interested in supporting Japanese Studies. He thereby collected enough money to pay for a language teacher, a secretary and a post-doctoral Junior Research Fellow (JRF), this last funded by the Rank Organisation: the first holder was Brian Powell, an expert on modern Japanese theatre, who succeeded Bownas as the first dedicated Lecturer in Japanese Studies in 1966 when the latter moved to Sheffield to the

---

4   See the biographical portrait of Storry by Ian Nish in Hugh Cortazzi, ed., *Britain and Japan: Biographical Portraits*, volume V (Global Oriental, 2004).

foundation professorship in Japanese studies. Powell held the post for the following 38 years and played a key role in all the subsequent developments in Japanese studies at Oxford.

In a lecture in 2009, Powell described how, influenced by a visit to the States in 1963, he moved the teaching of Japanese away from the conventional model of Oriental Studies programmes ('full of imposing-sounding texts') towards a more interactive model ('a list of language classes').[5] The texts that were used were widened to include non-literary subjects such as history and politics. He and subsequent JRFs taught the texts (both classical and modern); the Lectors (the first of whom, Shimizu Shūyū, went on to become a distinguished professor at Keio University) taught all the language classes, and the specialist essay topics would be taught by anyone around the University with the necessary expertise, such as Richard Storry or Oliver Impey (1936–2005), who was based at the Ashmolean Museum and for many years was the only person teaching Japanese art in any university in the country.

James McMullen (an expert on Japanese Confucian thought who did his doctoral work at Cambridge under the supervision of Carmen Blacker) took up a newly-created second lectureship in Oxford in 1972. McMullen organised and taught a year-long survey course on Japanese history and culture, whose aim was to enable undergraduates to make more informed choices among the options open to them later; the course evolved over the years until by the 1990s every lecturer in both the Oriental and the Nissan Institutes was contributing to it. In the 1980s, he was also largely responsible for broadening the survey course to set Japan in an East Asian context by bringing in lectures on China and Korea. This later expanded to include the possibility of doing Japanese together with subsidiary courses in other East Asian languages such as Chinese, Korean and Tibetan.

The lectors, who had a teaching stint of only seven hours a week, were replaced in the 1970s by instructors, properly qualified language teachers with a teaching load of twenty hours a week, and the teaching of modern Japanese in all its forms was

---

[5]   Powell, 'Oxford and Japan', p. 10.

thereby greatly increased. Equally significantly, periods of study in Japan as part of the course were increasingly encouraged. These voluntary 'year outs' were largely made possible through the generosity of Japanese universities (including Kanazawa, Keio, Kyodai, Ochanomizu Joshidai, Osaka Gaidai, Waseda), companies and at least one charity which provided the funding for students to spend a year in Japan before they embarked on their final year of study in Oxford.

In 1984, the BA in Japanese was lengthened from three to four years, with students spending their first year concentrated on intensive language training at the Centre of Japanese Studies at the University of Sheffield which had been established by Geoffrey Bownas in the mid-1960s and had gone from strength to strength. Students who took the voluntary 'year out' at this time were, therefore, in effect now taking a five-year undergraduate programme.

While there was no doubt about the quality of language teaching which the students received in Sheffield, this programme was not without its critics, especially among those who argued that studying in Oxford was not only about what was studied but the mode of delivery of teaching and the 'Oxford experience'. There was certainly no other programme in Oxford at the time where students spent a year being trained elsewhere. By this time, though, the Nissan Institute of Japanese Studies had been established (see below), and Arthur Stockwin, its inaugural Director, strongly supported the arrangement with Sheffield, essentially on two grounds: firstly, that it was crucial for Japanese studies in Oxford that the course be extended from three years to four, but with existing resources it was not possible to do that in Oxford; and secondly, that for a student to spend their undergraduate years in two very different universities was a valuable life experience in its own right (indeed, this was borne out by feedback from many, though not all, the undergraduates who went through the course at that stage). Stockwin, and no doubt other academic staff, had to fight their corner with some vigour in the face of criticism from those of more traditional inclinations within Oxford and beyond.

In 1994, first year students were 'repatriated' to Oxford, not, as seems to be widely believed, because of traditionalist criticism but because Sheffield went 'modular', making it less practical to work with Oxford, which also by now had the resources to teach the first year of its four-year course in-house. Indeed, by the end of the 1990s, the undergraduate programme had grown, as Brian Powell put it, 'to a level not dreamed of in the 1960s'.[6] The fact that this was possible was greatly helped by the establishment of a third University Lectureship in Japanese which was established in 1988 as a result of the Parker Report on Oriental Studies and was filled by Phillip Harries who moved from SOAS. In 1988, the Tokyo Electric Power Company (TEPCO) also permanently endowed a Tutorial Fellowship in Japanese at Pembroke College to which James McMullen moved from St Antony's; in the same year the Industrial Bank of Japan endowed a fellowship at Keble College, to which Brian Powell in turn moved. Further funding during this era for Japanese studies in Oxford came from Mitsui, JUSCO, the Industrial Bank of Japan and the Yamamuro-Mitsubishi Memorial Fund. The Sasakawa Foundation also made a very generous endowment which enabled, and still enables, scholars and students from across the University, and not only those in Japanese studies, to travel to and undertake research in Japan.

The growth of the BA in Japanese Studies was, of course, linked with the growing interest in Japan itself in the period. While students who came to study Japan in the 1960s and early 1970s often came for more esoteric interests such as Zen Buddhism and Japanese martial arts, those who came in the 1980s increasingly saw the study of Japanese and knowledge about Japan as a shrewd career move. While the Japanese economy had grown to become the second largest economy in the world by the late 1980s (and widely predicted to overtake the US as the largest economy in the world by the year 2000), the number of Japan specialists and Westerners able to speak Japanese was still vanishingly small. Natural market forces prevailed meaning that the degree in Japanese could lead to very lucrative job offers particularly when, as we shall see, a candidate could also demonstrate a knowledge of Japanese economy, society or business. That said, while the number of students enrolling in the BA programme grew substantially during the 1980s, they were

---

6   Powell, 'Oxford and Japan', p. 11.

always modest compared to numbers at many other universities at the time such as Sheffield and SOAS. This was because even if there was greater demand for places, numbers were restricted, in part by the number of places which colleges were able to offer (it is not possible to be a matriculated student in Oxford without having a College place), in part by the capacity of the teaching staff to offer tutorials to students in groups of two or three at least once a week, and in part by agreements with institutions in Japan who looked after students on their year abroad. Currently, twelve students are admitted to read Japanese each year and competition for places is as fierce as it has ever been.

THE STORY OF THE NISSAN BENEFACTION

If the appointment of Geoffrey Bownas in 1954 can be seen as the origin of the undergraduate programme in Japanese studies at Oxford, then the appointment of Richard Storry in 1955 can be seen as the start of the process that led to the foundation of the Nissan Institute of Japanese Studies in 1981 and the development of the MSc in Modern Japanese Studies which took its first students in the mid-2000s. The link between his appointment and the subsequent developments, though, is considerably more difficult to trace.

Richard Storry's original appointment at St Antony's College was in the Far East Centre run by Geoffrey Hudson. With the establishment of the Nissan Institute, this was renamed in 1982 the Asian Studies Centre, as it is still called today. Storry was particularly effective in building up a Japanese 'research cluster' in the Centre from the beginning, in particularly inviting major Japanese figures, such as Maruyama Masao, Oka Yoshitake and Ishida Takeshi, to visit. He also built up a fine collection of books on contemporary Japan which subsequently became absorbed into the University's collection when the University (not the College, though somewhat confusingly the Institute has always been housed in buildings owned by the College) established the Nissan Institute.

It is a curious fact that neither Bownas nor Storry could be counted among the early supporters of the plan that a major Japanese industrial conglomerate should support a centre for the study of modern Japan. Some of the evidence for this comes from someone who has, until now, been less recognised than he should have been in the process that led to the founding of the Nissan Institute, namely Roderick MacFarquhar, who was at the time a Member of Parliament, and later became Director of the Fairbank Center for Chinese Studies at Harvard University.

In around 1977, MacFarquhar proposed to the Japanese Embassy in London that a new institute of Japanese Studies be established in the south of England at the cost of around £1.5 million. MacFarquhar had been an associate fellow of St Antony's in the 1960s and he clearly thought that the College would be a suitable home for such a new Centre because of its long-standing interests in area studies. In a long article in the *Financial Times* (17 March 1977), he proposed that this Centre should be named after Sir George Sansom who had done so much 'to explain Japan past and present to Western audiences'.

In late 1977, the Warden and certain Fellows of the College, including Brian Powell and James McMullen, met with MacFarquhar in London to confirm the College's interest. As it happened, Storry was in Japan at that time on sabbatical and also, in part, raising funds for Japanese Studies. He was extremely unhappy to discover that MacFarquhar had gone ahead with his proposal for the project without ever consulting him and seemed to think that the proposal might get in the way of his own fundraising efforts. In a letter (3 January 1978) to the whole Governing Body, which was to meet to discuss the proposal, he wrote:

> It is not for me to say who is the more effective fund-raiser; but I think I could stake a claim to a rather better understanding of Japan and Japanese psychology...So I must ask those concerned... in any negotiations to keep me well briefed as to their progress.... there should be no reluctance...to resort, if necessary, to the international telephone service.

Despite Storry's plea, according to the official account given in the College history by Christine Nicholls:

> The international telephone service was not resorted to; the Governing Body approved the proposal; St Antony's and Oxford were

signed up to bidding for the new Japanese Studies centre, if and when the funds were raised.[7]

Despite his unhappiness at the time, later on Dick Storry subsequently changed his view from opposition to the MacFarquhar initiative to support for it 'overnight', according to Sir Raymond Carr, at that time Warden of St Antony's.

The decision of where any new Centre for Japanese Studies should be located was passed by the Japanese Embassy to the Foreign Office and then over to the University Grants Committee, which took soundings widely. Ronald Dore, then at Sussex and widely seen as the doyen of the study of modern Japan in the UK at the time, strongly supported the funds going to Oxford and there can be no doubt that this played a major part in the final decision.

MacFarquhar's description of his own role in the establishment of the Nissan Institute is recorded in detail in Nicholls' history of St Antony's College:

> The breakthrough came in the 1979 election campaign, when the Foreign Secretary, David Owen, came up to make a speech in my constituency. I pressed him to raise the Japanese institute issue with his Japanese counterpart when he met him a few days later. This Owen did, and the Japanese were particularly impressed because Owen had raised a matter which was not on the agenda. This meant, the Japanese reasoned, that the matter must be particularly important to the British and therefore should be addressed...I was summoned to the Japanese embassy where the Foreign Minister told me he had told the Ambassador to do something about the matter. The Ambassador got busy, contacted the head of Nissan, who was a classmate of his...The rest is history.[8]

Since MacFarquhar's original possible donors, Mitsubishi and Mitsui, had both decided against funding the proposal, the link

---

[7]   C. S. Nicholls, *The History of St Antony's College Oxford, 1950–2000*, (Basingstoke: Macmillan Press, 2000), p. 89.
[8]   Nicholls, *The History of St Antony's College Oxford, 1950–2000*, p. 92. See also Robin Mountfield, 'Nissan investment in Britain: history of a negotiation 1980–84', in H. Cortazzi, ed., *Britain and Japan: Biographical Portraits*, vol. VI (Folkestone: Global Oriental, 2007), pp. 107–121, 343–364.

between the then-Ambassador Fujiyama and the then-President of Nissan, Ishihara Takashi, was crucial to the formation of the Institute. The notion that the Nissan Motor Company should support a new institute in Oxford, however, was not without its critics.

First, there were those who were suspicious about the establishment of a new centre for Japanese Studies at Oxford University. Chief among those who expressed this view was Geoffrey Bownas who argued, not without some logic, that it would make more sense to endow and expand the centre which he had established in the mid-1960s at Sheffield and which was already the leading centre for the study of modern Japan in the country. MacFarquhar (*Financial Times*, 5 March 1977) responded to Bownas's letter to the *Financial Times* on this topic in a feisty manner:

> Sir, - I was surprised at the letter from Professor Geoffrey Bownas (February 21) suggesting that I did not know about the centre of Japanese studies at the University of Sheffield...What I found astonishing in the letter and in the others which I have received from a number of Professor Bownas's colleagues (a correspondence almost as large as that which I have received on the Abortion Amendment Bill) was the apparent sense of outrage at the thought of expanding Japanese studies elsewhere. One might have hoped that my suggestion would have been welcomed by everyone in the Japanese field as designed to increase the resources and students entering it; that surely, it must be agreed, if we are to understand Japan better. Instead, the reaction has been parochial and self-protective. This has only confirmed me in my belief that a new centre would be desirable.

Once the Nissan Institute was established, any friction between the Japanese studies establishments in Oxford and Sheffield quickly evaporated and, indeed, with the first year BA students going to Sheffield to study, mutually advantageous arrangements between them were quickly established.

Second, there were those who were suspicious of Japanese intentions in investing in such a project in the UK at all. The UK in the 1970s was going through a particularly tough economic period which saw the collapse of much of its industrial heartlands and record levels of unemployment. The Thatcher government put a lot of effort into attracting foreign direct investment which many in the UK trade union movement thought was a way to circumvent the rights of its members. Nowhere was this sensitivity felt more than in Oxford which had been home to car manufacturing at Cowley since almost the beginning of the industry. When the first holder of the Nissan Chair of Modern Japanese Studies, Arthur Stockwin, was told of his appointment and wrote to his parents in Birmingham about it from Australia, his father wrote back: 'When you drive your Nissan car through Cowley, be careful they don't stone the car'. (For a detailed account of the establishment of a Nissan car manufacturing plant in the UK – which was not actually agreed until 1984 after many years of negotiations – see Mountfield, 2007.)[9]

A short piece in the *Oxford Mail* (31 October 1979) under the heading 'Yen for Learning' indeed could not avoid making an indirect reference to the Oxford car industry when announcing the Nissan benefaction:

> Japanese car giants Datsun have given a massive £1,500,000 gift to Oxford University. In a ceremony that took place just a few miles from British Leyland's Cowley plant Mr Takashi Ishihara...handed over a symbol of the gift to University Vice Chancellor Sir Rex Richards.

Articles in *The Guardian* and *Time Out* both suggested that Nissan's investment in Oxford was part of what today would be called 'soft power' as Japan tried to deflect attention from the massive trade surpluses that it was beginning to build with the UK at the time and the sense that its own markets were not fully open.[10]

A particularly strong visual satirical take on the general level of ignorance about Japan in the UK during this period was captured by the front cover of the magazine *Private Eye* (27 April 1990), showing the then-Chairman of the Conservative Party and Secre-

---

[9]   Robin Mountfield, 'Course of the Nissan Negotiation 1980–84', in Hugh Cortazzi, ed., *Britain and Japan: Biographical Portraits*, volume vi (Global Oriental, 2007).

[10]   John Cunningham, 'Art or Craft? Suspicions about efforts to interest us in all things Japanese', *The Guardian*, 24 October 1981; David Rose and John May, 'The soft edge of the hard sell?', *Time Out*, 16–22 October 1981.

tary of State for Trade, Norman Tebbitt, signing a trade agreement with the President of Nissan, Ishihara Takashi, and playing on his recent proposal for a 'Cricket test', also known as the 'Tebbitt Test', where he argued that whether people from ethnic minorities in Britain supported the England Cricket team (rather than the team from their country of ancestry) should be considered a barometer of whether they were truly British (see Fig. 1). This cover reinforced for colleagues in Oxford the need for a programme on contemporary Japan of exactly the type that the Nissan Institute was designed to develop.

Another episode from the era indicates the sensitivities of the time (though more on the British side than the Japanese). When a dinner to celebrate the granting of the Nissan benefaction was arranged to be held in London at Leathersellers' Hall, the home of the Worshipful Company of Leathersellers, Dick Storry was concerned that the Japanese guests might be offended because of possible sensitivities around the *burakumin* minority in Japan, some of whom were descended from tanners of animal hides. He discreetly sounded out the Japanese side on this. It seemed, however, that none had ever made the association, and Storry found they were unconcerned. They were, however, according to Powell, concerned that the date for the opening of the first Nissan Institute building should fall on a *kichijitsu* (a lucky day) according to the Japanese calendar.

The £1.5 million which Nissan gave as a benefaction to the University allowed for the appointment of a statutory professorship (Arthur Stockwin), a lecturer in Modern Japanese History (Ann Waswo), a lecturer in the Social and Economic Development of Japan (Jenny Corbett), a lector (Chihoko Moran), a visiting professorship (the first holder of which was Professor Tsuzuki Chūshichi), a secretary and the refurbishment of a large Victorian building (No. 1 Church Walk), owned by St Antony's College, which became the first home of the Institute. The Institute was officially inaugurated on 23 September 1981.

Once the Nissan Institute was established, it became important to rectify certain confused ideas about what it was supposed to be engaged in. Stockwin, for instance, had to fend off pressure from a persistent journalist from *Motor* magazine insisting that the Nissan

Fig. 1: Front cover of the satirical magazine, *Private Eye*,
27 April 1990

Institute, in conformity with its name, ought to concern itself principally with analysis of the economics and history of the motor industry. More amusingly, a few years later when a small annexe to the
original building of the Institute was converted into an office (funded,
incidentally, by the Tokyo Club from which Storry had been seeking
funds in Japan at the time that colleagues in Oxford were negotiating the Nissan benefaction) it was listed in the telephone directory
as 'Nissan Garage'. Its first user, Roger Goodman, who had been
appointed as a Junior Research Fellow, received so many calls for
spare Nissan car parts that the telephone number had to be changed.

The main objective which the Nissan benefaction imposed on the
Institute was the dissemination at an undergraduate level of a wider
knowledge of modern Japan, in addition to the reinforcement of
studies of Japanese language and literature. The press release which
the Nissan Motor Company[11] put out on 23 September 1981 in

---

[11]   The Nissan Motor Company was actually still trading in the UK at this time under the
name Datsun, a name concocted from 'son of D. A. T.', the initial letters of the surnames

relation to the opening of the Institute gives interesting insights into the company's reasons for supporting the project:

> Oxford is planning to put added emphasis on the study of Japanese affairs in all faculties and curricula, especially politics, economics, modern history and literature, and to expand the scope of the examinations to include questions on Japan in relevant areas of the curricula. It is hoped that in this way the Nissan Institute will stimulate students to become interested in Japanese affairs, and so contribute, not only to the future progress of Japanese studies at Oxford, but also better understanding and friendship between the two Countries.

A much more detailed account of both the guiding philosophy and the content of the activities of the Nissan Institute were laid out in Arthur Stockwin's inaugural lecture, appropriately entitled *Why Japan Matters* (1983).[12] Undergraduate options were quickly and for the first time introduced into the undergraduate degrees in history and PPE (Politics, Philosophy and Economics). A group of students doing doctoral work on contemporary Japan began to quickly grow and within 25 years from its founding around 50 doctoral theses had been completed on modern Japanese society with most of those who earned doctoral degrees going on to teaching positions in universities across the world. The number of non-language options available for students doing the undergraduate BA degree in Japanese increased substantially exposing students to the disciplines of the social sciences which added intellectual depth and authority to a programme which, while very hard work, had, according to McMullen, previously had more in common with the generalist approach of the Greats degree in Classics. The teaching of these options was helped, of course, by the huge growth in English-language scholarship on pre-modern and modern Japan from the 1980s onwards.

Interest in Japan indeed grew so rapidly at both undergraduate and graduate level that soon the new building at 1 Church Walk was

---

of the three investors in the first of the company's cars, Den, Aoyama and Takeuchi; since *son* in Japanese means 'damage' the spelling was changed to the more cheerful *sun*.

[12]   J. A. A. Stockwin, *Why Japan Matters: An Inaugural Lecture Delivered Before the University of Oxford on 27 January 1983* (Oxford: Clarendon Press, 1983).

clearly unable to contain it, and in June 1990 (timed in part to celebrate the tenth anniversary of the first gift) the Nissan Motor Company made a second generous donation, of £3.2 million, to build a
new institute, this time on the main campus of St Antony's College,
to house staff, an extended library and a lecture theatre and seminar
rooms. Negotiations between the University and St Antony's College were at times difficult, but were settled with an arrangement
that gave the College access to the 150-seat lecture theatre included
in the new building, and on the other hand allowed the Institute to
incorporate what became the Bodleian Japanese Library within the
Institute building. The first ceremonial turf for the new building
was turned by Prince Naruhito, the Crown Prince who had been
a graduate student in Oxford, in 1991 (see Fig. 2). Showing that
the best oiled arrangements, even in Oxford, can be all too easily
disrupted by contingent events, the ground-breaking ceremony was
delayed for some time by a delivery lorry that blocked much of the
visiting party from leaving a lunch at another college. The building
was completed in 1993, and this further benefaction allowed for
the appointment of two new permanent members of staff, Roger
Goodman in social anthropology and Mark Rebick in economics,
who took up their posts in 1993 and 1994 respectively.

JAPANESE STUDIES IN OXFORD TODAY

The activities of the Nissan Institute expanded considerably during the 1990s. By the end of the decade, there were up to thirty
doctoral students at any one time writing dissertations on Japan;
Master's courses in subjects such as anthropology, economics, politics and history as well as undergraduate programmes had options
on Japan; the Nissan Institute/Routledge Japanese Studies Series
which had published its first book under the Croom Helm imprint
in 1986 had become the largest series in the world dealing with contemporary Japan (and will publish its 100th volume in 2016); the
Institute was hosting five or six Japan-specialist academic visitors on
sabbatical from universities outside Oxford every year; the Bodleian
Japanese Library had built one of the finest collections of materials
on Japan in Europe; and the Institute Friday evening seminar had
become a fixture not only on the Oxford but indeed the national

scene and had been addressed by many of the best known scholars of Japan from across the world. Many of these early seminars were published as Occasional Papers and can still be accessed from the Institute's website today.

From the mid-2000s there were major changes in the personnel teaching about Japan in Oxford. Many of those who had dominated the scene for the past quarter-century retired: Andrea Boltho, Phillip Harries, the late Oliver Impey, James McMullen, Brian Powell, the late Marcus Rebick, Arthur Stockwin, Ann Waswo. Jenny Corbett moved to a position at the Australian National University. They were over time replaced by new colleagues: Jenny Guest, Linda Flores, Bjarke Frellesvig, Sho Konishi, Ian Neary, Clare Pollard and Hugh Whittaker.

In 2006, Carlos Ghosn who was the President of both Nissan and Renault (which had taken over Nissan in the mid-1990s) visited the Institute for the first time on its twenty-fifth anniversary.

Fig. 2: His Imperial Highness, Prince Naruhito, Crown Prince of Japan, breaking the gound for the new Nissan Insitute of Japanese Studies building, 18 September 1991, in the presence, from, left to right, Professor Arthur Stockwin, Lord (Roy) Jenkins, Chancellor of the University, Mr Ishihara Takashi (President of Nissan) and Professor Theodore Zeldin (Sub-Warden of St Antony's College).

During a speech to a packed lecture theatre, he announced a third benefaction to the Institute of £1.5 million which completed the endowment of all the existing posts in perpetuity. New posts were created in the sociology of Japan thanks to financial help from the GB Sasakawa Foundation and were filled by Ekaterina Hertog and Takehiko Kariya (who moved from a professorship at the University of Tokyo). Complementing an already existing MSt course in Japanese studies in the Faculty of Oriental Studies, the Nissan Institute (now formally part of a new School of Interdisciplinary Area Studies) launched a new programme in 2007/8 in Modern Japanese Studies which had at its core an intensive language programme, a compulsory course in research methods and options in Japanese politics, economics, anthropology, sociology, linguistics, history, literature, law and the history of art. The course was limited to taking only fifteen students a year and could be taken either as a one-year MSc or a two-year MPhil. Around twenty per cent of each cohort went on to do doctoral work on Japan.

Now in 2016 Japanese studies at the University of Oxford has been in existence for 62 years and the Nissan Institute of Japanese Studies can boast a 35-year history. Like Japanese studies elsewhere, the field has been affected by fluctuations in the fortunes of Japan itself. During the Japanese economic boom of the 1980s, demand for instruction in things Japanese boomed accordingly, but during the later 'lost decades' of the economy, Japanese demographic decline and the rival attractions of a resurgent China, interest tended to wane and 'Japan passing' became common. Despite this, demand for Japanese studies at Oxford has stayed at respectable levels, and the offering in teaching, supervision and related facilities and activities has operated at a high level. The total number of faculty listed as teaching about Japan and doing research on Japan in the most recent Oxford University Japanese Studies Newsletter has reached thirty (including emeriti).[13] Most significantly, the distinction between pre-modern (centred on the Oriental Institute) and modern Japanese Studies (based at the Nissan Institute) has become increasingly blurred. Most academics who worked on Japan in the two institutes had their research jointly

---

[13]   See http://www.nissan.ox.ac.uk/japanese-studies-oxford

submitted to the Area Studies REF panel in 2014. Academics in both institutes teach on the undergraduate BA course in Japanese. Perhaps most symbolically, from 2017 the separate MSt in Japanese Studies offered by the Oriental Institute (which has focussed on pre-modern, philological and literary research training) and the MSc in Japanese Studies offered by the Nissan Institute (which has focussed on contemporary Japanese studies training) will be amalgamated into a single programme. This will finally and completely link together the legacies of Geoffrey Bownas and Dick Storry who each brought so much to the development of the study of Japan at Oxford in the 1950s.

15

Oxford Brookes

O

Joy Hendry

THE PROGRAMME OF Japanese Studies at Oxford Brookes started in the 1980s on a small scale, with a single part-time Japanese teacher who was hired to add Japanese to the 'Languages for business' course and also taught some engineering students, and a half-time anthropologist, who had carried out her doctoral fieldwork in Japan. By the end of the twentieth century, thanks to continuing support from the Japan Foundation, the Japanese Embassy and the Great Britain Sasakawa Foundation, it could boast more anthropologists of Japan than any other university in Europe, possibly in the world, and there was a stream of successful doctoral students who are now imparting their skills in other departments in Japan, the UK and mainland Europe. Oxford Brookes has also hosted both the annual conference of the British Association for Japanese Studies (BAJS) and of the World Haiku Association. By 2014, the post-graduate field had declined somewhat with the loss of a unique MA course that did not recruit quite enough students to satisfy the increasingly demanding university coffers, but Oxford Brookes is now recruiting more undergraduates for its popular course on Japanese language and society than any other university in Britain, and its graduates are making their mark in all sorts of Japan-related careers. Thanks to the Great Britain Sasakawa Foundation, the post-graduate offering is also beginning to build up again.

The initiators of the programme were Kumiko Helliwell and Joy Hendry, already friends when they found themselves employed by Brookes, and they started out by creating a Japan Interest Group, bringing together other scholars scattered throughout Oxford Polytechnic, as it was then called, who had a range of diverse interests in Japan. They organised various events including talks and demonstrations of Japanese arts including tea, ikebana and taiko drumming, and the culmination was a huge Japan Arts Day in 2001. Kumiko also invited Liam O'Brien, Kyōshi 7th Dan, and president of United Kingdom Kyūdō Association (UKKA) to initiate a *kyūdō* (archery) class which has now become the Oxford Kyūdō Society. During the heyday of anthropological endeavours at Oxford Brookes, they founded the Europe Japan Research Centre (EJRC). At that time Rupert Cox, who later published *The Zen Arts: An Anthropological Study of the Culture of Aesthetic Form in Japan* (2008), held a post-doctoral position. Judy Chance from the geography department participated in the work of the Centre, as also did Louella Matsunaga (*The Changing Face of Japanese Retail: Working in a Chain Store*, 2000) in anthropology. The deputy directors were Catherine Atherton in the Fine Arts Department, and Mitch Sedgwick, whose *Globalisation and Japanese Organizational Culture: An Ethnography of a Japanese Corporation in France* was published in 2008, in the Business School. Joy Hendry was the first director. An interesting logo for the centre was created by a Japanese graphic designer working in the UK, Hidetaka Matsunaga.

The EJRC was inaugurated in 2001 with a conference on the History and Practice of Copying in Japan, supported by the Japan Foundation and the Fundação Oriente in Portugal, and the papers were published in a book edited by Rupert Cox (2008). The EJRC continues to publish a newsletter, very occasional papers, and holds regular seminars followed by a reception which encourages informal exchange with our visiting speakers, as well as offering a venue to hear about some of the latest research in the field. Alexander Jacoby is the present director. The seminars have recently become available as podcasts on the EJRC website at http://www.social-sciences. brookes.ac.uk/Research/EJRC, where details of earlier events may also be found.

In 2002, a carpenter from Japan, Kawaguchi Kiyotoshi, was engaged: he sent materials from Joy Hendry's initial fieldwork site in Kyushu and, with his son, Yuki, built a 6-mat Japanese room which is used for tutorials, entertaining guests, meetings and various arts activities. We have received several generous gifts for the Japanese room, including a hanging scroll from a paper-making family in the same community proclaiming 'The Way of the Arts is Infinite' (芸道無限), a set of beautiful ikebana vases and display containers collected by Professor Toshio Watanabe's late mother, several ritual garments such as a stunning wedding *uchikake*, some masks for Setsubun, a child's 7–5–3 festival kimono and various utensils for the tea ceremony. The Japanese room was formally opened by the Japanese Ambassador at the time, His Excellency Masaki Orita, who took part in a tea ceremony with his wife. Further details about the room and its construction can also be found on the EJRC website.

The formal programme of Japanese Studies at Oxford Brookes commenced in 1999 when the Deans of Social Sciences and Humanities agreed to cooperate in creating a programme that would expect students recruited to the course to back up their language learning with modules on other aspects of Japanese society. Initially these were mostly taught by anthropologists and linguists, but the expertise of the staff has gradually broadened to include Japanese history, religion, arts, film and linguistics. Market research revealed demand from new undergraduates for a course to build on the

Japanese they had studied at GCSE and A level in their schools, and the modular system made this possible from an early stage. Thus numbers that were small at first soon grew, and by 2013 the course was overwhelmed with some 70 new recruits. Usually the intake is in the 40s, however, and in 2013/14, more than 160 students were enrolled in either single honours or joint honours in Japanese Studies. In the graduating year of 2015, no fewer than 10 of those students gained first class honours and another 15 upper second class. Suzuko Anai presently leads the course, accompanied by John Lo Breglio, Alexander Jacoby, Hanako Fujino and Keiko Ikeshiro, with additional support for language teaching.

A course entitled 'Introduction to Japanese society' is also a requirement for students doing single honours in anthropology, and these and the Japanese Studies students are also offered modules on 'Work and the Japanese', 'Japan at play', 'Personhood, gender and the body', and 'Minorities and marginality in contemporary Japan' by Japan specialists Louella Matsunaga and Jason Danely. Within the Japanese Studies field options also include classical and contemporary Japanese cinema, the arts of Japan, and manga and anime, offered by Alexander Jacoby; history modules on 'The making of modern Japan', 'Japan: myth and reality', and 'Japanese religions', all taught by John Lo Breglio; as well as linguistics and the whole range of Japanese language modules. All students, both those doing single honours and those doing combined degrees, spend their third year at one of our fifteen partner universities in Japan. These currently are: Aoyama Gakuin University, Kansai Gaidai University, Kitakyushu University, Kyushu Sangyo University, Kyoto Gaikokugo (Gaidai) University, Gakushuin University, Meiji Gakuin University, Nagasaki University, Nagoya University of Foreign Studies, Obirin University, Ritsumeikan Asia Pacific University, Ryūkoku University, Tsukuba University, Tsuru University and Yamanashi University. While in Japan, students attend intensive language courses as well as lectures on various aspects of Japan, and many write dissertations based on their experiences when they return.

Postgraduate study in Japanese Studies resumes in 2015–2016, thanks again to the generosity of the Sasakawa/Nippon Foundation in providing funding for studentships. One will be for a doctoral programme, the other a Masters by Research. Both of these are to be in the anthropology department like most of our previous postgraduates, but the Japanese Studies department is also launching a Masters by Research in the coming year.

Many Oxford Brookes graduates go back to Japan for a while, some to teach English, others to do postgraduate work or to take up positions in tour and travel companies, for example. One is even a professional voice-over actress there! Others have entered video game companies like Nintendo, doing translation or developing video games, and a couple are usually to be found in London at the Embassy or the Japan Foundation, one in the British Film Institute. One of our first graduates, Chris Perkins, is teaching Japanese in Edinburgh now, and among those who achieved doctorates Sebastien Boret, Ayumi Sasagawa and Bruce White are teaching anthropology in Japanese universities, while Ruth Martin works with the Japanese community in London. Boret's thesis has now been published as *Japanese Tree Burial: Ecology, Kinship and the Culture of Death* (2014), and, together with Gordon Mathews, White has edited *Japan's Changing Generations: Are Young People Creating a New Society?* (2003). Anna Fraser brought an exhibition of Japanese children's wartime drawings to Oxford, Catherine Atherton brought the work of rural Japanese basket-makers to exhibit at Oxford Brookes, and Paola Esposito teaches and displays butoh dancing in Oxford. Stephanie Oeben works as Open Access Research Manager for the big publishing company, Elsevier.

Research in the two departments has been quite varied over the years, including many aspects of Japanese society, religion and ritual life, and the arts. A selection of the books published by staff members and our doctoral graduates is listed below, and there are several areas of continuing strength. Alexander Jacoby's research interests span various aspects of Japanese cinema and he is currently completing a monograph on director Hirokazu Koreeda; Jason Danely's research has focussed on rituals of mourning and memorial, experiences of old age, kinship and social care and in 2015 he published *Aging and Loss: Mourning and Maturity in Contemporary Japan*; his current work looks at sources of psychosocial strain and compassion among family carers of older adults in Japan. Louella Matsunaga's recent research is on three main areas: a comparison of notions of the body and the investigation of medical-related death in England and Japan; Japanese religions outside Japan; and anthropological perspectives on branding. John Lo Breglio's interests focus on *kindai Bukkyō* – Japanese Buddhism from the middle of the nineteenth century through to the Second World War. He is also interested in the study of Japanese religions from pre-history to the present, East Asian Buddhism generally and post-colonial approaches to the study of modern Japan. Hanako Fujino specialises in Second Language Acquisition and Japanese Language Teaching and is currently working on learners' perception of grammar and grammar lessons, with the goal of approximating grammar teaching to the actual learning process.

In September 2013, Suzuko Anai and Keiko Ikeshiro published the first two of a 10-volume series of Japanese reading materials graded in accordance with the Common European Framework of Reference for Languages (CEFR) and the American Council of the Teaching of Foreign Languages (ACTFL) targeting young adults learning Japanese language and culture. Entitled 'Let's read Japanese', these readers can be used along with any textbooks as well as for self-study, and contain Japanese folktales, traditional stories, well-known stories of the world and original stories. They were launched at the Annual Symposium of the Association for Japanese Teachers in Europe at Madrid and at the Japan Foundation in London, and performed at an Oxford Brookes festival event called Outburst. In July (2015) a further volume was published.

Other research published by staff and former students includes Wim Lunsing's *Beyond Common Sense: Sexuality and Gender in Contemporary Japan* (1997), James Roberson's *Japanese Working Class Lives* (1998), Meryll Dean's *Japanese Legal System: Texts, Cases and Materials* (2006), and Daniel Gallimore's *Sounding like Shakespeare: A Study of Prosody in Four Japanese Translations of* A Midsummer Night's Dream (2012). Hendry, who is now an emeritus professor, has published many books including *Wrapping Culture: Politeness, Presentation and Power in Japan and Other Societies* (1993) and *The Orient Strikes Back: A Global View of Cultural Display* (2000).

16

Sheffield University

○

Gordon Daniels

THE HAYTER YEARS, 1963–1980

WHEN THE UNIVERSITY Grants Committee's 'Sub-Committee on Oriental, Slavonic, East European and African Studies', chaired by Sir William Hayter, issued its report in 1961 only one individual in Sheffield University showed a serious interest in its contents. The professor of geography, Charles Fisher, read the report and proposed the establishment of a centre for South-East Asian Studies in Sheffield. Unfortunately for Fisher, Hull University had already been allocated Hayter funds for such a centre, so, as an alternative, Fisher proposed the creation of a centre of Japanese Studies. It is noteworthy that no other university made a similar proposal at this time. Fisher's plan was accepted by the University Grants Committee in 1962, although the academic role which the centre might play was not clearly defined.

Nevertheless, the Hayter sub-committee had already established some major principles for stimulating and consolidating area studies. Ring-fenced funds would be provided for studentships, travel, language training and research, and grants would be available for specialist library provision. Above all, the sub-committee wished to encourage language learning, research and teaching in modern studies and the social sciences.

With the future somewhat unclear, in 1963 Fisher appointed two postgraduate students from Oxford, Martin Collick and Gordon Daniels as centre staff, although they had not yet completed their doctorates. For two years a retired foreign office official, Henry Sawbridge, acted as deputy director of the Centre: he had qualified in Japanese as a member of the Japan Consular service and had been consul-general in Yokohama These appointments underline the great lack of fully-trained Japanese specialists in British universities at the time. In 1964 Fisher left Sheffield for a chair at the School of Oriental and African Studies in London. However, before he left he had persuaded the university that a new professorship of Japanese Studies should be created to ensure the successful development of the Centre.

In 1965, Geoffrey Bownas of St Antony's College, Oxford, was appointed to the new chair. Bownas had studied and taught Chinese at Oxford, and had learnt Japanese for military intelligence purposes during the war. Although Bownas was essentially a scholar with literary interests his inaugural lecture, in 1966, 'From Japanology to Japanese Studies', emphasised the value of the Japanese language for modern historical and social science research. Soon after his appointment Geoffrey Bownas, with Martin Collick and members of related academic departments, decided that undergraduate courses of a completely new type would be taught at Sheffield. These would all be dual degrees linking the Japanese language with history, economic history, economics, geography, politics and sociology. Despite the success of the Tokyo Olympics in 1964 and the increasing importance of the Japanese shipbuilding and electronics industries, harsh memories of the Pacific War remained, and the ability of Japan-related courses to attract students remained questionable.

As a result, attention was given to creating a curriculum which would enable students who found Japanese too difficult, to transfer to conventional courses. The new four-year degrees included an introductory year in which elementary Japanese (unexamined) was added to a normal first-year programme. Professor Bownas visited some schools to publicize the new courses and a special brochure was distributed. In autumn 1966 five students entered the Centre programme: two left the course and three graduated in 1970.

Even as late as 1966 teaching materials for undergraduates were extremely limited. Eleanor Jorden's two volume *Beginning Japanese* was the first major colloquial course incorporating sound tapes, which were constructed according to current linguistic ideas. However, the complex romanisation of these textbooks and novel terminology were unfortunate barriers to understanding. 'Romaji sickness' was at times a topic in staff discussions, referring to the problems caused by the Romanised text of *Beginning Japanese*, for Jorden's work provided no introduction to the Japanese script. In the late 1960s and early 1970s these problems were largely resolved by a new member of staff, Graham Healey, who had studied Japanese in Oxford. By 1974 he had produced four new teaching volumes entitled *Beginning Japanese*, which were used by Sheffield Students and sold to other universities.

In 1966, the first Japanese lectrice, Mrs Kitamoto Nobuko, joined the Centre staff, and a year later Professor Fujita Shōzō of Hōsei University arrived as the first visiting Professor to be attached to the Centre. Professor Fujita had been deeply involved in the anti-Vietnam war movement, and had written an acclaimed work on the Emperor system. He gave considerable stimulus to the educational and intellectual life of the centre.

Among the first three Centre graduates, Angela Davies later became a specialist interpreter and consultant in the fields of Japanese gardens and Japanese tourism. The second cohort of students who entered in 1967 had, rather exceptionally for the time, an opportunity to experience Japan at first hand. As a result of discussions between Professor Bownas and government officials in London, these undergraduates were employed as 'hosts' in the British Pavilion at the Osaka International Exhibition in 1970 (Expo 70). Among these undergraduates Janet Hunter later gained an Oxford doctorate, became a member of the Centre staff, and finally Saji Professor of Economic History at the London School of Economics. Another 1967 entrant, Lesley Connors (née Knapp), gained a doctorate under Graham Healey and taught at the School of Oriental and African Studies.

In these years, two additional members of staff added to the Centre's academic range. Douglas Anthony, originally in the Department of Economics, began teaching in the Centre's programme, and Dr Jiri Jelinek a Japanese language specialist from Charles

University in Prague, arrived in Britain in 1968 as a political refugee, and was attached to the Centre. Dr Jelinek was a specialist in linguistics and his presence led to the creation of a new dual degree in Japanese and linguistics. Before arriving in Britain Dr Jelinek had been interested in machine translation and he soon received a grant from the Office of Scientific and Technical Information (OSTI) to develop materials and courses to enable scientists and librarians to translate Japanese materials in their specialist fields. By 1974 the work of Dr Jelinek and his research assistants had produced four volumes of relevant translation aids, and summer courses for technicians, scientists and librarians were held at the University. Dr Jelinek's deep interest in technical translation later led the American pioneer in the field, Stanley Gerr, to donate his vast card index of scientific Japanese and Chinese terms to the University Library; recently, however, the card index has been transferred to the Needham Research Institute in Cambridge. As the OSTI programme indicated, the Centre had a continuing interest in developing innovative language teaching materials and spreading knowledge of the Japanese language beyond small groups of university students.

The deployment of the Centre's expertise in the commercial sphere began in the 1960s when Martin Collick assisted United Steel in its Japanese operations. Significant links with private companies continued in 1969 when Dutch and British employees of the Shell Oil Company studied Japanese in the Centre before taking up positions in Tokyo.

Officials working in government service also studied Japanese in Sheffield. In 1971–72 several young diplomats from the Foreign and Commonwealth Office spent a year in language training before being posted to Osaka and Tokyo. Among these was Stephen Gomersall who became ambassador to Japan in the 1990s. In the same academic year Sir Fred Warner also received language and background tutorials for some months, before taking up his post as ambassador in Tokyo. Among outstanding centre undergraduates in the early 1970s were Ian Neary, now a professor in Oxford, and John Crump, who followed a Sheffield PhD with posts in York and Stirling, before his premature death.

In these years, there were broader indications of Sheffield's rising significance in the field of Japanese language teaching and Japanese

Studies. With the election of Edward Heath as prime minister in 1970, the Government paid increasing attention to Japan, and in 1973 the Japanese Prime Minister, Tanaka Kakuei, was invited to London. During his stay he announced a gift of over £400,000 for the development of Japanese Studies. On this occasion Tanaka allegedly stated that Sheffield University was 'putting in the most effort' into Japanese studies, and it was decided that the new fund would be administered from Sheffield University. Its distribution and use would be decided by a committee representing the four centres of Japanese Studies (Oxford, Cambridge, the School of Oriental and African Studies and Sheffield) and the University Grants Committee. At almost the same time the Japanese Government established the Japan Foundation as its major international cultural agency. Consequently the new fund was formally named the Japan Foundation Endowment Fund.

The establishment of the Endowment Fund had both direct and indirect effects, which strengthened Japanese Studies in Sheffield and across British universities. Thus for the first time Sheffield and other British students of Japanese were able to visit Japan as part of their academic training, spending some ten weeks at Nanzan University in Nagoya. The programme continued for some ten years before students were sent to other universities. The fund also enabled postgraduate students to spend further time in Japan to extend their period of field work. An equally significant by-product of the so-called 'Tanaka Fund' was the creation of the British Association for Japanese Studies. The use of the Endowment Fund called for a greater degree of national cooperation, and Sheffield played a leading part in proposing the establishment of a specifically Japanese Studies organisation. This replaced the looser and more broadly based Association of British Orientalists. When the new Association held its initial planning conference in Cambridge in 1975 a Sheffield representative proposed that the Association hold annual academic conferences, and that to encourage staff and postgraduate research, conference papers should be published as the 'Proceedings' of the organisation. For several years the editing and printing of the 'Proceedings' was carried out in the Sheffield Centre, and the publishing costs were met by the Endowment Fund. By the 1990s this successful series had evolved into the professionally published journal *Japan Forum*.

One further development, which stemmed from the recommendations of the Hayter Committee and the resulting availability of government funds, was the development of postgraduate research on Japan in the Sheffield Centre. The Economic and Social Research Council aimed to encourage the training of a new generation of Japan specialists and awarded two 'earmarked' postgraduate awards each year to Sheffield. These awards not only provided opportunities for Sheffield graduates but also attracted graduates from elsewhere. Among these students John Clark had graduated from Lancaster, Ian Gow from Edinburgh, Michael Weiner from a university in the United States and Hamish Ion from McGill University in Montreal. All gained doctorates using Japanese source materials and later pursued academic careers in Australia, the United States, Canada and Britain. Almost all produced academic monographs from their publicly-funded research. Significant criticisms were made of students who failed to complete their doctoral work, or chose not to enter the academic world. However, in most cases such students learned Japanese successfully and had long-term careers in the financial services industry. Among them Christopher Mitchinson became a successful Japan specialist in the City, and Michael Connors followed his doctorate with a lengthy career with Barclays de Zoete Wedd.

In 1980, Sheffield also benefitted from Japanese public and private funding in organising an unprecedented academic conference. A visitor to the centre, Professor Shiratori Rei from the Institute for Political Studies in Japan, helped organise a particularly original meeting. This was attended by Diet members from the seven most significant political parties. All presented papers outlining their policies and platforms. In addition both Japanese and Centre academics contributed papers. One British Member of Parliament, and the distinguished authority on the Japanese economy Professor G. C. Allen, also participated in the conference. This meeting was remarkable in gathering together so many Japanese parliamentarians, including a future prime minister, but it also produced a significant book, *Japan in the 1980s*, published by Kodansha in 1982.

In many respects 1980 marked the end of a significant period in Japanese Studies in Sheffield. Several months after co-ordinating a BBC book, *Inside Japan* (with five chapters by Centre staff), Professor Bownas left the University for a new career as a business consultant. Equally significant was the impact of the new government's policies, which soon influenced every department of Japanese Studies in Britain.

BEFORE AND AFTER THE PARKER REPORT, 1980–1989.

Although austerity in universities had begun before 1979, policies became more severe under the new Conservative administration. The earmarking of funds for Japanese Studies came to an end and universities were instructed to be much stricter in their budgeting procedures. Staff/student ratios rather than broader criteria now became dominant factors in policy making. In Sheffield the Academic Development Committee, which had the task of planning strategic cuts, now concluded that in terms of staff/student numbers Japanese Studies was overstaffed - despite the particular requirements of intensive language teaching. By the spring of 1982 members of the centre were invited to accept early retirement terms. No one accepted these terms but in 1988 Dr Jelinek was given leave to transfer his activities to Japan to continue his research on machine translation for the Sharp Company. The University continued to hope that Dr Jelinek's research might bring some financial benefit, in the form of royalties, but these hopes were never fulfilled and Dr Jelinek never returned to Sheffield.

Nevertheless, the view that the Centre's linguistic and associated skills might be put to commercial use gained particular strength during this period of university austerity. This aim reached fulfilment in 1983 when the University established the Japan Business Services Unit. This existed independently of the Centre for Japanese studies, but it drew heavily on the expertise of Centre staff and was headed by Rosemary Yates, a Centre graduate with a first class degree in Japanese and linguistics. The Business Services Unit provided a broad range of support services, ranging from translation and interpreting to negotiation, social and cultural advice and the preparation of specialist reports.

At a time when the Japanese economy was expanding significantly the Unit also played some part in attracting groups of Japanese students and pupils to visit Sheffield for summer English language and culture courses. Not only did the Unit engage profitably with a large number of Japanese and British companies it also had one particular success in stimulating the economy of the North Midlands. When Derbyshire's local government sought to attract the Toyota Motor Company to establish a major factory in Burnaston the Unit played a key role, a role which was publicly acknowledged by the local officials concerned. In later years the Unit expanded its operations to cover China, South Korea and South-East Asia but reorganisation ultimately led to the transfer of the Unit's activities and some of its staff to the publicly-funded South Yorkshire International Trade Centre.

Another example of the reshaping of Centre activities to generate income and demonstrate inter-university co-operation was the scheme for Oxford undergraduates to lengthen their degree course by spending a first year of intensive language training in Sheffield. Oxford students first joined the Sheffield Centre in the academic year 1984–1985 and the programme continued into the 1990s, when Oxford increased its staff and extended its own degree course to four years.

In one respect, the Centre for Japanese Studies operated in the 1980s on a relatively low-cost basis. Following the departure of Professor Bownas, at a time when the University had somewhat restricted funds, the Centre was administered by non-professorial heads, avoiding the costly appointment of a professor. However, some Sheffield University leaders saw such economies as politically damaging, both locally and nationally. The Centre's administrative position, located in the Faculty of Social Sciences, may also have meant that its language teaching expertise was not fully appreciated within the University. Furthermore, at precisely this time Oxford, Cambridge and the London School of Economics received major Japanese benefactions for the development of Japanese Studies. This may have suggested that the Sheffield Centre was unappealing to potential donors, and therefore an appropriate target for academic criticism. Such criticisms were particularly difficult to counter as government policy increasingly aimed to link much university funding to research performance, a linkage which was unprecedented. In the first research assessment, the Centre achieved somewhat disappointing results.

Yet amid these complex difficulties the Centre did have significant academic successes. In 1983 it organised a conference which brought a distinguished Russian scholar of medieval Japanese literature to Britain for the first time. Other scholars also came from universities in Hungary, Poland and Western Europe. The timing of the conference could not have been more unfortunate. It followed shortly after the Soviet destruction of a South Korean airliner flying in East Asian skies. Despite Western travel sanctions, East Europeans managed to arrive in Sheffield and Dr Lvova from Leningrad proved to be an independent-minded scholar of the very highest intellectual calibre. Another more lasting international relationship was the Centre's formal agreement with Hitotsubashi University, an institution with an unchallenged reputation in the social sciences. This formal link was reinforced by significant awards from the newly-created Jerwood Foundation. Distinguished scholars such as Tsuzuki Chūshichi and Yamazawa Ippei lectured in Sheffield and Centre staff used the excellent research facilities of the Hitotsubashi campus.

A welcome indication of the Centre's public reputation at this time was the praise voiced by Sir Peter Parker when addressing the local business community. Nevertheless, the University continued to suggest reductions in the Centre's staff, at a time when Sir Peter Parker's report on area studies, 'Speaking for the Future', advocated increased spending. The University was ultimately persuaded that to make cuts in Japanese Studies would bar it from receiving any new Parker funds. In the end the University's views and those of the University Grants Committee coincided in favouring the establishment of a new chair in Japanese Studies.

Despite the Centre's somewhat disappointing research ratings in the 1980s, these years saw Graham Healey create a major international research and translation project. After an initial study of the Iwakura Mission's visit to Sheffield, he gathered together an international team of historians to translate Kume Kunitake's entire account of the Mission's travels in the United States, Britain and continental Europe. Scholars from Princeton, Cambridge,

Hitotsubashi and Sheffield cooperated over several years to produce five volumes of translations of the highest quality. The work not only involved the translation of Kume's sometimes florid writing but also a study of all the places and personalities mentioned in the text. The importance of the project was demonstrated by the remarkable group of scholars from Britain, the United States and Japan who gathered in Sheffield in 1989 to discuss papers which analysed the detailed history and significance of the Mission. The translation, with the original illustrations, was published in 2002 and won a Japanese publishing prize. In 2009 a volume of selections from the translation was published by Cambridge University Press.

A second more limited research venture, which received surprisingly little acknowledgement, was focused on the private letters and diaries of Captain Malcolm Kennedy. The Kennedy Collection had been donated to Sheffield in 1985, and a postgraduate student, Jon Pardoe, produced a printed transcript of the entire Kennedy diaries. Captain Kennedy had served in the Army, worked in Japan in journalism and the oil industry, and had wartime experience at Bletchley Park. Pardoe learnt Japanese at the Centre and already possessing an impressive knowledge of Russian, wrote a highly professional doctoral thesis on Kennedy's entire career.

EXPANSION AND INTERNATIONALIZATION, 1989–2015

Seeking to expand research activity in the Centre, the University selected Glenn Hook, who had done postgraduate work at the University of British Columbia, to the new chair of Japanese studies. The University also hoped that the new professor would strengthen academic links with Japan, and attract funds and Japanese students to Sheffield. In 1989 Professor Hook commemorated the twenty-fifth anniversary of the Centre's founding by holding a major conference on the 'Internationalization of Japan', a particularly relevant topic at the time. Arguably this brought the most prestigious gathering of Japanese public intellectuals to Sheffield ever. Ogata Sadako who served as United Nations High Commissioner for Refugees, Nagai Michio, a former minister of education, and Sakamoto Yoshikazu, who had trained United Nations personnel, all gave presentations. Sir Fred Warner, a former British ambassador to Japan, and the distinguished journalist Hugo Young also attended; the papers of the conference were published by Routledge. Following this successful initiative Professor Hook founded a Sheffield series of academic monographs, which provided a new opportunity for staff and postgraduate students to publish their research findings. Alongside Professor Hook three of his postgraduate students, Christopher Hughes, now professor at the University of Warwick, Hugo Dobson, now head of the School of East Asian Studies in Sheffield and Julie Gilson, now a reader at the University of Birmingham, all contributed to a well-received joint work, *The International Relations of Japan*.

Despite these notable successes the speedy expansion of research activities within the Centre was a difficult process. Douglas Anthony and Martin Collick left for posts in Cardiff and Japan but it was not easy to replace them with active researchers who found the British academic climate encouraging. In 1989 Herbert Bix, a well-established revisionist historian in the United States, joined the Centre as research fellow and later senior lecturer, but he found it difficult to accept the administrative and financial pressures of the British university system, and returned to the United States. Earl Kinmonth, a well-regarded specialist on the development of Japanese thought, also found the administrative pressures of the Research Assessment Exercise disruptive and returned to California.

In the early 1990s, the Centre adjusted to significant academic reorganization. Some years earlier, an initiative by Graham Healey had led to the establishment of a small Korean studies unit, attached to the Centre. With the rapid development of China's economic and political importance it was believed that Sheffield would gain academically and financially from the creation of a Chinese studies unit. By 2000 this development had been confirmed with the inclusion of degrees incorporating Chinese and the appointment of Professor Tim Wright as head of the Chinese studies programme. Nevertheless, for much of the 1990s the financial and academic strengthening of the Centre of Japanese Studies remained an important objective.

In 1990, the School of East Asian Studies was created to include the three units, Japanese, Korean and Chinese studies. Three years later Professor Ian Gow of the University of Stirling was appointed to head the new school and reinforce its academic and financial basis. Despite some criticism of the School's research achievements, the 1990s was a period of considerable intellectual advance. In 1989 Michael Weiner, who had become a member of staff, converted his doctoral thesis into an academic monograph, *The Origins of the Korean Community in Japan, 1910–23*; in later years Dr Weiner raised new questions regarding the supposed homogeneity of Japan's population. In addition, another new member of staff, Richard Siddle, carried out original research on another of Japan's minorities, the Ainu of Hokkaido. During these years postgraduate students explored themes which had been largely ignored in British universities. A mature student, Susan Townsend, learnt Japanese in the School and, based upon her interest in colonialist thought in Japan, completed a doctorate on Yanaihara Tadao's critiques of the British Empire, which was published by Curzon in 2000. Dr Townsend is now an associate professor at Nottingham University. Another graduate of the Centre of Japanese Studies, Jane Robbins, did extensive research in Britain, Japan and the United States to analyse Japan's wartime overseas broadcasting, a field largely neglected by Western scholars. Some years later her thesis was published in Italy. Tomida Hiroko, who taught advanced Japanese in the school, did pioneering research on early Japanese feminism. Her thesis on the career of Hiratsuka Raichō was completed in 2000 and published by Brill four years later. In addition, in the 1980s and 1990s several doctorates were completed on linguistic aspects of Japanese, with one successful student, Nick Tranter, becoming a member of the staff of the School.

In the late 1990s, both Professor Gow and Gordon Daniels were convenors within the Anglo-Japanese History Project which was initiated by the Japanese Government in 1995, fifty years after the end of the Pacific War. Professor Gow cooperated with Professor Hirama of the Japanese National Defence Academy in editing volume 3 of the *History of Anglo-Japanese Relations, 1600–2000 – The Military Dimension*. Gordon Daniels and Professor Tsuzuki Chūshichi planned and edited volume 5, *Social and Cultural Perspectives*. Contributors to this volume included former Sheffield postgraduate students Susan Townsend, Hamish Ion and Jon Pardoe.

The 1990s was also a decade when the teaching of Japanese received considerable stimulus from new streams of funding from public and private sources. Following a report by the Japanese language sub-committee of the UK-Japan 2000 group in 1988, the Department of Trade and Industry made a grant of £1,000,000 for language teaching initiatives directed towards British businessmen. In addition, the newly created Daiwa Foundation provided funds for new staff and developments in the field of Japanese teaching. Sheffield benefitted from both these sources of funding. One Daiwa-funded programme provided additional Sheffield staff to teach Japanese in Sheffield and at Huddersfield Polytechnic (now Huddersfield University), another resulted in Daiwa scholars spending a period of intensive language study in the Sheffield School. These scholars included the distinguished potter and author, Edmund de Waal.

Sheffield responded to these initiatives, and the need to increase the School's income, by launching new postgraduate courses in the Japanese language, courses which taught advanced translation and conversational skills. Among these additional courses perhaps the most original was the distance-learning programme, which was directed at Europeans and Americans resident in Japan who already possessed a relatively good knowledge of Japanese. The two courses, one leading towards the MA in advanced Japanese studies, and the other to an MA in Japanese language and society, were particularly attractive to graduates seeking a postgraduate qualification. These highly successful programmes included teaching by correspondence and electronic means, a residential programme in Hiroshima and Tokyo, and a dissertation on a major work of translation. At a later stage a diploma course was launched which enabled candidates who had little knowledge of Japanese to progress eventually to the MA programmes. These distance-learning courses which were launched in 1995 continued for some ten years, and over five hundred candidates successfully gained the MA qualification. These programmes, which were later paralleled by similar if smaller scale initiatives in teaching Chinese and Korean, had no obvious competitors in Europe, Japan or North America. The application of information technology to Japanese language and literature is also evident in Dr McAuley's creation of a Japanese poetry website with texts, translations and background information; this site is regularly updated and has a large international following.

In 1999 Professor Gow left the School for Nottingham University and Professor Wright, a historian of China, became the head of the School of East Asian Studies. Although the rapid growth of the Chinese economy has stimulated increased funding for Chinese studies rather than the study of Japan, Japanese studies has continued to develop strongly. In part the whole School has benefitted from the increase in student numbers, particularly non-European Union students. Furthermore, the entry of Eastern European states into the European Union has brought talented Polish, Lithuanian and Hungarian students to study Japanese in Sheffield. Above all, the large number of British students entering the Japanese studies division of the school has reinforced the strength of its programmes. In 1966 dual degrees linking Japanese language with the social sciences were the only undergraduate degrees in Japanese Studies available at Sheffield. Now numerous dual degrees link Japanese with other modern European and Asian languages. Other programmes join Japanese with Business Management, Linguistics and Modern History. In one other respect degrees today are significantly different from those in the past: it is now possible to study for a single honours degree in Japanese studies, and in 2015 this was the most popular Japanese Studies degree in the School.

The structure of Japanese studies degrees is also vastly different from those in the past. Now students begin with two years of language study largely taught by Japanese nationals, and spend their third year abroad, in a Japanese university. These Japanese universities are geographically spread across the country, providing diverse academic and social experiences. Thirty students graduated with 'Japanese major' degrees in 2015. Equally striking has been the growth of postgraduate activity in the field of Japanese studies: seventeen students are now carrying out Japan-related research at the doctoral level.

Yet perhaps the most striking development of recent years has been the greatly expanded range of staff specialisations in the field of Japanese Studies. These now embrace language, literature, linguistics, international relations, politics, popular culture, history and business studies. This diversity is further enriched by the fact that staff have received academic training in Australia, Canada, Germany and Japan, as well as the United Kingdom. The professionalism and diversity of Japanese studies in Sheffield has more than fulfilled the objectives of the early pioneers, and its public recognition is apparent from the School's participation in research seminars with members of the Foreign and Commonwealth Office.

(Note on sources: this essay is based on Sheffield University Archives, especially the Vice Chancellor's files on the Centre for Japanese Studies and the School of East Asian Studies, 1962–1993, and on conversations with past and present members of the academic and administrative staff of the School.)

17

SOAS, University of London

O

Andrew Gerstle and **Alan Cummings**

SINCE ITS FORMATION out of London's University College and King's College in 1916, the School of Oriental and African Studies (SOAS) has had the overt purpose, more than perhaps any other University college, of serving the British nation. As its motto 'Knowledge is Power' asserts, the School has had a mission to train experts and foster knowledge on the 'Orient' and Africa. From its beginnings, solid language training has been at its core, and this is certainly the case for Japanese Studies.

The first Professor of Japanese at SOAS was Frank J. Daniels (1900–1983), who was appointed in 1961.[1] However, the first Professor of Japanese at the University of London was Joseph Henry Longford (1849–1925), who was appointed in 1902 to the Oriental Department of King's College London but he retired in 1916 when his department was moved to the newly established SOS (School of Oriental Studies, the School's formal title until 1938).[2] Longford had had a career as a member

---

[1]   A biographical portrait of Otome and Frank Daniels by Ron Dore is in *Britain and Japan: Biographical Portraits*, volume I, ed. Ian Nish, Japan Library, 1994

[2]   A biographical portrait of J. H. Longford by Ian Ruxton is in *Britain and Japan: Biographical Portraits*, volume VI, ed. Hugh Cortazzi, Global Oriental, 2007.

of the Japan Consular Service for thirty-three years alongside Sir Ernest Satow and William George Aston before taking up the University of London post.[3] He taught about Japan but does not seem to have taught language. He published several books on Japan (*The Story of Old Japan*, 1910; *Japan of the Japanese*, 1911) and edited the third volume of Murdoch's *History of Japan* (1926).

In his Inaugural Lecture, 'Japanese Studies in the University of London and Elsewhere', Daniels outlined Britain's efforts to develop resources for Japanese language learning and teaching. He cites a series of early publications on the language including Rutherford Alcock's *Elements of Japanese Grammar* (1861), W. G. Aston's *Short Grammar of Spoken Japanese* (1869), and *Grammar of Written Japanese* (1871). He notes also that Basil Hall Chamberlain, appointed Professor of Japanese and Philology at Tokyo University in 1896, was the first 'British Professor of Japanese'.[4] Chamberlain's *A Simplified Grammar of the Japanese Language (Modern Written Style)* (1886) was another important work. This tradition continued at SOAS with Japanese language textbooks produced by Daniels and his wife Otome, P. G. O'Neill, Charles Dunn, and more recently by John Breen, Stefan Kaiser and Helen Ballhatchet, as well as research on Japanese language and language teaching by Lone Takeuchi, Stefan Kaiser, Kazumi Tanaka, Barbara Pizziconi, Hiroto Hoshi, Mika Kizu, Noriko Iwasaki, and others.[5]

On the whole, British expertise on Japan until the Second World War was not acquired or transmitted within universities. Initially,

---

[3]   Satow was British Minister to Japan from 1895 to 1900; he and many of his colleagues in the Japan Consular service, including George Sansom as well as scholar diplomats such as Sir Charles Eliot, are discussed in Hugh Cortazzi, ed., *British Envoys in Japan, 1859–1972* (Global Oriental, 2004). A biographical portrait of W. G. Aston by Peter Kornicki is contained in Hugh Cortazzi and Gordon Daniels, eds, *Britain and Japan, 1859–1991: Themes and Personalities* (London: Routledge, 1991).

[4]   A biographical portrait of B. H. Chamberlain by Richard Bowring is contained in Hugh Cortazzi and Gordon Daniels, eds, *Britain and Japan 1859–1991: Themes and Personalities* (London: Routledge, 1991).

[5]   Biographical portraits of P. G. O'Neill by Phillida Purvis and of Charles J. Dunn by Hugh Cortazzi are contained in Hugh Cortazzi, ed., *Britain and Japan: Biographical Portraits*, volume VIII (Global Oriental, 2013).

diplomats such as Satow and Aston, and teachers employed in Japan like Chamberlain (not a diplomat but hired to be a teacher of English), learnt Japanese in Japan in the late nineteenth century. The Japan Consular Service which was established in 1859, soon after the re-opening of Japan following the Treaties of 1858, required its members to reach a high level of expertise in the Japanese language and many of its members went on to become Japanese scholars. They included Sir George Sansom in addition to Satow and Aston. Protestant missions also expected their evangelists to try to master the Japanese language and some attained high levels of proficiency. The historian Charles Boxer (1904–2000) and others learned Japanese in Japan as army or navy language officers. It was not until the post-war period that UK universities became major centres of learning and teaching on Japan.

SOAS began its teaching programmes in 1917 and Japanese was taught from the outset, always with students attending, although there were only two who took degrees in Japanese, one each in 1938 and 1939. Both the army and navy sent students to SOAS for language training in the 1920s. Daniels mentions three who taught Japanese in the 1920s and 1930s: W. M. McGovern (from 1919 to 1922), Yoshitake Saburō (from 1923 to 1942) and Commander N. E. Isemonger (from 1921 to 1943).

William Montgomery McGovern (1897–1964), who was appointed to the School in 1919, served only a few years but later became famous for his exploits in illegally entering Tibet in 1922. His 1924 book *To Lhasa in Disguise: A Secret Expedition Through Mysterious Tibet* was a popular success. His adventures (including to the upper Amazon basin and Peru in 1925–1926, chronicled in his 1927 book, *Jungle Paths and Inca Ruins*) were well known in his day. He had learnt Japanese studying Buddhism in Kyoto at the Nishi Honganji temple before joining SOAS and he later had a long career at Northwestern University.

After the attack on Pearl Harbor and then the Japanese capture of Singapore, there was an urgent need for special courses at SOAS to train translators and interpreters for service in India and Burma. J. K. Rideout and F. S. G. Piggott (1883–1966) taught on these courses: Rideout was a specialist in Chinese while Piggott was a retired military officer who had been Military Attaché in Tokyo.[6] A number of Japanese nationals were also recruited to teach Japanese during the war: one of them was Yanada Senji who stayed on after the war and worked closely with O'Neill.[7] Another was Matsukawa Baikin. Of the Japanese nationals appointed, the School retains a personnel file on only one, Yanada Senji. After graduating from Tokyo Imperial University in 1931, he spent a year at Harvard University before coming to Britain in 1933. Between 1935 and 1941 he was the London correspondent of the *Yomiuri shinbun*. Briefly interned on the Isle of Man in 1942, he began teaching at the School from the September of that year. He remained a member of the academic staff until his death in 1972.

Arthur Waley (1889–1966), the renowned translator of Chinese and Japanese literature, who lived in the Bloomsbury area for much of his life, had various connections with SOAS and the nearby British Museum and Institute of Education.[8] In the pre-war period he published translations in the *Bulletin of the School of Oriental and African Studies* and was made an 'additional lecturer' in Chinese poetry in 1924 and honorary lecturer in 1948. Waley gave consultations to students on Japanese literature and served as an external examiner for Japanese. He lived in a SOAS flat at 50 Gordon Square for several years. Ivan Morris, who completed a PhD at SOAS in 1951, was one of those who benefited from his guidance. Waley gave occasional lectures at the School after the war.

Daniels, after spending several years teaching in Japan, was appointed senior lecturer in Japanese at SOAS in 1941, arriving just before the Pearl Harbor attack. His appointment was spurred by the British military's plan to begin sending increasing numbers of

---

[6]   A biographical portrait of Major-General F. S. G Piggott (1883–1966) by Antony Best is contained in Hugh Cortazzi, ed., *Britain and Japan: Biographical Portraits*, vol. VIII (Global Oriental, 2013).

[7]   A biographical portrait of Senji Yanada by Sadao Oba and Anne Kaneko is contained in Hugh Cortazzi, ed., *Britain and Japan: Biographical Portraits*, vol. IX (Renaissance Books, 2015).

[8]   A biographical portrait of Arthur Waley by Philip Harries is contained in Hugh Cortazzi and Gordon Daniels, eds, *Britain and Japan, 1859–1991: Themes and Personalities* (London: Routledge, 1991).

officers to SOAS for language training because of the impending war. He had gone to Japan in 1928 to work in the office of the Naval attaché in Tokyo hoping for a bit of adventure. He then worked at mastering the Japanese language and from 1933 he was a teacher of English at Otaru Commercial High School. He was head of the SOAS Japanese language programme under the general supervision of Professor Eve Edwards, professor of Chinese, during the war and afterwards until his retirement in 1967. He and his wife Otome were central to the language programme during the war and in the immediate post-war years.

The teaching of Japanese at SOAS during the Second World War (1942–1945) is relatively well documented with the book by Sadao Oba that was published in Japanese and then in English.[9] The War Office had proposed that SOAS begin training students in Arabic, Japanese and Turkish from around 1939, and posts in these languages were created, but the military did not actively send any students, and it was not until after Pearl Harbor and the fall of Singapore that a programme of scholarships was started. A number of bright young schoolboys thought to have linguistic competence were recruited in 1942 for intensive courses in Japanese, Chinese, Persian and Turkish. As they were given accommodation at Dulwich school they came to be called the 'Dulwich boys'. They included Ronald Dore, who became an outstanding Japanese scholar specializing in Japanese education and society, and Peter Parker (1924–2002), who later had a distinguished career in business, becoming chairman of British Rail, author of the 'Parker Report' in 1986 on Oriental and African Languages and Area Studies, and namesake of the 'Peter Parker Japanese Speech Contest'.[10]

The armed forces, however, required many more linguists than the 'Dulwich boys' could provide and SOAS had to arrange special crash courses for young uniformed soldiers, sailors and airmen. Many of these had to live in barracks in London while others were billeted in London homes. Although most were men, there were some women as well. For example, a group of seven women in the

---

[9]   Sadao Oba, *The 'Japanese' War: London University's WWII Secret Teaching Programme and the Experts Sent to Help Beat Japan*, translated by Anne Kaneko (Folkestone: The Japan Library, 1995).

[10] A biographical portrait of Sir Peter Parker by Hugh Cortazzi is contained in Hugh Cortazzi, ed., *Britain and Japan; Biographical Portraits*, volume VI (Global Oriental, 2007).

Women's Auxiliary Air Force learned Japanese at SOAS in 1943, before joining the very large contingent of women who worked at Bletchley Park, the centre for code-breaking during the War.[11]

Frank Daniels who had responsibility for organizing courses for the armed services was under the general direction of Professor Eve Edwards, who led most of the negotiations with the authorities and doubtless behind the scenes smoothed inevitable difficulties and staff problems. Despite the strains of working under pressure in London during wartime bombardment, morale was generally good and many of the service language students were keen to get out to Asia where they could practise the skills as they had learnt.

There were initially two main courses of a year to eighteen months. These were termed the translators' and the interrogators' courses: as the names suggest, the translators' course concentrated on the written language and the interrogators' course on the spoken language. For both courses, teaching materials had to be created from an almost non-existent base with a focus on military terminology.

Daniels and his assistants quickly had gramophone records made, in the old 78 rpm format, recording the voice of Yanada Senji using Japanese phrases which the students might need in conversation (e.g. *anata demasu ka? Hai demasu*). Those studying for the interrogators' course had to listen over and over again to these records mouthing what was said on the records. In small groups they would study elements of grammar and vocabulary and texts in rōmaji specially created for this purpose. Hugh Cortazzi, who was an airman on an interrogators' course between September 1943 and December 1944, recalls that the temporary teachers included retired missionaries such as Canon France and serving officers such as Squadron Leader Lomax.[12] Exceptional students, including Ronald Dore and Charles Dunn, were retained as assistant teachers and were not sent out to serve in the field. Those on the interrogators' courses also had daily 'one to one' sessions with temporary Japanese staff. Hugh Cortazzi recalls a Mr Takaira and Mr Shimizu, among former Japanese

---

[11]   Michael Smith, *The Debs of Bletchley Park* (London: Aurum Press, 2015), pp. 222–251. Correspondence from Val Salmond and Adrian Barker.
[12]   Cortazzi, *Japan and Back*, pp. 18–20.

businessmen, as well as Canadian army Nisei, including sergeants Yamamoto and Yamaguchi.

The translators' courses were drilled in Japanese characters by various teachers including Major-General Piggott, who had spent three years in Japan in the 1930s as an army language student. He took them through the most commonly used characters in Rose-Innes' *Beginners' Dictionary of Chinese-Japanese Characters and Compounds*. This dictionary, as well as the *Kenkyusha Japanese-English Dictionary*, had to be quickly reproduced by photolithograph process in sufficient quantities for the students to use.

It soon became apparent that the division between written and spoken Japanese was unsustainable and both courses were given tuition in both written and spoken Japanese. The courses were intense, with students expected to turn up every day Monday to Friday and work either in classes or tutorials from 9 to 5 with a good deal of home-work (not easy in a barrack room or perhaps unheated lodgings with food increasingly rationed).

SOAS was fortunate in having a building, which in those days was new and had not been destroyed in the blitz, although buildings nearby had been destroyed or badly damaged. The V1s (flying bombs) and the V2s (rockets) posed a threat to all in London in 1944. One V2 fell in Tottenham Court Road as some airmen were walking back to have some lunch at their barracks in Hallam Street. One airman studying Japanese was killed.

Student numbers gradually increased, and at the peak in the 1944–45 session, there were 183 in total (not just members of the armed forces) learning Japanese, all but six of them full-time. The intensive wartime courses were considered effective in getting students to a level of Japanese sufficient for work in Southeast Asia (mostly India and Burma) and conflict areas, where they were working on captured documents or interrogating Japanese prisoners. The programme organizers adopted a tightly structured and demanding approach to language teaching, driven by the Department of Phonetics and Linguistics under J. R. Firth, who had been its head since 1941 and was the first Professor of General Linguistics in Britain. This emphasis on the modern language with a strong foundation in the written language was to remain at the core of the SOAS approach to Japanese language teaching after the war.

Among the wartime students of Japanese who later became academics in Japanese Studies were Louis Allen (Durham University), John McEwan (Cambridge University), Douglas Mills (SOAS and Cambridge University) Carmen Blacker (Cambridge University), Ronald Dore (SOAS and LSE), P. G. O'Neill (SOAS), Charles Dunn (SOAS), and Kenneth Gardner (librarian at SOAS and the British Library).[13] Some of these were among the 'Dulwich Boys', who were given state scholarships to study language at SOAS and then entered the military. Many took degrees at SOAS after the war including Hugh Cortazzi, who eventually became British ambassador to Japan. William Beasley (1919–2006) was also of this generation but he was assigned to study Japanese at the US Navy Japanese Language School at Boulder, Colorado, as a Royal Navy officer.[14]

It has been remarked on by others that although many began learning Japanese when Britain was at war with Japan, the SOAS language programme still managed to instil in many of the students a respect for Japan that influenced their post-war development and the restoration of British relations with Japan. The programme's close links with the government continued in the post-war period, with special language training programmes being run for the Ministry of Defence and the Foreign & Commonwealth Office.

A new degree syllabus for the BA Honours in Japanese was introduced in 1946. As Daniels described it in his Inaugural Lecture, 'while including texts from the tenth century onwards, [it] put more emphasis on writing Japanese and included an oral examination. The practical aim we had set ourselves was to qualify students to begin research with only general supervision, either in the School or in a Japanese university.'

In 1946, as part of a review of provision for non-European studies in universities, the Scarborough Commission examined facilities for Oriental, Slavonic, East European and African Studies and

---

[13]   For biographical portraits of Louis Allen by Phillida Purvis, of Carmen Blacker and John McEwan by Peter Kornicki, of Douglas Mills by Richard Bowring, and of of Kenneth Gardner by Yu-Ying Brown, see Hugh Cortazzi, ed., *Britain and Japan: Biographical Portraits*, vol. V (Global Oriental, 2004), vol. VIII (Global Oriental, 2013) and volume X (Renaissance Books, 2016), and volume VII (Global Oriental, 2007) respectively,

[14]   A biographical portrait of W. G. Beasley is contained in Hugh Cortazzi, ed., *Britain and Japan: Biographical Portraits*, volume VII (Global Oriental, 2010).

recommended an expansion of Japanese studies into new disciplines. Daniels submitted an ambitious plan for the expansion of Japanese studies at SOAS to include social science disciplines, which was not followed initially but in the end resulted in several new 'language' posts and included a social science position filled by Ronald Dore. In the 1960s, positions in the social sciences increased after the 1961 Hayter Report's recommendations for the expansion of Oriental and African Studies. As Dore noted in his biographical portrait of Daniels, Daniels can be credited with creating the first programme of modern Japanese studies across a range of disciplines in Britain. Over the years, the expansion of specialists on Japan has never been easy; it has been driven by government reviews (Scarborough in 1946, Hayter in 1961 and Parker in 1987) and more recently by staff-expansion grants for three or five years partial or full funding. Grants from the following have greatly helped expand and maintain Japanese studies at SOAS: the Japan Foundation (Screech, Pizziconi, Surak, Miyamura posts), International Shinto Foundation (Dolce), Sainsbury Institute for the Study of Japanese Arts and Cultures (Carpenter), and the Great Britain Sasakawa Foundation (Gerteis). Over the years, in addition to the 'language' departments, new 'discipline' departments were created within SOAS, most of which included specialists on Japan.

Japanese language study was the initial focus at SOAS, and members of the Japanese Section in the Far Eastern Department continued to contribute to scholarship on both contemporary and classical language. In 1959 Senji Yanada published a textbook with Charles Dunn, *Teach yourself Japanese*. P. G. O'Neill produced a number of books on language including *Introduction to Written Japanese* (1963), *A Programmed Introduction to Literary Japanese* (1968) and *A Reader of Handwritten Japanese* (1984). Stefan Kaiser, who left in the mid-1990s to become Professor at Tsukuba University, published extensively on Japanese language including *Japanese: A Comprehensive Grammar* (2001). He also collaborated with Helen Ballhatchet on a completely revamped version of *Teach Yourself Japanese* in 1979, and was one of a group of scholars who wrote the influential *Situational Functional Japanese* (1991–1992). Lone Takeuchi, who was at SOAS from 1983 to 1996, is a scholar of historical linguistics and classical literature and produced *A Study of Classical Japanese Tense and Aspect* (1987) and *The Structure and history of Japanese: From Yamatokotoba to Nihongo* (1999). Young scholars from Japan were regularly recruited to assist with language teaching in the 1960s and 1970s, such as Matsudaira Susumu, a scholar of Japanese theatre, and Ikeda Tadashi, who wrote a book in English on Japanese classical grammar.

Tanaka Kazumi, a scholar of language pedagogy, ran the SOAS language programme from 1993 and then left in 2009 to become a professor at ICU in Tokyo. She was the driving force behind the establishment of the British Association of Teachers of Japanese (BATJ) in 1998.

Japanese studies staff also conducted research on various aspects of Japanese culture and society, with many working on literary subjects. Daniels worked on language and folklore, while Charles Dunn published two important books on Japanese theatre, *The Early Japanese Puppet Drama* (1966) and *The Actors' Analects* (1969, with Torigoe Bunzō). In addition to his work on language, P. G. O'Neill also published *Early Nō drama: Its Background, Character and Development 1300–1450* (1958) and *A Guide to Nō* (1954). Kenneth Strong (1925–1990) completed a BA in Japanese at SOAS in 1951 and then later taught at SOAS from 1964 to 1980. He published *Ox Against the Storm* (1977), a biography of Japan's conservationist pioneer Tanaka Shōzō, and several highly regarded translations of modern fiction: Niwa Fumio's *The Buddha Tree* (1966), Tokutomi Kenjirō's *Footprints in the Snow* (1970), Kinoshita Naoe's *Pillar of Fire* (1972), Shimazaki Tōson's *The Broken Commandment* (1974) and Arishima Takeo's *A Certain Woman* (1978). Other scholars in the Far Eastern Department in this period included Akemi Horie-Webber, a scholar of theatre, who retired in 1994, and Miyoko Uraguchi Docherty, a scholar of modern Japanese literature, who left SOAS in 1994.

Many scholars began their careers at SOAS in the postwar period before moving to other institutions: Stanley Weinstein (Yale), Douglas Mills (Cambridge), Christopher Seely (Canterbury), Phillip Harries (Oxford), Nicola Liscutin (Birkbeck), and Susan Napier (Tufts); art historian John Clark (Sydney University) is another among them, as is John Carpenter (Metropolitan Museum of Art, New York). Hugh Clarke, a scholar of Okinawan language and culture, taught at SOAS in the 1970s and then went on to become Professor of Japanese at Sydney University. David Chibbett who wrote *The History of Japanese Printing and Book Illustration* (1977) was librarian at SOAS before taking up a position in the British Library, but he died prematurely shortly afterwards. Helen Ballhatchet was both a student and then a lecturer at SOAS (1979–1991) before taking up a position at Keio University. Ivan Morris completed his PhD at SOAS in 1951 before taking up a position at Columbia.[15]

The Japanese programme was led by P. G. O'Neill from the late 1960s onwards. After his retirement in 1986, the School tried to expand the discipline range of Japanese studies in the department and in 1986 appointed Brian Moeran from the Anthropology Department to the chair of Japanese studies. Moeran resigned after a few years, however, to take up a position in Hong Kong. Andrew Gerstle was then appointed to the chair of Japanese studies in 1993. He was head of the AHRC-funded Centre for Asian and African Literatures (jointly with University College London) in 2000–2005, a project which stimulated comparative literature studies at SOAS, and he has co-organized two exhibitions at the British Museum on Osaka Kabuki in 2005 and *shunga* erotic art in 2013.

John Breen and Helen Ballhatchet report that in their time most professors and lecturers took a role in the language programme. O'Neill, Dunn and Kenneth Strong were all considered to be good language teachers and their textbooks were used in the courses. From around the year 1977, SOAS (and other programmes in the UK with honours degrees in Japanese) began to send students for a summer in Japan, initially at Nanzan University in Nagoya. Later SOAS developed its own programme of in-country language training at the Hokkaido University of Education for the third term of year one and the summer vacation. From 1997, SOAS undergraduate students have been sent to various Japanese universities for their entire second year (later third year). This in-country training altered considerably the teaching programme, and was a stimulus to learning and of course to students' fluency in the spoken language.

---

[15]   A biographical portrait of Ivan Morris by Nobuko Albery is contained in Hugh Cortazzi, ed., *Britain and Japan: Biographical Portraits*, vol. IV (Japan Library, 2002).

The language programme of the Japanese section continued to expand during the 1980s and 1990s and into the twenty-first century, and with it the number of Japanese native language teachers. Setsuko Cornish taught Japanese language for many years in the Department. Non-degree teaching of Japanese language is carried out by the SOAS Language Centre, which offers a variety of courses to the public. The leader of the team of Japanese language teachers is Okajima Shin'ichiro. Yoshiko Jones has been a key teacher in the Language Centre as well as in the degree programme for many years. The Centre collaborates with the London Japan Foundation office in teaching beginners' level courses, and in hosting the Japanese Language Proficiency Test.

The current staff in what is now the Japan and Korea department is as follows.

[Professors and Lecturers] Stephen Dodd (modern literature), Andrew Gerstle (literature, drama, visual arts), Griseldis Kirsch (media), Barbara Pizziconi (linguistics), Nana Sato-Rossberg (translation studies) and Isolde Standish (film)

[Senior Teaching Fellows] Alan Cummings (literature, drama), Satona Suzuki (history)

[Principal and Senior Lectors in Japanese language] Furukawa Akiko, Harumi Seiko, Kanehisa Misako, Kashiwagi Miwako, Shiraki Hitoshi and Taniguchi Kaori. The language staff continually produce teaching materials to supplement the language textbooks.

The Japan Research Centre (JRC) was founded in 1978 with William Beasley as inaugural chair. Sugihara Kaoru played an important role in expanding the activities of the JRC in the 1990s. The JRC supports research activities on Japan, such as regular weekly seminars, annual lectures (Meiji Jingu, Beasley, Tsuda), conferences/workshops, performance events, as well as hosting academic visitors from Japan and 'Research Associates' in the UK. It is also home to the SOAS Studies in Modern and Contemporary Japan series (editor, Christopher Gerteis), published by Bloomsbury Publishing. Currently it also hosts the journal *Japan forum*, edited by SOAS staff. The JRC includes all the SOAS staff who work on Japan in the various disciplinary departments, and they will be discussed below.

LITERARY STUDIES

Literature has been a key discipline in the programme. The publications of O'Neill, Dunn and Strong have been mentioned above. Other notable work on literature has been produced at SOAS by Douglas Mills (*A Collection of Tales from Uji: A Study and Translation of* 'Uji shūi monogatari', 1970), Christopher Seeley (*A History of Writing in Japan*, 1991), Phillip Harries (*The Poetic Memoirs of Lady Daibu*, 1980), Nicola Liscutin (*Cultural Studies and Cultural Industries in Northeast Asia: What a Difference a Region Makes*, 2009), and Susan Napier (*The Fantastic in Modern Japanese Literature: The Subversion of Modernity*, 1996).

FILM AND MEDIA

The area of film and media studies has from the late 1990s developed considerably at SOAS, with two centres, one for film and one for media studies, and recently a BA in Global Cinema and Screen Arts was created in collaboration with Birkbeck College. Current staff members Isolde Standish and Griseldis Kirsch focus on Japanese film and media.

HISTORY

Japanese history has been a core discipline from the outset with the appointment of Longford to King's College London. The eminent scholar of early European interactions with East Asia, C. R. Boxer (1904–2000), previously at Kings College London, was appointed Professor of the History of the Far East at SOAS in 1951.[16] However, he served for only two years and was succeeded in the Chair by William Beasley, one of the most important scholars of Japanese history in the twentieth century. He began teaching at SOAS in 1947, became Professor of the Far East in 1954 and retired from SOAS in 1983. His focus was on Japan's transition from the Tokugawa to Meiji periods and on diplomatic history. His first book was *Great Britain and the Opening of Japan* (1951); his monumental prize-winning work was *The Meiji Resto-*

---

[16] A biographical portrait of Charles Boxer by James Cummins is contained in Hugh Cortazzi, ed., *Britain and Japan: Biographical Portraits*, vol. IV (Japan Library, 2002).

ration (1973), and his most widely read book *The Rise of Modern Japan* (1990). His *Japanese Imperialism 1894–1945* (1987) is a bold and challenging reappraisal of Japan's colonial period. Beasley had many PhD students in both Chinese and Japanese modern history, including Ian Nish, who later taught at the LSE and wrote *The Anglo-Japanese Alliance: The Diplomacy of Two Island Empires, 1894–1907* (1966) and *The Origins of the Russo-Japanese War* (1995). Beasley continued to be active and to publish long after his retirement from SOAS and the annual Beasley Lecture was established in 2013 in his honour.

G. W. Robinson was at the School for two years from 1955 to 1957. Andrew Fraser, a scholar of Japanese local history who completed a PhD under Beasley and taught at SOAS in the early 1960s, moved to the Australian National University's Research School of Pacific Studies (*National Election Politics in Tokushima Prefecture, 1890–1902*, 1972). He was succeeded in 1966 by Richard Sims, who wrote *French Policy Towards the Bakufu and Meiji Japan, 1854–95* (1998) and *Japanese Political History Since the Meiji Restoration, 1868–2000* (2001). Sugihara Kaoru, a prolific scholar of economic history and of Japan's relations with Asia, was at SOAS in the 1980s to mid-1990s before moving to a Chair at Osaka University; he later wrote *Japan, China, and the Growth of the Asian International Economy, 1850–1949* (2005). He was very active at SOAS, particularly as Chair of the Japan Research Centre.

The historian John Breen had a long career at SOAS before becoming a professor at the International Research Center for Japanese Studies in Kyoto. His publications have been on state and religion, particularly Shinto; he is the author of *A New History of Shinto* (2010) and *Yasukuni, the War Dead and the Struggle for Japan's Past* (2008), as well as two books in Japanese on the Ise Shrine. He is also editor of the journal *Japan Review*. The current SOAS historians are Angus Lockyer and Christopher Gerteis; both focus on modern Japan. Japanese history is also taught in the art and religious studies departments.

ANTHROPOLOGY AND SOCIOLOGY

Anthropology (and sociology) were established early in the post-war era, with Christoph von Fürer-Haimendorf as head of department, initially with a particularly strong focus on South Asia. Ronald Dore was appointed initially as a social science specialist, but not in the anthropology department. Dore, one of the most eminent scholars of Japan, produced many books on a variety of topics, from educational history to city life and economics. They include *City Life in Japan: A Study of a Tokyo Ward* (1963), *Education in Tokugawa Japan* (1965), *Land Reform in Japan* (1984); *British Factory, Japanese Factory: The Origins of National Diversity in Industrial Relations* (1973) and *Shinohata: A Portrait of a Japanese Village* (1978).

Rodney Clark, who completed his PhD in the Department, was appointed lecturer in anthropology in 1974 but resigned in 1979 to work in the world of finance and to write plays. His book *The Japanese Company* (1979) is well known and still widely cited. Brian Moeran, after completing his PhD at SOAS, was appointed lecturer in 1981. He is well known for his many publications on the pottery industry, advertising and media: *Lost Innocence: Folk Craft Potters of Onta, Japan* (1984), *A Japanese Advertising Agency: An Anthropology of Media and Markets* (1996), and *Language and Popular Culture in Japan* (2011). Moeran gained some notoriety when his memoir on life as a professor of Japanese at SOAS was published in Japanese in 1988.

Dolores Martinez began teaching at SOAS in 1989, occupying a new post created following the Parker Report, initially as a replacement for Brian Moeran, who had moved to the Far East Department as chair of Japanese studies. After Moeran left for Hong Kong in 1991, she became the only Japan specialist in the department. Martinez published on social rituals and film, including for example *Remaking Kurosawa: Translations and Permutations in Global Cinema* (2009). She was very active and supervised a number of successful PhD students before her retirement in 2012, when Fabio Gygi replaced her.

ECONOMICS

G. C. Allen (1900–1982), a Fellow of the British Academy who taught for many years at University College London, was an important early scholar of the economy of Japan, and published many books on Japanese economic history including *Modern Japan and its Problems* (1927) and *A Short Economic History of Modern Japan, 1867–1937* (1946).[17] He had learned Japanese in Japan in the 1920s while teaching economics there. His connections with SOAS were considerable and he left £3000 to SOAS in his will to establish a prize in the Economics of Japan.

The Department of Economics has a long history of encouraging staff to learn Japanese for research and teaching on the Japanese economy. Seymour Broadbridge, an early appointment in the department, learnt Japanese while at SOAS, although he left to return to Australia before teaching on Japan. Broadbridge was already an established economic historian with a PhD on British railway history in the nineteenth century. He studied Japanese language, and then researched small-scale industrial firms and published *Industrial Dualism in Japan* (1966).

The first head of economics and politics at SOAS was Edith Penrose whose husband, E. F. Penrose, had been a major force in Japanese economic studies (*Population Theories and Their Application, with Special Reference to Japan*, 1934). He was another who had worked in Japan in the 1920s. This connection led her to agree to the suggestion that lecturer Christopher Howe take up Japanese. Howe, a specialist on East Asian trade, taught on the economics of the region for more than forty years at SOAS, retiring from teaching in 2015. His major work on Japan is *The Origins of Japanese trade Supremacy: Development and Technology in Asia from 1540 to the Pacific War* (1996).

Professor Machiko Nissanke is a specialist on Africa but has contributed to teaching on Japan. Costas Lapavitsas is another who was given time to learn Japanese language in order to conduct research on Japan. His field is comparative political economy and finance, and in 2015 he was elected an MP in the Greek parliament. Miyamura Satoshi is the current specialist on Japan and East Asia in the department, and Ulrich Volz also teaches on the Japanese economy. Sugihara Kaoru, who was in the History department, was an important figure in Japanese economics during his time at SOAS in the 1980s–1990s. Penelope Francks (Leeds University) is a notable graduate of the department; she has written *Technology and*

---

[17]   A biographical portrait of G. C. Allen by Sarah Metzger-Court is contained in Hugh Cortazzi and Gordon Daniels, eds, *Britain and Japan 1859–1991: Themes and Personalities* (London: Routledge, 1991).

Agricultural Development in Pre-war Japan (1984) and *Japanese Economic Development: Theory and Practice* (1999). Another recent graduate is Ralph Paprzycki, who wrote *Inter-firm Networks in the Japanese Electronics Industry* (2005).

LINGUISTICS

Linguistics and language research has been at the core of Japanese studies at SOAS. Kaiser and Takeuchi have already been mentioned. Barbara Pizziconi was appointed particularly with the aim of creating an Applied Linguistics & Language Pedagogy programme in Japanese and this has now been running for many years. Hoshi Hiroto taught theoretical linguistics from 1994 to 2004 before moving to Akita University. Mika Kizu replaced him and taught theoretical and applied Japanese linguistics until 2013. Noriko Iwasaki, a specialist on applied linguistics and language teaching, was appointed to a post in the linguistics department to develop this field at SOAS across its languages. Professor Peter Sells, who headed the SOAS linguistics department between 2007 and 2011, also contributed to research on Japanese theoretical linguistics, as did Andrew Simpson, who conducted several comparative studies including Japanese. Nana Sato-Rossberg was appointed in 2014 with the particular task of developing Japanese translation studies at SOAS.

BUSINESS AND FINANCE STUDIES

This field developed initially from the distance-learning programme, where Sonja Ruehl has been a key figure. The department of financial and management studies, initially only for postgraduates, has recently expanded to include undergraduate degrees, including a BSc in International Management that includes a year in Japan, which started in 2012. Helen Macnaughtan is the current specialist on Japan in the Department.

POLITICS

The politics department has been less successful in maintaining research and teaching on Japanese politics over the years. Richard Boyd, the author of *Asian States: Beyond the Developmental Perspective*

(2005), was lecturer in Japanese politics for many years before moving to Leiden University. Lesley Connors taught for a few years in the late 1990s, and Phil Deans and Kobayashi Yuka have included Japan as part of their teaching on East Asian international relations. Currently Kristin Surak is the specialist on Japan in the Department.

GEOGRAPHY

Japan was at the core of the geography department from the outset. Charles Fisher (1916–1982) founded the Department of Geography in 1965.[18] He had been a prisoner of war in Changi and on the Burma Railway after the fall of Singapore, and was a specialist on East Asian geography. He wrote *Three Times a Guest: Recollections of Japan and the Japanese, 1942–1969* (1979).

John Sargent, who died in 2013, began his PhD at SOAS in 1962 and was appointed to the newly established Geography Department in 1965.[19] He served as head for seven years and retired in 1999. He published *Perspectives on Japan: Towards the Twenty-first Century* (2000) and *Geographical Studies & Japan* (1993). The latter was co-authored with Richard Wiltshire, who began teaching at SOAS in 1979 after spending several years in Japan teaching at Tohoku University. He also published *Relocating the Japanese Worker: Geographical Perspectives on Personnel Transfers, Career Mobility and Economic Restructuring* (1995). Thus SOAS, unusually in the academic world outside Japan, had two specialists on Japanese geography able to use Japanese for research and teaching. Paul Waley of Leeds University, who published *Japanese Capitals in Historical Perspective: Place, Power and Memory in Kyoto, Edo and Tokyo* (2000), is a notable PhD graduate.

The department was small, however, and early in 2001 it merged with the larger one at King's College London. Joint degrees continue to be offered in geography in collaboration with King's College. SOAS's loss was King's gain. Richard Wiltshire reports that student numbers for Japanese geography are far greater at Kings than at SOAS.

---

[18] A biographical portrait of Charles Alfred Fisher by Gordon Daniels is contained in Hugh Cortazzi, ed., *Britain and Japan: Biographical Portraits*, vol. VIII (Global Oriental, 2013).

[19] A biographical portrait of John Sargent is contained in Hugh Cortazzi, ed., *Britain and Japan: Biographical Portraits*, volume IX (Renaissance Books, 2015).

ART HISTORY

SOAS produced a PhD in Japanese art in 1980 before the Department of Art and Archaeology was established. This was Sebastian Izzard (now an important Japanese art dealer in New York City), who was supervised by William Watson, then professor of Chinese Art at the Percival David Foundation, who had a strong interest in Japan and was a central figure in the Royal Academy's *Great Japan Exhibition* of 1981–1982.[20] The Department, which was founded in 1988, appointed its first Japan specialist, Timon Screech, in 1991. His position was initially supported by grants from the Japan Foundation and Sotheby's. Through his many publications, Screech has established himself as a world-renowned scholar of the art and visual history of the Edo period.

When the Sainsbury Institute for Japanese Arts and Cultures (SISJAC) was founded in Norwich in 1999, it was created with a London branch in SOAS, and Screech for the first five years was a joint appointment with SISJAC. John Carpenter was appointed to SOAS with SISJAC funding, and from 2004 was the SISJAC London office representative. After several years at SOAS, John Carpenter moved to become curator of Japanese art at the Metropolitan Museum of Art in New York. Carpenter's focus has been primarily on text and image in Japanese art, from the classical period to modern times, and he is the author of *Hokusai and His Age: Ukiyo-e Painting, Printmaking and Book Illustration in Late Edo Japan* (2005) and *Designing Nature: The Rinpa Aesthetic in Japanese Art* (2012). Recent PhDs include Alfred Haft, who is now at the British Museum and has written *Aesthetic Strategies of the Floating World: 'Mitate', 'yatsushi', and 'furyū' in Early Modern Japanese Popular Culture* (2013), and Maezaki Shinya, a lecturer at Kyoto Women's University.

From early on the Department has run a Diploma in Japanese art on its own or in collaboration with Sotheby's. Arichi Meri, who received her PhD from the Department, has been key as convenor of this programme. Many students over the years have gone on to

---

[20]   An account of this exhibition by Nicolas MacLean in Hugh Cortazzi, ed., *Britain and Japan: Biographical Portraits*, volume IX (Renaissance Books, 2015).

get postgraduate degrees in the Department after completing the Diploma.

RELIGIOUS STUDIES

SOAS has a long tradition of the study of religion, although the department was formed relatively recently. Timothy Barrett, now emeritus Professor of East Asian History, moved from History to Religious studies a few years after the department was created in 1993 as a specialist on East Asian religion. Brian Bocking, who has written *The Oracles of the Three Shrines: Windows on Japanese Religion* (2001) taught Japanese religion in the Department from 1999 to 2007 before moving to University College Cork in Ireland. John Breen played a crucial role in enabling SOAS to obtain a grant from the International Shinto Foundation for a post in Japanese religion and funding for the Centre for the Study of Japanese Religions. Lucia Dolce, a specialist on Japanese Buddhism, was appointed in 1998 and the Centre was launched in 1999. Under Dolce's leadership the Centre and the study of Japanese religions have flourished at SOAS. The department has also been the recipient of grants from the Numata Foundation, Bukkyō Dendō Kyōkai and Agonshū for research and positions on religion, and in that connection Vincent Tournier, a specialist on Buddhism, has joined the Department as Seiyu Kiriyama Lecturer in Buddhist Studies.

MUSIC

SOAS has had a long tradition of research on the traditional Japanese performing arts, with O'Neill (Noh), Dunn (Bunraku and Kabuki), Gerstle (Kabuki and Bunraku) and Cummings (Kabuki and contemporary music). However, the first specialist on music was David Hughes who taught at SOAS from 1987 to 2008. Upon arrival (before the Centre of Music Studies had become an official Department of Music), he covered the music of East and South East Asia, as well as general ethnomusicology. His main regional research focus was Japan, but he also worked on Indonesia. He has written *The Ashgate Research Companion to Japanese Music* (2008, with Alison Tokita) and *Traditional Folk Song in Modern Japan: Sources, Sentiment and Society* (2008).

Hughes has been particularly active in organizing musical events and in leading traditional music groups, with over 100 events small and large during his time at SOAS and for these activities he was awarded the Japan Society award. He was also active in building up resources at SOAS on Japanese music. The SOAS Library has an impressive collection of books and AV materials related to Japanese music and performing arts. The Department of Music owns a representative variety of Japanese instruments; several were gifts from individuals, while others were acquired through grants obtained in connection with various summer schools and short courses. After Hughes retired in 2008, he was replaced by a Southeast Asia specialist.

LAW

East Asian law was taught and researched at SOAS from early on in the expansion of law studies as a discipline in the 1980s. Donald Clarke, a specialist on Chinese law, taught Japanese law during his brief tenure at SOAS before moving on to the University of Washington and then George Washington University. Frank Bennett was the first appointment as a specialist in Japanese law in 1988. However, after he left in 1998 to take up a position in Nagoya University, there has not been a specialist of Japanese law at SOAS.

LIBRARY

The SOAS Library, as the National Library for Asian and African Studies, has had an important role to play in Japanese studies, not only at SOAS but nationally as well. SOAS has been able to have specialist librarians in order to enlarge and manage the collection. The list of successive Japanese librarians is: 1950–1955 K. B. Gardner (Far East); 1955–1955 G. W. Bonsall (Far East); 1958–1969 Miyamoto Shōzaburō (Far East; Japan from 1968); 1969–1972 D. G. Chibbett [Japan and Korea]; 1972–1995 Brian Hickman; 1973–2010 Yasumura Yoshiko; 1995-present Kobayashi Fujiko.

The Library holds over 160,000 items for Japanese studies as of 2015. The Library has collected research and teaching materials in a wide range of academic disciplines except for the sciences (although it includes books on the history of science) and books for children.

The origin of the collection was a few hundred books, mainly in European languages, which were transferred from the London Institution to the newly founded School of Oriental Studies in 1917. During the first 30 years, the collection was slowly but steadily expanded by purchase and donations. Notable donations included the collections of Richard Ponsonby-Fane (1878–1937), who resided in Japan from 1919 until his death, and Sir Henry Partlett (1842–1921) in the mid-1920s, and some 400 volumes of mainly nineteenth-century Japanese woodblock printed books donated by Ms S. de Watterville in memory of her brother Lieut.-Col. E. F. Calthrop, one time military attaché in Tokyo, in 1927.[21] Other early donations include books and prints from Frederick Anderson, the Ernest Satow collection of early books, Arthur Waley's collection and Japanese books brought back from Japan by the Duke of Gloucester, during the 1928–1929 academic session. The School purchased confiscated materials from the embassy of Japan in London in 1947. The total holding of Japanese-language books at that time was still less than 3,000.

The major step in building up the collection was a special grant received as a result of the Scarborough Report in 1947. In 1949 the substantial sum of £4,000 was spent on Japanese books, partly from School funds and partly from a special non-recurrent grant made available by the University Grants Committee. Also, £1,000-worth of Japanese Sinological materials was acquired. Walter Simon, the Professor of Chinese, and Frank Daniels visited China and Japan to obtain Chinese and Japanese texts to build up the Library.

During the 1950–1951 academic year, the retiring Chairman of the Governing Body, Lord Harlech, presented to the School some eighteenth-nineteenth century Japanese colour prints, book illustrations, and sketch albums, which formed a major part of the Japanese prints collection together with the works presented as a gift from Frederick Anderson, governor of the School from 1917 to 1939.

---

[21]   On this donation see S. Yoshitake, 'Notes on Japanese literature', *Bulletin of the School of Oriental and African Studies,* vol. 4 (1928), pp. 679–688.

In the 1952–1953 academic year, the School received some 2,000 volumes formerly kept in Japanese embassies and consulates in Europe during the Second World War, which included many classified documents relating to Japanese foreign policy and activities abroad. Those books are still easily identified by the stamp of the Imperial crest, a chrysanthemum with sixteen open petals, inside the books.

The Hayter Report on Oriental and African Studies (1961) recommended that the Library should operate as a national library in buying important material published in, or relating to, Asia and Africa. It also recommended that the main expansion in Oriental and African studies during the next ten years should be in fields such as history, geography, law, economics and social studies. Accordingly, the Library increased acquisitions relating to post-Meiji Japan.

Once SOAS was recognized as a National Library, the Library received grants and donations from external sources, including the Ford Foundation Far Eastern Studies Program (£10,000 in 1967–1968), Mitsui and Co. Europe Ltd. (£5,000 for six years from 1982 to 1983), TDK Ltd. (£5,000 to update the Japanese business collection in 1984/85) and Hamada & Matsumoto (£5,000 for the purchase of Japanese law-related materials in 1987/1988). The Japan Foundation, Toshiba International Foundation, Kasumi Kaikan, Shoyu Club, the Metropolitan Center for Far Eastern Art Studies and the Sainsbury Institute for the Study of Japanese Arts and Cultures are among the donors who have been supporting the collections in recent years.

Between 1975 and 1992, the UK Japan Library Group organized the National Co-operative Scheme for the Acquisition of Japanese Vernacular Monographs, financed by a grant from the Japan Foundation Endowment for the Promotion of Japanese Studies. SOAS focused its acquisitions on language, modern literature, law, folklore, and geography.

Two book-buying tours to Japan were made by SOAS librarians in order to improve the collection: Miyamoto Shōzaburō in 1968 on a grant from the Ford Foundation Far Eastern Studies and the School, and Brian Hickman in 1975 on a grant from the Japan Foundation Endowment Committee and the School. They also established contacts for exchange programmes with leading institutions and some are still active today.

The Burma Campaign Memorial Library, which includes over 300 Japanese-language books, was inaugurated in May 1999. This is a comprehensive collection of writings about the war in Burma (1942–1945). The Japanese books cover official military records, memorial publications from some Infantry Regiments, memoirs, and novels.

Electronic resources have become an increasingly important part of the Japan collection. Teaching and research now benefit from using databases, and the Library provides access to many Western-language databases of primary sources, e-books, and journals. The number of e-resources available in Japanese is increasing every year, and major newspapers (*Asahi, Yomiuri* and *Nikkei*) and important reference works are available in the Library. The development of full-text Japanese journal databases for arts and humanities in Japan has been very slow so the Japan collections will depend on traditional paper copies for Japanese language resources for some time to come. The Japan collection will continue to change its focus to follow academic trends while it keeps the traditional materials as treasures of knowledge.

———

NOTE ON THE SOURCES USED

Correspondence received from the following: Meri Arichi, Helen Ballhatchet, Adrian Barker, Timothy Barrett, Frank Bennett, John Breen, Ian Brown, Sir Hugh Cortazzi, Christopher Howe, David Hughes, Kobayashi Fujiko, Peter Kornicki, Dolores Martinez, Adrian Mayer, Machiko Nissanke, Adele Picken, Val Salmond, Timon Screech, Richard Sims, Tanaka Kazumi, Richard Wiltshire and Thomas Young.

SOAS Archives of Personal Files and Annual Reports.

Obituary of P. G. O'Neill, *The Times*, 23 March 2012.

Obituary of John Sargent, SOAS website (https://www.soas.ac.uk/news/newsitem86103.html)

Ian Brown, 'Teaching languages to the armed forces', draft chapter in *History of SOAS*, (forthcoming).

Frank J. Daniels, *Japanese Studies in the University of London and Elsewhere: An Inaugural Lecture Delivered on 7 November 1962* (London: School of Oriental and African Studies, University of London, 1963).

John W. de Gruchy, *Orienting Arthur Waley: Japonism, Orientalism, and the Creation of Japanese Literature in English* (Honolulu: University of Hawaii Press, 2003).

Koyama Noboru, 'Eikoku ni okeru nihon kenkyū hatten no rekishi', *Nihon kenkyū: Kyōto Kaigi*, 1994.

Brian Moeran. *Rondon Daigaku Nihongo Gakka: Igirisujin to Nihonjin to* (Jōhō Sentā Shuppankyoku, 1988).

Ivan Morris, *Madly Singing in the Mountains: An Appreciation and Anthology of Arthur Waley* (New York: Walker and Company, 1970).

P. G. O'Neill, *Collected Writings of P.G.O'Neill* (Japan Library, 2001).

Sadao Oba, *Senchū Rondon Nihongo gakkō* (Chūōkōronsha, 1988).

Sadao Oba, *The 'Japanese' War: London University's WWII Secret Teaching Programme and the Experts Sent to Help Beat Japan*, trans. Anne Kaneko (Japan Library, 1995).

Michael Smith, *The Debs of Bletchley Park* (London: Aurum Press, 2015)

Tayama Hiroko, 'Dainiji sekai taisenchū no igirisu ni okeru nihongo kyōiku: tekiseigo toshite manabareta nihongo', in *Yamaguchi Kōji kyōju taishoku kinen ronbunshū; kotoba to sono hirogari (Ritsumeikan Hōgaku* Bessatsu, 2005).

18

The White Rose East Asia Centre: Collaboration in Japanese Studies Between the Universities of Leeds and Sheffield

○

Glenn Hook

THE WHITE ROSE East Asia Centre (WREAC) was established jointly between the universities of Leeds and Sheffield as one of the five centres for excellence funded by the Language-Based Area Studies (LBAS) initiative.[1] It is the only centre with a focus on Japan and this account of it focuses on Japanese studies, although both the National Institute of Chinese Studies, based at Leeds, and the National Institute of Japanese Studies, based at Sheffield, together constitute WREAC.[2]

This account covers the aims and activities of WREAC, especially in terms of the training of postgraduate students. It demonstrates how national funding for Japanese studies at the postgraduate level

---

[1]   https://www.llas.ac.uk/news/2584 (accessed 19 September 2015); Pamela Moore, 'Evaluation Report on the Centres for Excellence in Language-Based Area Studies' (undated). http://www.esrc.ac.uk/files/research/evaluation-and-impact/language-based-area-studies-centres-lbas/ (accessed 19 September 2015).

[2]   The White Rose East Asia Centre is part of the White Rose University Consortium, a strategic partnership between the Yorkshire universities of Leeds, Sheffield and York formed in 1997. The partnership was named the White Rose University Consortium after the White Rose, which has been associated for more than 600 years with Yorkshire, England's largest county. For further details, see http://www.wreac.org/about.

has been crucial for improving the research environment for the training of the next generation of specialists as well as for funding students to pursue postgraduate work. While the lack of funding at the postgraduate level can be a major deterrent to potential students in Japanese studies, this does not yet seem to be the case at the undergraduate level: so far recruitment has not been adversely affected by the government's decision to transfer the cost of studying at university from the state to the student with the introduction of £9,000 fees from the 2012–2013 academic year.

The early twenty-first century has seen the increasing marketization of higher education in Britain. While some praise the way the market spurs competition between higher educational institutions and helps to ensure that at least some of Britain's best institutions remain in the top tier in the global ranking of universities, others instead worry about the survival of certain subjects if universities are left purely to market forces. This is particularly so in the case of subjects with a small number of students registered for postgraduate degrees. The question thus becomes: should the state intervene in the higher education market in support of these subjects? In order to address this question the late Sir Gareth Roberts chaired the Higher Education Funding Council for England (HEFCE) Chief Executive's Strategically Important Subjects Advisory Group. The group's initial report, issued in June 2005, became the basis for HEFCE's advice to the Secretary of State on future policy in higher education. Although the report gives pride of place to market-based solutions to support specific subjects 'wherever possible', state intervention is also recognised as part of the mix in cases where subjects meet the dual criteria of being 'both strategically important *and* vulnerable'.[3] The report provides advice on how to define 'strategically important and vulnerable subjects in higher education', on the one hand, and agrees at the same time to support cooperation between higher educational institutions as a means to meet national goals, on the other.

Historically, Japanese studies in British higher education has developed as in the case of other subjects at single institutions, apart

---

[3] Higher Education Funding Council for England (2005), 'Strategically important and vulnerable subjects. Final report of the advisory group'. http://webarchive. nationalarchives.gov.uk/20100202100434/http://hefce.ac.uk/pubs/hefce/2005/05_24/ (accessed 15 September 2015), p. 1 (original emphasis).

from exceptional instances, such as the now defunct MA in Japanese Studies offered between the universities of Newcastle and Durham in the early 1990s. In this sense, the group's report can be viewed as an important incentive in encouraging universities to think outside the context of their own institution and to seek opportunities to collaborate with other universities while simultaneously accepting the continued role of the market in stimulating competition between them. In the wake of the group's report, the Language-Based Area Studies (LBAS) initiative for funding strategic and vulnerable subjects in language-based area studies was announced to universities for competitive bidding by a consortium of universities. Bids by single institutions were ineligible. This pooling of resources provided an opportunity to share expertise and facilities between institutions as well as to create an academic environment with a critical mass of researchers and postgraduate research students, while continuing to compete for students at the undergraduate level and to operate undergraduate programmes independently.

Japanese studies fell within the remit of the LBAS initiative in being viewed as both strategically important and vulnerable, that is, important for Britain in terms of commerce and diplomacy, yet vulnerable due to the lack of a critical mass of postgraduate students making the subject viable solely by relying on the market mechanisms of supply and demand. The LBAS funding of approximately £25 million was jointly furnished by the Arts and Humanities Research Council (AHRC), the Economic and Social Research Council (ESRC), the Higher Education Funding Council for England (HEFCE), and the Scottish Funding Council (SFC). The initiative attracted competitive bids from a range of universities with established programmes in language-based area studies, including the successful bid from Leeds and Sheffield. Under the umbrella of WREAC, the two institutions submitted a bid to establish a centre for excellence in East Asian Studies with a focus on both Chinese and Japanese Studies. The departments included in the bid were the Department of East Asian Studies with the Centre for International Business at Leeds and the School of East Asian Studies at Sheffield.

The strategic and vulnerable subjects falling under the rubric of the LBAS initiative included not only Chinese and Japanese studies, but also Middle Eastern area studies (Arabic and Turkish language studies), former Soviet Union, Caucasus and Central Asian studies, other East Asian languages and area studies, and studies of Eastern European and Baltic countries, including European Union accession countries Bulgaria and Romania. The successful bids to establish centres in language-based area studies were from the following consortia of universities: the British Inter-University China Centre (universities of Bristol, Manchester and Oxford, with Oxford as the lead institution); the Centre for the Advanced Study of the Arab World (universities of Edinburgh, Durham and Manchester, with Edinburgh as the lead institution); the Centre for East European Language-Based Area Studies (University College London, the universities of Bath, Birmingham, Cambridge, Kent, Manchester, Oxford, Sheffield and Warwick, and the School of Oriental and African Studies, with UCL as the lead institution); the Centre for Russian, Central and East European Studies (universities of Glasgow, Aberdeen, Edinburgh, Paisley, Strathclyde, Newcastle and Nottingham, with Glasgow as the lead institution); and WREAC (universities of Leeds and Sheffield, with Leeds as the lead institution).

WHITE ROSE EAST ASIA CENTRE (WREAC)

WREAC was launched formally in 2007 with an inaugural symposium and a plenary presentation by Carol Gluck of Columbia University addressing the question of the patterns of change: a grand unified theory of Japanese history. The National Institute of Japanese Studies (NIJS) was launched separately in the same year with a workshop and plenary presentations by Tessa Morris-Suzuki (Australia National University), Naoki Sakai (Cornell University) and Yoshimi Shunya (Tokyo University). They addressed the theme of 'Shifting boundaries: negotiating identities and challenges for scholarship'. More formally, His Excellency Nogami Yoshiji, Japanese ambassador in London, launched the Centre at a reception at the University of Sheffield, describing NIJS as 'one of the landmarks for Japanese Studies' in the United Kingdom.[4]

---

[4]   NIJS [National Institute of Japanese Studies] News (2007), 'Ambassador launches International Centre of Excellence on Japan', issue 1, p. 1.

The launch of WREAC at the start of the first phase of funding with approximately £4.1 million over five years (2006–2011), including the value of linked studentships for postgraduate students, created the opportunity for members of staff with specialist interests in East Asia in the relevant departments at Leeds and Sheffield to work together with postgraduate students to realise the aims of the LBAS initiative. It started operations 'with the aim of creating a world-class cadre of researchers with the necessary language skills to undertake contextually informed research' on East Asia. More concretely, this meant to carry out 'high quality research training for the next generation of scholars in Japanese studies covering the humanities, business and social sciences; organise new research initiatives to conduct cutting-edge research in Japanese studies; develop existing research through the appointment of research fellows and post-doctoral fellows; nurture and train young scholars through world-class postgraduate programmes; organise conferences and workshops; and build up national and international networks in Japanese Studies around the world'.[5]

A second, much smaller amount of funding from 2012 to 2014 was awarded through the AHRC's Delivery Plan (2011–2015) and the British Academy's Language and Quantitative Skills Programme. Of the original funders only the AHRC continued to support the general work of the LBAS centres after the first five-year phase. A subsequent and final tranche of money was approved by the AHRC from 2014 to February 2016. These two new awards enabled WREAC to build on the achievements and impact of the original LBAS funding. In these years greater emphasis was given within the limited funding available to strengthen collaboration between the centres, build up knowledge exchange and further promote WREAC's engagement with users outside the academic community.

The quintessential element of the grant during the first phase was the award of linked postgraduate studentships in order to build up national capacity in East Asian studies. The linked studentships provided sixteen PhD awards and twelve masters two-year awards divided between Japanese and Chinese Studies. The award of the

---

5   *Ibid.*

linked studentships also proved crucial in helping WREAC to raise additional funds for supporting students. All research students in East Asian studies at the two institutions became part of the WREAC community, even if they were not awarded a linked studentship through the LBAS initiative. After the end of the first five years of funding, no linked studentships were awarded to the LBAS centres, and the area studies department at Leeds and Sheffield were required to bid under the AHRC and ESRC national schemes with other disciplines, although the ESRC provided a 'steer' to the two universities to offer a postgraduate studentship for those studying social science subjects on the East Asian Studies 'pathway' at the White Rose Social Science Doctoral Training Centre.

As far as staffing is concerned, funding was awarded for a small amount of staff time to administer WREAC for two academics at Leeds (executive director and director of NICS) and one member of academic staff at Sheffield (director of NIJS). In addition, the salaries of one administrator or part-time administrator at each institution were paid for throughout the different stages of the awards. The grant also allowed for the appointment of four one-year postdoctoral fellows and four early career fellows divided between Chinese and Japanese studies, with one postdoc and one early career fellow hired in Japanese studies at each institution during the first stage of the awards. These new posts helped to consolidate and expand both the research and teaching programmes at the two institutions, as illustrated by the research expertise contributed by the early-career fellows in Japanese history with research interest in topics related to consumerism in its historical context at Sheffield and Japanese politics at Leeds with research interest in topics related to Japan-Africa relations. At the same time, these two appointments enriched the teaching programmes of undergraduate and taught postgraduate students by adding modules on topics such as Modern Japanese History and Twentieth-Century History of Japan at Sheffield. At Leeds, new teaching was added with modules on topics such as Economics, Politics and Contemporary Society and Japan Inside-Out. Finally, all members of the departments with an interest in the work of WREAC became part of the Centre's community. All interested staff and students became a member of one of the Centre's four research clusters.

The four research clusters emerged out of the intellectual interests of staff and research students. Staff and students from the departments joined one or more of these clusters, along with a number of associate members from outside the two institutions. The clusters have been modified over time to take account of changes in the region as well as in the staff employed by the two institutions and their research interests. The clusters focus on business, political economy and development, East Asian identities and cultures, social change and transition in East Asia, and regionalization and globalization. During the period 2012–2016, a number of distinct projects were organised within the overall context of the clusters and the commitment to strengthen collaboration with our LBAS partners, as seen below.

In terms of governance, the centre has drawn on the experience of the White Rose University consortium set up in 1997 by the three 'white rose' universities of Leeds, Sheffield and York in order to strengthen collaboration between and among the three universities. WREAC is governed by an executive board which is now made up of the executive director of the Centre (chair), along with director of each national institute, the directors of the four research clusters, the directors of postgraduate studies and the heads of department of the two area studies departments. An international advisory board monitors the performance of the Centre. It is composed of the WREAC executive director and national institute directors, the chief executive of the White Rose University consortium and a range of stakeholders with an interest in East Asia such as representatives from the Foreign and Commonwealth Office, the Daiwa Anglo-Japanese Foundation and the Great Britain Sasakawa Foundation, as well as overseas academics specializing in China and Japan. It was chaired by the Vice-Chancellor of the University of Sheffield during the first phase of funding and then chaired by a pro-Vice Chancellor.

TRAINING OF POSTGRADUATE STUDENTS

The overriding purpose of WREAC during phase one of funding was to increase national capacity in East Asian studies through the joint training of the next generation of researchers. In a sense, the intervention of the state in order to support the training of Japan experts through linked scholarships helps to address the tension between a globalised labour market and Britain's need for human resources in strategic and vulnerable subjects. As British universities aim to attract the best and brightest from the global pool of specialist labour in order to maintain and hopefully improve their global rankings, the staffing in Japanese studies departments is the result of competition between applicants from outside as well as inside the United Kingdom. But attracting staff from outside the UK may not meet the needs of the nation in terms of commerce, diplomacy and other fields as, for a range of reasons, British rather than foreign nationals trained in the subject may be the target of employers. So state intervention in the funding of British postgraduate students can help to fill the gap between supply and demand in strategically important and vulnerable subjects. However, market forces can mean that, once the supply of PhD award holders has been increased through initiatives such as LBAS, the demand for employees with expertise in Japanese studies at British universities and elsewhere in the economy may not match the supply. This means that the newly minted PhDs may themselves become part of the global pool of experts on Japan and seek employment outside the UK.

With these issues as the background, WREAC has trained the LBAS-linked scholarship-holders by exploiting the existing training programmes at the two institutions as well as by developing new collaborative degrees, although these continued to be awarded by a single institution. At the MA level, students were able to equip themselves with Japanese language and other skills on the existing one-year MA degrees programmes. The extra funding from the LBAS initiative provided WREAC with the means to create a new two-year MA in Advanced Japanese Studies at Sheffield for those with existing competence in the language. The new MA programme drew on the expertise the two institutions had developed in providing online training with an innovative programme of face-to-face 'short, fat' language modules concentrated in a few days of intensive teaching instead of maintaining the 'long, thin' modules as normally taught over the twelve-week period of the semester. This limited the inconvenience to the students in commuting between the two institutions.

As far as the PhD training is concerned, students were able to continue their language training when on fieldwork in Japan by taking advantage of the ESRC's Difficult Language Training Scheme. This enabled a number of the LBAS students to take additional training at Waseda University and at the Kai Japanese Language School in Tokyo. Overall research training was carried out through the programmes run at the two institutions, with additional East Asia-specific training offered through WREAC. For instance, LBAS students were supervised by Japanese studies staff from both institutions, rather than just the university where they had enrolled for their degrees. This innovation meant that the students were able to draw on the additional expertise available at Leeds or Sheffield to strengthen their training programme. The opportunity for interaction with staff from both institutions was embedded more widely through WREAC's regular away days, where research students could present their work for feedback from staff and students from both institutions. The students funded through the LBAS scholarships pursued a range of topics in their theses, both in the humanities and the social sciences. Illustrative of the former is work on the reception of Japanese horror movies in the UK and the role of shamanism in Japan. In the social sciences, work on the effects of globalization on Japanese security was carried out as well as research on the role of the Yasukuni shrine in China's Japan policy (for further examples, see the WREAC website, http://www.wreac.org/people/students).

In order to offer opportunities to improve Japanese language competence outside the formal classroom setting, WREAC also organised a tandem-learning scheme with research students from Hokkaido University. The UK-side and Japan-side students are paired in order to provide them with an opportunity to improve their skills in the target language through regular online interaction. The online work was then followed by a workshop in Hokkaido where the WREAC students presented their research findings in Japanese to an audience of staff and research students from WREAC and Hokkaido. The programme has helped to equip research students with the skills necessary to make a formal academic presentation in Japanese. The Hokkaido programme also included both WREAC and Hokkaido staff offering training seminars for the students on how to publish in leading journals, make grant applications to funders and other topics of help in their future careers.

After the completion of the PhD, students in Japanese studies have gone on to careers in academia as well as in other professions. For instance, one of the students who completed his PhD at Leeds is now teaching at Chiba University in Japan and one of those from Sheffield is working in the European Union monitoring mission in Georgia.

PROMOTING KNOWLEDGE OF JAPAN IN WREAC AND OUTREACH

Postgraduate students as well as staff have been able to benefit from attending a range of events funded by WREAC, far beyond the weekly or biweekly seminar series in East Asian studies already in place before the LBAS initiative. The main vehicles for promoting knowledge of Japan outside the formal training programmes have been through the annual distinguished lecture, conferences and workshops. At the same time, WREAC has sought to develop knowledge exchange and outreach opportunities beyond the two institutions, thereby helping to strengthen the impact of the work carried out by staff and research students. In combination, promoting knowledge both inside and outside the two universities has helped to embed WREAC in the wider community of those with an interest in Japan.

The annual distinguished lectures have been given by scholars from Japan and elsewhere, with Fujiwara Kiichi of the University of Tokyo offering the inaugural lecture in 2007. His topic was postwar Japanese literature and the politics of wartime representation in Japan. Most recently, his colleague in the Faculty of Law, Takahara Akio, presented the latest lecture in 2015 on public diplomacy in Japan-China relations. International workshops and conferences have focussed on topics such as: Japan's multinational enterprises and cross-cultural management practices in East Asia; symbols, images and knowledge: shaping historical memory; decoding boundaries in contemporary Japan: the Koizumi administration and beyond; China, Japan and regional leadership in East Asia; ruptured pasts, uncertain futures: imagining historical and social time in East Asia;

and transitions in Japanese and Japanese language training, among others. These events have provided postgraduate students and staff with the opportunity to gain exposure to different methodological and theoretical traditions in Japanese studies and related disciplines as well as to network with scholars from within the UK as well as overseas.

As well as between the two institutions, WREAC events have been organised with external partners as part of our outreach and knowledge-exchange activities. This is illustrated by workshops and conferences organized together with government ministries, business and non-governmental organisations (NGOs). The workshop on 'Opportunities and challenge for the G8: lessons for Japan and the UK', organized with the Foreign and Commonwealth Office, examined the current and potential future role of the UK and Japan in the G8 summit with speakers from academia, government and NGOs taking part in the event. Another workshop, this time in collaboration with the Embassy of Japan in London, focussed on 'Rethinking security in East Asia: which areas? which actors?' This brought together a number of leading experts, including Kitaoka Shinichi, former deputy permanent representative of Japan to the United Nations, who also gave the WREAC distinguished lecture. Other events have focussed on developing outreach in the local community, as in the case of the international workshop on 'Interrogating Okinawa: meaning, memories and images', which brought together specialists in the humanities and social sciences to investigate issues related to politics as well as popular culture in Okinawa. This was carried out in cooperation with the Showroom Cinema in Sheffield. The film *Unta magiru*, by the well-known Okinawan filmmaker Takamine Go, was shown as part of the event. Another example of WREAC's outreach and knowledge exchange activities is the project on 'Japan's shrinking regions', where partnerships have been developed with the Japanese Ministry of Internal Affairs and Communication as well as the Japan Local Government Centre in London.

The additional funding for WREAC during the last two phases of funding has enabled us to boost WREAC's outreach and knowledge exchange activities further. As seen above, knowledge exchange with the Foreign and Commonwealth Office has been a part of

WREAC's activities in jointly holding workshops, but, in addition, staff have been involved in briefings for Britain's new ambassador to Japan, as well as in presenting a seminar series at the FCO for participants from across Whitehall. Most recently, WREAC and the FCO organised an international workshop on soft power and public diplomacy. Meanwhile, the extra funding has enabled WREAC to pursue closer collaboration with the other LBAS centres, as illustrated by the workshop on informal political actors in East Asia, Russia and the Arab world held in Sheffield.

Finally, as far as knowledge exchange with industry is concerned, WREAC funding has proved crucial in developing a project on negotiating with Asia. This project has enabled students to spend time as interns in Japan, as in the case of a student who was an intern in the Marketing, Communication and Brand Management Department of Mitsubishi Fuso Truck Company in Tokyo. Through such internships, students have been able to apply their language and intercultural skills in a Japanese setting. Students have also collaborated in the project by helping to produce an on-line library of Japanese language templates of critical use in negotiating your way around Japanese academia. These templates serve to help Japanese studies researchers during their fieldwork and later career with the task of communicating in formal written language to potential informants, research institutes, publishers, and so on.

The aim of developing an international network of experts on Japan has served to embed the research students, postdoctoral fellows and early career researchers into a range of Japan-related networks. This is illustrated by the development of the Sino-Japanese relations network, which has grown to include around forty postgraduate research students, postdoctoral students, early career researchers as well as established academics from Europe and further afield. The network's activities have included workshops and conferences on Sino-Japanese relations as well as training workshops, as illustrated by one held on research methods.

Similarly, WREAC research students and fellows have enjoyed the opportunity to develop their own personal networks more broadly in Japan and Europe. In conducting research in Japan, for instance, research students and fellows have been hosted at our universities' partner institutions, such as at the University of Tokyo and Waseda University. Strengthening our network further, WREAC established new links with the German Institute of Japanese Studies in Tokyo and scholarly visits between the two have facilitated a number of exchanges, as when Alex Klein (now at Duisburg-Essen University) presented lectures on Japanese politics at Sheffield.

In Europe, WREAC has developed strong links with East Asia Net, a network of leading institutions in Europe with programmes in East Asian studies. Research training in Japanese studies is part of well-established programmes at a number of the member institutions, such as Duisburg-Essen, Lyon, Venice and Vienna. In the case of Duisburg-Essen, WREAC students have been able to attend workshops and training activities organized by the Institute of East Asian Studies both in Duisburg and in Tokyo. The network organizes conferences and workshops and other research and networking activities. Both Leeds and Sheffield have organized workshops as part of East Asia Net, bringing together staff and students in East Asian studies at Leeds and Sheffield with their partners in the network. The workshop organized in Leeds focussed on the topic of 'Risk in East Asia and Mis-taking Asia,' with papers by WREAC members on intersecting risks in Okinawa as well as an invited contribution from a WREAC visitor on risking externalities in energy and the environment. The workshop organised in Sheffield took up the theme of memory in East Asia, with papers by WREAC members on contested memories over the war and bases in Okinawa, the memories of Kamikaze pilots, and memory and heritage in Hashima (Gunkanjima, Battleship island) in Nagasaki.

CONCLUSION

I have outlined above some of the key roles and functions of WREAC during the past decade, with a focus on activities aimed at enriching and enhancing the training experience of postgraduate students made possible by the LBAS funding. The LBAS-linked studentships proved crucial in increasing the supply of Japanese studies specialists trained in the United Kingdom. The extra funding for studentships meant students who would otherwise have been unable to pursue a postgraduate degree in Japanese studies were able to do so. Given the globalized nature of the labour market, WREAC graduates have taken up careers both at home and overseas on completion of their training. For strategic and vulnerable subjects like Japanese studies, the balance between supply and demand seems destined to be met globally rather than nationally, given the needs of higher education institutions to employ the best and brightest in seeking to maintain their global competitiveness. Precisely because labour is global, however, graduates who have moved overseas to gain employment due to lack of demand for their skills at home can just as easily move back to the UK as new opportunities for Japan experts arise.

By bringing together a consortium of universities, the LBAS initiative provided the funding to enable the two WREAC universities to develop deeper collaboration at the postgraduate level. Some of the joint training drew on innovative ideas at the level of both the taught MA and PhD. The former is illustrated by the advanced training in Japanese language online and in convenient 'short, fat' modules for advanced MA students, drawing on the experience at both institutions in distance learning programmes. The joint supervision of PhD students by experts from both institutions was another way for the two institutions to cooperate in order to improve the training experience of the students. And the regular WREAC away days with staff and students from both institutions provided a stimulating setting where students could present their research. The relatively close geographic proximity of Leeds and Sheffield proved an advantage in pursuing this deeper and closer collaboration, building on the experience of the White Rose University Consortium. This meant that, when WREAC organized workshops, conferences and general training events, students were able to attend the events without having too far to travel.

With the end of the linked studentships after the first five years of LBAS funding, WREAC was still able to use funds to enrich the training experience of students funded from other sources, as in the ongoing away days and workshops and in the integration of research students into the Sino-Japanese Relations Network. In the wake of the ending of the studentships, the Nippon Foundation and the Great Britain Sasakawa Foundation have launched a programme to support postgraduate students. The five-year programme started in 2014 and offers support for up to thirty postgraduate student-ships per year. Leeds and Sheffield as well as many other universities have received support. In this can be seen the dynamic relationship between public and private funding as universities face the ongoing challenge of training experts in Japanese studies.

(Apart from those mentioned in the notes, the sources drawn upon in this chapter include Arts and Humanities Research Council Language-Based Area Studies (LBAS) http://www.ahrc.ac.uk/ Funded-Research/Funded-themes-and-programmes/Language-based%20area%20studies/Pages/Language-Based-Area-Studies. aspx; White Rose East Asia Centre, *East Asia in 2013. A region in transition* (White Rose East Asia Centre, 2013); and the White Rose East Asia Centre website http://www.wreac.org/home.)

19

Japanese Studies at Other Universities in Britain

○

Hugh Cortazzi

THERE ARE A number of other British universities, in addition to the ones featured in the preceding essays, which do not offer degrees in Japanese but where Japanese language is taught or where there is significant research or teaching about Japan. Here will be found brief accounts of each of them, thus ensuring that this volume provides as complete a picture as possible of the current state of Japanese studies in Britain.

BIRKBECK, UNIVERSITY OF LONDON

Birkbeck does not offer single honours degrees in Japanese studies, but it does offer joint honours degrees through its Japanese Cultural Studies Programme, which is housed in the Department of Film, Media and Cultural Studies. Japanese studies may be combined with journalism, film/media, management, history, French/German/Spanish/Portuguese, global politics, linguistics, English or international law for a BA (honours). Five modules related to Japanese studies are offered at undergraduate level: 'Rethinking Japan', 'Theorising Japanese cinema', 'Popular culture in Japan and East Asia", 'Manga and anime', and 'Advanced seminar in Japanese culture and society'. The Department of History offers an MA module on 'Empires in modern East Asia', which includes a substantial component on Japan.

Birkbeck employs two full-time staff members (a lecturer in Japanese studies and a teaching and research assistant) plus a part-time tutor. It does not have a study abroad programme as the majority of the students of Japanese are working fulltime during the daytime and it is difficult for them to take time off from work. The number of students taking Japanese/Japanese studies courses has grown from 17 in 2010/2011 to 39 in 2015/2016.

BIRMINGHAM

Birmingham offers Japanese as a minor programme in 'Languages, Cultures, Art History and Music'. This is a 4-year programme including a year's study in Japan in the third year. The university employs two Japanese as language teachers. In 2014/2015 there were 14 students on this programme as part of joint honours courses.

BRISTOL

There are no BA or MA programmes focusing on Japanese studies, but there are a number of undergraduate and master's level units which include the study of aspects of Japanese society and international relations. Junko Yamashita is lecturer in contemporary Japanese society in the School of Sociology, Politics and International Studies.

CENTRAL LANCASHIRE (PRESTON)

The university offers joint honours degree courses with Japanese in Asia-Pacific studies, modern languages, TESOL (Teaching English to speakers of other languages), linguistics, law with international studies. Japanese can also be studied as a 'free elective'. In addition to studying the language students learn about Japanese society and culture. Three members of the university staff are involved with the teaching of Japanese. Three others have carried out Japan-related research. The university claims to have 22 partner universities in Japan. The number of students taking

Japanese or Japanese studies courses had risen from 45 in 2010/2011 to 58 in 2015/2016.

GOLDSMITHS, UNIVERSITY OF LONDON

Goldsmiths does not have an independent Japanese studies department, but the departments of sociology, politics, theatre and performance have modules related to Japanese culture and society.

IMPERIAL COLLEGE, LONDON

'Imperial Horizons' Japanese language courses are open to all undergraduates, who may take the course as credit or non-credit. The college has a full-time Japanese coordinator and five part-time Japanese lecturers.

KING'S COLLEGE, LONDON

The Department of War Studies runs a module which examines the transformation of North East Asia as a result of the conflicts of the last two hundred years. Japanese language courses are also available at the College's modern languages centre where there are five native speakers of Japanese. Alessio Patalano lectures and does research on Japan-related war studies.

KINGSTON UNIVERSITY

The Faculty of Art, Design and Architecture has a particular focus on Japanese art, film, performance, design and architecture from the 1960s.

LIVERPOOL JOHN MOORES UNIVERSITY

Liverpool Screen School leads the university's research and teaching related to Japanese culture and international relations within the context of East Asian studies. Japan-related topics are taught in courses offered on International Relations and International Journalism.

NOTTINGHAM

Two members of staff in the history department teach and research on the history of Japan in the context of the history of East Asia. The university language centre runs some Japanese classes.

PORTSMOUTH

Portsmouth University offers evening classes in Japanese.

READING

The university 'offers Japanese language courses as part of the Institution Wide Language Progamme (WLP).' The main aim of the programme is to develop practical communication skills. Two Japanese lecture and undertake research in Japanese studies.

ST ANDREWS

Japanese studies is a new subject at St Andrews. Konrad Lawson in the History Department runs modules on 'The Japanese Empire and its Aftermath, 1873–1952' and 'The city in East and Southeast Asia 1850–1950'

STIRLING

Stirling University no longer offers any dedicated courses in Japanese studies although it has modules which relate to aspects of Japan in a number of disciplines including film and media journalism, politics, history and management.

UNIVERSITY COLLEGE, LONDON

UCL welcomed the first group of Japanese students to come to study in Britain in 1865. The students, who came from Satsuma, were befriended by Professor Alexander Wiliamson FRS, then Professor of Chemistry at UCL. Many Japanese have studied at UCL since then. Sir Ernest Satow, Japanese scholar and British diplomat, studied at UCL in 1859–1861 before going to Japan. In his memory UCL in 1989 created the Satow chair in Japanese Law. The UCL Japan Society offers members free weekly Japanese lessons.

WARWICK

Warwick University has optional modules in Japanese provided by the university's language centre to complement the curriculum of degrees in politics and international studies. For the master's course in Politics and International Studies the university runs courses on 'Japanese colonialism: leaving Asia and joining the West' and 'Japan and the Asia Pacific: independent agent or agent of US power?'

YORK

There are no modules at undergraduate level with Japan-related content but the university hopes to develop a Japanese studies programme in the future with a particular focus on the postgraduate level. Oleg Benesch in the History Department offers a postgraduate module on 'Japan's empire and the making of the East Asian order from the 1860s to the Cold War'.

PART III

FOUNDATIONS AND OTHER ORGANIZATIONS

The British Association for Japanese Studies (BAJS)

○

Caroline Rose[1]

ORIGINS AND DEVELOPMENT

THE BRITISH ASSOCIATION for Japanese Studies (BAJS) was established in 1974, and its first President was Douglas Mills, University Lecturer in Japanese at Cambridge. The Association was launched in order to promote the study of Japan both in the United Kingdom and internationally, in particular by stimulating teaching and research. The initial idea behind the formation of BAJS originated in discussions during a European Association of Japanese Studies conference, and was developed by a relatively small group of scholars working in the main centres for Japanese Studies in the UK.

Once BAJS was launched, the annual BAJS Conference was the showcase event, hosted annually by the centres of Japanese Studies around the UK, which at first were few but gradually increased. The Conference has received regular support from the Great Britain Sasakawa Foundation to fund, in particular, the costs of bringing plenary speakers to the conferences. Funding has also been provided by the Japan Foundation, and the Embassy of Japan has also played a supportive role in the growth of the Association,

---

[1] With thanks to former BAJS Presidents for their help in compiling this chapter.

with attendance in some years by the incumbent ambassador. While the Conference was a relatively small event in the initial period, attended mainly by historians (reflecting the field at the time), this soon changed as Japanese Studies in the UK began to attract new PhD students and junior scholars working across the humanities and social sciences. As the conference calendar became more crowded, the schedule was adjusted to a three-year cycle consisting in turn of the BAJS Conference, the European Association of Japanese Studies Conference, and the Joint East Asian Studies Conference (a collaborative effort by BAJS, the British Association of Chinese Studies, and the British Association of Korean Studies). In EAJS conference years, BAJS runs a one-day postgraduate workshop.

BAJS membership rose in the 1980s and 1990s as Japanese Studies flourished in the UK, and managed to maintain healthy numbers despite the closures of several centres in the early 2000s. The BAJS Council played an active role in lobbying the government against the closures, and worked with the Embassy of Japan and the Foreign and Commonwealth Office to voice the concerns of the Japanese Studies community about the potential loss of much-needed language-based expertise. The contraction in the number of Japanese Studies centres during this period did not, however, lead to a reduction in the level of interest in Japan from the many undergraduates and postgraduates seeking to study Japanese, and BAJS was able to increase its support for training and scholarship from the early 2000s with a number of funding initiatives (see below).

A further boost to BAJS development came in 2009 with the launch of the BAJS Japan Chapter, which reflected the increasing number of UK-trained Japanese Studies academics based in Japan. Coordinated by Philip Seaton at Hokkaido University, its two main aims are to hold symposia and workshops in Japan presenting the research of members and other invited guests, and to promote links and collaboration between Japan-based BAJS members. In addition, it affords Japanese Studies scholars and students from the UK a virtual home and ready-made network during periods of research or study in Japan. The success and popularity of the BAJS Japan Chapter means that it is able to hold two events per year (in spring and autumn), which alternate between Tokyo and other parts of Japan.

GOVERNANCE

As the Association expanded over the years, so too did the administrative work associated with it and the need for willing pairs of hands to ensure its smooth running. BAJS is run by its Council, which is comprised of the President, Honorary Secretary, Honorary Treasurer, BAJS Secretariat representative (*ex officio*), the Immediate Past President, a *Japan Forum* representative (*ex officio*), elected members and co-opted members. Council meetings take place twice a year, with the Annual General Meeting held during BAJS or the Joint East Asian Studies conferences. Since 1991, the normal term of office for the president has been three years, while other officers have a two-year term; there have been 26 presidents since BAJS was established. When Japanese Studies in the UK boomed in the 1980s and the membership increased in size, it was agreed that the Association would benefit from dedicated administrative assistance. The Secretariat was, therefore, set up in 1991, with generous pump-priming from the Japan Foundation, in order to support the day-to-day work of the Council. BAJS has also developed a strong on-line presence in the last decade or so, with a website (re-launched in spring 2016), a Facebook page and Twitter account (see http://www.bajs.org.uk).

JAPAN FORUM

The proceedings of the BAJS annual conferences were published in the *Proceedings of the British Association for Japanese Studies* until 1989, when *Japan Forum* was launched as the official journal of the Association, published by Oxford University Press. From 1996 the journal was published by Routledge (later Taylor and Francis), a major publisher in the area of Japanese Studies. The primary objective of *Japan Forum* is to publish original research in the field of Japanese Studies, making available scholarship on Japan to an international readership of specialists and non-specialists. It is a multidisciplinary journal, publishing contributions from across the arts and humanities and social sciences.

A significant development in BAJS history was the renegotiation of the publishing contract in 2001, when BAJS entered into discussions with a number of publishers who submitted competitive bids. Ultimately, the decision was made to stay with Routledge, but under much improved terms, which in turn created a sound financial basis for BAJS to develop its activities and funding opportunities for the Japanese Studies community. Linked directly to *Japan Forum*, two new annual prizes were created in the early 2000s in cooperation with other funding bodies: the Daiwa Anglo-Japanese Foundation/Japan Forum Prize, which ran from 2001 to 2013, was awarded to the best article published in *Japan Forum* by a junior scholar, and the Toshiba International Foundation/Japan Forum prize, which ran from 2002 to 2011, was for the best article submitted to *Japan Forum* during the year. Many of the recipients of these prizes have gone on to pursue highly successful academic careers in Japanese Studies centres around the world

In 2010, as a result of a review of the editorial team structure of *Japan Forum*, significant changes were made. An editorial team based at the Universities of Leeds and Sheffield was appointed, and the post of Managing Editor was created to oversee the day-to-day running of the journal. This latter role was supported through the Japan Forum PhD Scholarship, filled by a PhD student at Sheffield from 2010 to 2011, and a PhD student at Leeds from 2011 to 2014. In addition, the journal adopted an online system of submission. It also moved from three to four issues per year, reflecting the increase in high-quality submissions and the demand for the journal. With the intention that the responsibilities and benefits of hosting the journal could be shared across the country, the Yorkshire-based team completed their term of appointment in the summer of 2014 and were succeeded by a team based at SOAS from 2014 to 2017. In 2015, the *Japan Forum* contract was renewed, with Taylor & Francis continuing to provide a competitive service.

BAJS ACTIVITIES

The continued success of *Japan Forum* has provided BAJS with the financial means to provide generous support to the Japanese Studies community in various ways. In addition, generous benefactors and close cooperation with UK-based Japanese funding bodies has resulted in a number of prizes and funding opportunities which have helped to raise awareness of the high-quality research being carried out by UK-based Japanese Studies scholars.

BAJS has been keen to nurture new generations of Japanese Studies doctoral and master's students through schemes such as:

> BAJS Studentships. These are awarded once per year to students registered for doctoral study in the UK. They were introduced in response to the increasingly challenging competitive funding environment in the UK for postgraduates and the need to continue to attract high quality research students into the field. While the studentships only partially cover maintenance costs or fees (awards are up to £4000), they have proved to be essential in enabling students to embark on a PhD who would otherwise have been unable to do so for lack of funding.[2]
>
> John Crump Scholarships (since 2008). In memory of former BAJS President John Crump, these awards are intended to help students who are in the final writing-up period of their doctoral studies. Successful applicants are expected to submit an article for consideration by *Japan Forum* upon completion of their PhD, as a means of encouraging them to embark on their publishing career.
>
> BAJS also offers a conference attendance fund for postgraduates presenting papers at conferences either in the UK or internationally.

BAJS has been working closely with the Japan Foundation since 2011 to run an annual BAJS/Japan Foundation Postgraduate Studies Workshop aimed at bringing together postgraduate students, early career fellows and more senior academics to discuss research, funding strategies, and career development. The events have regularly attracted 30–40 postgraduate students every year, and have helped to develop a network of junior scholars.

BAJS has also been fortunate to receive support from various sources to award prizes to students and scholars at different

---

[2]   The Toshiba International Foundation also funded postgraduate studentships from 2000 to 2011.

points in their academic careers. BAJS administers the annual Ivan Morris Memorial Prize for an outstanding piece of work (extended essay, dissertation or thesis) in Japanese Studies. The funds for the Prize were provided by an anonymous benefactor to BAJS in 1979, with a Board of Trustees appointed to maintain oversight of the prize. The Japan Forum Prize (formerly the Daiwa-Japan Forum prize) is awarded to the best article by a junior scholar.

Finally, BAJS support has not been restricted to the postgraduate community, but has been offered, on a competitive basis, to more established scholars. The 2009 Daiwa Foundation/BAJS scheme supported projects on 'The economic history of everyday life in modern Japan' (see Janet Hunter and Penny Francks, *The Historical Consumer: Consumption and Everyday Life in Japan, 1850–2000*, Palgrave Macmillan, 2012), 'Re-presenting the past: Japan, China and World War Two in the twenty-first century' (Caroline Rose, Leeds), and 'Words and things in early Meiji Japan' (Angus Lockyer, SOAS). In 2014–2015, BAJS project funds were awarded to SOAS for their Translation Initiative in Japanese Studies, 'Translations from the Japanese history of the senses', and to Sheffield for a project on 'Post-doctoral career progression in Japanese Studies'.

IN CONCLUSION

Having passed its fortieth anniversary, it is safe to say that BAJS has achieved, indeed surpassed, its original aims. The Association boasts a growing membership and a highly successful journal. It offers a range of funding schemes for postgraduate students and established scholars, and runs a busy calendar of research and training events in the UK and Japan. In cooperation with the other Japan-related organisations in the UK, BAJS has played a significant role in the maintenance and development of Japanese Studies. The number of participants at BAJS events and the high quality applications for the various scholarship and prize schemes reflect the currently healthy state of affairs, and the Association remains committed to nurturing scholarship and teaching in this thriving field.

LIST OF OFFICERS OF BAJS

President 3 year term started *	Hon Secretary 2 year term	Hon Treasurer 2 year term	From April	To April
D.E. MILLS	I. NISH	G.H. HEALEY	1974	1976
G.R. STORRY	I. NISH	G.H. HEALEY	1976	1977
C. DUNN	P. LOWE	J. HUNTER	1977	1978
I. NISH	P. LOWE	J. HUNTER	1978	1979
L. ALLEN	J.P. LEHMANN	G. DANIELS	1979	1980
P.G. O'NEILL	J.P. LEHMANN	G. DANIELS	1980	1981
C. BLACKER	J. HUNTER	R. AKROYD	1981	1982
G.H. HEALEY	J. HUNTER	R. AKROYD	1982	1981
D. STEEDS	I. NEARY	B. BOCKING	1983	1984
P. LOWE	I. NEARY	B. BOCKING	1984	1985
K. GARDNER	J. HENDRY	P. FRANCKS	1985	1986
G. DANIELS	H. BALLHATCHET	R. BOWRING	1986	1987
K. THURLEY	L. OKAZAKI-WARD	M.G. BROWNING	1987	1988
B. POWELL	R. GOODMAN	M.G. BROWNING	1988	1989
W. MENDL	R. GOODMAN	M.G. BROWNING	1989	1990
M. COLLICK	M. WILIAMS	N. WARD	1990	1991
I. NEARY*	M. WILLIAMS	N. WARD	1991	1992
I. NEARY	M. CONTE-HELM	D. STARR	1992	1994
A. STOCKWIN	H. PARKER	K. SUGIHARA	1994	1995
J. HENDRY	H. PARKER	K. SUGIHARA	1995	1996
J. HENDRY	C. ALDOUS	W. McCLURE	1996	1997
J. McMULLEN	C. ALDOUS	W. McCLURE / J. WESTE	1997	1998
J. CRUMP	J. BREEN	J. WESTE	1998	2000
G. HOOK	J. BREEN	J. WESTE	2000	2001
G. HOOK	I. ASTLEY	J. WESTE	2001	2002
G. HOOK	I. ASTLEY	C. HOOD	2002	2003
J. HUNTER	P. MATANLE	C. HOOD	2003	2004 +
J. HUNTER	H. MACNAUGHTAN	D. KELLY	2004 +	2006 +
M. WILLIAMS	H. MACNAUGHTAN	D. KELLY / G. OLCOTT	2006 +	2007
M. WILLIAMS	H. MACNAUGHTAN	G. OLCOTT	2007	2009 +

M WILLIAMS / C HUGHES	A COBBING	M. DUSINBERRE	2009 +	2010
C HUGHES	A COBBING	M. DUSINBERRE	2010	2011
C HUGHES	A COBBING	U. HEINZE	2011	2013
C. ROSE	S.TOWNSEND	U. HEINZE	2013 +	2014
C. ROSE	S.TOWNSEND	P. MATANLE	2015	

+ Sept AGM

21

The Daiwa Anglo-Japanese Foundation and Japanese Studies in UK Universities

○

Jason James

THE DAIWA ANGLO-JAPANESE Foundation was established in 1988, generously funded by donations from Daiwa Securities totalling £20 million over its first two years. From the beginning, education was its core mission. The first of the Foundation's three charitable objects, set out in the Trust Deed, is 'The advancement of the education of the citizens of the United Kingdom and the citizens of Japan in each other's institutions, business organisations, economy, culture, heritage, history, language, literature, art, music and medical and scientific achievements.' The other two objects also refer to education, and describe the Foundation's objectives of giving scholarships and grants respectively.

Although the Trust Deed itself implies a symmetrical education of both countries about each other, there was always a perception that it was more at the UK end that education was required. With English as the *lingua franca* of international exchange, there was no shortage of Japanese people with knowledge of the UK's language, but very few British people had knowledge of Japanese. One undated early document in the Foundation's archives states that 'underlying the establishment of the Foundation lay the belief that the emergence of Japan as a world power...had left large gaps in the United Kingdom's and Europe's understanding of modern Japan...[R]esources were still needed if...the United Kingdom were to begin to have the same understanding of Japan that Japan already had of the West.'

Similarly a note dated February 1992 states that:

> The history of Anglo-Japanese links until now indicates that Japan has been learning and importing from Britain educational skills, culture and the rules of society and this movement has been slightly one-sided. However, from now on we would like Britain to learn more about Japan...

Within a couple of months of the Foundation's establishment Sir Hugh Cortazzi, then Chairman of the Japan Society, wrote to Chino Yoshitoki (then Chairman of Daiwa Securities and Vice-Chairman of the Foundation) on 4 October 1988 stating that he was 'very interested in the development of Japanese studies in the UK', and attaching an article he had recently written on the subject for the *Nihon Keizai Shinbun*, in which he emphasised that while 'we need no longer be ashamed of our efforts in Japanese studies', 'resources are not yet adequate to build up a significant corps of Japanologists'.

Japanese studies departments at UK universities were quick to follow Cortazzi's lead in approaching the Foundation. Some of them – most notably Cambridge, where Japanese Studies owed its very survival through the late 1980s to his intervention – had been struggling with funding, and when they heard of the substantial resources controlled by the Daiwa Foundation, they rapidly starting making proposals to it for using the money.

Support for university Japanese studies departments immediately became the main topic discussed at early trustees' meetings as a possible use for the Foundation's resources. At the second meeting, in January 1989, it was proposed that approximately half of the Foundation's total spending should go on a 'main theme to be selected. It was suggested that the teaching of the Japanese language might be an appropriate initial theme.' By the third meeting, in September that year, it was agreed that, 'as a general guideline, the sum of...£2,500,000 should be allocated...for grants to Japanese studies and related activities at British universities and other institutions, and selected projects of a more general nature…' Of this the lion's share, £2 million, was to go to universities to support Japanese studies.

A number of grants were made by the Trustees on an *ad hoc* basis in the early days of the Foundation's existence, and several of these supported Japanese studies in universities. In 1989 the following grants were made: the University of Cambridge was given £20,000 towards computer cataloguing of the Japanese language holdings in its library, Liverpool John Moores University Business School was given £72,000 towards the cost of introducing Japanese as part of its BA Hons International Business Studies degree, and £47,000 was given (through the Japan Foundation Endowment Committee) to fund two PhD students in Japanese studies.

The development of a formal strategy, however, did not begin until the appointment of Christopher Everett in January 1990 as the Foundation's first Director General. The rather haphazard and unfocussed nature of their early grant-giving was a concern for the Trustees, and in their January 1990 meeting they 'considered that from now on this focus would be supplied by the £2 million to be allocated to universities, and beyond that by the programme of Daiwa Scholarships if the Director General's study showed this to be feasible'. In the end it was the Daiwa Scholarships programme, launched in 1991, that became the Foundation's flagship activity.

Nevertheless, the first really substantial spending undertaken by the Foundation was a set of grants made in 1990, focussed on funding Japanese studies posts at UK universities. Christopher Everett embarked on a series of visits to universities early in the year, and the resulting grants were awarded in May. In the end the grants made under this programme were as follows:

£140,000 to Downing College, Cambridge for three 3-year Research Fellowships in Japanese Studies;
    £130,000 to Cardiff University for a lectureship in Japanese Language;
    £140,000 to SOAS for a lectureship in Japanese economics;

£140,000 to Manchester University for a lectureship and a lectorship in Japanese language;

£125,000 to Newcastle University for a lectureship in Japanese language;

£140,000 to Oxford University for a lectureship in Japanese linguistics, attached to a Fellowship at Hertford College;

£130,000 to Stirling University for a lectureship in Japanese;

£100,000 to Sheffield University for a lectureship in Japanese linguistics;

£122,980 to Sheffield University/Huddersfield Polytechnic for a joint lectureship in Japanese language and studies;

£115,000 (following an initial £35,000 granted in 1989) to Imperial College London for a lectureship in the Japan/Europe Industry Research Centre; £80,000 to Essex University for research projects. These were two collaborative projects with Japanese institutions, and were not in the field of Japanese studies.

£72,000 to the Needham Research Institute, Cambridge for two 2-year Visiting Fellowships for Japanese historians of science.

£50,000 to The Royal Society for Japanese language instruction for postdoctoral researchers going to Japan.

£100,000 to the Japan Library Group to enable post-1968 holdings of Japanese books in all British university libraries to be recorded on a single computer database accessible to all. This project was led by Dr Peter Kornicki of Cambridge University.

The above list of grants falls a little short of the planned £2 million, but there were some additional grants made later in the same fiscal year – for instance £10,000 was given to the University of York in November to help establish a lectureship in Japanese music, while £130,000 was given to the University of Stirling in January 1991 to fund a post in Japanese linguistics. In the end the total size of the programme probably reached the target level. It can be seen from the list above that the focus at this initial stage was very much on posts in Japanese language or linguistics.

The various posts were not permanently endowed, but were funded for as long as each grant would cover – generally 5–7 years. When the Foundation made its awards it expressed the hope that universities would make the lectureships permanent, but this was not a formal condition. Some posts duly became 'permanent', though permanence is an elusive concept in the university sector, and some 'permanent' posts were terminated when the relevant department was later closed. Other posts simply expired when the funding from the Foundation ran out. The lectureship at Imperial College was terminated even earlier, when the Japan/Europe Industry Research Centre was closed in 1993, with the unused balance of £22,000 being returned to the Foundation.

There was some unhappiness among the universities themselves about the non-permanent nature of the Foundation's funding. The 1993 report on 'Japanese Language Teaching at British Universities and Centres of Higher Education', produced by the UK-Japan 2000 Group, noted that '[w]hilst all institutions were enormously grateful for any outside help, many pointed out that the uncertainty and short-term nature of this funding makes planning for the long-term extremely difficult'.

There were several reasons why the Foundation was not prepared to endow posts on a permanent basis. One was that the Trustees did not entirely trust that the universities, if given permanent control over the funding, would not divert it to other areas at some point in the future. Even within the time frame of the 1990 grants, Hertford College, Oxford, attempted to divert their funding to a fellowship in mathematics when the initial holder of their Japanese linguistics fellowship moved on (though Everett got wind of this and nipped it in the bud). Perhaps a more important reason was that the Foundation was not 'absolutely confident that the expansion in Japanese studies was permanent, and we weren't entirely confident that every university would succeed' (Everett). There was a deliberate decision to spread the funding beyond the established centres of SOAS and Oxbridge, but the Trustees were aware that not all the seeds they were sowing would take firm root. Where they did, the feeling was that the universities should in the longer term be happy to fund posts out of their own resources. A final factor, perhaps, was that while Japanese *departments* would have welcomed permanent endowed funding, the broader *universities* of which they were a part may have been less enthusiastic: permanent posts can prove troublesome in the very long term, if they outlive their usefulness.

This funding of university Japanese Studies posts was the Foundation's first major programme, but there was a feeling among the trustees that they should be taking a more proactive role than simply doling out money in response to university requests, and should develop their own independent programmes. The Daiwa Scholarships scheme was the first tangible result of this policy, and remains the Foundation's flagship programme to this day. This programme sends young British graduates to Japan and trains them in Japanese, but it specifically excludes candidates who already have a degree in Japanese studies, though some of them (such as Professor Hugo Dobson of the University of Sheffield) ended up moving into the field at a later stage. The Daiwa Scholarship programme appears to have been Christopher Everett's idea, and as it came to fruition, with the first Scholars selected in 1991, it gained enthusiastic backing from the Trustees, not least from Mr Chino. He remained an enthusiastic supporter of the Scholarship programme over the years, commenting in 1998 (according to a hand-written note by Everett) 'Daiwa scholar is the core grant of the Foundation, it must be maintained (most adamant).' This programme was one factor diverting the Foundation's attention away from university Japanese Studies departments, though of course the funding for university posts provided in 1990 continued for a number of years thereafter.

In 1993, Everett produced a paper for the Trustees reviewing the effect of the university grants made in 1990/1991. The overall conclusion was that they had 'made a significant impact on Japanese Studies at University level'. Although the grant to Imperial College London had not worked out, the Trustees 'were pleased to see that as many as five of the ten fellowships and lectureships might become permanent posts'. Where posts proved unsustainable beyond the initial funding round, the Foundation was inclined to accept that result, rather than take on the burden of funding them indefinitely. Everett noted in his paper: 'I suspect that some universities may apply to us in due course for renewal of grants but all are aware that we are unlikely to be able to give a positive answer.' In fact, Christopher Everett's successor as Director General, Professor Marie Conte-Helm, commented to me that she believed only a very few of the posts funded by the Foundation survived in the longer term, singling out the one at Birkbeck established in 1994.

Consistent with its view that if posts were to prove sustainable, universities should ultimately prove willing to provide the necessary funding themselves, the Foundation only part-funded the next round of posts it provided. In 1994, grants of £75,000 each were made to Birkbeck College, University of London, and Pembroke College, Cambridge, neither of which had received funding in the 1990/1991 round. These grants were for five-year posts, and were conditional on the colleges providing matching funding. Interestingly, these two posts were both in Japanese history, by contrast with the focus on Japanese language and linguistics in the 1990/1991 round. Similarly, in 1995, £30,000 was given to the University of Hull as a contribution towards, rather than full funding of, the cost of a Japanese language teaching post.

In the mid-1990s, the Foundation was engaged in various projects to assess the value of its grant-giving, and its focus on Japanese studies in the university sector was also continued by its production of two reports. One, produced in 1996 for the Japanese Embassy, reported on the specific issue of Japanese 'study tours', while the other, with support from the Japan Foundation, was a broader survey of the Japanese studies sector entitled *Japanese Degree Courses, 1996–7*. The field of Japanese studies was showing encouraging growth at the time, suggesting relatively little need for the Foundation to fund more posts. The main funding problem identified in the report was the expense of sending Japanese studies undergraduates on study tours to Japan as part of their course.

Some funding for study tours had been provided by local councils as part of the overall tuition payments made by them to universities – but this funding tended to be inadequate, given the very high costs of travel to and subsistence in Japan. The Japan Foundation Endowment Committee (JFEC) provided support in this area for a while, but withdrew in 1993 to focus instead on research funding.

In its early days, the Foundation periodically chipped in from its general grant programmes to help universities, or individual students, with the cost of study tours. There was a £3,000 grant in 1990, for instance, towards the cost of students from Durham University attending an intensive Japanese language course in Kyoto, while £25,000 was given to the Japan Foundation Endowment Committee in the same year to support its work in this area. Grants to support study tours were also made to a number of individual students. But the Foundation never initiated a dedicated programme to support study tours to Japan, and was unwilling to replace the JFEC funding when this was withdrawn. The amounts of money required were just too large, given the Foundation's other commitments. Another factor was that 'some of the trustees felt strongly that we shouldn't be doing the work of government and providing replacement funding for sources of official funding that had dried up' (Marie Conte-Helm). As government funding, not only for study tours but also for student living expenses and tuition fees, gradually dried up over the years, the Foundation remained reluctant to fill the gap. It remains the Foundation's policy that 'school, college or university fees' and 'research or study by an individual school/college/university student' are specifically excluded from the Foundation's general grant programmes.

The environment changed significantly after the turn of the millennium, with Japanese studies starting to shrink after its growth in the previous decade. The changes are brought out in the publication *Japanese Degree Course, 2001–2002*, an updated version of the 1997 edition, jointly produced by the Foundation together with the Japan Foundation. Stirling closed its Japanese department in 2001, and Durham announced in 2003 that it would follow suit. The Foundation complained about these decisions, but having seen its role as the provision of seed corn for departments that subsequently might or might not prove sustainable, did not feel it was in a position to 'buck the market', as Mrs Thatcher might have put it. As the sector continued to face funding difficulties, it was eventually the Great Britain Sasakawa Foundation, with funding from the Nippon Foundation, that stepped up to provide a major programme of funding for Japanese Studies lectureships, announced in 2007. This, in turn, led the Daiwa Foundation to shift its focus away from universities, towards developing a programme to support Japanese language teaching in schools – though in the end budget pressures meant that nothing much came of this.

In recent years, the Foundation has continued to provide substantial resources to universities through its regular grants programmes, but Japanese studies departments have had to compete with a wide variety of UK-Japan collaborations or other projects going on elsewhere within universities. An analysis of Daiwa Awards and Small Grants made since 2010 suggests that, in total, around half of all grants made by the Foundation go to universities in the UK or Japan. If larger scientific grants made through the Royal Society-Daiwa Anglo-Japanese Foundation International Exchanges Scheme (which ran until 2014) are included, grants made to universities have probably accounted for around two-thirds of all grant-giving by the Foundation in recent years. Grant-giving to universities includes grants to support projects in Japanese studies departments, or sometimes East Asian studies departments, but my analysis suggests that these have accounted for only around 4% of overall grant-giving (excluding grants made via the Royal Society programme) – around £50,000 over the period, out of total grant-giving of £1.2 million. While this percentage may seem low, it nevertheless implies that, as one would expect, Japanese studies departments are punching well above their weight in terms of the grants they receive from the Foundation, given that these departments account for only a tiny part of the overall universities to which they belong.

As for funding for Japanese studies students, the earlier concerns about the cost of 'study tours' seem like a distant dream. It seemed reasonable to worry about this in the days when students had both their tuition fees and a (means-tested) maintenance allowance paid by the government; in the current environment, in which students take out large loans to cover their tuition fees and living expenses, the cost of study in Japan is the least of their problems, and indeed (given lower Japanese tuition fees and a weak yen) it may well work out cheaper than the cost of study back at home. It seems clear that as state funding for university students in general was steadily withdrawn, any contribution the Foundation might have made to help Japanese studies students would have had to be very tightly targeted, so as not to risk overwhelming its other activities.

Nevertheless, the Foundation has become increasingly concerned about the difficulties faced by students, particularly since the trebling of domestic undergraduate tuition fees to a maximum of £9,000 in 2012. While this does not seem to have discouraged many young people from undertaking a first degree, there must be a real worry that, having already built up debts probably in excess of £50,000 during their BA, Japanese studies students will be reluctant to continue into postgraduate work.

So in 2015, following a similar initiative from the Great Britain Sasakawa Foundation, and supported by generous additional funding from Daiwa Securities, the Daiwa Foundation announced a new scholarship programme aimed specifically at helping postgraduates in Japanese Studies, the Daiwa Scholarships in Japanese Studies. From the very early days of the Foundation, the Daiwa Scholarship programme was occasionally criticised for the fact that graduates in Japanese studies were specifically excluded from it. Since the core part of the Daiwa Scholarships is an intensive course in Japanese, it was reasonable enough to exclude those who had already done a full university course, but this stricture did have the effect that the young people who had made the deepest commitment to Japan were the only ones unable to benefit from the Foundation's scholarships. (This, too, is not entirely unreasonable: the Foundation's objective is to spread interest in and knowledge of Japan in the UK, so giving scholarships to established Japanese specialists would have felt a bit like preaching to the converted.)

The new scheme, for an initial trial period of five years, will fund at any one time up to six British postgraduate students in Japanese studies, attached to either UK or Japanese universities; the first two recipients were selected in 2015. The Foundation hopes through this scholarship scheme to ensure that the next generation of British experts in Japanese studies can be nurtured, and themselves nurture future generations of British students.

22

The Great Britain Sasakawa Foundation: Japanese Studies Funding and Policy, 1985–2016

O

Stephen McEnally

THE GREAT BRITAIN Sasakawa Foundation was founded in 1985 following an initial endowment of ¥3,000,000,000 (£9.5 million) from the Japan Shipbuilding Industry Foundation (now called The Nippon Foundation). The objective was to create an exclusively grant-giving body that could offer financial support towards joint projects and initiatives that would 'advance the education of the people of both nations in each other's culture, society and achievements' and so promote and maintain close relations between the United Kingdom and Japan.

The endowment had by the end of 2015 reached almost £26 million. Over the years the Foundation has awarded almost 5,000 grants, totalling over £14 million, to projects and initiatives in all fields of Japan-related activity ranging from arts, culture and society to science, technology and medicine, from the humanities to youth exchange and sport. Whilst emphases between activity fields have naturally shifted over the years, it is support for the study of Japan and its language that has remained a cornerstone of the Foundation's work.

The inaugural press release, whilst describing a background in which 'more effort should be made in promoting mutual understanding between (our) two peoples', observed that 'the British people should have greater opportunities to learn about Japan'. The Foundation's first Annual Report similarly referred to 'a need to encourage in various ways a greater understanding of Japan and its people'. At a time of relative disparity in mutual understanding, with significantly less known in the UK about Japan than vice versa, these were unsurprising statements. Japan, after all, was a country of growing political and economic consequence, both to the UK and to the world.

By 1988 there was specific mention of emerging priorities:

> …it is the teaching of Japanese in British universities, schools and in adult education classes which has come to receive a significant measure of our support. (Annual Report, 1988)

And records of early trustees' meetings also begin to reveal a recurring concern among founding trustees that not enough was being done at 'the national level' to promote Japan and Japanese studies, for governments 'seemed to review the health of the field of Japanese studies only about every twenty years, and then only when forced to do so'. (Internal meeting note, 1987). A Board minute of the same year points to 'a clear need, *in the national interest* (italics added), for a deeper awareness in the UK of a country of increasing economic and strategic importance to the UK'.

There was considerable truth in both these observations, and the trustees were sensible of the generally held view that the study of Japan itself was of 'rather low priority' to governments of the day. Indeed, Japanese studies had received only two 'waves' of government attention and review: the 1961 Hayter Report on the teaching of Oriental, Slavonic, East European and African Studies and the 1986 Parker Report. The Hayter Report had helped move the physical study of Japan to other parts of the country and away from 'Oriental studies' at Oxford, Cambridge and London (as a result, three 'northern' centres were established: Asian studies at Hull University, Chinese studies at Leeds University and Japanese studies at Sheffield University). It had also helped to broaden the study of Japan from the humanities into the social sciences and to shift the study of Japan from the historical to the contemporary period. And, of course, this was all in line with the government's view of the national interest in commerce and diplomacy.

Trustees were particularly encouraged, however, by the publication of the Parker Report because it dwelt on the importance of the study of Japan. Written at a time of high economic growth in Japan, the Report's principal recommendation, that the UK should in the 'national interest' devote more funds to promote the study of Japan, came as little surprise. But were UK governments prepared to invest in the field? After all, it was in the 1980s that corporate funds had already started to flow into Japanese studies, which had resulted in the establishment of the Nissan Institute of Japanese Studies at Oxford University and the establishment of a chair of Japanese at Cambridge funded by the Keidanren.

The findings of the Parker Report, coming just one year after the Foundation's establishment, were timely and helped trustees focus upon how the Foundation might better support the field. For it was evident to all that, in spite of these few corporate benefactions, funding (UK or otherwise) was by no means secure. And although the Foundation had already awarded, albeit reactively, a large number of substantial grants to Japanese studies centres (two examples of which were to Newcastle University to support Japanese at its newly formed East Asia Centre, and to the Essex Centre for the Study of Contemporary Japan towards a specialist Japan library), trustees now began to recognise a need to take a more 'proactive role' than hitherto. It was a question of, 'not simply responding to the calls made upon us, although we shall never lack for good applications' but exploring 'what initiatives the Foundation ... should take to foster strong and permanent links between Japan and Britain' (Annual Report, 1986). And they wisely decided that a number of these 'initiatives' should be in Japanese studies and the study of the language.

A first step, in late 1986, was to commission and fund a major survey by the School of Oriental and African Studies into the possibility of sending UK students of Japanese to Japan to study and work. It led to the setting up of a full programme in 1988, again supported with considerable Foundation funding. Other 'targeted initiatives' followed – sporadically, it has to be said. One major initiative in 1989, however, was a grant of £79,000 over three years awarded to Sheffield University to construct a national database for Japanese studies in the UK. Another hugely significant initiative in 1994 was to commission and fully fund (£20,000), in cooperation with the Japan Studies Working Group of the UK-Japan 2000 Group, the first detailed UK survey of the state of the teaching of Japanese at tertiary level, a survey that has subsequently been updated regularly culminating in the most recent 2016 report compiled by the Japan Foundation.

Over the decade that followed, however, the vision of 'proactive and targeted initiatives' was rapidly overtaken by a need to respond to an ever-increasing stream of applications from universities seeking (often core) funding merely to keep Japanese studies alive, as the effect of reduced government funding was beginning severely to pinch. At this point, in 1991, the Daiwa Anglo-Japanese Foundation stepped in with support for a number of university lectureship posts followed by a second, smaller programme in 1994. But with limited recurrent resources the Foundation itself was unable to make a similar commitment. It nonetheless, continued to award (often significant) grants to the sector in five principal areas.

The Foundation's 1988 Annual Report had noted '…the assistance … given to British universities to enable students to travel to Japan for training in the language' and this area – the undergraduate 'year abroad' and summer schools – became a principal target for substantial and recurrent funding well into the early 1990s. A grant in 1986 of £19,000, for example, was given to Sheffield University towards Japanese Summer Schools for students at Cambridge, London, Oxford and Sheffield and in 1988 £12,500 was awarded to SOAS for a course in Japan to provide language training, home-stay and business experience. In 1991 three scholarships totalling £15,000 were awarded to the North-West Centre for Japanese Studies for study in Japan and regular grants for similar amounts were made annually to other institutions across the sector.

A second area was support for the teaching of the Japanese language at secondary school level. 'It is recognised that if better advantage is to be taken of what the universities have to offer in the teaching of Japanese studies and the Japanese language, greater attention must be given to study at secondary level' (Annual Report, 1988). This was the first indication of a desire to do more to nurture the 'successor generation'. As a result, a large number of grants were made to schools, mainly for new teaching materials and for exchange visits. In 1988, for example, £20,000 was invested in the construction of a three-year Japanese language course at Hiroshima University for UK secondary school teachers and, in 1990, £18,000 was granted to the University of Wales for the training of Japanese language teachers in Welsh schools. A further grant of £20,000 was awarded to Tavistock College, Devon, to provide additional staffing to enable expansion of its language teaching provision. A further important opportunity for the Foundation to make a difference at this level arose during the mid 1990s at a time when a number of UK secondary schools were seeking 'language college' status and were beginning the teaching of Japanese. During this period the Foundation awarded over £75,000 to twelve schools: in retrospect an excellent investment, as most are still teaching Japanese to this day.

The third broad area of Foundation support was to the (non-academic) professional bodies involved in the promotion of Japanese studies and the teaching of the language. The Foundation was pioneering, for example, in supporting the fledging British Association for Japanese Studies when in 1988 it was granted £96,500 to set up and maintain an institute to provide intensive Japanese training for university students and staff, secondary school teachers, and company staff doing business with Japan. It gave £14,000 to the 1991 Japan Festival towards the general support of Japanese teaching in the UK and £10,000 to the Japan Festival Education Trust for a 'Discovering Japan' exhibition, a touring resource for secondary schools. In 1992, the National Educational Resources Information Service was awarded £20,000 to establish a database of Japanese teaching resources for schools and higher education centres. Regular financial support to the activities of the Japan Foundation London Language Centre and to the British Association for the Teaching of Japanese continues.

The fourth area, support for publications/materials and Japan-related resources, has always been a key one for the Foundation and over the years it has provided financial subsidies towards the publication of over 100 works on Japan in a wide range of fields and has consistently financed moves in the universities to coordinate and simplify national access for the separate holdings of material relating to Japanese studies.

The fifth principal area was support for posts. In spite of the Foundation's inability to launch anything to match Daiwa's 1991 and 1994 post initiatives, it was nonetheless able to fund and/or co-fund a number of new lectureships:

> 1990 a teacher of Japanese in a Welsh secondary school (£22,500)
> 1991 Durham University, Visiting Japanese teacher of Japanese (£15,000)
> 1992 Sheffield University, Language Resources Officer (£20,000)
> 1995 Birkbeck College, Japanese History Lectureship (£25,000)
> 1998 Oxford Brookes University, Lectureship in Japanese studies (£18,000) and University College, London, Lectureship in Japanese Archaeology (£10,000)

By 1996, just ten years after its establishment, approximately 25% of the Foundation's £6 million total grant expenditure had been devoted to Japanese studies and language support.

Yet for all the resources that the Foundation had awarded to the field, with the exception of those few targeted initiatives described above, most of its grants continued to be 'scatter gun and *ad hoc*', as an internal board minute of the time described them. What the Foundation lacked was the means to initiate a programme that could inject serious funding into the field, one that would have impact and provide a firmer foundation for potential development. The late 1990s and early 2000s continued to witness further deterioration in the health of the Japanese studies field, as a number of centres and university departments began to retrench, some closing entirely. Victims were Sussex University, the University of Essex Contemporary Japan Centre, the Birmingham University Japan Centre, and the Scottish Centre for Japanese Studies at Stirling University. But the closure of the East Asian Studies Department at the University of Durham in 2003 was a critical turning point. Durham at the time was training some 20% of all East Asian Studies undergraduates in the UK and was one of the bastions of Japanese studies.

It was evident to trustees that these retrenchments and closures were not due to a falling demand for Japanese, nor to decreasing undergraduate applications. Indeed, a Japan Foundation survey at the time showed that nearly 10,000 secondary school students were taking Japanese language courses and demand for university places was growing rapidly. UCAS statistics had revealed a huge 40.9% increase in 2006 in the number of applications to Japanese degree courses and numbers applying to study Japanese as the sole or main focus of their undergraduate degree had been rising steadily year on year with 532 applications in 2002, rising to 744 in 2004, and to 1,126 in 2006. This trend, moreover, had been visible for at least a decade before that. In short, universities willing to support full single and joint honours undergraduate degrees were shrinking to leave a mere handful struggling to meet the demand. At the time only seven universities offered single honours degrees in Japanese studies with a further nine providing postgraduate courses that included elements of Japanese studies. The decline in provision had happened, therefore, despite growing interest and a concomitant demand for courses. What was clear was the need for the UK to maintain an adequate provision of degree programmes to serve both the rising interest and the requirements of employers. Evidence had also shown that graduates in Japanese were very much in demand in the job market with a respectable number of graduates in Japanese studies moving into Japan-related work, and contributing to the promotion of British interests in various ways. Students coming to the UK from overseas to pursue higher degrees in Japanese Studies were also on the increase and making a significant economic contribution.

By 2006, the third and most recent Government review had just taken place with an 'expansion' of East Asian studies resulting from the Language and Area Studies Initiative under which five international Centres of Excellence, jointly funded by the HEFCE, ESRC and AHRC, had been created. Two of these centres focused on East Asia. The first was 'The White Rose East Asia

Centre (WREAC) comprising the National Institute of Japanese Studies (NIJS) and the National Institute of Chinese Studies, a joint initiative by Leeds University and Sheffield University and which combined the study of Japan and China. The second was the British Inter-university China Centre (BICC), a collaboration between the universities of Oxford, Bristol and Manchester that focused exclusively on China. The NIJS was the only centre to have received funding for Japanese studies under this new initiative and therefore the only designated international Centre of Excellence on Japan in the UK.

On the one hand, Foundation trustees were encouraged to see that the university funding agencies, for all the concentration on China, were including Japan, still by some considerable distance the world's second largest economy, as one of the areas of 'key strategic importance' and that it was to be given a funding boost. On the other hand, the results of the initiative posed two further challenges for Japanese studies nationally and the Foundation was quick to identify them. The first was that all other UK universities teaching Japanese were to receive no government funding at all for their teaching and research. The second was that only half of one of the five new Centres of Excellence (the NIJS within the White Rose East Asia Centre) had a specifically Japan-related remit. It was important, therefore, to devise a funding mechanism that might help boost funding for Japanese Studies to the kind of level that could have been envisaged had the HEFCE initiative resulted in a discrete Japan Centre of Excellence, whilst at the same time ensuring that other UK centres/departments of Japanese also benefited from increased funding.

Trustees saw this as an opportunity. Concerns were already being raised more widely about the longer-term sustainability of these multi-disciplinary Centres once the five-year HEFCE funding expired. Were additional funding to be made available to NIJS there would be a firmer base upon which UK Japanese studies could be sustained. And if, at the same time, funding could also be obtained to support Japanese studies at other UK universities then the Foundation could make a real difference. Fortunately, The Nippon Foundation (the Foundation's initial benefactor) was itself looking to widen the scope of its grant-making activities and to expand its international programmes into higher education. It shared the Foundation's concerns and stepped boldly into the breach.

Minutes of the Foundation's 2006 Annual General Meeting, attended by representatives from The Nippon Foundation, reveal a detailed discussion, similar to the one in 1986, on the importance of the 'national interest'. Trustees talked of the potential 'far-reaching repercussions for relations between our two countries' that the Japanese studies funding crisis could wreak, if not properly addressed. The UK was 'losing its national pool of Japan specialists at an alarming rate', experts who had been 'instrumental in fostering and sustaining the close partnership that the UK and Japan had enjoyed in trade and investment, cultural and scientific exchange and in a number of multilateral contexts'. The meeting regretted that for what appeared 'purely financial reasons', the study of Japan was no longer important and that Japanese was becoming a vulnerable subject 'merely because it was expensive to teach'. Japanese was being cut back 'in favour of subjects that brought in more revenue' and the government mantra remained constant and at arms length: decisions of this nature had to remain the preserve of the universities themselves and complete autonomy in the decision-making process had to be honoured. The meeting also regretted the declining number of mid-career academics as more UK scholars were seeking research opportunities and work overseas. Not only were we losing our pool of experts 'but we are also passing up the opportunity to encourage the next generation of such experts to take its place'.

Something had to be done. Both Foundations quickly agreed that the area of greatest need was support for new lectureships. Grants would be made available to universities to cover the direct salary costs and would run for a full five years. This would make it easier for universities to appoint on indefinite contracts, help the posts to become established and (at least in theory) make it more difficult for universities to 'discontinue' them after the funding ceased. The idea of endowing one or two lectureships only was never an option: for if the Programme was to have national impact the funding eggs needed to be placed into many baskets.

The Programme was announced by both Foundations at a Press Conference at the Embassy of Japan in September 2007 as a joint partnership. The Nippon Foundation would fund the Programme and the Great Britain Sasakawa Foundation would administer it. It would place £2.5 million into the establishment of the posts in order to 'help maintain that vital pool of expertise and sensitive understanding that is essential for the continuing health of the British-Japanese relationship'. It was to be 'the biggest leap forward in the history of the Great Britain Sasakawa Foundation' and 'one of the largest injections of recurrent external funding that the discipline has ever received'. It was designed to target the study and research of contemporary Japan, primarily in the social sciences. It was hoped that the posts created would not only strengthen the UK's teaching and research capacity but also broaden the range of options on offer within current Japanese studies programmes. They would also facilitate the establishment of new courses and, importantly, they would cross-fertilize into discipline departments to include Japan-related courses in other faculties. All appointments would be with younger lecturers in mind – the next generation of Japan experts.

The spread of subject field and width of geographical coverage was pleasing: the 13 posts at 12 universities nationwide ranged from Japanese political history and economics to science policy, from the economic anthropology of Japan to Japanese visual media, and from the sociology of Japan to the Japanese creative industries, cultural policy and contemporary visual cultures. A particularly welcome placement was in the area of science and technology policy at Cambridge University, and Newcastle University chose to place the appointment in the Department of History. The Foundation would have welcomed an application from Scotland but Japanese studies at Stirling had ceased, Glasgow had poor provision and Edinburgh's department had become small. And Japanese studies had all but disappeared in Northern Ireland.

THE POSTS CREATED WERE AS FOLLOWS:

Birkbeck College, University of London, Department of Media & Cultural Studies: Research and Teaching Associate in Japanese Creative Industries Studies

University of Bristol, School of Sociology, Politics & International Studies: Lectureship in Contemporary Japanese Studies

University of Cambridge, Faculty of Middle East & Asian Studies// Needham Research Institute: Research and Teaching Associate in Japanese Science and Technology

Cardiff University, Cardiff Japanese Studies Centre: Lectureship in Japanese Studies

University of Leeds (National Institute of Japanese Studies): Lectureship in Japanese Studies

University of Sheffield (National Institute of Japanese Studies): 1. Lectureship in Japan's Economy and Management; 2. Lectureship in Japanese Studies

University of Manchester, School of Languages, Linguistics and Cultures: Lectureship in Japanese Visual Cultures

University of Newcastle, School of Historical Studies Lectureship in Modern Japanese History

University of Oxford, Department of Sociology/School of Interdisciplinary Area Studies: Career Development Fellowship in the Sociology of Japanese Society

Oxford Brookes University, Dept of Anthropology and Geography: Lectureship in the Anthropology of Japan

University of London, School of Oriental & African Studies, Department of History: Lectureship in the History of Contemporary Japan

University of East Anglia, Faculty of Arts & Humanities//Sainsbury Institute for the Study of Japanese Arts & Cultures: Lectureship in Contemporary Japanese Visual Media

With additional funding from The Nippon Foundation for outreach activities, the Foundation was also able to organise two international conferences at which the Sasakawa lecturers presented their research alongside leading UK specialists and invited speakers from Japan. The first, 'Japan Matters - Redefining Power, Politics and Culture in the Age of Globalisation', was in 2009 and the second, 'Keeping Japan on the Map', was held in 2011, both attended by audiences of over 200.

The Programme was completed in 2013. In an address at a reception at the Embassy of Japan, the Japanese Ambassador commented that 'it was hard to think of another programme related to Japanese studies in this country that has achieved its aims in such spectacular fashion'. The lectureship at Birkbeck, for example, allowed Japanese to be studied from undergraduate level to PhD for the first time. The Bristol post contributed significantly to the growing success of the Centre for East Asian Studies and a new MSc degree programme with a major Japan component was created as a result. The post at Cambridge was the first in the UK to specialise in the cultural and historical analysis of science, technology and medicine in Japan and although it did not continue, the initial incumbent moved on to create a course based on her expertise in the field of science, technology and medicine at the University of Manchester. At Cardiff University's growing Japanese Studies Centre, the only centre in Wales to teach Japanese, the lectureship was instrumental in ensuring that Japanese continued at a time when the Centre itself had been under threat of complete closure. The post at Leeds fulfilled one of the Programmes's principal objectives and became established there as one of the 'next generation' of experts. Manchester's appointment was unique in being the first in the UK to specialise in and teach Japanese popular culture, a new area of interest and research. The Newcastle lectureship enabled students, unlikely to have studied Japan during their university degrees, to specialise in Japanese history and helped establish its first MA with a Japan component. The post's success led directly to staff expansion into the School of Modern Languages with the establishment of a Japan Foundation-funded permanent lectureship there. The Sheffield post helped equip students, and potentially the next generation of experts on Japan, with the tools to analyse and understand Japan's economy and management and helped build and maintain long-term academic expertise for media representations and for briefings for policy makers. At Oxford the appointment provided the means for further expansion in Japanese studies with the recruitment of a senior Japanese sociologist to a second post there and the Japanese studies programme at Oxford Brookes was able to strengthen greatly its expertise in the anthropology of Japan. At East Anglia the lectureship fulfilled its objective in enabling the University to offer teaching in a new area, contemporary Japanese visual media, adding value to existing strengths in Political, Social and International Studies, and Film and Television Studies. It was also the major catalyst and impetus in the University's decision to create a new Centre for Japanese Studies in 2011. Finally, at SOAS the future of Japanese Studies, history in particular, was far better secured as a result of the lectureship.

The Lectureship Programme had been conceived originally as having a studentship component, but for budgetary and other reasons, The Nippon Foundation had advised the Foundation that this 'might form the basis of a future funding bid'. In the meantime, the Foundation had been providing much needed support – and this support continues today – in the form of travel grants to doctoral students wishing to undertake fieldwork in Japan in a range of Japan-related disciplines.

Although the lectureships had helped to create depth and had encouraged the teaching and research of new specialisms within the field, with a funding crisis still acute, now exacerbated by the new funding structure that had brought swingeing increases in undergraduate fees, there was a renewed need to encourage study at masters and PhD level. Research Council postgraduate funding, moreover, which now designated East Asian studies as a whole with no separate category for Japan, was becoming increasingly difficult to secure. Trustees felt that the Foundation was in a good position again 'to make a difference' if it could offer a number of postgraduate studentships across the sector.

Therefore, following a successful bid to The Nippon Foundation for renewed funding totalling £1.5 million, the Foundation succeeded in 2014 in launching the Sasakawa Japanese Studies Postgraduate Studentship Programme and it is currently providing up to 30 postgraduate studentships annually over the period 2014–2019 to UK universities. Critical mass was again a major consideration in crafting the Programme. Rather than offering 'full fees plus maintenance' studentships, at some £25,000, it was decided that £10,000 units - which would more than cover tuition fees – would have the greatest impact. And it would make all the difference in attracting the greatest number of the brightest undergraduates to proceed to postgraduate study who might otherwise have been deterred for reasons of affordability. It was also decided that the studentships should be open to UK, EU and overseas students. Universities would make their own selection for Foundation approval. Now in its third year, the Programme has supported students at the following universities: Birkbeck, Bristol, Durham, Cambridge, Cardiff, Edinburgh, LSE, King's College London, Leeds, Manchester, Newcastle, Oxford, Oxford Brookes, St Andrews, Sheffield, SOAS, UEA, University College London, Warwick and York.

It is clear that the Great Britain Sasakawa Foundation continues to play a valuable role in the promotion of Japanese studies in this country. Since its inception it has contributed consistently and effectively to the field with grants to the secondary and higher education sector that in the last ten years alone have amounted to some £4.5 million. But with a broader remit that extends into wider areas of Japan-related activity, the resources that it is able to commit to Japanese teaching, study and research will always be limited. It can only nibble at the edges of a deeper and more fundamental funding crisis. The necessity for a UK government strategy that can significantly increase and sustain core funding for Japanese studies, as recommended thirty years ago by the Parker Report, is as imperative today as it was then.

23

The Japan Foundation's Support for Japanese Studies in Britain

○

Ishikawa Yui

ORGANIZATION

THE JAPAN FOUNDATION (JF) was established in October 1972 as a special legal entity supervised by the Ministry of Foreign Affairs with the objective of promoting international cultural exchange through a comprehensive range of programmes in all regions of the world. In October 2003, it was reorganised as an independent administrative institution.

With a global network consisting of the Tokyo headquarters, the Kyoto Office, two Japanese-language institutes (the Japan Foundation Japanese-Language Institute, Urawa, and the Japan Foundation Japanese-Language Institute, Kansai), and 22 overseas offices in 21 countries, JF operates programmes in partnership with other organisations in and outside Japan, with a focus on three major fields: arts and cultural exchange, Japanese-language education overseas, and Japanese studies and intellectual exchange.

JF activities can be divided into two main categories. The first is a series of events and projects such as exhibitions, performance, language courses, symposiums, the development of networks and the creation and sharing of databases and surveys. The second is a range of grants programmes available to institutions and individuals all over the world to encourage them to engage with Japan-related projects.

The Japan Foundation (London) was opened in 1972 as one of the first overseas offices and since then we have worked closely with Japan-related organizations in the UK, such as the Daiwa Anglo-Japan Foundation, the Great Britain Sasakawa Foundation, the Japan Society and other entities. We also collaborate with other organizations which do not necessarily focus only on Japan, such as British universities, think tanks, museums, theatres, schools, etc.

In 1973, then Prime Minister Tanaka Kakuei decided to donate a fund of 300 million yen (then worth £455,000) for the continuation of Japanese studies in the UK through JF. This fund is now maintained by the Japan Foundation Endowment Committee, and continues to help many scholars and projects in the field of Japanese Studies (see separate essay in this volume).

SUPPORT FOR JAPANESE STUDIES: OVERVIEW

Since its establishment JF has supported Japanese studies in the UK on three levels: individuals, institutions and networks. Our activities cover a wide range of topics across the social sciences and humanities and are designed to contribute to the enhancement and deepening of Japanese studies.

In the decades since the establishment of the JF office in London, there have been various changes in the areas of interest and research in Japanese studies. These have reflected the changes taking place in Japanese society and the way in which these changes are viewed in the UK.

Up to the 1990s, economics, business, politics and international relations were dominant themes, probably reflecting the dramatic changes taking place in the Japanese economy and Japan's role in the world. History was another major interest. The Scarborough Report of 1947 had called for a wider approach in area studies to include the study of history, literature, economics and religion in addition to language. Because of the focus on these fields, research in other areas such as arts, sociology and anthropology was limited and JF received few application projects for support in these areas.

After 2000, however, JF received more applications related to the humanities and there was less emphasis on economics, politics and international relations. There has also in recent years been an increasing interest in issues such as environmental problems and ageing societies where Britain and Japan have common concerns as well as in aspects of art. This shift and diversification demonstrate the changes in Japan's role and status in the UK and the world, and at the same time, the enrichment of Japanese studies in the UK. As British academics' research into Japan has increased, researchers and scholars have been able to delve more widely in their areas of specialization.

Japan Foundation is keen to encourage research in all these areas, as they are important factors in understanding Japanese culture and its society. JF has accordingly produced a Japanese Studies Survey (see below) to provide information about developments in Japanese studies.

JF SUPPORT FOR INSTITUTIONS

JF support includes funding and resources for academic staff expansion, research conferences, symposiums, expansion of library materials, visiting professors, language teachers, study trips, etc. More than 35 universities and institutions across the UK have been supported through one or more of these schemes during the past four decades. Some universities have been awarded funding several times; so some 150 projects have received JF support in the UK alone.

Among British institutions which have received support are the Universities of Oxford, Cambridge, Sheffield and Edinburgh, the School of Oriental and African Studies, the Sainsbury Institute for the Study of Japanese Arts and Culture (SISJAC) and Chatham House. In providing support for institutions we attach great importance to ensuring that the universities involved are fully committed to any project in which we are involved. One of the characteristics of our institutional support is the emphasis we place on commitment by the universities involved. For example, when offering staff expansion support we require that the university provide matching funding. After the support ends the universities are expected to maintain and fund the academic post. By obtaining this engagement from the universities, we hope that both the post and course will become permanent.

INTELLECTUAL EXCHANGE CONFERENCES

This programme is designed to strengthen intellectual exchange between Japan and other countries, and to increase Japan's intellectual contribution by supporting dialogue on regionally or globally shared issues as well as on key global agendas. Past topics have included environmental problems, ageing society, international relations and security issues, and migration. Through relatively large-scale symposiums and conferences focussing on common issues or Japan related topics, we aim to facilitate a greater understanding of Japan overseas and to develop Japanese bilateral and multilateral relations with foreign countries.

Awards to British institutions have, JF believe, strengthened the relationship between the UK, Japan and the rest of the world. These symposiums and workshops have involved academics and practitioners not only from the UK and Japan, but also from other parts of the world and have helped to build worldwide networks. Recent successful projects in the UK have focussed on such subjects as art history, international relations and security, as well as on disaster risk reduction.

LOCAL PROJECT SUPPORT PROGRAMMES

JF (London) also provides smaller-scale grants to support local Japan related activities such as conferences, symposiums and research projects, which have shorter lead times. There is no fixed deadline and applications are accepted up to two months before the project starts. Recent projects, which have received support, have included a research conference focussing on art history and a workshop on cultural studies.

SUPPORT FOR INDIVIDUALS

Japanese studies fellowship

The Japanese studies fellowship is a long-running programme for scholars and post-graduate students in Japanese studies. The fellowship programme started in 1972, with the aim of enabling outstanding scholars and researchers to visit Japan to conduct their research. As the human factor is most important for cultural exchange, we place the highest priority on inviting people to come and experience Japan first-hand. So far under this programme over 130 scholars have gone to Japan from the UK. They cover a wide range of research areas from ancient to modern and from literature to economics.

a) *Short term fellowships* lasting from 2 to 59 days. Recent research topics of awardees have included literature, anthropology, international relations and environmental sociology.

b) *Longer-term fellowships* lasting from 2 to 12 months for research in Japan. Applicants are required to be affiliated with an institution in Japan during their fellowship. Recent awards have been for research in fields such as art history, linguistics and politics.

c) *Doctoral candidates.* 12 to 14 months fellowships are awarded for doctoral candidates who are in the closing stages of their PhD study, and need to conduct research in Japan in order to complete their dissertation. Applicants are required to have an affiliation with an appropriate institution in Japan, which can provide help and supervision. Recent awardees have conducted research in areas such as film studies, literature and economics.

STUDY SUPPORT PROGRAMME

JF (London) also offers a local grant programme to support individual scholars. The programme provides for a number of travel grants to contribute to the costs of air fares to and from Japan. The scale of support offered is smaller than that for the fellowships. However, the programme is operated on a rolling deadline so that JF can be flexible in meeting the needs of scholars. Recent recipients of such grants have included scholars conducting research in such areas as media studies, archaeology, art history, and international relations. JF has also awarded funding to practitioners such as a council officer in charge of development planning whose research into Japanese *machizukuri* – まちづくり – urban planning) has led to the development of interactive and practical bonds between Japan and the UK.

JF has recently accorded priority to students interested in specializing in aspects of Japanese studies who seek an academic career. JF recognizes the need to nurture future upcoming generations of Japanese studies scholars to fill posts at universities as they become available through natural turnover as senior scholars retire. This has become even more important as a result of the recent increase in tuition fees and the financial problems facing those seeking to advance to post-graduate studies.

SUPPORT FOR NETWORKS

JF also supports academic networks in Japanese studies. The biggest Japanese studies network in the UK is the British Association for Japanese Studies (BAJS) established in 1974. JF has continued to support BAJS's activities including annual conferences and workshops. BAJS's annual conferences provide opportunities for Japanese studies scholars to present their own research to fellow scholars and also to build a professional network within and beyond the UK. Beyond the UK, there is the even larger European Association for Japanese Studies (EAJS), with which JF also enjoys a good relationship. In 2014, the president and secretary were selected from British universities, and they will be in charge until EAJS's next international conference in Lisbon in 2017. This shows the significant influence of British Japanese studies in Europe and we hope it will encourage more UK-based scholars to be involved in this network.

Every three years, JF has funded EAJS conferences, attended by many UK researchers. Meetings of the EAJS enable scholars to work actively throughout Europe rather than only in one country and also provide opportunities for collaborative research in the region.

JF has also supported issue-oriented networks. For example, one recent recipient of an award was a group of librarians who wished to develop new strategies for dealing with historical

Japanese materials held in their university libraries. In many cases, these valuable materials had been overlooked, simply because the librarians did not have enough skill and knowledge to include them in their catalogues. The group held workshops to train librarians in how to tackle this problem and learn how to manage, catalogue and handle antiquarian manuscripts and printed material.

Networks bring various advantages to scholars. These include links with fellow researchers around the world, new information related to research subjects, comparative ideas from other regions, opportunities for collaborative research projects or practical skills to deal with shared problems.

EVENTS ORGANIZED BY JF

JF offers a wide range of public seminars and workshops throughout the year. The aim of these events is to deepen understanding of Japanese society and culture as well as to encourage the development of the Japanese studies community.

Public seminars are held regularly once or twice a month, and the topics cover a wide range of humanities and social sciences areas such as literature, history, sociology, economics and politics. Recent seminars topics have included:

a) *Kon-katsu* (婚活, a Japanese word for 'marriage hunting') which examined the difficulties relating to marriage, which many Japanese young people face today;

b) An anthropological study examining Tohoku after the disaster in March 2011 covering the immediate reactions to the disaster, and the current situation in the devastated areas;

c) The life and philosophy of a Japanese mathematician whose work was influenced by Zen Buddhism.

Some seminars have also dealt with issues of interest in both Japan and Britain such as ageing societies and the revitalization of communities.

JF aims to raise the awareness of British audiences towards aspects of Japan which are not widely known in the UK, but also to provide opportunities for Japanese studies scholars to present the outcome of their research to the general public beyond academia. In some cases JF invites speakers from Japan to tour universities around the UK conducting seminars and workshops, in order to provide more opportunities for students outside London to meet these experts.

JF has also organised annually since 2012 a Japanese studies postgraduate workshop in collaboration with BAJS. This workshop is designed for PhD candidates in Japanese studies in British universities. The workshop consists of sessions focussing both on academic research and on practical skills. In the academic sessions, some of the students have the opportunity to present their research and receive feedback from senior scholars and fellow students. The practical workshops by senior scholars have included sessions on publishing, getting funding for research, and conducting fieldwork and interviews in Japan, all crucial skills for young scholars wanting to pursue their career as an academic.

In 2014 and 2015 representatives from funding organisations based in London (Daiwa Anglo-Japan Foundation, Great Britain Sasakawa Foundation and the Japanese Society for Promotion of Sciences London) also joined the workshop to explain their funding schemes and activities together with Kinokuniya Publishing and Nikkei Europe, organisations which provide databases of Japanese materials.

In 2015, JF held the fourth workshop in Leeds. This brought together more students from central and northern England who have relatively less opportunities to obtain such information compared to those based in London. JF now plans to alternate the workshop between London and other cities in order to reach more students across the UK.

JAPANESE STUDIES SURVEY

JF conducts a Japanese studies survey throughout the world, the UK being included in the section devoted to Europe. The most recent survey completed in 2008 led to the creation of a directory of Japanese studies specialists and institutions with individual country reports in its appendix.

In addition to this worldwide survey, JF (London) has also conducted once every 3–4 years since 1996 a smaller survey focusing only on the UK. (In 1996 and 2001 the survey was conducted in collaboration with the Daiwa Anglo-Japan Foundation.) This local survey consists of statistics relating to institutions and students, based on questionnaires completed by staff and students in Japanese studies courses at universities. The most recent results are available on the website of the JF (London).

The past two surveys have shown that the number of Japanese studies courses in the UK increased in the late 1990s and dropped in the early 2000s, but that the total number of students enrolled in these courses has steadily increased. In 2016, JF updated the survey and published the results on the JF (London) website.

MID-AND LONG-TERM GOALS

JF aims to continue to maintain its range of support for Japanese studies in the UK, but in order to maximize limited resources it needs to develop a more targeted strategy based on a realistic assessment of its current achievements. JF's long-term goal is the enhancement and enrichment of Japanese studies, which will lead to a greater understanding of Japan in the UK.

a)   Development of the next generation of Japanese studies experts in the UK

British universities face a difficult financial situation, which threatens existing Japanese studies posts. In order for Japanese studies to survive, young, promising scholars are needed to secure these posts in universities and academia in the UK. JF provides direct support for up and coming scholars through the Japanese studies fellowships and JF (London)'s study support programmes, which allow PhD students and scholars in the early stage of their academic career to visit Japan for their research. JF (London)'s public seminars and the Japanese studies post-graduate workshops provide opportunities for valuable exchanges as well as practical information for all who are interested in Japanese studies.

b) *Support for regional activities*

Although JF funding has always been used to support Japanese studies throughout Britain, JF events have tended to be held mainly in London. However, as the number of universities with Japanese studies courses has increased across the country, a London-centric approach is no longer appropriate and JF are now increasingly expanding events around the country in order to provide more opportunities for the increasing number of students outside London to interact with first class experts from Japanese studies fields.

c) *Greater diversity in areas of research*

The scope of Japanese studies has broadened in past decades, enabling scholars to analyse and develop their own research through multiple disciplines. This integrated analysis has contributed to the deepening of understanding of Japanese society. It has also helped to promote the status of Japanese studies and ensure that they are recognized as valuable components of university education and research. JF, in the light of the 2015 Japanese studies survey, will give priority to weaker areas over more strongly resourced research fields. Recent applications for JF support suggest increased interest in anthropology, history and sociology, and declining interest in the fields of politics and economics.

d) *A broader approach to the study of Japan*

Recently, more and more universities are bringing area studies such as Japanese studies under other disciplines or establishing joint/dual degrees to provide opportunities for comparative or combined study. The reasons for this include the greater efficiency of an integrated approach at a university management level as well as the appeal of such integrated study to potential students.

Single honour Japanese studies degrees are still the most fundamental way to begin study about Japan and gain expertise as a Japan specialist, but recent trends suggest that this is not the only way to approach Japan today. The study of Japan can also be pursued within other disciplines such as politics, history or sociology. An interdisciplinary approach ensures that wider perspectives can be maintained and avoids a too limited approach to Japanese studies.

e) *Working with other organisations*

JF (London) will continue to work closely with other organizations in the UK interested in Japanese studies for example in co-organising seminars and workshops. JF aims to develop its funding programmes to focus on targets different from those of other funding bodies. It will continue to share information with other organisations and to collaborate in various ways to revitalise the Japanese studies community as a whole.

JF believes that the five points described above are key factors in developing the next generation of scholars in Japanese studies and in stabilising the future of Japanese studies in the UK. JF will try to reflect these principles in its grant programmes and its own events for the coming years.

24

The Japan Society and Japanese Studies in the UK

○

David Warren

THE JAPAN SOCIETY was founded in 1891, during the International Congress of Orientalists, following a resolution proposed by Arthur Diosy (1856–1923), one of the honorary secretaries of the Japanese Section of the Congress, to establish a society for the encouragement of Japanese studies and to bring together people interested in Japan. The Society's objectives were the 'encouragement of the study of the Japanese Language, Literature, History and Folk-Lore, of Japanese Art, Science and Industries, of the Social Life and Economic Condition of the Japanese People, past and present, and of all Japanese matters'.

The reference to the 'study' of Japan and things Japanese did not in that era specifically denote academic study. As the other essays in this volume indicate, there were very few opportunities in British academic institutions, until well after the Second World War, to engage in academic study of the Japanese language or of Japanese society – or, indeed, of the history and philosophy of Japan, other than as part of broader academic fields of study. There were of course Japanese students formally enrolled at British universities as early as the 1870s (earlier indeed, if we include the Chōshū and Satsuma pioneers, before the Meiji Restoration, in the 1860s). But the discrete study of Japan came later. The Japan Society, as it developed, was therefore able to play something of a role as a forum for public discussion of Japan, and for dissemination of relevant information – although on the whole to an audience of those already persuaded of the significance and value of a closer bilateral relationship between Britain and Japan – at a time when such activities were rare.

It is certainly the case that the Society, in its early years, attached importance to its status as a centre of learned enquiry about Japan. In August 1892, the honorary secretaries described the work of the Society as 'Encouragement of Research, Dissemination of Information and Stimulation of a Demand for Information [about Japan]'. A number of distinguished scholars were elected as honorary members, including a number active, then or later, at British and Japanese universities. The nucleus of a library was established, and the Society established its own 'museum' in the form of a 'Collection of such specimens of Japanese Works of Art and Industry, and of the Natural Products of Japan, as are not usually found in Public or Private Collections, and which may serve to illustrate various phases of Japanese life, Manners and Customs'. As Sir Hugh Cortazzi explains in his history of the Japan Society, to which this paper is indebted, there were no great treasures in this modest collection.[1]

The Society reflected the spirit of intellectual enquiry and educational proselytising that marked the late Victorian era. And from its inception, an important element in the Society's work has been a programme of regular lectures on all aspects of Japan. The first few years of the Society's activities saw lectures on 'Ju-Jitsu, the Ancient Art of Self-Defence by Sleight of Body', and 'The Uses of Bamboo in Japan', as well as Japanese crêpe printers, Japanese naturalistic art, mountaineering in Japan, Japanese railways, and other Japanese pastimes and amusements. The emphasis was on arts and crafts, but not exclusively – an 1895 lecture on 'Japanese Shipping' presented a more challenging analysis – for some members – of the longer-term threat posed to British imperial dominance by the acceleration of Japanese industrial strength. However, the Society remained actively involved in exhibitions, both of Japanese artefacts and more

---

[1]   Hugh Cortazzi, 'The Japan Society: a hundred-year history', in Hugh Cortazzi and Gordon Daniels, eds, *Britain and Japan 1859–1991: Themes and Personalities* (London: Routledge, 1991), pp. 1–53.

general art shows in which Japan could be included. It is difficult to assess how effectively the Society played its self-appointed role as a disseminator of Japanese art and culture. It covered a reasonably broad field of Japanalia, but the membership of the Society appears to have been drawn mainly from those whose interest in Japan had already been sparked by exposure through overseas diplomatic and commercial postings, or through travel. Moreover, the activities and ethos of the Society reflected as much the nurturing of high-level diplomatic and social relations between the British and Japanese elites as the development of a wider understanding of Japan as a field of study. This role grew in importance as Britain and Japan drew closer after the signing of the Anglo-Japanese Alliance in 1902. Perhaps partly in reaction to the admonition of the departing Japanese Ambassador, Hayashi Tadasu, to the *Daily Mail* in March 1906, that '[the Japanese] study English works far more than those of other European countries.... I wish that a similar desire were evinced on this side to know more of Japan's conditions and aspirations,' the Society joined a deputation to the Prime Minister, Sir Henry Campbell-Bannerman, later that year, urging more systematic consideration of Government grants for the teaching of Oriental languages (which of course included South as well as East Asian languages, and Arabic), in comparison with the much greater strength in depth of the German educational system. The initiative led eventually to the establishment of the School of Oriental and African Languages as part of London University in 1917. But Japanese, then as now, was a relatively small part of what was perceived as a wider problem.

The Society played a supportive role in 1910, when the Japan-British Exhibition was staged from May to October at White City, Shepherds Bush, West London, under the auspices of the Japanese Government, both as part of the planning process and in contributing its own display of objects designed to illustrate the growth of commercial relations between Britain and Japan. These began, according to the contemporaneous report in *The Times*, with documents relating to William Adams and his voyage to and residence in Japan in the early 1600s, but also suits of armour and relics associated with HMS *Beagle*, which had been purchased by the Japanese Government and had become a naval training ship. This event was indisputably the high-watermark of the process of raising the Japanese profile more generally in Britain during the period of the Alliance.

The Japan Society continued, before, during and after the First World War, to maintain an extensive programme of lectures and meetings. A number dealt with educational themes: the Dean of Peterhouse, Cambridge, spoke in 1905 on 'Japanese Undergraduates at Cambridge University', proposing that a chair of Japanese studies should be established there. As Sir Hugh notes in his history, it took another eighty years before this could happen, supported in the event by funds provided through the Japanese Keidanren (Federation of Economic Organisations). After the War, the Society's work to support art exhibitions also resumed – an exhibition of ukiyoe prints was staged in 1925, and scholarly lectures, many by figures of great distinction such as Marie Stopes and Arthur Waley, also featured in the Society's calendar of events. Even as relations between Britain and Japan deteriorated in the 1930s, the commitment of the Society to maintaining and strengthening cultural links in this way continued: a Japanese paper on 'The Foundation of Buddhist Culture in Japan' was read to the Society as late as May 1940. But although the Society remained a forum in which scholarship on Japan could be publicly shared, there was no direct activity by the Society in the interwar years that could be described as furthering the development of academic studies on Japanese themes.

When the Society, which had suspended its activities in 1942, was revived in 1949, the cultural and educational role weakened somewhat. A new constitution was adopted in 1958, and the first objective of the Society was now the 'promotion of mutual understanding and good feeling between the British and Japanese peoples'. The aim was more to support broader diplomatic objectives of facilitating Japan's re-entry to the commonwealth of nations after the trauma of the 1930s and 1940s, less to be a centre of, or at least a platform for, scholarly expertise on Japan and an organisation designed to encourage the study of the country. As political and diplomatic contacts resumed, the Society's role became defined more as a friendship organisation, hosting distinguished visitors from the Japanese Government and Imperial Family, and establishing or assisting with social networks to support the growing Japanese community in London. Lectures continued on a wide and imaginative range of historical and cultural subjects, but, in the words of Sir Hugh Cortazzi, 'the *Bulletin* in post-war years contained fewer contributions to scholarship in Japan'.

As the community of British scholars expert in Japan grew with the successful establishment of Japanese studies in a wide range of British universities described elsewhere in this volume, a number of distinguished academics became associated with the Society, either as lecturers or participants in the Society's other activities. The story of the expansion of Japanese studies is told more fully in those essays, and owes more to successive official reports on the importance of improving the nation's linguistic as well as international skills through more focussed higher education resources, particularly the Scarbrough Commission of 1947, the Hayter Report of 1960 and Sir Peter Parker's 1985 survey, 'Speaking for the Future: A Review of the Requirements of Diplomacy and Commerce for Asian and African Languages and Area Studies'. The Society revised its Constitution again in 1988, this time ensuring that the promotion of the study of Japan and its people 'in all its aspects, traditional and modern' was a primary objective, together with the need 'to make the results of that study more accessible to the general public'. The Society was associated with the Great Japan Exhibition at the Royal Academy in 1981, at which many art treasures never seen outside Japan were shown; and ten years later, when the Society celebrated its centenary, the Japan Festival was mounted, to reflect the increasingly important commercial and political relationship between Britain and Japan, but also in the year in which it would be possible to mark this important anniversary. The Japan Festival of 1991 was memorably wide-ranging. The Society was fully involved in its organisation, although it did not have the resources to run what eventually amounted to over 360 events, across the whole of the United Kingdom, many, such as the 'Visions of Japan' exhibition at the Victoria and Albert Museum and the Grand Sumo Tournament at the Albert Hall, mounted on a massive scale.

The aim of the Festival was to expose as many people as possible in some way to aspects of Japanese culture. There was a strong educational element in all of this and an important legacy of the Festival was the Education Trust (later Japan 21), which worked with British schools to raise awareness of Japan. With the merging of the Japan Society with Japan 21 in 2007, the Society took over responsibility for this activity, and for the 'Japan in Your Classroom' programme, which takes Japanese volunteers into schools in the UK, as well as running the 'Japan UK Live!' bilingual website and other activities to facilitate exchange between British and Japanese primary and secondary schools, and through which the Society provides training and teaching resources, as well as expert assistance.

In addition to its own *Proceedings*, in which the texts of many of the lectures and talks given to the Society are preserved, the Japan Society has since 1991 published a number of books. The *Britain and Japan: Biographical Portraits* series (ten volumes to date) is a unique record of the lives of distinguished Japanese and British politicians, diplomats, artists, writers, and other individuals who have played a part in the development of the relationship between Japan and Britain over the last 150 years. These essays – which now number over 550 – are a resource of great importance to historians looking at different aspects of what has been, and indeed remains, a relationship of great significance. The Society is now digitising much of its publications output to ensure that this resource can become publicly available.

As the Society enters its 125th year, its role as the leading independent organisation in the United Kingdom dedicated to the enhancement of the British-Japanese relationship remains strong, and its objectives remain to promote learning and advance education on Japan, to promote the study of Japan and its people in all their aspects, to promote the study of Britain and its culture by Japanese people and to further educational exchanges between Britain and Japan. The Society has over 1000 members and is strongly supported by many Japanese and some British corporate sponsors and donors. It has never been a political or lobbying organisation although it has made its views on the importance of educational opportunities and of increasing the scope of Japanese studies at both secondary and further education level known when appropriate. The scope of the Society's activity – lectures on cultural and educational themes, business and political talks, conversation groups for Japanese speakers, publications about Japan, schools outreach, and the provision of a supportive social network for the Japanese and Japanophile communities in the UK – has made a valuable contribution to the growth of the bilateral relationship over many years.

As other countries grow in relative economic power and political influence compared with Britain and Japan, there is a concern that the importance attached by both countries to what remain strong and friendly links might weaken. It would be bad if that were allowed to happen, and the continued provision of centres of excellence in the academic study of Japan in the UK is a crucial element in ensuring that it does not. The Japan Society's role in the growth of interest in Japanese studies over the past hundred or more years has been supportive rather than instrumental. But the Society was the organisation that represented this area of study and scholarship when there were virtually no other fora for the purpose. So it still has a role to play in working to sustain recognition of the importance of academic study as a basis for better mutual understanding.

25

Japanese Studies in the UK: The Role of the Japan Society for the Promotion of Science

O

Polly Watson

THE BEGINNINGS OF JSPS

THE JAPAN SOCIETY for the Promotion of Science (JSPS) was established in 1932, in response to calls for the promotion of academic activities, in order to support academic research. While government finances at that time were under severe pressure, the Emperor (Hirohito) donated a sum of 1.5 million Japanese yen for the promotion of arts and sciences. One of the main projects of JSPS in its early years was the provision of grants for individual research. These grants were awarded to research projects based on the original ideas of individual researchers, who were pioneers in their areas, and represented various research fields ranging from arts, humanities and social sciences to natural sciences, engineering and medicine. The spirit of JSPS as a non-profit, governmental organisation to support bottom-up curiosity-driven research without setting priority areas has been maintained and JSPS has consistently been Japan's core institution for supporting basic scientific research.

ESTABLISHMENT OF JSPS IN LONDON

In the 1960s, JSPS greatly expanded and developed its ability to strengthen its international credibility and to work closely with government policies related to science. Based on the success of the visiting research associate programme that began in 1960, JSPS established some programmes to involve researchers from outside Japan. Since there were no programmes at that time inviting foreign researchers to Japan, JSPS's new programmes constituted a landmark in promoting international academic exchange. In 1963, the Japan-US joint research programme (a bilateral programme with the USA) was launched. In the 1970s the JSPS concluded agreements with The Royal Society and the British Academy to promote Japanese science in the UK. The Royal Society and the British Academy have since then acted as nominating authorities for JSPS bilateral programmes and fellowships and have undertaken the entire selection process with the aim of sending high calibre researchers from the UK to Japan to carry out collaborative research activities.

In 1994, JSPS Tokyo headquarters decided that a JSPS London office should be opened to promote knowledge in the UK of Japan's scientific research strengths and forge a greater level of exchanges between the UK and Japan in the natural sciences as well as in the humanities and social sciences. JSPS London was also tasked with distributing information on JSPS activities to local researchers and organizations, as well as gathering information and reporting to the Ministry of Education (known as MEXT) on scientific trends in the UK.

In 2014, JSPS London celebrated its twentieth anniversary. During the twenty years since its establishment here it has played a key role in the administration of an increasing number of scientific and academic programmes and has supported the reform and internationalisation of Japanese universities. The 'Super Global Programme' involving thirty universities in Japan was launched in 2014 with the aim of promoting Japanese universities to the world's highest level and improving the standard of research and education in Japan. JSPS London has been given the task of supporting the Japanese universities selected to pursue their internationalisation activities in the UK. In addition, JSPS London promotes this programme as a way of offering funding opportunities for UK academics wishing to carry out research in Japan.

In the past twenty years, over 2,000 researchers from the UK have visited Japan, and nearly 3,000 Japanese researchers have come to the UK, to participate in JSPS programmes and joint activities. The UK is currently the second most popular destination for Japanese researchers in Europe after Germany.

INTERNATIONAL COLLABORATIVE PROGRAMMES

In the past decade especially, JSPS has placed special emphasis on building and expanding international networks through each of its current eight overseas offices. Advancement of international collaboration has been achieved on three levels – the individual, the group and the institution. Every year JSPS London staff visit between ten and fifteen universities and research institutes across the UK and Ireland to promote JSPS and its funding schemes and to advise researchers on how to begin or develop their collaboration with Japan. They also ask alumni to talk about their research experiences as JSPS fellows. JSPS's international programmes are designed mainly to support researchers based in Japan, but by learning about their experiences, new possibilities for collaboration often become clear.

INSTITUTIONAL/MULTILATERAL

Two JSPS international programmes operate on an institutional level to promote multilateral collaboration. Firstly the 'Programme for Advancing Strategic International Networks to Accelerate the Circulation of Talented Researchers' funds a two-way exchange of researchers both by sending early-career Japanese researchers overseas and by inviting overseas researchers to Japan. The aim of this programme is to build networks for international collaboration. Funding is at a level of thirty million Japanese yen per year for a project of one to three years. This programme started in April 2014 and UK institutions have not yet become involved.

The second JSPS programme, which operates on an institutional level to promote multilateral collaboration, is called the 'Core-to-Core Programme'. This programme for Japanese universities aims to facilitate multilateral research collaboration between institutions internationally and supports the connection of research hubs in Japan with those in countries around the world in cutting-edge research areas. The aim is to form sustained collaborative relationships and establish world-class centres, which will create research cores and foster early career researchers of the next generation. JSPS provides support to the Japan side of up to twenty million yen per year for a maximum of five years. These funds can be used to cover international and domestic travel expenses, costs for attending and holding conferences, exchanges of scientists and project-related research expenses of the researchers based in Japan only. Collaborators in partnering countries are required to get matching funds from funding agencies in their respective countries to cover such costs involved in their participation in the project. Up to 2015, out of a total of 110 projects supported by this programme, thirty-nine have involved research hubs in the UK.

To encourage more multilateral collaboration in the social sciences, JSPS in 2014 became an associate partner of a programme called the 'Open Research Area for the social sciences'. This programme is led by research councils in Europe, namely the the French National Research Agency (ANR), the German Research Foundation (DFG), the Netherlands Scientific Research Organization (NOW), and the UK's Economic and Social Research Council (ESRC) which have concluded framework agreements. Through its involvement in supporting Japanese researchers taking part in this programme, JSPS aims to foster a wide variety of researchers in the social sciences who can play an active role in tackling pressing problems facing humanity. It emphasises, in particular, participation by young researchers.

GROUP/ BILATERAL

On a group level JSPS operates the 'Open Partnership Scheme'. Under this scheme, support is provided for joint projects carried out by research teams in Japan and a counterpart country based on a one to two year research project or on a small-scale seminar.

Up to 2.5 million yen per fiscal year is provided by JSPS to the Japanese side for projects that last up to two years or for a small-scale seminar organised by either side for a period of one week. This support from JSPS is to provide funds to enable Japanese researchers to attend and for direct research-related costs.

Counterpart countries are expected but not required to secure matching funds from funding sources in their own country to cover costs for their participation in the project or seminar. If the counterpart country cannot provide matching funds but are willing to host the Japanese researchers and can provide in-kind contributions such as venue, teaching supervision and data and equipment sharing, JSPS will take this into account.

Since the programme started in 2005, JSPS has made ninety-one awards for bilateral projects involving the UK, which includes a joint seminar agreement between JSPS and the ESRC that ran from 2010 to 2012.

INDIVIDUAL AWARDS

JSPS awards around one thousand fellowships each year to enable international researchers to experience Japan's world-class research facilities and work alongside leading Japanese academics. The current international fellowship system began in 2000, and includes fellowships for researchers at all stages of their career and in all research fields. Stays can be long or short, and researchers can be awarded repeat fellowships. Researchers are fully funded with allowances for subsistence and additional research-related costs. JSPS also provides welfare support, including Japanese-language training. These fellowships include a postgraduate level summer programme, a short and standard (longer term) postdoctoral fellowships, long and short 'invitation fellowships' for mid-career scientists, and a 'special invitation' fellowship for senior researchers. The level of funding between fellowships varies but will include a return airfare, maintenance allowance and health insurance.

Each type of fellowship is designed to provide UK researchers with first-hand experiences of the research and living environment in Japan, whilst expanding academic exchange between the two countries. These fellowships are a stepping-stone to involvement in our group and institutional level projects to support UK-Japan research projects over a longer term.

Applications for most JSPS fellowships should be made to JSPS Tokyo via a host in Japan. The exceptions are the summer programme and the postdoctoral fellowships. The summer programme is only open to some nationalities. UK applicants can apply directly to the British Council in Tokyo. In addition to an application to JSPS Tokyo, for the short-term postdoctoral fellowship, UK applicants can also make an application directly to JSPS London and apply for the standard type of postdoctoral fellowship; UK applicants can apply directly to The Royal Society or the British Academy, depending on their research field.

More information about all of these funding opportunities can be found on the JSPS London website: http://www.jsps.org/funding/index.html. On this website there are also case studies from those who have benefitted from JSPS international programme funding; these explain about their research experiences in Japan, how the collaboration started, how they benefitted from being involved in the programme and collaborative developments since the project's completion.

FINDING A HOST IN JAPAN

As well promoting its funding opportunities, JSPS London offers forums for UK researchers to find a host in Japan or develop a network. The JSPS London website provides a link to the 'ReaD & Researchmap' system and JARC-Net. Both are comprehensive databases for research and development activities, and information about Japanese researchers in universities and institutions. From here the researcher can start a fundamental search to find scholars in Japan in a similar research area and can make contact with them. The majority of scientists listed have experience of collaborating with overseas researchers.

JSPS PROGRAMMES FOR INVITING JAPANESE RESEARCHERS TO THE UK

For the future of science in Japan, to encourage a rich international viewpoint and to foster a generation of talented researchers, there are two fellowship programmes for early-career Japanese researchers to allow them to work at a research institution in the UK for up to 2 years. They are called 'The Research Fellowship for Young Scientists and Postdoctoral Fellowship for Research Abroad'. Both fellowships provide travel expenses, a stipend and a research grant. More information can be found on the JSPS London website: http://www.jsps.org/scheme/scheme.html. Every year about fifty researchers from Japan are engaged in research in the UK under these programmes. These researchers are also encouraged to join the network managed by JSPS London for 'Japanese Researchers Based in the UK' (JBUK). JBUK allows Japanese researchers to develop their professional networks and obtain practical support to help them get the most out of their research and living experience in the UK and provides a forum for exchanges of information. There is also a symposium scheme for JBUK members to organise UK-Japan academic events.

THE JSPS ALUMNI ASSOCIATION OF THE UK AND IRELAND

Former beneficiaries of any type of JSPS international funding programme who are based in the UK or the Republic of Ireland are encouraged to join the 'Alumni Association' managed by JSPS London. Membership is free. This association was established in 1994 and membership currently stands at over 550. The association consists of an executive committee representing different regions within the UK and the Republic of Ireland to help with and act as a focal point for alumni activities. Alumni are encouraged to become involved with the committee so that they can help to shape the future direction of the association.

The association offers a number of funding schemes exclusive to members. The JSPS London office was the first overseas office to devise a re-visitation grant to Japan for JSPS alumni in order to create and expand academic links. This was called the FURU-SATO Award. A total of 41 such awards worth £2,000 each were made between 2009 and 2013. This award was superseded by the BRIDGE Fellowship under which since 2010 twenty-three awards worth £8,000 each have been made

There is also a symposium scheme to allow alumni to organise UK-Japan academic conferences with a phase 2 element as follow-on events to build on these achievements. JSPS London supports five large-scale symposia annually under this scheme to stimulate scientific partnerships between Japanese and British scientists. The scheme started in 2010 and since then JSPS London has made nine awards worth £30,000 each to its alumni.

In all, over £500,000 has been awarded since the inception of these schemes. The aim of the alumni association is to build on these achievements and maintain academic links with Japan.

Other benefits for members of the alumni association include networking events that are organised throughout the year at well-known venues across the UK. Members are also encouraged to advertise their academic accomplishments linked to Japan on the alumni association website. There is also a help forum for JSPS fellows and alumni to communicate with one other to solve issues regarding research activities and living in Japan.

FUTURE MISSION

JSPS London Office will continue to encourage and facilitate scientific and academic collaboration between Japanese and UK researchers and also hopes to broaden its activities to include other countries in the near future.

***

APPENDIX

Approximately 10% of fellowships in Japanese studies progress to the JSPS group level bilateral funding scheme for 1 to 2-year projects or a 1-week seminar. Themes and institutions involved in the UK in JSPS projects include:
Japanese Economy at the School of East Asian Studies, University of Manchester.

Japanese International Relations, Security Policy, Diplomatic History, Legal and Political Philosophy at the School of East Asian Studies, University of Sheffield and University of Manchester and Politics and International Relations Departments at the Universities of Oxford, Cambridge, Essex, Warwick, Aberdeen and Coventry.

Rural development at the School of Agriculture, Food and Rural Development, University of Newcastle, and School of Social Policy, University of Birmingham.

Sociology and Anthropology at the Department of Sociology and Anthropology, Universities of Exeter, Manchester, Oxford and SOAS.

Japanese film and Literature at the Centre for Media and Cultures at Birkbeck College and Royal Holloway, University of London, the Department of Japan and Korea at SOAS and the School of Modern Languages and Cultures, University of Leeds.

History of Modern Japan at the Department of History, Universities of Oxford, Edinburgh and Manchester.

Japanese Art and Archaeology, Departments of Art History at SOAS and the University of East Anglia.

The Sainsbury Institute for the Study of Japanese Arts and Cultures

O

Nicole Coolidge Rousmaniere

IN 1998, SIR Robert and Lady Sainsbury, long devotes of Japanese art, decided to sell Amadeo Modigliani's 'Portrait of Baranowski', the commemorative wedding present they had given each other, in order to create an institute dedicated to Japanese art studies in Norwich. This visionary gift was meant to build on their earlier gift to the Norwich community, the Sainsbury Centre for Visual Arts, which they had previously endowed at the University of East Anglia. The Sainsbury Institute for the Study of Japanese Arts and Cultures (SISJAC) was registered as a charity in 1999. In endowing this institute the Sainsburys particularly wished to promote the wider dissemination of knowledge and understanding of Japanese art and culture, and to this end they appointed Dr Nicole Rousmaniere to be the founding director. Nicole Rousmaniere is now also Professor of Japanese Art and Culture at the University of East Anglia but when she was a lecturer at the University she developed a close relationship with the Sainsburys based on their mutual love of early Japanese art. With her appointment and with the guidance as a Trustee of Dame Elizabeth Esteve-Coll, former Director of the Victoria and Albert Museum and Vice-Chancellor of the University of East Anglia, the Institute was launched in 1999.

Since its inception, the Institute has expanded both its base of trustees and its affiliations with its main institutional partners, the University of East Anglia (UEA), the School of Oriental and African Studies (SOAS) and the British Museum in London. At present, the Sainsbury Institute has become a vital part of a much larger scholarly network and its activities have flourished as well. The Sainsbury Institute organises an extensive programme of research activities, fellowships, public lectures and international workshops.

Recent activities of the Institute include a workshop on 'Radio Carbon Dating in Japanese Archaeology', a symposium on 'Deconstructing Boundaries: Is "East Asian Art History" possible?' and the lecture series 'Tokyo Futures, 1868–2020'. The Institute disseminates the results of these research activities in a variety of ways, including through its website (www.sainsbury-institute.org), an annual report and an e-magazine available on line. There have also been a number of publications that have resulted from research carried out by fellows and others associated with SISJAC, such as Dr Christine Guth's *Hokusai's Great Wave* (University of Hawai'i Press, 2015), Dr John Szoztack's *Painting Circles: Tsuchida Bakusen and Nihonga Collectives in Early Twentieth-century Japan* (Brill, 2013), and Dr Gennifer Weisenfeld's *Imaging Disaster: Tokyo and the Visual Culture of Japan's Great Earthquake of 1923* (University of California Press, 2012). SISJAC has also joined with the Japan Society to publish several books by Sir Hugh Cortazzi on Japanese art and culture: *Japan in the Late Victorian London: The Japanese Village in Knightsbridge and the Mikado, 1885* (2009), *Images of Japan 1885–1912: Scenes, Tales and Flowers* (2011), and *A Miscellany of Japanese Sketch Books and Print Albums (1840–1908)* (2013). In addition, the Institute promotes outreach and educational activities mostly within the United Kingdom and Japan. The intensive outreach and continually evolving scholarship has served to promote the Sainsbury Institute for the Study of Japanese Arts and Cultures as an internationally recognised centre well beyond its East Anglian base.

Professor Nicole Rousmaniere served as founding director from 1999 to 2010. The present Executive Director of the Institute is Mizutori Mami. In addition, there are currently two permanent senior academic staff members: Dr Simon Kaner, who works on the archaeology of Japan, and Professor Nicole Rousmaniere, who works on ceramics and East Asian trade networks. They are partially seconded to the University of East Anglia and to the British Museum, respectively.

An integral part of the Institute is the Lisa Sainsbury Library. The Library's collections focus on the arts and archaeology of the Japanese archipelago and Japan's relations with Europe, and the materials are shared with scholars and students throughout Europe. In addition, the Library holds Sir Hugh and Lady Cortazzi's unique collection of historical maps of Japan as well as other primary source material. The Institute's Lisa Sainsbury Librarian, Hirano Akira, maintains the collections while mentoring Institute Fellows and helping associates with their research projects. Hirano Akira also acts as Honorary Librarian to the Japanese Section, Department of Asia at the British Museum. The library has substantial holdings in books and journals focussing on Japanese arts, archaeology and cultures both in English and Japanese totalling over 30,000 volumes. Funding for the library both financially and through donations of volumes has come from multiple sources, some institutional but also private individuals. Particular mention should be made of Professor Sir Raymond Firth, Professor Matsushima Ken, Professor Matsushita Masaaki, Professor Kawai Masatomo, Professor Kano Hiroyuki, and Sir Hugh and Lady Cortazzi, all of whom have made significant donations to the Lisa Sainsbury Library and have thus helped to create one of the most comprehensive collections of Japanese art research material in Europe.

Apart from the library staff, three full-time and two part-time staff members help to maintain the Institute's programmes and physical plant. In addition there are a number of postgraduate fellows in the Institute at any one point. The main fellowship programme is the Robert and Lisa Sainsbury Fellowships for postgraduate research and publication projects. Other fellowships include the Handa Fellowship in Japanese Archaeology, the Sotheby's Senior Scholar and the Fellowship for Japanese Studies Young Scholars. The Fellowship programme has been in place since 2001 and since then fifty fellows have benefitted from the various fellowship programmes. Visiting research fellows play an integral part in the research culture of the Sainsbury Institute and its partner institutions. While working on their own publication and research projects, they contribute to seminars and conferences in the UK and elsewhere in Europe. The Sainsbury Institute's two principal fellowship programmes are designed to encourage scholars in the fields of Japanese art and archaeology to complete a substantive piece of research. The Robert and Lisa Sainsbury Fellows for the academic year starting in 2015 are Dr Radu Leca (SOAS), who is focusing on the late-seventeenth-century impact of representations of the vernacular experience of space in Japan as expressed by the concept of the spatial imaginary, Seung Yeon Sang (Boston University), who is concentrating on the Japanese practice of appreciating and collecting ceramics in *chanoyu*, and Dr Tsuchikane Yasuko (Cooper Union, NYC), whose current focus is the interdisciplinary examination of art history and religious studies of the parties dedicated to the production and reception of modern art in historical Buddhist temples. All fellows are chosen through a competitive process that involves an external examiner and participation from members of various academic communities in the UK.

The Institute's activities as well as the library holdings are all digitalised. The Lisa Sainsbury Library has catalogued the holdings both in Japanese and English and they are accessible through the Institute's website, along with a database of prints and maps donated by Sir Hugh and Lady Cortazzi. The high-resolution digital database of these works, which date from the sixteenth century onwards, was created by the Art Research Center, Ritsumeikan University, in Kyoto. This database was one of the Art Research Center's initial international projects. The relationship has since grown and Ritsumeikan University has a close relationship not only with the Institute but also the University of East Anglia, a telling example of the Sainsbury Institute's reputation.

In the diplomatic sphere, the government of Japan has recognised the achievements of the Sainsbury Institute. For her services to Japanese art over a long period of time, Lady Sainsbury was awarded the Order of the Rising Sun with Neck Ribbon from the Japanese government in 2003. The Sainsbury Institute's most active Trustee, Dame Elizabeth Esteve-Coll, was also awarded the same honour in 2005 for her services to Japan and the promotion of the understanding of Japanese art. In 2011, Nicole Rousmaniere was awarded a Japanese Foreign Minister's Commendation.

The Institute is currently overseen by a set of Trustees working closely with the University of East Anglia and is run by a Management Board, both of which are chaired by the Vice-Chancellor of the University of East Anglia, at present Professor David Richardson. There are eight members of the Management Board, including Professor Kawai Masatomo, Director of the Chiba City Art Museum, and Baroness Amos, the Director of SOAS, and there are also a number of participating observers as well.

A Trust Deed governs the funding of the Institute. The Trustees have the responsibility for investing the original Trust Fund and applying the income to support the costs of running of the Institute in accordance with the provisions of the Trust Deed. The Management Board acts as the governing body of the Institute, overseeing the nature of its activities and approving its budget and staffing.[1] The income from their original endowment, together with generous annual grants from the Gatsby Charitable Foundation (established by Lord Sainsbury of Turville), provides the greater part of the Institute's funding. The Institute raises funds from other sources to support workshops, publications, lectures and other projects. It also receives non-financial donations, especially library materials and other support in kind.

To help deliver its remit of dissemination and outreach both in the United Kingdom and in Japan, the Sainsbury Institute holds three annual named lecture series, which are separately funded. These are the Toshiba Lectures in Japanese Art and Science, the Carmen Blacker Lecture Series held in London and Norwich, and the Ishibashi Foundation Lecture Series held in Japan. In addition, there is the popular monthly Third Thursday Lecture Series, which started soon after the Institute was founded at the suggestion of Professor Kano Hiroyuki of Doshisha University. Quite unexpectedly, this programme has made the Institute a significant part of the cultural scene in Norwich. The Third Thursday Lectures are held in the Hostry of the Cathedral Close in

---

1   *Annual Report 2012–3, Sainsbury Institute for the Study of Japanese Arts and Cultures* (Dorchester: Henry Ling Ltd, 2014), 30.

Norwich next to the Institute, and nearly 180 of them have been held so far. They are supported by the Great Britain Sasakawa Foundation and Yakult UK Ltd along with the Robert and Lisa Sainsbury Trust.

The Institute also houses the Centre for Archaeology and Heritage headed by Dr Simon Kaner. The Centre for Archaeology and Heritage at the Sainsbury Institute develops projects to realise the potential of Japanese archaeological and artistic heritage, engaging students and researchers from Japan, Europe and elsewhere, and leading a consortium of European universities and other research partners interested in Japanese archaeology and heritage studies. Current research projects include a major new survey of Japanese archaeology and studies of the response to disasters and their impact on cultural heritage.[2] Other projects currently being undertaken by the Centre for Archaeology and Heritage include the Archaeology of Ritual and Religion, the Origins of Agriculture in Japan and the Shinano-Chikuma River Project.

The Sainsbury Institute currently has joint research and project cooperation agreements with the British Museum and the School of Oriental and African Studies in the United Kingdom, with Ritsumeikan University's Art Research Center in Kyoto, and with the Centres of Excellence in Kokugakuin University for Jōmon studies and in Kyushu University for international archaeology, as well as an agreement of cooperation with Niigata Prefectural History Museum. In addition, the Sainsbury Institute has active research agreements and conducts collaborative research projects with the British Museum, the Centre Européen d'Etudes Japonaises d'Alsace and the Museum of Asian Art, Corfu, in Europe and Kokugakuin University, Kyushu University, Nagawamachi, Nara National Research Institute for Cultural Properties, Niigata Prefectural Museum of History, Research Institute for Humanity and Nature, Ritsumeikan University, Tohoku University, School of Humanities in Tokyo University and the National Research Institute for Cultural Properties, Tokyo, in Japan. These agreements involve members of the Institute and its affiliates, Fellows

---

2   Sainsbury Institute for the Study of Arts and Cultures website, http://sainsbury-institute.org/research/centre-for-archaeology-and-heritage/ accessed 1 December 2015.

and associated visiting scholars travelling between Europe and Japan to complete specific projects and disseminate the results of the research conducted. A recent innovative project that is now in its sixth year is based around the William Gowland Collection of Kofun archaeological material that is housed in the British Museum with some additional materials held by the Society for Antiquaries, London. This collaborative international research project involves a number of Kansai-based specialists from Japanese universities, museums and archaeological institutes working at the British Museum with SISJAC and UEA affiliated staff and students. A major NHK one-hour long film, multiple publications, seminars and workshops and an AHRC British Museum-UEA collaborative doctoral award all testify to the efficacy of the powerful network and the spirit of collaboration that is at the core of the Sainsbury Institute.

The relationship with SOAS has always been fundamental to the Sainsbury Institute. In the early years of the Institute, Professor Timon Screech of the Department of the History of Art and Archaeology at SOAS contributed significantly to forming its mission and its London base. Subsequently, Dr John Carpenter, who at the time was teaching at SOAS but is now at the Metropolitan Museum of Art in New York, worked closely with the Institute and helped develop and mentor its Fellowship, publication and academic programmes. The relationship with SOAS continues to evolve as the Institute looks towards teaching provision at UEA.

The Norwich base of the Sainsbury Institute is a Georgian building at 64 The Close, adjacent to Norwich Cathedral. This was originally part of the twelfth-century Cathedral and has generous proportions, harmonious with a specialist Japanese arts and cultures library. On the 20th anniversary of its creation, the Sainsbury Institute for the Study of Japanese Arts and Cultures will relocate to the campus of the University of East Anglia and embark on a new phase of its development, one that is focussed on teaching and nurturing the next generation of scholars working on Japanese art, material and popular culture and archaeology.

The Institute's founders have both passed away. Sir Robert died on 2 April 2000 and Lady Sainsbury died on 6 February 2014 at the age of 101. Lady Sainsbury always took an active interest in the Institute and was a regular visitor. She was always proud that the Institute she created along with her husband had become a vital organisation within Norwich and the United Kingdom, as well as Europe and Asia. Her comments were as acute as her passion for the Institute was sincere. It is certainly fitting that the space which houses the Institute's research collections, to which she was the major donor, will continue to bear her name. The Institute is in fact a tribute to Sir Robert's and Lady Sainsbury's ideals. The acorn they planted in 1998 has grown into an impressive oak.

The Tanaka Fund and its Impact on Japanese Studies Library Collections in the UK through the JFEC and the JLG Cooperative Acquisitions Scheme

○

Gill Goddard

IN 1973, THE then Prime Ministers of Japan and Great Britain, Tanaka Kakuei and Edward Heath, released a joint communiqué announcing, *inter alia*, the donation by the Japanese government of the considerable sum of 300 million yen (then £455,000), for the promotion of Japanese studies in UK universities. The donation was to be made through endowment via the Japan Foundation and to be administered in the UK by the Japan Foundation Endowment Committee (JFEC), which was established for this purpose in 1974 under the auspices of the University Grants Committee (UGC).[1]

Membership of the JFEC was drawn from the UK Japanese studies community, under an independent chair elected by the University Grants Committee (UGC). Although the JFEC is now

---

[1] This chapter is based on the following sources: Yu-ying Brown, 'The Japan Library Group in the U.K.', *Japan Forum*, 5 (1993), pp.257–261; W. Hayter, *Oxford Review of Education* 1.2 (1975), pp.169–172; Japan Foundation Endowment Committee, *A Review of the First Twenty-five Years, 1974–1999* (Sheffield: JFEC, 1999); P. W. Carnell, *Check-list of Japanese Periodicals Held in British University and Research Libraries* (Sheffield: Sheffield University Library, 1976–1978; Japan Library Group, *Minutes*.

based in the offices of the British Association for Japanese Studies (BAJS) at the University of Essex, the original host institution, the University of Sheffield, continues to provide financial administration.

Amongst the many benefits to the UK Japanese studies field which flowed from the establishment of the Japan Foundation Endowment Committee was support for the UK Japan Library Group's Co-operative Acquisitions Scheme. In many ways it was, ultimately, as with many other initiatives, to become a victim of the success of the Japan Foundation's original aim to promote knowledge about Japan in other countries through cultural exchange and education. What follows is the story of the Cooperative Acquisitions Scheme, based on notes and correspondence between the Japan Foundation Endowment Committee and Japan Library Group (JLG).

When the JFEC was set up, the Japan Library Group was already at work, founded in 1966 by what were then the four main academic centres of Japanese Studies (Cambridge, SOAS, Oxford and Sheffield) and the British Museum Library and the National Lending Library (later merged within the British Library), with the aim of providing co-ordinated library support through the sharing of resources and expertise.

The first major achievement of the group was the publication of a checklist of Japanese language serials held in the UK, an invaluable resource in those pre-electronic days, and this led to the successful identification of gaps in the holdings, and the amalgamation of title runs by donations between member libraries, a process that is still relevant though somewhat less so with the gradually developing availability of digital versions of journals. The various editions of the *Check-list of Japanese Periodicals Held in British University and Research Libraries* were edited at Sheffield by Peter Carnell, and were published and distributed with the financial support of the JFEC.

Following on from the success of the serials project, the members of JLG turned their attention back to the more problematic area of how to provide the UK academic community with the broadest possible range of Japanese language material in monograph form across the full range of subjects. Initial JLG discussions as to the desirability of a co-operative purchasing scheme for monograph acquisition had taken place as early as 1968, but the limited and varying budgets of the individual member libraries, coupled with falling exchange rates, rising book prices, and rapid growth in the Japanese book trade output all conspired to make it impossible to acquire all academically desirable titles, including the growing body of important reprint material.

It was not until the JF's endowment scheme was announced in 1973/1974 that the group could see a way forward. JLG members re-examined their current situation, and prepared a proposal to put to the JFEC, with the aim of meeting the need to provide access to current Japanese scholarship for the students and researchers of the UK academic community.

The scheme they devised was based on the principle that each library should concentrate its acquisitions in the specific subject areas which corresponded with the areas of academic interest of their institution. Thus the Bodleian and Oriental Institute Libraries at Oxford would concentrate their purchasing and collection within the areas of religion, philosophy, art, and archaeology and history up to the end of the Tokugawa era, Sheffield University would focus on the modern social sciences of economics, politics, sociology, education, agriculture and trade plus modern history from Meiji onwards, SOAS would focus on language, modern literature, law, folklore and geography, and the British Library Oriental and India Office Collections on general and reference works plus pre-modern history and literature. The University of Cambridge is notably absent from the list, only opting in later when sufficient funds became available. The proposal was for a two-stage scheme: the participating libraries would use their existing library funding to purchase new publications as far as that funding would allow, whilst important material not thus purchased would be requested for purchase through bids to the JFEC. The intention of the scheme was to maximise the value of existing funding at the individual institutions by reducing unnecessary and expensive duplication of material, whilst encouraging the development of broad subject specialist coverage at particular institutions, that material being available to all via the Inter-Library Loans system.

In order to streamline the process, members of the group were all required to mark up their copies of the same catalogue of new publications. For this purpose, the quarterly New Editions News (NEN) issued by Gannando Overseas Inc. was chosen as offering the most complete selection of academically valuable titles available. Twice a year, Japan Library group members met to go through the lists, coordinate and de-duplicate titles, and then to identify what titles amongst the remainder should be requested from the JFEC, and by which library. On approval by the JFEC, purchase orders were then sent to Gannando, and on receipt of the titles, the accompanying invoices were sent to the JFEC at Sheffield for payment, utilising a proportion of the annual income from the capital investment. For a few heady years between 1975 and 1992, virtually every newly published title of significance to Japanese studies was acquired by one or other of the member libraries.

Together with the undergraduate study tour, the Cooperative Acquisition Scheme was at the heart of the JFEC's programme of support for Japanese studies in the UK until the early 1990s. Between 1975 and 1992, the JFEC awarded approximately £470,000 to the study tour scheme, and in the same period allocated nearly £180,000 to library support.

The JFEC also provided grants to individual libraries, outside the auspices of the JLG, enabling the enhancement of collections through requests for specific titles such as reference materials and major sets beyond the reach of their own budgets. Together with the JLG scheme, the JFEC provided funding support to UK libraries of some £267,000, approx. 16% of their total outgoings.

However, even by the late 1970s/early 1980s, not only was inflation and the falling exchange rate putting pressure on the JFEC, but other demands on the JFEC's resources were also growing as interest in Japanese studies grew and new courses and new programmes at other universities created extra demands. It became inevitable that the scale of support could not be maintained across the board. It was recognised that allocating funding support to the libraries of only four UK institutions (five from 1991/1992) was increasingly seen as being unfair to the libraries of the newer Japanese Studies centres. The demands of the latter were of course different from those of the established collections, and ultimately there was simply too little to share usefully between the larger number of institutions and students. Following a series of reviews of its support for Japanese studies in the UK, the JFEC reluctantly withdrew its support for the JLG's Cooperative Acquisitions Scheme. Member libraries have subsequently relied for purchasing power on their share of individual institutional resources, and in some cases the impact has been a return to *ad hoc* reader-request-led purchase policies, rather than broad coverage of new publications on their institution's subject specialist areas.

The JFEC's support has since 1992 concentrated on individual academic research projects, and library support has been achieved by approving research-led purchases for individual researchers. Materials thus acquired for particular subject-specific projects should, according to the JFEC, be placed in the appropriate institutional library for general use and available to all via the Inter-Library Loan system, on completion of the research project. It is regrettable that this principle is interpreted in a way that is not necessarily to the advantage of national collection building. However, it is in part being balanced by the gradual development of freely available online resources, particularly in certain fields such as science and technology, but also in pre-modern literature and history.

As the Cooperative Acquisitions Scheme began to wind down in the late 1980s and early 1990s, the UK Japan Library Group began to concentrate its efforts on online catalogue developments for Japanese language collections, at a time when UK library management systems were in their infancy, and university IT systems certainly could not cope with foreign scripts. With the cooperation and generous support of Japan's principal academic information network, NACSIS (later NII), and vital financial support from the Daiwa Anglo-Japanese Foundation and other donor bodies, JLG has developed both a collaborative cataloguing system and an online catalogue of Japanese language material available in the UK.

This chapter is not the place for the full story of the ultimate establishment of the UK (later European) Union Catalogue of Japanese Materials, but it is thanks to the continuing efforts of Japan Library Group members that current students, librarians and researchers can today easily locate Japanese-language material which may be of relevance to their studies.

Bibliography

Bownas, Geoffrey, 'From Japanology to Japanese studies', inaugural lecture, University of Sheffield, 14 December 1966, p. 6. The lecture is reprinted in Bownas, *Japanese Journeys: Writings and Recollections* (Folkestone: Global Oriental, 2005), pp. 228–246.

Britain and Japan: Biographical Portraits: ten volumes of biographies of men and women from Japan and Britain who have in some way or other been involved in Anglo-Japanese relations. The first and second volumes were edited by Ian Nish, vol. III by James Hoare and the remainder by Hugh Cortazzi (1994–2016).

Cortazzi, Hugh, *British Envoys in Japan, 1859–1972* (Folkestone: Global Oriental, 2004).

Cortazzi, Hugh, *Japan Experiences: Fifty Years, One Hundred Views: Post-war Japan Through British Eyes 1945–2000* (Richmond, Surrey: Japan Library 2001).

Cortazzi, Hugh, and Gordon Daniels, eds, *Britain and Japan 1859–1991: Themes and Personalities* (London: Routledge, 1991)

Cortazzi, Hugh, 'The Japan Society: a hundred-year history', in Cortazzi and Gordon Daniels, eds, *Britain and Japan 1859–1991: Themes and Personalities* (London: Routledge, 1991), pp. 1–53.

Daniels, Frank J., *Japanese Studies in the University of London and Elsewhere: an Inaugural Lecture Delivered on 7 November 1962* (London: School of Oriental and African Studies, University of London, 1963);

Kenrick, Douglas Moore, 'A century of Western studies of Japan: the first hundred years of the Asiatic Society of Japan 1872–1972', *Transactions of the Asiatic Society of Japan (TASJ)*, Third Series, vol. 14 (1978).

Koyama Noboru, *Japanese Students at Cambridge University in the Meiji Era, 1868–1912: Pioneers for the Modernization of Japan*, trans. by Ian Ruxton (Morrisville, NC : Lulu [2004]).

Nish, Ian, 'The growth of Japanese studies in Britain', *Hosei Occasional Papers* 6 (1989), pp. 1–12.

Nish, Ian, 'Introducing Japanese studies in Britain', in J. W. M. Chapman, ed., *European Association for Japanese Studies 1973–88* (Ripe, E. Sussex : Saltire House Publications Society, 1988), pp. 52–57.

Nish, Ian, 'Japanese Studies in Britain', in Yu-ying Brown (ed.), *Japanese Studies* (London: British Library, 1990).

Report of the Committee Appointed by the Lords Commissioners of His Majesty's Treasury to Consider the Organisation of Oriental Studies in London (London: HMSO, 1909). [Reay report].

Report of the the Interdepartmental Commission of Enquiry on Oriental, Slavonic, East European and African Studies (London: His Majesty's Stationery Office, 1947) [Scarbrough report].

Report of the the Sub-Committee on Oriental, Slavonic, East European and African Studies (London: Her Majesty's Stationery Office, 1961) [Hayter report].

Speaking for the Future: A Review of the Requirements of Diplomacy and Commerce for Asian and African languages and Area Studies (1986) [Parker report].

Index

Abe Shinzō, Prime Minister xi
Adams, William 4, 149, 280
Adolphson, Mikael 84
Agonshū 206
AHRC: *see* Arts and Humanities
    Research Council
Akroyd, R. 241
Alcock, Sir Rutherford 5, 54, 58, 61
Aldous, Chris 241–242
Allen, George Cyril xxvii, 50, 177,
    201–202
Allen, Louis xxvii, 21, 94, 96,
    194, 241
Amos, Baroness 298
Ampiah, Kweku 113
Anai Suzuko 169, 171
Anderson, HMS 17
Anderson, Frederick 208
Anderson, William xxvii, 11
Ando Miko 11
Anesaki Masaharu 48
Anglo-Japanese Alliance 7, 10, 22,
    25, 66, 200, 280
Annesley, A. 53–54
Anthony, Douglas 90, 174, 182
Aoi Tadao 84
Aoki Masahiko 135
Arichi Meri 205
Armstrong, Helen 106
Arts and Humanities Research
    Council 33, 125–126, 197,
    214, 216–217, 226, 259, 300
Asher, Ron 113
Asiatic Society of Japan 6, 47, 59

Astley, Ian 113, 242
Aston, William George xxvii, 4–5,
    11, 42–43, 60–61, 63, 69,
    87–88, 188–189
Aston University 31
Atherton, Catherine 167, 170
Aya Hōmei 140

Babb, James 145, 147
Baffelli, Erica 141
Bailey, Paul 105
BAJS: *see* British Association for
    Japanese Studies
Ballhatchet, Helen 188, 195,
    197, 241
Barclay, Craig 106
Barnes, Archie 95
Barnes, Gina 31, 83, 97–98, 102, 105
Barr, Michael 146
Barrett, Timothy 206
Batchelor, John xxvii, 7, 42–43,
    45–46, 51
Bath, University of 31
Beasley, William G. xxvii, 23, 134,
    194, 198–200
Bedford School of Japanese 15–17
Bennett, Frank 207
Bentliffe, David 17
Best, Antony 131, 133
Bettelheim, Bernard Jean 44
Bird, Isabella: *see* Isabella Bishop
Birkbeck, University of
    London 196, 199, 227–228,
    248, 258, 263–264, 266, 293

Birmingham, University of 31,
    182, 215, 228
Bishop, Isabella Bird 49
Bix, Herbert 182
Blacker, Carmen xxvii, 21, 23,
    74, 78–80, 83, 95, 151, 194,
    241, 298
Bletchley Park 8, 10, 14, 16–18,
    21–23, 26, 68, 95, 181, 192
Bocking, Brian 32, 206, 241
Boltho, Andrea 163
Bonsall, G. W. 207
Boret, Sebastian 170
Boulding, Toshimi 84
Bownas, Geoffrey xxvii, 17, 23,
    26–27, 150, 152, 154, 157,
    165, 173–174, 178–179
Bowring, Richard, xii, 79–80,
    83–84, 141, 241
Bowring, Sir John 53
Boxer, Major Charles xxvii, 9,
    68–69, 189, 199
Boyd, Richard 203
Bradbury, Malcom 108
Bradford, University of 31
Breen, John 188, 197, 200, 206, 242
Breglio, John lo 169, 171
Breslin, Shaun 145
Brinkley, Francis (Frank) xxvii, 42, 65
Bristol, University of 12, 228, 260,
    263–264, 266
British Academy 201, 216, 286, 290
British Association of Teachers of
    Japanese 196
British Association for Japanese
    Studies xv, 111, 166, 176,
    235–242, 272
British Library 35, 39, 87, 194,
    197, 303–304
British Museum 35, 68, 87–88,
    190, 197, 205, 295–296,
    299–300, 303
Britton, Dorothy xxvii
Broadbridge, Seymour 202
Brown, Mika 109
Brown, Samuel Robbins 44, 54
Browning, Mary Grace 241

Bukkyō Dendō Kyōkai 206
Bunt, Jonathan 139
Buxton, Barclay Fowell 46

Calthrop, Lt.Col. R. F. xxvii,
    66–68, 208
Cambridge, University of 15, 25,
    27, 31, 33–34, 39, 56, 73–86
Campbell–Bannerman, Sir
    Henry 280
Cardiff University 30–31, 89–93,
    182, 245, 263–264, 266
Carpenter, John 195–196, 205
Carroll, Tessa 32
Cave, Peter 140
Ceadel, Eric xxvii, 16–17, 23, 25,
    74–75, 88
Central Lancashire, University
    of 31, 37, 228–229
Chadwick, John 18
Chamberlain, Basil Hall xxvii, 7, 42,
    47, 68, 87–88, 149, 188–189
Chemulpo 58
Chiba Kazuo 131
Chiba-Mooney, Sakie 115
Chibbett, David 197, 207
Chino Yoshitoki 244, 248
Cholmondeley, Lionel 45
Churchill, A. G. 67
Clark, John 177, 196
Clark, Rodney 201
Clarke, Donald 207
Clarke, Hugh 196
Clements, Rebekah 105
Clifford, Capt. J. 75
Clunas, Craig 38
Cobbing, Andrew 38, 242
Cocks, Richard 4
Collcutt, Martin 34
Collick, Martin 173, 175, 182, 241
Columbia University 6, 34, 64, 74,
    133, 197, 215
Connors, Lesley 174, 204
Connors, Michael 177
Conte-Helm, Marie 241, 248, 250
Cooper, Arthur 18
Corbett, Jenny 159, 163

Cornish, Setsuko 198
Cortazzi, Sir Hugh 21, 39, 79, 192, 194, 244, 279, 282, 295–297
Cotton, James 144–145
Cowan, F. M. 53
Cowling, David 105
Cox, Rupert 167
Craig, Albert 134
Craigie, Sir Robert 9–10, 15
Cross, Naomi 97
Crump John 32, 175, 239, 242
Cummings, Alan 198, 206
Cunningham, W. B. 57
Curzon, Lord 149

Dairen (Dalian) 58, 63
Daiwa Anglo-Japanese Foundation xiv, 107, 218, 238, 243–252, 256, 306
Danely, Jason 170
Daniels, Frank xxvii, 9–10, 20, 23–24, 28, 187–195, 208
Daniels, Gordon 173, 183, 241
Daniels, Otome xxvii, 20, 188, 191
Davidson, Colin 57
Davidson, Robert Young 45
Davies, Angela 174
Dawson, Raymond 95, 106
Dean, Meryll 171
Deans, Phil 204
Dening, Sir Esler 7, 57
Dening, Walter xxvii, 6, 42–43, 45–47, 51
Denison, Rayna 110
Department of Trade and Industry 31–32, 184,
Dickins, Frederick Victor xxvii, 7, 12, 60, 65, 88
Diosy, Arthur 278
Dobson, Hugo 182, 248
Dodd, Stephen 198
Dohmen, Martin 53
Dolce, Lucia 195, 206
Dore, Ronald 19, 21, 131–133, 141, 156, 191–192, 194–195, 201
Downing College, Cambridge 245
Drifte, Reinhard 145–146

Dulwich Boys 19–22, 25, 29, 191, 194
Dummett, Michael 17
Dunn, Charles J. xxvii, 23, 188, 192, 194–197, 199, 206, 241
Durham University xv, 27, 29, 31–32, 35, 83, 94–107, 144–145, 147, 194, 214–215, 249–250, 258–260, 266,
Dusinberre, Martin 146–147, 242

EAJS: see European Association for Japanese Studies
East Anglia, University of, 37–38, 105, 108–111, 263, 265, 293–300
East India Company 4, 63, 65, 148
Economic and Social Research Council xvi, 125–126, 147, 177, 214, 217, 259, 288–289
Edwards, Eve 191–192
Eliot, Sir Charles xxviii, 6, 48, 63
Enslie, J. J. 53–54
Esposito, Paolo 170
ESRC: see Economic and Social Research Council
Essex, University of 28–29, 31–32, 35, 246, 255, 258, 293, 303
Esteve-Coll, Dame Elizabeth 294, 297
European Association for Japanese Studies 28, 236, 272
Eusden, Richard 53–55
Evans, Eileen 21
Everett, Christopher 245, 247
Expo 70 (Osaka International Exhibition) 174

Falkus, Malcolm 131
Faulds, Henry 48
FCO: see Foreign and Commonwealth Office
Field, Patrick 16
Firth, John 21, 193
Firth, Sir Raymond 296
Fisher, Charles 172–173, 204
Flores, Linda 163

Foreign and Commonwealth
    Office xii, 23, 41–42, 55, 57,
    156, 175, 186, 218, 223, 236
France, Canon 192
France, Walter Frederick 48
Francks, Penelope 119, 135,
    202–203, 240, 241
Fraser, Andrew 200
Fraser, Anna 170
Frellesvig, Bjarke 163
Fujino Hanako 169, 171
Fujita Shōzō 174
Fujiwara Kiichi 221
Fukuda Haruko 82
Furukawa Akiko 198
Fyson, Philip Kimball 45
Fürer-Haimendorf, Christoph
    von 200

Gallimore, Daniel 171
Gardner, Kenneth xxviii, 39, 194,
    207, 241
Garrett, Philip 147
GBSF: see Great Britain Sasakawa
    Foundation
Germer, Andrea 146
Gerr, Stanley 175
Gerstle, Andrew 34, 197–198, 206
Gerteis, Christopher 195, 198,
    200
Ghosn, Carlos 163–164
Gifford, Patrick 82
Giles, Lionel 68
Gills, Barry 145
Gilson, Julie 182
Gloucester, Duke of 208
Gluck, Carol 215
Goldsmiths, University of
    London 229
Gomersall, Sir Stephen 175
Goodman, David 144–145
Goodman, Roger 160, 162, 241
Gow, Ian 32, 177, 182–183, 185,
Gower, A. J. 53
Grant, Annie 109
Great Britain Sasakawa
    Foundation xiv, 35, 98, 107,

    109, 166, 195, 218, 225, 235,
    250–251, 253–266
Greene, Daniel Crosby 44
Griffis, William Elliot 42
Grocke, Rachel 106
Gubbins, John Harrington xxviii,
    5, 11–12, 60–61, 63–64, 66,
    69, 149–150
Guest, Jennifer 163
Guth, Christine 295
Gützlaff, Karl Friederick August 44
Gygi, Fabio 201

Haft, Alfred 205
Hall, J. C. 60
Hamada Kōichi 131
Hansen, Gitte Marianne 147
Harlech, Lord 208
Harries, Phillip 153, 163, 196, 199
Harumi Seiko 198
Hawes, Lt. A. G. S. 62, 65
Hawkes, David 17
Hawley, Frank xxviii, 10, 24
Hayasaka Makoto 111
Hayashi Keiichi 107
Hayashi Tadasu 280
Hayes, Carol 98–99
Hayter, Irena 126
Hayter, Sir William 26, 117, 172
Hayter Report 26–27, 29–30, 34,
    117, 119, 136, 172, 177, 195,
    209, 254, 282, 308
Healey, Graham 174, 180, 241
Hearn, Lafcadio 47, 128–129
Heath, Edward 176, 302
Hebbert, Michael 134
HEFCE: see Higher Education
    Funding Council for England
Heinze, Ulrich 109, 242
Helliwell, Kumiko 167
Hendry, Joy 167–168, 171, 241
Henitiuk, Valerie 108
Hepburn, James Curtis 42, 44–45
Hertford College, Oxford 245, 247
Hertog, Ekaterina 164
Hickman, Brian 207, 209
Higgins, Chris 106

Higher Education Funding Council
for England 33, 107, 124–126,
213–214, 259–260
Higher Education Funding Council
for Wales 33
Hirado 4
Hiraiwa Gaishi 79
Hirano Akira 296
Hirschmeier, Johannes, 135
Hitotsubashi University 131, 137,
180–181
Hoare, James 39
Hoffmann, Johann Joseph 13
Hokkaido University 220, 236
Hokkaidō 7, 20, 43, 45–46, 50,
141, 183, 197, 220, 236
Honolulu 58
Hood, Christopher 90–92, 242
Hook, Glenn 181–182, 242
Horie-Webber, Akemi 196
Hoshi Hiroto 188, 203
Hoshino Reiko 113
Hounshell, David 133
Howe, Christopher 202
Huddersfield University 184, 245
Hudson, Geoffrey 154
Hughes, Christopher 182, 242
Hughes, David 105, 206–207
Hull, University of 118, 124, 172,
249, 254
Hunter, Janet 131, 133, 135, 174,
240–242

Igarashi Kazuyo 113
Ijuin Kimitaka 80
Ikeda Tadashi 196
Ikeshiro Keiko 169, 171
Imperial College London 229,
246, 248
Impey, Oliver 151, 163
Innami Fusako 105
Inoue Tetsujirō 48
Ion, Hamish 34, 177, 183
Iriye, Akira 134
Isemonger, Commander N. E. 19,
189
Ishida Takeshi 154

Ishida Toshiko 98
Ishiguro, Kazuo 108
Ishihara Takashi 157–159, 163
Ishii Nobuko 112
Itasaka Gen 75
Itō Motoshige 134

Iwakura Tomomi 149
Iwasaki Noriko 188, 203
Izzard, Sebastian 205
Jacoby, Alexander 167, 169–170
James Capel & Co. 82
Jamieson, R. A. 54
Jansen, Marius 49
Japan Consular Service 4–6, 12,
18, 52–65, 69, 173, 188–89
Japan Festival Education Trust 257
Japan Forum 177, 198, 237–240
Japan Foundation xiv, 267–277, 302,
Japan Foundation Endowment
Committee 27, 35, 209, 245,
249, 268, 302–306
Japan Library Group xv, 27, 35,
209, 246, 302–306
Japan Society 3, 11, 35, 49, 60–61,
68, 111, 187, 244, 268, 278–
284, 295
Japan Society for the Promotion of
Science 285–293
Jelinek, Jiri 174–175, 178
Jenkins, Lord Roy 163
Jenkins, Michael 95
JF: *see* Japan Foundation
JFEC: *see* Japan Foundation
Endowment Committee
JLG: *see* Japan Library Group
John Rylands Library (Manchester)
141Worboys, Michael 140
Jorden, Eleanor 174
JSPS: *see* Japan Society for the
Promotion of Science

Kaiser, Stefan 188
Kanehisa Misako 198
Kaner, Simon 295–296, 299
Kano Hiroyuki 296, 298
Kariya Takehiko 164

Kashiwagi Miwako 198
Kasza, Robert 102
Kawabata Miki 84
Kawaguchi Kiyotoshi 168
Kawahara Hiromi 113
Kawai Masatomo 296, 298
Kawashima Hiroshi 83
Keehn, Barry 83
Keene, Donald 25, 34, 74
Keidanren 35, 79, 255, 281
Keiō University 135, 137, 151–
    152, 197
Kelbie, Sakino 115
Kelly, D. 242
Kennedy, Captain Malcolm xxviii,
    8–9, 18, 68, 181,
Kenworthy, Joan 98
Khan, Robert 99, 102
Kikuchi Dairoku, Baron 129
Kilindini (Mombasa) 17
King Alfred's College of Higher
    Education 31
Kingston University 229
King's College London 12, 31,
    61–62, 64, 68, 144, 187, 199,
    204, 229, 266
Kinmonth, Earl 182
Kinokuniya Publishing 274
Kinsella, Sharon 140
Kirby, E. J. W. 18
Kirsch, Griseldis 198–199
Kitamoto Nobuko 174
Kitaoka Shin'ichi 222
Kizu Mika 98, 102, 188, 203
Klein, Alex 224
Kobayashi Fujiko 207
Kobayashi Yuka 204
Kōji Taira 135
Konishi Sho 163
Koreeda Hirokazu 170
Kornicki, Peter xii, 79–80, 84,
    88, 141, 246
Koso Ritsuko 104
Koyama Noboru 39
Kume Kunitake 180–181
Kunin, Seth 103, 105
Kurokawa Mikiko 113

Kushner, Barak 85
Kyōto University 137

Language Officers 7–9, 15, 67, 189
Lapavitas, Costas 202
Large, Stephen 82
Laslett, Peter 22
Lattimore, Owen 118
Laurie, Haruko 78, 82–84
Lawson, Joseph 147
Lawson, Konrad 230
Leeds, University of 30, 33, 37,
    117–127, 202, 204, 212–226,
    238, 240, 254, 260, 263–264,
    266, 274, 293,
Lehmann, Jean-Pierre 32, 241
Liggins, John 44
Liscutin, Nicola 196, 199
Liverpool John Moores
    University 229, 245
Lloyd, Arthur xxviii, 6, 42–43,
    47–49, 51
Lloyd, John 18
Lloyd-Jones, Sir Hugh 17
Lockyer, Angus 200, 240
Loewe, Michael 17
Lomax, Sq/Ldr 192
London School of Economics 22,
    28, 128–138, 174, 179, 194,
    200, 266
Longford, Joseph Henry xxviii, 12,
    61–62, 64, 66, 187–188, 199
Lowe, Peter 241
LSE: see London School of
    Economics
Lunsing, Wim 171

McAuley, Thomas 184
McClatchie, T. R. 60
McClure, W. 241–241
McClure, William 97–98
McEwan, Ian 108
McEwan, John R. xxviii, 23, 25,
    74, 194
MacFarquhar, Roderick 155–157
McGovern, William Montgomery
    289

McMullen, David 79
McMullen, James 151, 153, 155, 161, 163, 242
Macnaughtan, Helen 203, 242
Maezaki Shin'ya 205
Manchester Metropolitan University 139
Manchester, University of 31, 38, 139–143, 215, 245, 260, 263–264, 266, 292–293
Manila 58, 63
Martin, Captain 10
Martin, Ruth 170
Martinez, Dolores 201
Marui Co. 84
Maruyama Masao 154
Matanle, Peter 242 Hosoya Chihiro 131
Matsuda Akira 109
Matsudaira Susumu 196
Matsukawa Baikin 20, 190
Matsumoto-Sturt, Yoko 113–115
Matsunaga, Hidetaka 167
Matsunaga, Louella 167, 170
Matthews, Gordon 170
Meade, Ruselle 92
Medhurst, Walter Henry 43
Mehl, Margaret 113
Mendl, Wolf 241
Mills, Douglas xxviii, 74–75, 77–78, 95, 194, 196, 199, 235, 241
Minority Subject funding 32–33
Mitchinson, Christopher 177
Mitford, Algernon 42–43, 55–56
Mito Takamichi 80, 83
Mitsubishi 156
Mitsui 156
Mitsui Kaijō Kasai 84
Miyamoto Shōzaburō 207, 209
Miyamura, Satoshi 195, 202
Moeran, Brian 197, 201
Moran, Chihoko 159
Moran, Joseph 32
Moretti, Laura 85, 147
Moriguchi Chikashi 135
Morimoto Kazuki 98, 102
Morishima Michio 132, 137

Morley, Jamese 133
Morris, Ivan 34, 190
Morris, Mark 83–84
Morris-Suzuki, Tessa 215
Moubray, Guy de 22
Munro, Neil Gordon xxviii, 45
Murdoch, James 47, 62
Myburgh, C. F. 53

Nagasaki 4, 44, 57, 169, 224
Nakai Norihiro 134
Nakamura Takafusa 133
Nakane Chie 135
Nanking, Treaty of 52
Napier, Susan 196, 199
Naruhito, Prince 162–163
Narumi-Munro, Fumiko 114–115
National Defense Education Act 35
Neary, Ian 144–145, 163, 175, 241
Needham Research Institute, Cambridge 175, 246, 263
Newcastle, University of 31, 97, 100, 103, 144–147, 214–215, 246, 255, 262–264, 266, 293
Newman, Denise 17
Nicholls, Christine 155
Nikkei Europe 274
Nilsson-Wright, John 83–84
Ninagawa Yukio 113
Nippon Foundation 35, 91, 108, 126, 169, 225, 250, 253, 260–64, 265
Nish, Ian 22–23, 131, 133, 149, 200, 241
Nissan Motor Company 35, 157, 162
Nissanke Machiko 202
Nitobe Inazō 47
Nogami Yoshiji 215
Nottingham, University of 31, 38, 183, 185, 215, 230
Noyce, Wilfrid 17
NSK 31, 35, 98, 107
Numata Foundation 206

Oba Sadao 191
O'Brien, Liam 167

Odaka Kōnosuke 134
Oeben, Stephanie 170
Ogata Sadako 181
Oka Yoshitake 130, 154
Okahisa, Etsuko 103
Okajima Shin'ichirō 198
Okakura Kakuzō 129
Okakura Yoshisaburō 129
Okazaki-Ward, Lola 241
Okinawa 222, 224
Olcott, George 242
O'Neill, Patrick G xxviii, 19, 95, 194–197, 206, 241
Onishi Ryoko 114
Oriental Museum (Durham) 105–107
Orita Masaki 168
Ōshima Hiroshi 22
Owen, David 156
Oxford Brookes University 37–38, 166–171, 258, 263, 265–266
Oxford, University of 5, 10, 12, 15–17, 26–28, 31, 35, 38–39, 56, 61, 64–65, 76–78, 81, 83, 85, 95, 148–165, 173–176, 179196, 215, 246–247, 254–256, 260, 263–264, 266, 269, 293, 303–304
Ozaki Kōyō 6

Paprzycki, Ralph 203
Pardoe, Jon 181, 183
Park Jin 145
Parker Report 30–31, 34, 82, 89, 95, 97, 119, 144, 153, 178, 180, 191, 195, 201, 254–5, 266, 308
Parker, Helen 112, 241
Parker, Sir Peter xii, xxviii, 19, 21, 29–30, 34–35, 144, 180, 191,
Parker, Steven 139
Parkes, Sir Harry xxviii, 53, 55–56, 59–60
Partlett, Sir Henry 208
Paske-Smith, Montague 63
Patessio, Mara 140
Pearl Harbor 14, 189–191

Pembroke College, Cambridge 248
Penrose, E. F. 202
Penrose, Edith 202
Perkins, Chris 115, 170
Peterhouse, Cambridge 281
Piggott, Maj. Gen Francis S. G. xxviii, 9, 20–21, 24, 66–68, 189–190, 193
Pilcher, Sir John 18, 20
Piper, John 44
Pizziconi, Barbara 188, 195, 198, 203
Plunkett, Sir Francis Richard 56
Pollard, Clare 163
Ponsonby-Fane, Richard 208
Portsmouth, University of 230
Posen, Adam 134
Powell, Brian 149–153, 155, 159, 163, 241
Power, Eileen 129
Powles, Cyril 42
Pratt, Keith 95
Pratt, Peter 63
Prince of Wales, HMS 14

Ranis, Gustav, 135
Rapley, Ian 92
Rawson, Barbara 106
Rawson, Philip 106
Reader, Ian 32 139–140, 142
Reading, University of 230
Reay, Lord 12
Rebick, Mark 162–163
Redman, Sir Vere 18
Reischuer, August Karl 48
Repulse, HMS 14
Richards, Janet 92
Richards, Sir Rex 158
Richardson, David 111
Richardson, Lauren 116
Riddell, Hannah 46
Rideout, J. K. 189–190
Rising Sun Petroleum Company 9
Ritsumeikan University 297
Robbins, Jane 183
Roberson, James 171
Robert Fleming & Co, 82

Roberts, Sir Gareth 213
Robertson, Russell 54
Robinson, G. W. 200
Robinson, John Coooper 49
Rodrigues, João 4
Rose, Caroline 242
Rosny, Léon de 13
Rousmaniere, Nicole 294–296, 298
Rowley, Gaye 90
Royal Asiatic Society 59–61
Royal Society 246, 250–251, 286, 290
Ruehl, Sonja 203
Russell, Bertrand 130
Russell, Donald 17, 23

Saigō Hideki 98, 102
Sainsbury Institute for the Study of Japanese Art and Culture xvi, 109, 111, 205, 269, 294–301
Sainsbury of Turville, Lord 298
Sainsbury, Lady 294, 297, 299–301
Sainsbury, Sir Robert 294, 299–301
Saitō Osamu 134
Sakai Naoki 215
Sakamoto Yoshikazu 181
Salford University 139
Salmond, Air Chief Marshal Sir Geoffrey 8
Samuels, Richard 133
Sansom, Sir George xxviii, 5, 24, 57, 60. 63–64. 67–69, 155, 188–189
Sanwa Bank 31, 35
Sargent, John 204
Sasagawa Ayumi 170
Sasamoto-Collins, Hiromi 102
Sato-Rossberg, Nana, 109, 198, 203
Satow, Sir Ernest Mason xxviii, 4–6, 12, 42–43, 54–55, 57, 59–60, 62–64, 69, 87–88, 188–9, 208, 230–231
Sawbridge, Henry 65, 173
Scarbrough Report 23–25, 34, 76, 88, 95, 195, 282, 308
Scarbrough, Earl of 23

School of Oriental and African Studies 3, 8–10, 14–15, 17, 19–21, 25, 27–28, 30–31, 34–35, 38, 68, 76, 94–95, 134, 153–54, 187–211, 238, 240, 245, 247, 256, 265–66, 293, 295, 297–98, 300, 303–304
Scottish Centre for Japanese Studies 29, 32, 114, 258
Scottish Funding Council 32–33, 214
Screech, Michael 17
Screech, Timon 195, 205, 300
Seaton, Philip 236
Sebald, W. G. 108
Sedgwick, Mitch 167
Seely, Christopher 196, 199
Seligman, Charles 129
Sells, Peter 203
Seoul 39, 58
Seung Yeon Sang 297
Severini, Antelmo 13
SFC: see Scottish Funding Council
Shadwell, Admiral Sir Charles 65
Shand, William 10–11
Shaw, Alexander Croft xxviii
Shaw, Ronald Duncan 50
Sheffield, University of 27, 29, 31, 33, 65, 76, 90, 118, 125–126, 150, 152–154, 157, 172–186, 212–226, 238, 240, 246, 248, 255–256, 258, 260, 263–264, 266, 269, 293, 303–305
Sheldon, Charles 74–75, 77
Shimizu Shūyū 151
Shimizu, Mr. 192
Shiraki Hitoshi 198
Shiratori Rei 177
Shores, Matthew 85
Showa Shell Sekiyu 9
Siddle, Richard 183
Siebold, Alexander von 54
Siebold, Heinrich Philipp von 88
Simon, Walter 208
Simpson, Andrew 203
Sims, Richard 200

SISJAC: *see* Sainsbury Institute for
  the Study of Japanese Art and
  Culture
Skillend, William 17
Smethurst, Richard 134
Smith, Joanne 146
Smith, Rosemary 92
SOAS: *see* School of Oriental and
  African Studies
St Andrews, University of 230
Standen, Naomi 146–147
Standish, Isolde 198–199
Starr, Don 95, 102, 241
Steeds, D.. 241
Steger, Brigitte 85
Stein, Peter 17
Stevenson, Lord Dennis 98
Stirling, University of 28, 31–32,
  113–114, 175, 182, 230, 246,
  250, 258, 262,
Stockwin, Arthur 39, 152, 158–
  159, 163, 241
Stopes, Marie xxviii, 11, 281
Storry, Richard xxviii, 10, 23,
  150–151, 154–156, 159–160,
  165, 241
Stranks, Charles 50
Stranks, James 50
Strong, George Noel 50
Strong, Kenneth 21, 196–197, 199
Sugihara Kaoru 134, 198, 200,
  202, 241
Sugiyama Shin'ya 135
Surak, Kristin 195, 204
Sussex, University of 257
Suzuki Satona 198
Suzuki Yoshitaka 134
Swinnerton–Dyer, Sir Peter 34
Szoztack, John 295

Tachibanaki Toshiaki 135
Taipei 63
Taiwan 58, 64, 120
Takada Kazuki 102
Takahara Akio 221
Takaira, Mr. 192
Takeda Hiroko 91

Takeuchi, Lone 188, 195–196
Tanaka Fund 176, 302–306
Tanaka Kakuei 176, 268, 302
Tanaka Kazumi 188, 196
Taniguchi Kaori 198
Tavistock College, Devon 257
Tawney, R. H. 129
Tebbitt, Norman 159
Teeuwen, Mark 90
Teikyo University 96–99
TEPCO: *see* Tokyo Electric Power
  Company
Thacker, T. W. 94, 105
Thoburn, John 110
Thompson, David 45
Thurley, Keith 131, 133–134, 241
Tiltman, Brigadier John 14–15, 18
Tokita, Alison 206
Tokugawa Ieyasu 148
Tokyo Electric Power Company 79,
  153
Tokyo, University of 104, 109,
  129–130, 133–134, 137, 164,
  188, 215, 219, 221, 224,
Torigoe Bunzō 75
Toshiba International
  Foundation 110, 209, 238, 298
Tournier, Vincent 206
Townsend, Susan 38, 183, 242
Tranter, Nicholas 183
Troup, J. J. 60, 88
Trübner and Co. 5
Tsuchikane Yasuko 297
Tsuda Ume 149
Tsuzuki Chūshichi 159, 180, 183
Tuck, Captain Oswald 9, 15–16, 68
Turvill, Angus 103

UEA: see University of East Anglia
Uehara Etsujirō 129
UGC: see University Grants
  Committee
Ulster University 31–32
Umemura Maki 91–92
University College London 17,
  187, 197, 201, 215, 230–231,
  258, 266

University Grants Committee 27, 29–32, 34, 82, 89, 95, 156, 172, 176, 180, 208, 302–303
University of Manchester Institute of Science and Technology 139
Uraguchi Docherty, Miyoko 196

Valentine, James 32
Ventris, Michael 18
Verbeck, Guido 45
Victoria University of Manchester 139
Viney, Robert 148
Volz, Ulrich 202

Waal, Edmund de 184
Wada Kazuo 133
Wales, University of 257
Waley, Arthur xxviii, 11, 190, 208, 281
Waley, Paul 204
Wallas, Graham 129
Walton, William Howard Henry 50
Ward, N. 241
Warner, Sir Fred 175, 181
Warren, Charles Frederick 45
Warwick, University of 29, 145, 182, 215, 231, 266, 293
Waseda University 104, 137, 152, 220, 224
Waswo, Ann 159, 163
Watanabe Takeshi 130
Watanabe Toshio 168
Watson, R. G. 59
Watson, William 205
Watters, Thomas 88
Watterville, Ms S. de 208
Webb, Beatrice 129
Webb, Sidney 129
Webster, Sir Charles 130
Wein, Roland 145

Weiner, Michael 177, 183
Weinstein, Stanley 196
Weisenfield, Gennifer 295
Weste, John 97, 102, 242
Weston, Walter 45, 49
White, Bruce 170
White Rose East Asia Centre xv, 125, 212–226, 259–260
Whittaker, Hugh 83, 163
Wiles, Maurice 17
Williams, David 91
Williams, Mark 241–242
Wilson, Angus 108
Wiltshire, Richard 204
Wireless Experimental Centre 17, 26
Wright, Tim 182

Yakushiji Katsuyuki 109
Yamaguchi, Sgt 193
Yamamoto, Sgt 193
Yamanouchi Hisaaki 75
Yamazawa Ippei 180
Yanada Senji 20, 190, 192, 195
Yanaihara Tadao 130, 183
Yasuda Trust and Banking 83
Yasumura Yoshiko 207
Yasutomi Ayumu 135
Yate, Major Charles 8
York, University of 175, 231, 246, 266
Yoshikawa Tomoko 113
Yoshimi Shun'ya 215
Yoshioka Shiro 147
Yoshitake Saburō 19, 189
Young, Hugo 182
Yu, Sabrina 147

Zachmann, Urs Matthias 115
Zeldin, Theodore 163
Zheng, Binghan 103